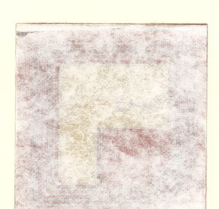

VICTORIAN
LINCOLN

TO MEMBERS AND OFFICERS, PAST AND PRESENT, OF THE
LINCOLNSHIRE ARCHIVES COMMITTEE

VICTORIAN
LINCOLN

BY

SIR FRANCIS HILL
C.B.E., LL.M., LITT.D., F.S.A.

CAMBRIDGE UNIVERSITY PRESS

Published by the Syndics of the Cambridge University Press
Bentley House, 200 Euston Road, London NW1 2DB
American Branch: 32 East 57th Street, New York, N.Y.10022

© Cambridge University Press 1974

Library of Congress Catalogue Card Number: 73-82461

ISBN: 0 521 20334 1

First published 1974

Printed in Great Britain
at the University Printing House, Cambridge
(Brooke Crutchley, University Printer)

CONTENTS

ILLUSTRATIONS

PLATES

Between pages 150 and 151

1 The Brayford Pool and Lincoln Cathedral (1858) by James Wilson Carmichael. Usher Gallery, Lincoln. Reproduced by permission of the Mayor, Aldermen and Citizens of Lincoln

2 City of Lincoln, south view from Canwick, c. 1870

3 January 1850. Protectionist meeting in the Corn Exchange. *Illustrated London News*

4 February 1850. Great Protectionist meeting in the Castle Yard. *Illustrated London News*

5 August 1869. Agricultural meeting at Lincoln: Messrs Clayton and Shuttleworth's works and the show yard. *Illustrated London News*

6 May 1870. Lincoln Horse Fair. *Illustrated London News*

7 January 1871. Floods at Lincoln. *Illustrated London News*
   (a) Lincoln, from Bracebridge
   (b) A street in Lincoln

8 Catching a poacher! Cobden and Sibthorp by H.B. (1845)

MAPS

PREFACE

WITH the completion of this, my fourth book on the history of Lincoln, I have gone as far as seems possible in the leisure moments of a busy life to achieve a youthful ambition to write a history of my native city. I send it forth with mixed feelings. First, after living with the work for more than forty-five years I shall miss it sadly: it has so long provided an escape from the concerns of the day. Secondly, it is pleasant to reflect that I have been more fortunate than my predecessors as historians of Lincoln – Thomas Sympson in the eighteenth century and Edward James Willson and John Ross in the nineteenth – in getting my writing into print: but they had not the advantages that we have in these latter days of ready access to records and relative ease of publication. Thirdly, I am increasingly aware of weakness, error and omission, leading to the reflection that I could do it all so much better if I could begin again.

I can at least say that if I were to begin again my books would be of the same kind. I have merely sought to know what happened in Lincoln, and how it came to be what it is, and put the results into narrative form. I hope I have given interest and pleasure to my fellow-citizens and others; and if my books are of value to scholars concerned with the same or wider themes so much the better.

Many of the sources used in *Georgian Lincoln* have continued to be of use. New sources in the Lincolnshire Archives Office include the Bishops' Correspondence, Visitation Returns, Larken MSS, Hebb MSS, Monson MSS (and especially the papers of the sixth Lord Monson), and parish records. Methodist records are being assembled there by the devotion of Mr William Leary, and other Free Church records have for the most part been gathered there.

Lieutenant Colonel Sir Weston Cracroft-Amcotts of Hackthorn Hall, Lincoln, kindly lent me the diary of his grandfather Colonel Weston Cracroft (afterwards Amcotts), and though some parts of the diary are missing, it has been of great value, giving a charming impression of a public-spirited country gentleman of the mid-nineteenth century. Mr Anthony Jarvis of Doddington Hall, Lincoln, kindly lent me the diary of his great great uncle G. K. Jarvis, with family correspondence and a letter book. The Bishop of Lincoln lent the diary of Edward Lee Hicks, Bishop of Lincoln 1910–1919. Volumes of letters to Sir Charles Anderson of Lea near Lincoln, together with his diary, were deposited in the

Lincolnshire Archives Office for my use by the Earl of Feversham, and I am grateful to him. Mrs Smeeton kindly sent me a brief diary of her aunt Elizabeth Wordsworth. Lieutenant Colonel Sir Benjamin Bromhead's collection of the MSS of Sir Edward Bromhead at Thurlby Hall, Lincoln, were still of value for the earlier part of the period.

The late Canon W. W. Leeke wrote some of his memories for me shortly before he died, and the late Dr Godfrey Lowe gave me a copy of some notes of his. Memories recorded by the late E. F. R. Woolley at the prompting of Canon Hubert Larken are in the cathedral library. The notes of Colonel J. G. Williams (as to whom see *Medieval Lincoln*, pp. xiv–xv), some of them annotated by G. R. Sharpley, a nephew of Joseph Ruston, are in my possession, as is a manuscript by Edward Peacock. Mrs Olive Riggall gave me letters in verse from Dean Fry to her father Dr G. J. Bennett, the cathedral organist.

I did not become aware of the existence of a file of the *Lincoln Gazette* at the *Lincolnshire Echo* office until a very late stage, and I have decided that rather than postpone publication for a further period I must do without it. I have used extensively the files of the *Lincoln Rutland and Stamford Mercury* and the *Lincolnshire Chronicle*, both in the Lincoln Public Library, and I am grateful to the proprietors of both papers for allowing me to borrow them to study. It is only fair to say that I read the *Mercury* file many years ago, and the *Chronicle* file more recently, when I knew better what might matter; hence the more numerous citations from the latter source.

There is such a mass of printed material available for this period that I have abandoned the idea of giving references for statements that are easily verifiable; my pages are still laden with footnotes.

It is pleasant to acknowledge the help of friends. Mr Michael Lloyd and his colleagues at the Lincolnshire Archives Office have never failed; and Mr F. T. Baker and Miss E. Jahn at the Lincoln Public Library have helped in all manner of ways, and Mr Lawrence Elvin has allowed me constantly to use his great knowledge of the local collection there. Mrs Craven abstracted for me from newspaper files biographical notes of many leading citizens, constituting a local gazetteer.

I am especially grateful to Mrs Joan Varley, not only for the help and advice she gave when she was County Archivist, but for reading my typescript and making valuable suggestions, and searching out and supplying precise references to papers which I read before they were calendared, a task the thought of which made me quail. Similarly Dr Richard Hunt of the Bodleian Library has provided references to the Wilberforce MSS there. Dr Richard Olney not only lent me his own unpublished thesis, but he read my typescript and made useful comments.

Miss Winifred Hunt, my secretary for forty-five years, has helped throughout my work. Mrs Jean Huggins and Mrs Cooke have produced new drafts at short notice. Mr Alan Lyons checked some statistics. Mr Charles Martin has drawn the maps. To all of them I am grateful.

To the Syndics and officers of the University Press I am indebted for their generosity and patience.

J. W. F. HILL

Lincoln
Midsummer 1972

ABBREVIATIONS

A.A.S.R.	*Reports and Papers of the Associated Architectural Societies*
Anderson Diary	Diary of and volumes of letters addressed to Sir
Anderson Letters	Charles Anderson deposited in L.A.O. by the Earl of Feversham
B.M.	British Museum
Bromhead MSS	Correspondence of Sir Edward Bromhead, Bart., in the possession of Lieutenant Colonel Sir Benjamin Bromhead, Bart., Thurlby Hall, Lincoln
C.M.	Minutes of Lincoln City Council
Cracroft	Diary of Colonel Weston Cracroft (Amcotts) in the possession of Lieutenant Colonel Sir Weston Cracroft-Amcotts, Hackthorn Hall, Lincoln
D.N.B.	*Dictionary of National Biography*
G.L.	*Georgian Lincoln*, by J. W. F. Hill (1966)
E. L. Hicks Diary	Diary of Bishop Edward Lee Hicks in the possession of the Bishop of Lincoln
G. K. Jarvis Diary	MSS in the possession of Mr Anthony Jarvis, Doddington Hall, Lincoln
Jarvis Corr.	
Jarvis Letter Book	
L.A.O.	Lincolnshire Archives Office
L.C.	*Lincolnshire Chronicle*
L.C.S.	*Lincoln Cathedral Statutes*, ed. Bradshaw and Wordsworth
L.D.M.	*Lincoln Diocesan Magazine*
L.L.	*Lincoln Leader*
Lincs. N. & Q.	*Lincolnshire Notes and Queries*
L.P.L.	Lincoln Public Library
L.R.S.	Publications of the Lincoln Record Society
M.L.	*Medieval Lincoln*, by J. W. F. Hill (1948)
P.D.	*Parliamentary Debates*
Ross Letter Books	Correspondence of John Ross in the possession of J. W. F. Hill
S.M.	*Lincoln Rutland and Stamford Mercury*
T. & S. L.	*Tudor and Stuart Lincoln*, by J. W. F. Hill (1956)
Wilberforce MSS	Papers of Bishop Samuel Wilberforce in Bodleian Library
Willson	E. J. Willson Collection in the Library of the Society of Antiquaries

CHAPTER I

THE EARLY VICTORIAN SCENE

A casual visitor to Lincoln at the time of Queen Victoria's accession might have thought it little changed since the brothers Buck depicted it in their engraving of 1743. There was the cathedral dominating the scene, supported by the castle and the cluster of houses round them. This was the upper city, virtually consisting of the original Roman *Colonia*. On the steep hillside, virtually the second Roman enclosure, was the high street, the Roman Ermine Street, flanked by houses; and the street punctuated by church towers strode across the river Witham and the valley to the southern edge of the gap in the limestone ridge running north and south through the county. To the west of the high street was the inland port of Brayford Pool, the commercial centre of the city, with access by water both to the sea down the Witham, and to the river Trent and the Humber by the Roman Fossdyke canal. The most obvious changes of the century were that the western towers of the minster had lost their spires, and a little turret had been added to the eastern mound of the castle.

Yet on a closer view the city had changed much. There was new building, mostly of brick, contrasting with the older stone houses. There were new churches and chapels. Above all, there were the houses needed to accommodate a population that had doubled in the course of the century. Most of the new houses, however, were small and poor, and tucked away in yards and alleys, or spread along the banks of the waterways, and were not likely to be much noticed by tourists.

This growth of population was to continue at an increasing rate: between 1831 and 1871 there was an increase of 150 per cent. Most of the new inhabitants came from neighbouring rural areas, and most of them from the poorest classes. Richard Sibthorp commented on the changing scene:

10 February 1858. This old city is becoming increasingly populous, and one or two considerable branches of business have, within the last ten years, been introduced here and with great success. There is an iron foundry employing six or seven hundred workmen weekly, and doing an immense business; besides large corn mills. But on the whole, the poor are increasing, and its richer inhabitants diminishing; for, like most old cathedral towns, it used to be the residence of many independent persons, widow ladies, etc., and this class of inhabitants is quitting it. We are in hopes that a Loan Society would be of much use here.[1]

[1] J. Fowler, *Life and Letters of R. W. Sibthorp* (1880), p. 126.

When Richard Mason retired from the town clerkship in 1855, he having been appointed in 1826, he too referred to the change. When he first came to Lincoln, he said, it was a mere straggling place of 7,000 or 8,000 inhabitants, and a trade which supplied the mere wants of the inhabitants. Now, the population comprised a race of intelligent merchants and tradesmen, and the tall shafts of the steam mills were emblems of advance in material wealth, with moral and social advantage. It was a triumph that the Stamp End Works could prosper, because coal and iron had to be brought to an agricultural district, and yet the foundry could beat those with coal and iron at their command.[1] He might have added that it was the railways that had made this possible; it was not a long haul from the coalfields of south Yorkshire, and in Lincoln were men of enterprise, a pool of labour, and wage rates related to agricultural rates.

Railways and factories were not then the commonplaces that they have since become. About 1857 Edward Peacock, a countryman and a small squire, described Lincoln as having become 'a semi-manufacturing town in the centre of an agricultural district'. But in spite of the daily train of operatives he saw extending three or four abreast for a distance of nearly half a mile, Lincoln was still an agricultural market: 'It is almost incredible what a vast quantity of horses and vehicles, to say nothing of numerous droves of other cattle, pass daily through the streets, leaving behind them unmistakeable traces of their presence.'[2]

This predominantly agricultural atmosphere persisted until the later years of the century. In 1883 one of Charles Dickens' successors found a busy, thriving, brewing, malting town, with the reek of brewers' grain in the air, with horsy men, always ready for a deal or a bet, thronging its principal inns; and over the railway crossing its main street there was always going on a vigorous shunting of cattle trucks and pig waggons. But a different stage of existence marked each stage of ascent to the hilltop.[3]

The industrial revolution, if it can be so described, reached Lincoln a century after it reached the great industrial areas of the country. Its advent, accompanied by rapid increase of population due in part to increased opportunities for work and in part to the townward drift of surplus rural labour, changed the economic and social scene and completed that transfer of the centre of gravity from the upper to the lower city which had begun with the growth of agricultural markets at the

[1] *L.C.*, 26 October 1855.
[2] Peacock MS in my possession.
[3] *All the Year Round*, 27 October 1883.

beginning of the century. Local leadership was taken by prosperous commercial men, mostly liberal and even radical, and many of them dissenters, quick to show resentment of the old social superiority of gentry and cathedral clergy, expressed in the single pejorative term 'uphill'. This geographical expression of social division continued until the geographical division of society was itself erased by the building of great housing estates both above and below hill in the years following the First World War. The term however can still be used by anyone wishing to air a prejudice against anyone or anything he dislikes.

All these changes came gradually and almost imperceptibly, and a visitor could continue to describe the city in terms which would have been appropriate in earlier times. The attempt to depict the city as it appeared just before the industrial development had made much mark is helped by a record left by a transatlantic visitor in 1857.

In that year, when Nathaniel Hawthorne was United States Consul in Liverpool, he made a pilgrimage to Boston in Lincolnshire.[1] He left Manchester at 1.45 p.m., travelling by the Manchester, Sheffield and Lincolnshire Railway, and reached Lincoln shortly after 6 o'clock. The last stage of the railway line had only been opened in 1848;[2] before that, travelling by coach, it would have taken him all day. Arriving at the Midland station (now St Marks), with its Ionic portico, he found no cab – cabs had not arrived in Lincoln[3] – and so he took the Saracen's Head omnibus for the few hundred yards' journey to the hotel. There he and his party were hospitably received, and he thought it looked comfortable enough, 'though, like the hotels of most old English towns, it had a musty fragrance of antiquity, such as I have smelt in a seldom-opened London church where the broad-aisle is paved with tombstones'. The entrance into the courtyard was through an arch, in the side of which was the door to the hotel. Inside, there were long corridors and an intricate arrangement of staircases 'amid which it would be no marvel to encounter some forgotten guest who had gone astray a hundred years ago, and was still seeking for his bedroom while the rest of his generation were in their graves'. He thought there was no exaggerating the confusion of mind that seized upon a stranger in the bewildering geography of a great old-fashioned English inn.

The hotel stood in the high street immediately without the Stonebow,

---

[1] See his *Our Old Home* (1890), I, 231–58. For the date see Julian Hawthorne, *Nathaniel Hawthorne and his Wife* (1885), II, 138.
[2] Below, pp. 113–15.
[3] A cab first appeared on the streets in 1863, and though cabdriver and horse vanished in the following year, a cab-stand built in 1865 implies their reappearance. Uphill got a cab-stand on Castle Hill in 1877.

which had been the southern gateway of the medieval walled city. The city walls had gone, and many of the gates, but the mostly Tudor Stonebow stood across the street with a similar arch for foot-passengers on each side: 'a gray time-gnawn, ponderous shadowy structure, through the dark vista of which you look into the Middle Ages'. Although the street was narrow and contained many antique peculiarities, English domestic architecture had lost its most impressive feature: and he thought there were finer old towns than Lincoln – Chester, for instance, and Shrewsbury – with houses once the homes of the gentry. These he was later to see in the uphill city. His sentimental regrets were not shared by the local newspaper, which had hailed the most striking improvements in street architecture: many of the old shops in High Street, formerly of a most miserable and squalid appearance, had given place to others that would not disgrace any city in England.[1] Hawthorne was right in noting that the modern brick or stucco fronts hid the older houses behind them.

That evening, between 7 and 8 o'clock, his party set out to pay a first visit to the cathedral, ascending a street which grew steeper and narrower till at last it got to be the steepest street he had ever climbed – it reached a gradient of 1 in 4 – passing the Jew's House with a stone portal and carved ornaments, which had become a dwelling-place for poverty-stricken people.

Certainly, the Bishop and clergy of Lincoln ought not to be fat men, but of rare spiritual, saint-like, almost angelic habit, if it be a frequent part of their ecclesiastical duty to climb this hill; for it is a real penance, and was probably performed as such, and groaned over accordingly, in monkish times.

Entering the precincts of the cathedral through the Exchequer gate, one of the gateways of the once embattled Close, they saw the houses of Minster Yard, built as habitations of its dignitaries and officers: 'some of them are still occupied as such, though others are in too neglected and dilapidated a state to seem worthy of so splendid an establishment'. Except for Salisbury he remembered no more comfortable picturesque precinct round any cathedral.

The following morning they took a fly up the hill by the oblique ascent – the Lindum Road. They visited the cathedral, saw the castle – part of it still used as a prison – and the Roman Newport Arch: they saw, 'on the broad back of the hill' some stately and queer old houses and many mean little hovels; and little houses clustering in the castle moat looking like toadstools from the mould of a decaying tree.[2] He concluded, with

---

[1] *L.C.*, 23 June 1848.
[2] The ditches had been granted away in the time of Charles I. *M.L.*, p. 99.

exaggeration but with a hint of truth, that all or most of the life of the day had subsided into the lower town, and that only priests, poor people and prisoners dwelt in the upper regions.

Here were the fine old houses that he had missed below hill. Some of them had been the town houses of the gentry, who had come in for the Color Ball[1] or the high sheriff's ball, or on county business, until the improved turnpike roads made it less difficult to get to Lincoln and back home again in a day. The upper city was still the capital of the county and the diocese. The residentiary canons usually resided only during their statutory periods of residence, some three months in the year, then moving on to other preferments; and the other houses were, many of them, occupied by the widows and unmarried daughters of clergy and gentry, some professional men, and a few other residents of private means. Merchants of substance were finding their way into the circle. Hawthorne, it seems, did not meet any of the higher clergy on his visits to the minster. As a representative of a republican government (and lately rebels at that) he would hardly have been welcome; and certainly he would never have been received at the table of Chancellor Pretyman – if he were in residence – with a footman behind every chair.

If he had known, he could have stayed at the White Hart near the cathedral: it had (in 1844) been repaired, and a new front with a balcony put up. Dr Dibdin, the bibliophile, had complained before then that there was no inn in the neighbourhood of the cathedral at which a civilised traveller could stay.[2]

The next day, on his return to the Saracen's Head, Hawthorne found the high street enlivened with a great bustle and turmoil of people all the evening, because it was Saturday night, and having accomplished their week's toil and received their wages, they were making their small purchases against Sunday, and enjoying themselves as well as they knew how.

This was the social heart of the city, and the business centre too. The shops of the principal tradesmen, interspersed with private houses, homes of doctors and lawyers and retired people, and a few private boarding schools were within a stone's throw. The shops which had not yet been refronted had old-fashioned bow windows with small panes of glass in them, and doorways divided in the middle. Except on market days and on Saturday nights it was all sleepy enough, and one could walk up and down the high street and not meet more than three or four people.

---

[1] Below, p. 79.
[2] *Bibliographical Antiquarian and Picturesque Tour in the Northern Counties of England and in Scotland* (1838), I, 89.

Hawthorne was no doubt told during his stay that his inn was the Lincoln headquarters of Colonel Sibthorp, the eccentric tory M.P. for the city, the whig stronghold, the Reindeer, being opposite. The whig-radical interest had been much strengthened by the Reform Bill of 1832, which had enfranchised the middle-class citizens, the £10 householders, who now shared the franchise with the resident freemen, upon whose well-paid support Sibthorp especially relied. The gradual removal of the disabilities of the dissenters had, with the vote, given them self-confidence, and they were emerging from the back streets and building chapels and schools; and they found plenty of abuses in the Church of England to denounce. The bishop for the first time for centuries had a home near the city, and Bishop Kaye was to be seen from time to time as he went about his slow but steady campaign against absentee and pluralist clergy. After municipal reform in 1835 the whigs and radicals had captured every seat in the city council, and were busy removing ancient landmarks and upsetting time-honoured institutions. Habits of deference were being undermined, especially for the clergy: a cathedral dignitary could walk the length of High Street without a single man touching his hat to him. What would happen next?[1] But the next thing did not happen. Reaction set in.

Hawthorne went on to Boston. His journey could most quickly have been completed by the Great Northern Railway, whose line along the river bank had not long been open. Instead, observing in the guide book that a steamer ran on the river between Lincoln and Boston, he thought the river trip would be a pleasant variation on their usual mode of travel.

The steamer proved to be small, dirty and altogether inconvenient, the sky lowering, and, presently, an ugly wind from the German Ocean blowing in their teeth. He thought they never accomplished more than six miles an hour; and the authorities would have been horrified if they had, fearing that the wash of the boat would damage the banks. They were constantly stopping to take up passengers and freight anywhere along the green banks. This gave them plenty of time to see the objects on the shore, but unfortunately there was next to nothing to see, the country being an unvaried level, over the whole thirty miles, save only the cathedral, which at last rather faded out than was hidden by any intervening object. The river retained its canal-like aspect all along; and only in the latter part of its course did it become more than wide enough for the little steamer to turn itself round; at broadest, not more than twice that width. And so to Boston.

The steam packets were soon to be driven off the river, as the coaches

[1] Thomas Cooper, *Wise Saws and Modern Instances* (1845), II, 121.

were driven off the roads, by the railways. But before a steam packet first appeared on the Witham, about 1814, there was only the horse-drawn packet; and on the road the mail coach was the best transport to be had. Long afterwards, when railway travel had become commonplace for the upper classes, Charles Anderson of Lea near Lincoln recalled the conditions of travel in his youth. Men were content to jog along in jackboots on palfreys of sober and constitutional pace, or to crawl through miry lanes in leathern conveniences called coaches or flies, truly like flies in a gluepot:

Even in later times, within our own remembrance, leaving Lincoln by the mail at 2 p.m. supping at Peterborough at 9, the traveller, after composing himself for an uneasy slumber about Yaxley Barracks (from whence the waters of Whittlesea Mere might be seen shimmering in the moonlight) grumbling through a weary night at the obstinate legs of his opposite neighbour, and sorely pinched in the small of the back, was duly delivered, cold and cross, at the Spread Eagle, Gracechurch Street, about 5 the next morning. He had then the choice of going to bed, with feet like ice, in a fireless room, opening out on an open-air gallery (where a box was fixed for the barber to shave travellers), or of sulking in a fusty coffee-room till the waiters were astir and the world was aired. But the days of Yaxley Barracks, where the French prisoners used to make toothpicks and models of machines of the bones which remained of their dinners, are long gone by – Whittlesea Mere has been pumped dry by machinery, and the Iron ways have superseded the old North Road.[1]

Gentry and business men were relieved of this discomfort by the railways. Within a few years they could reach London in little over three hours instead of thirteen, spend a few hours there, and return within the day. Most people, however, had no occasion to go, and could not afford the cost. It was a sensation when cheap trains were put on for the Great Exhibition in 1851; a third-class return fare to London was only 4s.; the Midland, trying to compete, would take a party of twelve at 2s. 6d. each. The pawnshops were crowded by people determined to seize the chance. Thereafter cheap holiday trains were provided; in 1856, a ticket to Grimsby and Cleethorpes cost only a shilling return.

Meanwhile, instead of the shriek of the steam engine and the whistle of the guard there was the clatter of the hooves of the coachhorses on the cobble stones and the blasts of the guards' horns as the four or five mail coaches passed up and down the street. Gentlemen and farmers rode in on horseback or in gigs to sessions or the market; the waggons crawled in with heavy goods; and the carriers' carts came rumbling in on market day, about a hundred of them from villages all around, putting up at 15 or 20 different inns, unloading the farmers' wives and daughters with

---

[1] *Lincoln Pocket Guide* (1st edition 1874), p. 1, 'To the Curious Reader'.

their butter, eggs and poultry for market, loading up again in the afternoon and rumbling home. And there were the country butchers and the fish and game dealers making for the butchery or the fish market. Teams of horses and waggons always tried to get to Lincoln by 6 a.m. and to do so might have to start by 2 a.m. Flocks of sheep would start for the fair on Monday and try to arrive by Tuesday night, resting on Wednesday. By Thursday they would be ready for the fair.[1]

Life in Lincoln was not only slow: it was isolated. For ordinary people the despatch or receipt of a letter was a rare event. Until the advent of the penny post in 1840 the total volume of letters was small.[2] The Lincoln post office consisted of a small room at the corner of Swanpool Court in High Street. There was only one delivery per day, but this was a great advance on the three posts a week to which they had been accustomed until 1790. There was only one messenger, Mrs Mimmack, an active old lady who went out in all weathers with skirts so short as scarcely to reach her ankles, and a large basket with two lids wherein she carried the letters. The post boy had to ride to Grantham for the mail, and in wintertime there was no knowing what time he would return. John Wold Drury was postmaster at a salary of £124, with perquisites from private boxes which made the job worth about £200. He resigned after many years, in 1846, and a room near the Stonebow was taken for the post office. When the penny post came in the number of letters passing through the Lincoln office multiplied nearly fourfold. It was only after much agitation that full advantage of railway transport was taken by the post office in getting mails to and from Lincoln. By 1887 the Lincoln office had about 50 officers and messengers besides those at five branch offices.[3]

Until the reform movement roused new interest in public affairs there was only one local newspaper, and that not very local, the *Lincoln Rutland and Stamford Mercury*, one of the oldest of provincial newspapers, published on Fridays at Stamford by Richard Newcomb.[4] He was a liberal and an opponent of the Exeter interest at Stamford, but he was regarded as undependable in his views. His local correspondents, 'often men of substance and influence in their respective neighbourhoods, were allowed a fairly free hand in their weekly report'.[5] The *Chronicle* commented that at Stamford it was for Church and State; at Lincoln for

[1] *Lincolnshire Magazine*, III (1938), no. 12.
[2] The postal charge depended on the distance the letter travelled. It was about 10d. from London to Lincoln.
[3] *L.C.*, 2 July 1887.
[4] *G.L.*, pp. 291–4.
[5] Dr R. J. Olney's unpublished thesis, 'Lincolnshire Politics, 1832–1885'.

the radical Seely; in the county for the whig Cholmeley and protection; at Boston, anti-church and free trade.[1] The Lincoln column was generally radical, especially from 1836 to 1838, when it was written by Thomas Cooper. The price of the paper was 4½d., and in 1852 its circulation, spread over several counties, averaged 12,060.

Growing concern with public affairs stimulated the appearance and growth of other newspapers. A *Lincoln Herald* was started in 1828 by James Amphlett, which veered to the tories when the radical James Hitchens issued the *Lincoln Times* in 1839; the latter only lasted a year. The *Herald* moved to Boston in 1832. Another liberal paper, the *Lincoln Gazette*, was begun about 1835 by W. S. Northhouse with the support of Lord Yarborough; Sir William Ingilby called it 'the Brocklesby Gazette'. In 1836 it was taken over by Edward Drury, and ceased in 1841. A tory *Lincolnshire Chronicle* began at Stamford in 1833. T. J. N. Brogden became its Lincoln correspondent in 1834 and its lessee in 1850, moving it to Lincoln. He resigned in 1856. A *Lincolnshire Times* was founded in 1847 by the liberal William Gresham; E. R. Cousans bought it about 1856, and merged it in the *Chronicle* when he became the latter's lessee in 1861; he surrendered his lease in 1870. A tory *Lincoln Standard* began in 1836, published by Brogden, but it was short lived. Brogden became a liberal in 1859, and started a new *Lincoln Gazette*, publishing it with his son J. E. Brogden until 1870 when Cousans bought it.[2]

The circulation of these papers, other than the *Mercury*, was small, and within a narrow radius. Edward Drury said in 1834 that only one in 20 people saw a newspaper, and that only once a week. He raised the circulation of the *Gazette* from 400 to 800; and he said that the circulation of the *Standard* in 1838 was 150.[3] What these papers lacked in circulation they sometimes made up in virulence, for which at a time of public controversy there was ample scope. Eatanswill was a caricature, but it contained some truth, and certainly some of the Lincoln journalists showed in their writings that they had read their *Pickwick Papers*, which began to appear in parts in 1836.

Most people took it for granted that if they wanted to go anywhere in the town they would have to walk. Hence men lived as near as they could to their work. Hence also the importance for health and recreation of the preservation of footpaths across the fields or by the river. They had not far to go to reach them. Lincoln was deeply embedded in the countryside, and the built-up area did not extend far from the heart of the city.

[1] *L.C.*, 7 May 1852.
[2] Dr Olney's thesis; *L.C.*, 29 December 1876, 7 May 1880.
[3] *G.L.*, p. 294.

High Street virtually ended with a few straggling houses below the future Midland station and the stables of Mr Chaplin and Mr King (both commemorated in street names). On the west of the city there was only one house beyond the Park, and the way from Newland to Carholme lay through the fields. In Newport there were a few stone farmhouses and cottages; on Wragby Road building ceased at the Peacock Inn, and on Monks Road at the Sessions House. Anyone wishing to go to Canwick or Washingborough could walk south from Broadgate, over the river by a swing bridge, and through the fields; or by St Mary Street over St Mary's Bridge on the Sincil Dyke into the same fields; or by a gate opening from the south end of High Street across a path on the South Common. The common, not as yet broken up by roads railway and cemetery, stretched to the future Great Northern Terrace, including the present Cowpaddle. Dwellers on the long ribbon of High Street to Bargate were imprisoned by water, the Witham on the west and Sincil Dyke on the east, with few bridges in either direction.

The *Mercury* said in 1835 that there was no place with less convenience of public walks than Lincoln.[1] But there were several walks. In 1833 Charles Mainwaring, the owner of the Monks estate towards Greetwell, built a granite head for the spring called 'the Spa' in the Monks fields.[2] A little to the north of it was the Monks lane, a sylvan way giving a superb view of the minster much favoured by De Wint and other artists. After many complaints about it being impassable, St Swithin's parish undertook its repair, with a footpath on the north side.[3] Thomas Cooper wrote of walks with Charles Seely by the Witham, or along the Canwick fields, or by the venerable minster.[4] George Boole, living in exile at Cork, wrote 'Oh! that the Greetwell fields and those with whom I have so often walked through them could be transported here!' And again, 'I adjure you by the "fen" and the "hayth", by Skellingthorpe wood and the memory of Swanpool, yea finally by the little hostelry at Fiskerton in which you once read to me Smith's *Polite Conversations*, that you come and see me here at Cork.'[5] Another choice of walk was added when a footpath was made by public subscription along the crest of the South Common in 1844.

New developments brought new threats to the footpaths. The walk

[1] *S.M.*, 25 December 1835.
[2] A. C. Benson, *The Trefoil* (1923), p. 150, remembered visits to fetch medicine bottles of chalybeate water from the spring, which was supposed to have an instantaneously strengthening effect.
[3] *S.M.*, 29 April 1836.
[4] *Life* (1872), p. 120.
[5] Letters (24 October 1854, 18 June 1855) to W. Brooke, per Mr A. P. Rollett.

along the Monks was blocked by the Manchester, Sheffield and Lincolnshire Railway; the path to Fiskerton disappeared; a Greetwell tenant
ploughed up a footpath; and stiles were erected that daunted the ladies.
Lord Yarborough promised to take up the grievances with the railway
board. The Great Northern Railway blocked a path along the south side
of Brayford in breach of a promise not to do so. From time to time,
beginning in 1842, the corporation took action to abate these nuisances,
starting in the Greetwell fields. In 1849 their officers went forth (the town
clerk saying he would go with them) with saw and hatchet to open the
blocked paths and bring the offenders before the magistrates. A new drive
began in 1857 with the mayor as chairman and Dr Elmhirst as secretary; they were to go beyond the city boundary within a radius of seven
miles. In 1873 Brogden with a handsaw and Maltby with an axe went out
removing obstructions to paths: there was another expedition in 1875.

There were other obstructions. Urchins beset the paths on Sundays,
breaking hedges, gambling and chasing animals; and policemen in plain
clothes were sent to prevent such desecration of the sabbath. The streets
too were noisy with waggons, carts and drays, rumbling over the cobble
stones; and of course they were constantly fouled by livestock passing
over them. The pavements were becoming cluttered with perambulators; in 1868 they were officially allowed to use the footpaths, though
they had so greatly multiplied that it was feared that they would become
a nuisance. Peg tops and whipcord, marble-playing, rope-skipping and
hoop-trundling had to be endured. In winter boys and girls would make
slides on the paths and pelt passengers with snowballs. A policeman,
looking on, would not interfere; it was not his job. The inspector of
nuisances ought to look to it; or the Lighting and Paving Commissioners
should sprinkle the slide with ashes. The proverb was constantly in the
mouths of inhabitants that the grievance was not likely to be redressed
until an alderman had broken his leg. Things have not changed in that
respect.

Street amusements ranged from pitch and toss almost to manslaughter.
Idle hulking vagabonds, the moral scourings of the Castle Dyke, infested the streets, and seemed to find it difficult to refrain from seizing
you by the throat and rifling your pockets. There were beggars everywhere, their plight being due, said Peacock, in 99 cases of 100 to idleness
and improvidence. The female beggar would have a child in her arms,
perhaps borrowed for the purpose, and others running along beside her,
occasionally impudent, especially if half drunk.[1]

Walking continued (horses excepted) to be the only means of loco-

[1] Many of these details are taken from the MS of Edward Peacock in my possession.

motion until the advent of bicycles in the late 1860s. At first they
appeared only in the better seasons, being dormant in winter, and they
were for the audacious rather than the sober and respectable; and
certainly it needed courage to mount one of the penny-farthing variety
whose front wheel might be five feet high. Markham Hill was the first
clergyman to ride a bicycle in Lincoln streets. Mounted on a 48-inch
Coventry machine he caused some scandal; until one day, at a dinner
party at the deanery, Dean Blakesley (1872–85) called down the table:
'Mr Hill, I am told you ride a velocipede round the cathedral.' 'Yes, Mr
Dean', was the reply. 'Well', added the dean, 'I wish I could.'[1] By the
1890s the 'safety' bicycle was equipped with pneumatic tyres and free
wheels.

Bicycle sports were established in 1879, and soon included motor cycle
racing, and the Cycle Club's first annual road handicap followed in
1883. Motor cars – rich men's toys – were to make no impact on the life
of the city until much later. Under the Motor Car Act of 1903 the chief
constable was instructed to issue registration certificates of motor cars
and motor cycles, and in 1908 a motorist was fined for travelling at the
Stonebow at six miles an hour.

Other sports were coming in as the gradual reduction of working hours
provided opportunity.[2] Cricket was already becoming a popular game
in the early years of the century. By 1834 there were two cricket clubs in
Lincoln, the Independent and the Sociable; in 1842 the Commercial
Cricket Club advertised for home and away matches within a 30-mile
radius, stipulating that clubs must consist only of *bona fide* resident
members. There was a Lincoln Cricket Club in 1848. The clerks in
Clayton and Shuttleworth formed the Stamp End Cricket Club in 1854,
and the United Lindum came into being two years later.[3] Enthusiasm
for the game owed much to the Monson family, who had matches at
Burton between an All-England XI and a Lincolnshire XXII. A like match
was played on the racecourse in 1854. The first Lincolnshire side was
formed in 1880.[4]

Football was being seen as a means of combating the degeneracy of
town life. The Football Association was formed in 1863, and many of the
famous clubs came into being in the 1870s. The Lincoln Football Club
was formed in 1884 by the union of three older clubs (one which joined

[1] *L.L.*, 8 September 1900.
[2] Below, p. 155.
[3] In 1857 G. K. Jarvis was told of its ambition to make the club one of the first in the
neighbourhood. The mayor was a patron, Richard Hall president and Councillor
Mortimer treasurer. L.A.O. Jarvis, vi/2/17.
[4] *Lincolnshire Magazine*, III (1938), no. 9.

the London Association was in being in 1863), and it at once grew to 70 members. All the players were amateurs, the first professional being engaged in 1886. Originally they played in a field at 'John of Gaunt's', acquiring their Sincil Bank ground in 1895.

There was a rowing regatta in 1841, and later this became an annual event. The usual course was on the Witham between Stamp End lock and Washingborough, spectators watching from the Monks fields, and being entertained by the militia band. A Lincoln Rowing Club was formed in 1847, and this and other clubs organised sports at Saxilby and Drinsey Nook on the Fossdyke, the inns there being popular ports of call. From 1861 there was a regatta on Brayford every year. More sober transport was provided for Sunday school treats, William Rainforth and other kindly barge owners taking parties to Burton Lane End, Drinsey Nook or even to Torksey. There were swimming events also, and great fishing expeditions to Fiskerton, where the landlord of the inn provided giblet pies. For the more roisterous there were the village wakes: drinking and fighting might go on for hours at Bracebridge. The appearance of billiard tables and bagatelle boards with their incitement to gambling, also caused alarm among the sober.

Temple Gardens, on the hillside between the Old Palace and Lindum Road, had been leased as pleasure gardens. Subscribers could buy either family or single tickets. The City band played there every Wednesday evening during the summer, and the Bluecoat band sometimes. There were brass band contests and flower shows and Sunday school galas, and even exhibitions of arts and sciences, and an occasional balloon ascent provided a sensation. In 1863 Mr Collingham bought the gardens in order to build a house for himself, and the lack of such a place no doubt stimulated the demand for an arboretum.[1] But by then there were many demands, some of them much greater and more important.

[1] This is now the site of the Usher Art Gallery. Brass bands, following the invention of the piston-valve instrument, became popular in the 1850s.

CHAPTER II

POLITICS 1832-68

Although the Reform Bill of 1832 set in motion a succession of changes which eventually led to universal suffrage, the changes the Bill itself effected were limited, and indeed included provisions which favoured the old order. Colonel Sibthorp, the eccentric tory member for Lincoln, moved that in the counties there should be added to the forty shilling freeholders who had immemorially enjoyed the county franchise the £50 tenants at will. The radicals backed the proposal on general principle, and with their aid the tories carried their point.[1] Clearly tenants at will as a class were more amenable to influence than freeholders, and so the gentry were able to strengthen their hold on the county seats. The point is neatly illustrated by the practice of Lord Yarborough's steward, who never canvassed freeholders on behalf of his master's heir but thought it his duty to claim the votes of tenants at will.[2]

The decision to give four members instead of two to a number of counties, including Lincolnshire, promised increase of weight to the landed interest; and the cutting of these counties into two electoral divisions upset members on both sides of the House of Commons. In undivided Lincolnshire the largest single interest was that of Lord Yarborough; but in north Lincolnshire his interest would be so strong as to turn it into a nomination borough. In Grimsby, too, he had the largest influence, though smaller interests, Heneage or Tennyson or the independents, might secure one of its two seats. The Lincolnshire boroughs all kept their two seats save Grimsby which was deprived of one member – it had a population of only about 4,000 – and the remaining seat was safe for a Yarborough nominee. The inclusion of several additional parishes within the constituency strengthened the whig interest still further.

At the other end of the county, Stamford, the stronghold of Lord Exeter at nearby Burleigh House, was made more secure for him both by the inclusion in the parliamentary borough of the parish of St Martin, which was part of his estate, and the abolition of the scot and lot franchise – every householder having a vote – and the substitution of the £10 householder, which reduced the number of voters.

On the other hand the result in Lincoln did not aggrieve the reformers. The non-resident freemen had lost their votes. It was thought that there

[1] Sibthorp was much aggrieved that Lord Chandos got the credit.
[2] D. Southgate, *Passing of the Whigs* (1962), p. 93.

had been about a thousand of them; where they lived in considerable numbers, as in London, they had been able to negotiate collectively for the sale of their votes, bringing in an election jobber who sold them to a prospective candidate. So vanished the worst and most conspicuous form of corruption.[1] The resident freemen, who in the first draft of the Bill would also have been disfranchised, had been reprieved. There were about 600 of them; as a class they too were by custom corrupt. It might be expected that they would continue to look for the payment of 'compliments' by the candidates they supported; but they would no doubt also remember, at least for a time, that it was the tories whom they had to thank for defending their interests.[2] Sibthorp defended the old system, in which he was an experienced practitioner, and opposed a Bill against bribery as being so loose and indefinite that it might inhibit acts of hospitality and charity; and going over to the offensive, pointed out that a dinner given to ministerial members in Downing Street, and the feeding and fattening of them by His Majesty's Government, that they might have their votes, were indisputable specimens of corruption.[3]

The new class of voters, the £10 householders, would owe their votes to the whigs who had enfranchised them; and the greater number of them would belong to the lower middle class, dissenters and radicals among them, who could be relied upon to support the whigs until they had a chance of supporting liberals and radicals. There were about 450 £10 householders, some of them resident in the Bail and Close, which had been brought into the parliamentary constituency for the first time, and in which the influence of clergy and gentry would be strong. These latter voters would reinforce the tory interest.

As Sibthorp had forecast in the debates on the Bill, the electorate had been reduced, though not as much as he had expected. In the election of 1826, 1233 had voted; in 1832 it was computed that 1,083 would be entitled to vote. In fact the number that voted was 878. The strength of Sibthorp's argument had been reduced by the reprieve of the resident freemen.[4]

An election soon followed the passing of the Bill. The retiring members

[1] *G.L.*, pp. 225–36.
[2] At a magistrates' dinner in 1850 old Humphrey Sibthorp recalled events at the election of 1818. He went to the bank in the morning and drew £3,000, the whole of which was spent in the course of the day, and £300 more besides, merely in paying Coningsby Sibthorp's voters *mileage* and *subsistence* money, in addition to payment for their votes. 'Unluckily', wrote Cracroft 'I could not catch the exact sum, as the waiters came in with the tea at the moment, but I think it was ten [guineas].' Cracroft, 7 June 1850.
[3] *P.D.*, 3rd Series, xiv, 1157.
[4] The number of resident freemen who were not £10 householders steadily declined, and their importance was much reduced by the introduction of household suffrage in 1867.

for the county were Yarborough's son Charles Pelham, an aristocratic whig, and Sir William Amcotts Ingilby, an eccentric whig of increasingly radical tendencies, who had come in at a by-election in 1823 on the Yarborough interest.[1] His violence of speech and his constant attacks on the clergy – the 'sable gentry' – were to be his undoing. In the meantime he was the hero of the reformers, and his whimsical speeches had their publicity value. He stood again.

Presently Sir Robert Sheffield emerged as the tory candidate. He was a much liked and respected county figure, but not of any special ability.[2] The other whig candidate was Charles Pelham, who did not campaign vigorously: his family interest was enough.

This was in the new northern division of the county. In the new southern division there was no tory opposition to the whig candidates, Henry Handley, a private banker, and Gilbert John Heathcote, son of Sir Gilbert, who was probably the largest landowner in the south of the county.

In the city the retiring members were Sibthorp and the whig George Fieschi Heneage, son of the squire of Hainton.[3] He was a respected though not a popular figure, but he had the double advantage of being local and able to bear his own expenses. Some years later he was described by Weston Cracroft in his diary:

25 June 1849. What a singular being George Heneage of Hainton is – sometimes apparently in a trance and dead as it were to all around him, and then starting up, making some absurd observation, and then laughing the most curious laugh at his own wit...However, with all his oddities, George Heneage is a clever man, exceedingly well read, and can converse well on most subjects. Hainton is a very agreeable house to stay at.

22 November 1854. He is an oddity, and the most high minded and high principled excellent man, answers to the description of a 'queer fish' – no man has a kinder heart. See him sit at dinner sometimes for 5 minutes at a time without opening his lips, then all of a sudden he'll tell a story apparently quite foreign to the conversation, and burst into an uncontrollable fit of laughter.....often he'll repeat the anecdote (a good one, for he tells them well) and burst out again.[4]

[1] He was a Yorkshire baronet who had inherited Kettlethorpe near Lincoln from his mother. *G.L.*, p. 230.

[2] Anderson wrote of him 'dear excellent man, to think of thus losing his right hand (in a shooting accident) which was of more use than half the right hands in the county put together'. Diary, 2 September 1838. Cracroft said 'though utterly devoid of talent, and a very poor speaker, no man ever gave more satisfaction as chairman of quarter sessions'. 4 July 1856.

[3] No doubt his second name was the origin of his nickname of 'Fish'. Ellen Tennyson wrote (1 January 1833): 'Fish is going to be married to a Miss Tasburg(h), a Catholic who lives near Doncaster. She is not at all pretty, but on a very large scale. Fish seems to have been the best of the bunch at the Lincolnshire election, as he supported Papa *most manfully* for such a lethargic character.'

[4] Heneage's aunt Mrs Hoare used to say that he was the greatest bore she knew. It was said that the grand library at Sir John Thorold's at Syston was a dangerous one. It has a

The reformers needed a second candidate, and the whigs in London found for them Edward Lytton Bulwer, who had been member for St Ives, and was already known as a novelist and editor of the *New Monthly Magazine*. He was helped from the party purse,[1] and had chosen to stand for Lincoln because the whigs there, like himself, were defenders of the corn laws. He was a clever and foppish young man, and in a moment of triumph after the election was to refer in his *England and the English* to Sibthorp as a small second rate country squire.[2]

The most famous of all the local candidates was Charles de Laet Waldo Sibthorp, who had succeeded to the family estates at Canwick on the southern border of Lincoln, and to many estates elsewhere, on the death of his elder brother Coningsby. Several of his family, including his father and his elder brother, had represented the city. Charles had been a captain in the 4th Dragoon Guards and was happily married. According to Cracroft the change in his circumstances changed the man, and he became heartless and purseproud, leading a life of intemperance, riot and wickedness. His wife divorced him. 'A perfect mountebank in manner and appearance,' wrote Cracroft, 'yet I must do him the justice to say that he was a most fearless public man.'[3]

It is these aspects of him that are chiefly remembered. Charles Dickens described him in his *Sketches by Boz*:[4]

You see this ferocious looking gentleman, with a complexion almost as sallow as his linen, and whose huge black moustache would give him the appearance of a

gallery round it, and someone engaged in reading there heard a murmur of voices in the room below, and looking over the gallery, saw George Heneage on his knees proposing to Miss Tasburgh. Anderson Letters, II, a note preceding letters from G. F. Heneage, 11 July 1864. The note was added by Anderson long afterwards. Heneage succeeded to the family estates in 1833.

[1] Lord Broughton (John Cam Hobhouse), *Recollections of a Long Life*. VI (1911), 208. Bulwer was recommended by Fazackerley, a former member for Lincoln on the Monson interest.

[2] The phrase was removed from later editions. Sibthorp, who hated reading, may never have seen the reference, and if he did would be likely to dismiss it with the most lofty contempt. For a description of Bulwer at this time of his life, see James Grant, *Random Recollections of the House of Commons from the Year 1830 to the Close of 1835, by One of no Party.* (1836), pp. 331–3.

[3] 25 July 1850, 16–19 December 1855: 'the only good point of his past life to look back to with any comforting thought of him is his reconciliation with his wife, and his family surrounding him in his last days – else all's blank, and much worse.' His weaknesses were of course well known to his family. His brother-in-law Henry Hawkins wrote to Humphrey Sibthorp c. 1831 about the disadvantages of working with an unstable character: 'I would advise him to regain if possible his lost popularity among the more respectable portion of his constituents, and those who under the new bill are likely to become his constituents. I am at a loss to know how he will get into parliament when all the close and rotten boroughs are annihilated.' L.A.O. 3 Sibthorp 1/19.

[4] Published 1833–6: 'A Parliamentary Sketch'.

figure in a hairdresser's window, if his countenance possessed the thought that is communicated to those waxen caricatures of the human face divine. He is a militia-officer, and the most amusing person in the House. Can anything be more exquisitely absurd than the burlesque grandeur of his air, as he strides up to the lobby, his eyes rolling like those of a Turk's head in a cheap Dutch clock? He never appears without that bundle of dirty papers which he carries under his left arm, and which are generally supposed to be the miscellaneous estimates for 1804, or some equally important documents. He is very punctual in his attendance at the House, and his self-satisfied 'He-ar, He-ar' is not infrequently the signal for a general titter.[1]

Another writer described this cause of frequent merriment in the House:

Lo! far up the mountain of benches, close by one of the pillars of the side-gallery, there stands a figure which defies classification. It is unique. It would, at first glance, merely excite ridicule; but at a second, you perceive a something indicative of strength, of manliness, of self-possession, which mingles a kind of involuntary respect with your laughter. It looks like the *débris* of what must have been a *magnifico*. A majestic air of tawdry grandeur reminds you of how King Joachim might have looked when he found that the game was up at Naples.[2]

He spoke constantly on every subject, though he was not capable of making a long speech. He could denounce an opponent without there being the slightest ill-feeling on either side. He enjoyed bickering with Ingilby, especially about the latter's smoking habits. He was the favourite butt of *Punch*, which often filled up a corner with some dictum or pun attributed to him.[3]

The Reform Bill had not changed the electoral scene as much as was no doubt expected by reformers. It was still the gentry, local or otherwise, to whom the parties looked for candidates.[4] The whigs, it is true, had lost the influence of the Monson family. For some generations they had generally been able to hold one of the Lincoln seats, but the family interest had been weakened by a long minority; and the young fifth lord, who had lately come of age, was not a reformer.[5] The whigs, therefore,

---

[1] The forest of hair upon his face gave O'Connell an opportunity to parody Dryden's verses when Sibthorp and two other colonels opposed a grant to Maynooth College in 1845:

> Three colonels, in three different counties born,
> Did Lincoln, Sligo and Armagh adorn;
> The first in gravity of face surpassed,
> The next in bigotry – in both the last.
> The force of nature could no further go;
> To beard the one she shaved the other two.

[2] *Fraser's Magazine*, xxxvi (July–December 1847), 462–5.
[3] Towards the end of Sibthorp's life the sixth Lord Monson passed judgment on him and the electors of Lincoln: 'I think it is very disgraceful the way Sibthorp is always received and the horrid stuff he talks that they cheer.' L.A.O. Monson 25/10/3/2/52. 8 July 1852.
[4] Stamford, Grantham and Grimsby were virtually nomination boroughs; Boston sometimes returned one of the gentry.   [5] *G.L.*, ch. IX.

had to look to other local families or to the whig caucus in London. In coming years they were to have increasing difficulty in holding the more positive reformers, and the strains in the party began to show almost at once. On the other side also there was a growing difference between the old tories like Sibthorp and the modern conservatives who looked to Peel as their leader. This rift did not show quite so quickly.

When Heneage arrived he found whigs and radicals working together in an electoral committee, the latter acting as pacemakers. He did not like it, and on their part the committee did not like his wish to have a committee of his own. The Saints – the evangelicals – were asking candidates for their views on the emancipation of slaves, and thought Heneage not as explicit on the subject as he ought to have been. Sibthorp declared in favour of gradual emancipation: his brother the Reverend Richard was a leading Saint. Charlesworth shrewdly commented, 'We are sold to Bulwer: the election will be a rough one, and all Sibthorp's courage will be needed: his bodily stamina will scarcely be adequate.'[1]

When voting began Sibthorp was in the lead, but on the second day of the poll his brother Humphrey accepted defeat on his behalf. Heneage headed the poll with 543 votes, Bulwer following with 448, and Sibthorp polled 402, of which 312 were plumpers.[2] It was the only time in a long public life that he was defeated, and he took his defeat with courage and self-possession.

The reformers took to rejoicing. Yet the rift had shown, and at one point Heneage had been tempted to make off. The radicals had been prepared to throw him over if it were necessary to secure Bulwer's return by plumping for him. In fact, they had each only five plumpers; they had kept together in confidence of the result. Charlesworth reviewed the battle:

12 December 1832. Notwithstanding the first chair majority of Heneage ceded to him by Bulwer, to whom as an alien it was not an object, I am still of opinion that if the Reform ship had not been found equal to its whole burthen, Heneage would have been recklessly thrown overboard. I dare say he has paid for his whistle. Sibthorp's fate had been decided by the Dissenters, who voted to a man against him, openly perhaps on grounds of his private character, but really because he supported the Church. His vices did not alarm the consciences of the Dissenters when they answered to the holy call of St Richard wearing a pink cockade. It is understood that this righteous interest will for the future always return *one* representative at least...I hear that Sibthorp is paying cheerfully, liberally and promptly.[3]

[1] Bromhead mss (6 June 1832).
[2] I.e. the voters who polled only one of their two votes.
[3] Bromhead mss.

Charlesworth was impartial in his dislikes; he did not realise that the dissenters were bound to support the whigs as the party most likely to relieve them of their civil disabilities.

In the northern division of the county Pelham and Ingilby defeated Sheffield; several drafts of an inscription to be placed on plate to be presented to Ingilby have survived, of which the most polished reads:

> These gilded toys
> From the Lindsey Boys
> To their Comical Knight
> The Yorkshire Bite
> Wot laid the Nobs
> At the feet of the Snobs
> In 1833.[1]

Towards the end of 1834 there were rumours of another election. The tories were rallying their forces, forming clubs and paying great attention to the registration of voters. On the other side, reforming zeal had ebbed; exaggerated hopes were dashed by the government's dull record and still more by the unpopular New Poor Law.[2] Locally too Ingilby had lost ground. It was thought in north Lincolnshire that he might be dropped for both his violence and his irresponsibility; and that his place might be taken in the county by Heneage, and that Yarborough might send a younger son to Lincoln. Such a change would have suited the Lincoln radicals, who wanted a more decided reformer than the lukewarm Heneage. The electoral committee, which tried to hold together whigs and radicals, was unpopular. A caucus was a new thing, and Charlesworth denounced it:

13 December 1834. They have emancipated the town from the 'tyranny' of Canwick and Burton to establish a new oligarchy. The town should call upon Colonel Sibthorp to rid them of the tyranny of that crew: a printed list of their names would disband them at once...Shall we have a Pelham sent to us?[3]

The tories also hated the electoral committee as 'a band of petty tyrants'.

As some of his supporters were saying that they would reserve their votes until they were sure of Bulwer's election, Heneage withdrew, and Captain Phipps was imported as a second reform candidate. Sibthorp was returned at the head of the poll with 565 votes, of which 456 were plumpers, and Bulwer held the second seat. In the northern division Pelham headed the poll, and Ingilby lost his seat to Thomas George Corbett, then a tory.[4] The prime mover of the tory campaign was

---

[1] L.A.O. Tennyson d'Eyncourt, H30/36.
[2] Below, p. 131.   [3] Bromhead MSS.
[4] He had been a radical, then a tory and protectionist, and later was said to be a free trader. In the Lincoln district Ingilby headed the poll, followed by Corbett and Pelham.

Robert Swan, the registrar of the diocese, no doubt urged on by Ingilby's attacks on the clergy; it was said that he had an agent – the parish clerk – in every village ready to begin an immediate canvass.[1] Faced with the need for money and organization Ingilby did not stand again.

Enthusiasts were soon looking to another election. The Lincoln radical James Hitchens wrote to Charles Tennyson, now become d'Eyncourt:

16 August 1836. We are in a delightful position. Tomorrow's paper will contain Sir William Ingilby's retirement from the Lindsey Division. The cause is indeed to be deplored for his coming to this decision. A Conservative Association is upon the *tapis*, in conjunction with that formed in the South Division.

As to the city he added:

In addition to the *horror* of a *military* merry andrew we are to have tried a *legal* merry andrew in the person of Sir Charles Wetherell. It will however in this case be a sorry event for them, for *both* must go out should they try it. The Tories are very active in the Registration, the *Parish Clerks* are again foisted upon the Cits. Shall we in the absence of Sir William have any champion, or shall we tamely submit to be ridden over?[2]

Tory thinking was not as Hitchens thought it was. It was the conservatives of a Peelite kind, headed by Bromhead, who sought to put up a candidate. The Sibthorps did not like this idea, as the colonel depended largely on the number of plumpers he could muster; and hints were put about that votes might be divided between Sibthorp and Bulwer. However, the new candidate, Henry Ellis,[3] appeared, and Bromhead explained to him that Sibthorp's vote was partly personal, and that he (Ellis) ought to have a separate committee.[4]

The reformers also had to rely on a carpet-bagger for their second candidate, Bulwer remaining the first, and they put forward Colonel Churchill, whose versatility was described by Anderson:

18 November 1837. Colonel Churchill, a red roaring Rad., is in Lincoln waltzing with the cits' daughters at night and speechifying the dissenters at public breakfasts in the morning, with a converted Caffre chief, poor wretch, from the Wesleyan Missionary Association, and it is said will turn out Bulwer, whose books the dissenters begin to think improper. What a world of humbug this is![5]

At the election in that year, caused by the accession of Queen Victoria,

[1] L.A.O. Tennyson d'Eyncourt, H29/34, 25 December 1834, E. B. Drury to Tennyson. The curate of Orby wrote that his vote for Ingilby would be almost unique, as his only church vote. Diary of John Rashdall in the Bodleian Library; typewritten copy L.A.O. Misc. Don. 125. p. 87, entry for 20 January 1835.
[2] L.A.O. Tennyson d'Eyncourt, H34/78.
[3] He was half-brother to the Countess of Ripon, and had once been returned for Boston, but was unseated on petition. Later he was ambassador to Persia.
[4] Bromhead MSS (30 June, 31 August 1837).
[5] Wilberforce MSS, d25, fol. 175.

Sibthorp kept his place at the head of the poll, and Bulwer held the second seat. It was complained with justice by Ellis' supporters that some tories did not vote for their man but plumped for Sibthorp; the latter had 36 plumpers and Ellis only lost by 44. Humphrey Sibthorp lamely explained that some of them would have given a second vote to Bulwer.

Bromhead was soon in touch with William Rickford Collett, who had just been defeated at Boston, as a possible candidate at Lincoln. He was a banker and railway projector, and owned a slate mine in Tipperary, in which, as he told the House of Commons in 1846, he had for nine years employed 900 labourers and spent £90,000.[1] He was described as 'a big handsome man with large features, swarthy complexion, copious curling whiskers, and a great deal of hair, amateur painter in oils, fond of music'.[2]

Collett was willing; and he approached Sibthorp, who was polite and complimentary, but said he never directly interfered. When a meeting with Sibthorp was suggested, the latter said he was willing to come, and he would take the chair himself. This, said Brogden to Bromhead, would never do.

December 1838. If Colonel Sibthorp takes the chair we shall be inundated with nonsense, but that is not the worst. It is my firm persuasion he will embrace the opportunity which his position will give him to give a knock down blow to Mr Collett. If you are not present there will not be a soul that dare open his mouth in condemnation of such conduct.

Swan and some other extreme tories refused support; Swan even accused Bromhead of carrying on Conservatism on republican principles. But by then there was a club of tory working men, called the Pitt Club, whose members were determined to have Collett. He had, however, some shortcomings as a candidate. Brogden commented that if he would remain long enough, and not pass along the streets without bowing to the people, he would succeed; he must not confine his attention to above-hill ladies of conservative principles, but condescend – at the Cake Ball – to dance with the tradesman's wife or daughter even of blue principles, provided he did not make his own friends jealous.[3] Elections – and human nature – have not changed much.

Bulwer had lost ground. He was a supporter of the new Poor Law, pointing to the great saving it had effected in taxation, and claiming that as pauperism had diminished the moral tone of the working classes had risen in proportion. Furthermore, he was regarded as halfhearted about the corn laws; this would upset the tories, and the liberals were veering to

---

[1] *P.D.*, 3rd Series, 85,727.   [2] Ex inf. Sir William Hart.
[3] Bromhead MSS, *c.* 31 December 1839.

free trade. His matrimonial affairs and the tone of his books were against him.[1]

Charles Seely had emerged as a radical leader. He was a portent. His father had been a miller and baker in Lincoln – he himself used to be described as 'the baker's boy' – and he had several mills, becoming a partner in the firm of Keyworth and Seely, corn merchants and millers, in 1835;[2] and he was to become a wealthy man, with coalmining interests in Derbyshire. He was elected to the city council in 1837, and was mayor in 1840; it was said on his election that there were no persons so proper for mayor as those who had erected such chimneys as Mr Seely's chimneys. A steam flour mill was progress indeed. Writing of an early friendship with him, Thomas Cooper said:

He would have me, almost every Sunday, at his table; and often we sauntered by the Witham, or along the Canwick fields, or by the venerable Minster, in the dusk of evening; and sometimes I rode with him, in his mercantile journeys, to Boston or Sleaford. Our conversations were on politics, or human character and society, or on general literature; but how often during the years that have passed since I left Lincoln, have I thought of the one strong deep impression I caught of my friend's character – 'This is the man whose purpose is formed, and he will accomplish it', and how completely that impression has been realised![3]

His purpose was to become member for Lincoln, and in pursuing it he made no attempts at conciliation; he quarrelled with the whigs, and even his friends regarded him as selfish.

Feeling ran high about the corn laws, and there was a great county meeting in their defence, at which whigs and tories combined. When the election came in 1841 there was no talk of tories plumping for Sibthorp; they voted for Collett as well. As the contest went on, Seely, finding that he could not win, tried to save Bulwer by throwing his interest to him. It was in vain. The tories won both seats, a thing they were never able to do again, and Seely was at the bottom of the poll. Lincolnshire was almost solidly for the corn laws.[4]

[1] When he presented a copy of his play *Richelieu* to the Mechanics Institute, his wife presented a copy of her novel *Cheveley; or the Man of Honor*, in which she satirised him unmercifully.   [2] As to the Keyworths, see *G.L.*, p. 204.
[3] *Life* (1872), p. 120. When Cooper republished his *Wise Saws and Modern Instances* as *Old Fashioned Stories* in 1874, he dedicated the book to Seely in memory of a forty-year friendship. Seely's mother said she put down £3,000 towards his election expenses. Bromhead MSS, 16 June 1841.
[4] It was alleged that the rewards for voting for Sibthorp were not promptly paid, and a crowd of placemen went to Washingborough to demand payment from Humphrey Sibthorp, threatening to pull his house about his ears. When Sibthorp went to the races he was besieged by ragged and drunken freemen.
The Swedish artist Rylander was lodging in Lincoln at the time of the election, and he depicted a scene in the contest in a drawing given by the late Dr W. H. B. Brook to the

The long reign of the whigs had ended, and a conservative government under Peel took office. Peel had been Sibthorp's hero, and his adulation must have been an embarrassment to Peel.[1] But he watched the premier with mounting suspicion as he veered towards free trade. The corn laws were repealed in 1846, and Sibthorp's idol was broken.

He does not like to turn round and abuse Sir Robert, after his eloquent praises of that statesman which are on record; nor, on the other hand, does he like openly to laud Lord John Russell and the Whigs, whom he has so often denounced, amidst the cheers and laughter of his friends, as the incarnation of everything that is wicked and despicable in statesmanship. He halts, therefore, between the two, and his vocation is for a time partially suspended. He is sorely puzzled between the present, the past, and the future; and his demeanour in his new position is very comical. But there is hope for Colonel Sibthorp. Ere long parties must settle down, and there will then again be afforded scope for that frankness of disposition, and that habit of unflinchingly uttering the most *bizarre* truths, which have made the colonel so famous, and from which it is only justice to say, that the House and the public have been accustomed to receive no small portion of instruction together with their amusement.[2]

When the government soon afterwards was defeated, the whigs under Russell took office, and manoeuvres began for the next election. Bulwer – now become Lytton – was a doubtful starter on grounds of health, and he sounded Rudgard, his leading supporter, upon the idea that his place might be taken by his friend Charles Tennyson d'Eyncourt's son George. Rudgard replied that nothing but old associations with Lytton would prevent the liberals from going in a body with Seely. Lytton thought he would have no chance unless Collett withdrew, and to this end there were approaches between Sibthorp's and Lytton's friends; but they had no success. Lytton was still a whig, though the liberal parliamentary agent told him in 1848 that he was half tory, half protectionist,[3] and

Usher Gallery. The figures were identified in the *L.C.*, 15 September 1876, as follows: 'There are half a dozen figures, evidently portraits, and of this number Col. Sibthorp, the candidate, Powell, the Canwick gardener of that time, and that electioneering celebrity "Judy Day", were mentioned as being easily recognised. A correspondent supplies the following identification of the remaining figures: The one smoking the cigar is Louis, a young Frenchman, who was on a visit to the Rev. – Adcock, Master of the Grammar School. The one with paper in his hat is Charlie Robson, a livery stable keeper, who had stables at the rear of the Black Boy, now pulled down. The remaining one is undoubtedly Dick Muller, an old "Worthy and Independent", the hero of 100 electioneering fights, although he often came off second best.' The scene is placed on the Castle Hill, where the Black Boy stood. William Day was the keeper of the Red Lion in Hungate. The small figure in the background on the left is Sibthorp.

[1] *Punch* described one occasion when Peel's anguish under Sibthorp's eulogy seemed intolerable. 'He reminded us of the sufferings of the *Clown* as promised by *Autolycus*; a hapless creature smeared with honey, and then set over a wasps' nest.'

[2] *Frasers Magazine*, XXXVI, 462–5.

[3] Broughton, *Recollections of a Long Life*, VI (1911), 208.

plain men thought he was neither one thing nor the other. Seely's partner, Keyworth, tried through d'Eyncourt to convince Lytton that he had no chance: he argued that the 380 new voters added to the register since the 1841 election were nearly all Seely men.[1] There was another question: should the liberals and free traders put up a second candidate? John Norton – Calico John – thought they should:

16 May 1847. Seely will risk nothing for the sake of principle – so that he gets returned he cares not who his colleague is. I have never been sanguine enough to think we could return two liberals at the next election, but I feel assured that if a gentleman like your friend [D. W. Harvey] stood the contest he would run our celebrated colonel very hard and injure his seat on the next occasion. The majority of our electors are liberals in politics, and only want a bold and energetic man to arouse them to the proper discharge of their duty...

Collett was very unpopular, and attempts had been made to get him to retire, and bring out Lytton to defeat Seely. Seely was understood to have nearly 600 *written* promises, and if they proved faithful he must succeed.[2]

In the event the two tories and Lytton and Seely all went to the poll. It was alleged afterwards that on election eve Seely's supporters went about in disguise, kidnapping voters and making doubtful men drunk so as to keep them safe. Alderman Gresham, it was said, was arrayed in a blue smock frock and a low crowned waggoner's hat, but a wag called out 'Twig his legs' and he was discovered; another was arrayed in a soldier's coat, and patriots were there in fancy costume. On the day Seely's strength was brought up early by plumpers, and for a time he was at the head of the poll. The mob, in his interest, broke into a granary and drank all the ale they could find in a brewhouse, and a desperate riot outside the Saracen's Head was at last quelled by the mayor and others. At the end Sibthorp headed the poll with 659 votes, Seely coming second with 518. Lytton polled 436 and Collett only 273.[3] Seely was drawn through the city in a triumphal car, in his procession an effigy of Rudgard on a kind of gallows, labelled 'The Newland Dictator' which was burnt near Bargate.[4] This proved costly. Collett had been defeated by cross voting:

[1] L.A.O. Tennyson d'Eyncourt, H23/34.   [2] *Ibid*, H23/7.
[3] Collett had been in trouble with the Methodists for voting for a grant to the Roman Catholic College of Maynooth. He was gazetted bankrupt in 1851.
[4] An election squib of 1841 was devoted to Rudgard's determination to beat Seely:

> I over the Charity trust preside,
> Christ's Hospital Governor am beside,
> I'm Magistrate too – I have been Mayor
> Then what for the people need I care.
> I won't be beat (etc.)

This no doubt alludes to the charge that while the Sibthorps paid money to voters *for past*

while 226 voted for Sibthorp and Collett, 266 voted for Sibthorp and Lytton. Only 124 voted for Seely and Lytton, whilst Seely had 215 plumpers and Lytton only 39.

The radical Northhouse, noticing how ill Sibthorp looked, wrote to Tennyson d'Eyncourt that in the event of an early vacancy there would be a chance to return young George cheaply. He added:

16 August 1847. I pity Sir Edward Bulwer Lytton. I am afraid his pretended friends have ruined *his* cause for ever in Lincoln. In my various speeches at the Theatre and in the open air I spoke as I felt of his intellectual grandeur and excellent qualities to such an extent that Mr H. Williams adroitly used my eulogium as a sufficient reason for plumping for him and not voting for my client Seely.[1]

Rudgard prompted a petition against Seely's return on the ground of corruption, some tories subscribing to the petition fund. At the hearing before the Commons committee Seely acknowledged that he had lent money freely, though more borrowers voted against him than for him, and he referred to the practices of Sibthorp and Collett. The committee found that a system of treating had for a long time prevailed in Lincoln by candidates or their agents distributing at public houses to electors and others drink and other entertainment. Seely was unseated. He clearly expected this result, and had a candidate ready. Thomas Benjamin Hobhouse, brother of Sir John Cam Hobhouse, a liberal minister, at once set off to contest the seat. His brother wrote to Lytton asking for support, saying that he understood Lytton did not intend to stand. Lytton was justifiably furious, and denounced the action as an act of political discourtesy and ingratitude without parallel. They should have known that no reliance was to be placed on anything Seely or his friends might say about his intentions. He was sure his friends would bring him forward, and he would be supported by all but Seely's special faction.[2] He said later this course had been agreed during the hearing of the petition, and that the appearance of Hobhouse had naturally led the tories to suppose that he was not standing, and to bring forward a candidate.[3] Lytton visited Lincoln, found his position hopeless, and

services, the liberals distributed municipal charities on like principles. To all this the 'people' replied with equal contempt for English grammar:

> We won't be beat! We won't be beat!
> Seely shall have a member's seat.
> What care we for treacherous Will?
> United and free we'll conquer still.

[1] L.A.O. Tennyson d'Eyncourt, H44/31.
[2] B.M. Add. MSS 36471 (Broughton MSS), ff. 361–405.
[3] *Life of Edward Bulwer first Lord Lytton*, by his grandson the Earl of Lytton (1913), II, 156.

after an interview with Hobhouse, handsomely advised his friends to support him. Hobhouse came to something like an engagement not to oppose Lytton thereafter, and he agreed that his conduct deserved acknowledgment. Hobhouse told his brother of the pains of election-eering, having to go to church with Keyworth and hearing a sermon from Richard Sibthorp. He did not like his supporters; they were decidedly the low party, and more radical than their candidate.[1]

The tories put forward one Humfrey, a barrister on the midland circuit, who declared that he had told the Lytton group that if they could show that Lytton had a better chance than he had he would withdraw. Hobhouse was returned; G. K. Jarvis noted in his diary that many tories refused to vote, thinking that their party should have supported Lytton rather than bring forward a tory candidate.[2]

In July 1849 there were rumours of Sibthorp's death, and Tennyson d'Eyncourt was again putting out feelers for young George. Lytton's agent Loaden wrote that if Lytton were not standing he was free to start his son.

3 August 1849...but you must be careful in your first step so as to avoid the danger of being claimed by either party, but you must use the elements of strife, hatred and sulkiness which are abundant among the parties when excited in an election at this time in Lincoln. The Bulwer party will not vote for a nominee of Seely, or do anything that may increase the influence of Seely, and they will not like a Tory, therefore although small in number they hold the balance, but must be managed tenderly, and both Tories and Seelys must be imbued with a conviction of the power of Bulwers. The way in which I managed them for Mr Hobhouse showed the Tories the power I possessed with such a force at my disposal.

Two days later he added that when the Sibthorps were not exerting them-selves the liberals were the strongest by full 50 and perhaps 100, but in an election between Sibthorp himself and a liberal the figures would be re-versed. Lytton's plumpers were about 80. They were therefore in a strong position.[3] But this did not help them, because Sibthorp was not dead.

When in 1846 Lord Worsley went to the House of Lords on the death of his father Lord Yarborough, Sir Montague Cholmeley was returned unopposed in Lindsey. He was a moderate whig and a protectionist. Cracroft gives a pleasant picture of the man:

there is something so charming in his offhand nervous manner, something so noble in his fine intellectual countenance, something so winning in his inexpres-sible gentleness that Willie [Cracroft's wife] says she could have married him, old clothes and all. He certainly does not think much about dress.

And some years later, at an agricultural show at Market Rasen, Cholmeley

---

[1] See p. 26, n. 2.   [2] Jarvis Diary, 16 March 1848.
[3] L.A.O. 2 Tennyson d'Eyncourt, H51a/68, 69.

'put in anything but a beaulike appearance, his hair uncombed, shirt all over egg – dear fellow, how we all love him'.[1]

A great protectionist meeting was held at Lincoln castle in 1850, the audience being estimated at 20,000.[2] Cracroft, himself a free trader, noted that he had never seen so many respectable farmers at such a gathering, with such unanimity and such good humour.

Every one, even that scoundrel Mr John Norton, had the most patient hearing given him, and from first to last for at least four hours, the proceedings were a pattern of respectability, order and decency, a credit to the sheriff, farmers, mob, in short to the county of Lincoln…there is now no doubt whatsoever of the great mass of opinion in the county being protectionist.

He thought eight or nine tenths of the crowd were farmers, there being no fewer than 300 small freeholders from the Isle of Axholme.[3] Cracroft was not a very strong partisan.

Early in 1852 Russell's whig government was defeated, and the tories under Lord Derby took office, with Disraeli as Chancellor of the Exchequer. It was announced that the government would abide by the decision of the country at the next election on the question of free trade, which was thought a feeble line by the protectionists.[4]

At the general election that followed the Lindsey tories produced James Banks Stanhope of Revesby to run with Christopher against Cholmeley. Sir John Thorold described Stanhope as 'a dear bargain to any woman that gets him – he is noisy, fidgetty, dirty, stingy'. Cracroft quoted this, adding:

At any rate Stanhope has much to recommend him, being perfectly unaffected, kind and hearty in manner, and much to be praised for building a house, improving his property, and living on it as a country gentleman ought to do…he often reminds me of the pictures I have seen of Billy Pitt, who was his near relation – his nose is retroussé like his, but Stanhope makes terrible faces when nervous, twitching his nose up in a wonderful sort of way.[5]

---

[1] Cracroft, 6 May 1846, 30 July 1856.
[2] The clerk to gaol sessions estimated it at 10,000–12,000. These are the figures given by the *Illustrated London News*, 2 February 1850.
[3] Cracroft, 27 January 1850. He noted that no gentry of the free trade party took any part.
[4] R. A. Christopher, M.P. for north Lincolnshire, became chancellor of the duchy of Lancaster, and Sir John Trollope, M.P. for the southern division of the county, a poor law commissioner. When Christopher stood for re-election on appointment he was severely heckled on the government attitude to protection.
[5] Cracroft, 10 November 1849. About 1884, Stanhope, after years of helping tenants with linseed cake, money and other doles, declared at the midsummer rent audit that 'Revesby has become an intense blister to me'. He had given his estate to his cousin Edward Stanhope. T. Kime, *Some Reminiscences of the Stanhopes of Revesby about 1855–1914*. According to Kime he was testy but a good sort. He died in 1904. For a prank played on him by Lord Charles Beresford at the Carlton Club, see Lord Frederick Hamilton, *The Days before Yesterday*, ch. VII.

The tories won both seats, and their men Trollope and Burghley were unopposed in the southern division. Edward Heneage, brother of George, and a whig who had four times been elected for Grimsby, was defeated there by a tory.

Manoeuvres continued in the city. The whigs tried to bring Lytton back again, but he was committed to Hertfordshire as a conservative.[1] The more democratic tories did not like the alliance between the Sibthorp and Lytton parties, and wanted Collett back again. In the end George Heneage was brought out of retirement as a whig protectionist. He must have been obtuse; Cracroft noted in 1856 that he was talking about representing Lincoln for ever, and his son after him, when from all he (Cracroft) could hear and see nothing could exceed his unpopularity.[2]

Sibthorp and Seely were in the field again. The battle raged chiefly round Seely and his conduct. He had an enemy in Brogden, then of the *Chronicle*, who described him as 'this eccentric little politician', wearing 'the wonderful jackboots and that inimitable hat, a cross between the *crowner* of the brigand and the Italian hurdy-gurdy grinder, both of which form a part of the canvassing costume of our *mealy* friend'.[3]

Seely's partner in the milling trade, Keyworth, said he had committed the unpardonable crime of elevating himself in mercantile pursuits above several of his fellow citizens by his industry, integrity and indomitable perseverance – a thrust at Rudgard in particular; and that the petition against him had been founded in hatred, malice and petty jealousy. It had been complained in the press that 400 men and boys had been released from the firm of Clayton and Shuttleworth, in which Seely was a partner, to take part in the election. On the contrary, during the election the foundry bell had rung regularly to summon the men to work, and those who did not attend would not receive one farthing for the time they were absent. In the foundry wages alone amounted to £17,700. In seconding the nomination, Battle asked who more promoted the success of the trade and town of Lincoln than the man who had raised up a large corn market through the origination of large mills.

Seely himself said that he had various kinds of workmen, millers, engineers, smiths, colliers and others. In his mills he paid the same wages as he did when flour was 3s. a stone. He appealed to his partner, who managed the foundry, to say whether the wages he paid then were not as high, and in many cases higher, than he ever paid before. He heard from

---

[1] His brother Sir Henry Bulwer also declined an invitation to stand for Lincoln.
[2] Cracroft, 9 December 1856.
[3] *L.C.*, 28 February 1851. It reported on 27 October 1854 that Seely had purchased the Derbyshire coalmine belonging to John Coupland.

his colliery manager of the decided increase in comforts and conditions of the working classes in Derbyshire. In short, he had no doubt about the benefits of free trade. He had always refused to join a millers' league, which was organised for the purpose of obtaining a duty on foreign flour. His opponents were members of a great league of landowners for raising the prices of agricultural produce.

Feeling ran high. A drunken rabble broke into Heneage's headquarters, and troops were brought in to quell the riot. Out of 1,362 registered voters, no fewer than 1,169 voted. Fear of the effects of free trade was decisive, and Sibthorp and Heneage were returned.

The government's acceptance of the country's verdict on free trade was a bitter blow to full-blooded protectionists, and Sibthorp, who meant what he said about the corn laws, talked of their duplicity. Heneage and Stanhope also disapproved of the government's course. Disraeli, however, was a realist, and he sought to find a way of compensating agriculture by raising some of the burdens on land.[1] When his budget was defeated, a government of whigs and Peelites was formed under Lord Aberdeen.

A long chapter of history came to an end with the death on 14 December 1855 of Charles Sibthorp. He was a strange mixture; a man of public principle and private vice; of great courage, good temper, and consistency, and a hard worker; of limited intelligence; shrewd, with flashes of wit, but a buffoon. His greatest moment came when he carried against the leaders of both parties a motion to reduce the annual grant to Prince Albert from £50,000 to £30,000.[2] He had opposed Catholic Emancipation, the Reform Bill, municipal reform, the new Poor Law, and the Great Exhibition of 1851. He hated railways, saying that he would vote for no railroad save one that would take ministers to hell.[3] One of his last sallies was upon the Militia (Service Abroad) Bill during the Crimean War. He moved to omit a clause providing that no militia officer should rank higher than a lieutenant colonel. Sibthorp,

---

[1] John Bright later made merry over the poll book of the Lindsey election commemorating 'the glorious Protectionist triumph'.

[2] H.B. drew a cartoon of him as 'the leader of the opposition', patronising Peel.

[3] The *Annual Register*, 1855, p. 325, refers to his frequent admixture of very genuine humour and often real wit. There were many stories about him. It was said that his best hit was made when Paul Methuen was boring him in the House. Sibthorp suddenly jumped up, and with outstretched arm, pointing to the tormentor, he exclaimed 'Paul! Paul! Why persecutest thou me?' Laughter almost lifted the roof of the House.

On hearing that he was sinking, Cracroft wrote, 'What will the House of Commons do without the facetious old Polonius and his speeches, which are always sure to end in a grand eulogium on "the regiment which I have the honour to command", viz. the South Lincoln Militia.' Cracroft, 23 October 1855.

who was 71 and a full colonel, asked what his own position would be. Palmerston seized his opportunity:

The gallant officer is one of those persons of rank, position, fortune, and social connection in this country whom – with great deference may I be allowed to say – I should wish to see employed in exercising their beneficial influence at home, rather than in the command of regiments of militia abroad. And though I should have the greatest confidence in a regiment going into action commanded by the gallant officer, nevertheless he must be conscious that his influence in his own circle at home might be attended with greater advantage to the nation.[1]

Punch commented that 'Sibthorp at Home' offered a rich field, much richer than the battlefield, for the contemplation of those who were familiar with the gallant colonel's peculiarities.

The end was foreseen, and the day after it his son Gervase issued an election address: he declared himself a conservative, a protestant, and a friend of civil and religious liberty. He supported the war with Russia. It was a more liberal address than was expected: what, asked Lord Monson, would the colonel say to his degenerate son? But Gervase no doubt seized the chance of striking out a new line; he was at home in the circle of moderate whig and tory gentry near Lincoln from which his father had entirely cut himself off.[2]

Seely was in the field. Monson's son William (the future seventh lord) had aspirations, of which there had been hints in 1849, when he was not yet of age, and there was correspondence about a second liberal candidate. The prospects were reviewed by Henry Williams, a liberal lawyer, to William Monson:

17 December 1855. My own idea is that Sibthorp will have the seat, for he is rather popular than not in the Town, and he has issued an address...which is much approved...Added to Major Sibthorp's popularity there is the family interest, which bolstered as it has been for many years by lavish expenditure is as you know very powerful, indeed so powerful is it that with two exceptions the old Colonel, Tory and Jack Pudding as he was, has always been returned considerably at the head of the poll.

There was strong prejudice against Seely, though he had a powerful party among the lower orders, and at a general election might defeat Heneage. There would be no hope for two liberal candidates if Seely were one of them.

On the 22nd Williams reported that Seely had resigned the contest. He thought that if a good whig stood at the next election he would have a good chance to come in with Major Sibthorp, even if Seely were the third

---

[1] *P.D.*, 3rd Series, 136, 479.
[2] He was generous and kind hearted, and it was reported that unlike his father he intended to live at Canwick.

candidate, basing himself on union between the tories and the anti-
Seelyites; but, he added, the whig must not be Heneage – 'I am afraid
his sun is set here.'[1] But by the time the next election came Monson had
been returned for Reigate, which he represented until 1862, when he
succeeded his father.[2] In the end Sibthorp was returned unopposed
(16 January 1856).

There was a move – or Charles Chaplin thought there was a move – to
put up a liberal candidate in the southern division, which was a tory
stronghold. Chaplin suspected it came from the north, where Cholmeley
had held a seat. Doubtless Chaplin knew that Christopher (who had
become Nisbet Hamilton on his succession to large estates in Scotland)
was disposed not to stand for Lindsey again. He therefore proposed to the
Lindsey liberals that if they would discourage an attempt in the south,
Hamilton would withdraw in Lindsey, provided no second liberal candidate was brought against the sitting tory member Banks Stanhope. The
liberals knew their weakness, and they accepted the offer.[3] Hamilton
almost at once issued his retirement address; the plan went through, and
Stanhope and Cholmeley were elected.

In the city it was assumed that when the next general election came
Seely would be in the field, with of course Sibthorp; and Heneage was
likely to find the liberals putting forward another candidate in place of
himself – perhaps Charles Tennyson d'Eyncourt, or young Lord God-
erich, or Major Cracroft – the liberals being tired of him and his sponsor
Rudgard. Presently the liberals heard that Seely would not be standing;
and it emerged that he had bought a house in the Isle of Wight and had
decided to contest Newport there.[4] They then invited John Hinde
Palmer, the son-in-law of Tennyson d'Eyncourt and a barrister, who was
in favour of extension of the franchise and the ballot. When the contest
came Sibthorp and Heneage were returned. But the position of Heneage
was weakening.[5] He relied on conservative votes plus those of a few
whigs: he could only muster 32 plumpers, including the Monson tenants.

[1] L.A.O. Monson 25/13/1, 22/6/14.
[2] He was created Viscount Oxenbridge in 1869, and held office in the liberal government
of 1892–94.
[3] Cracroft, 14 January 1856.
[4] The Rev. E. R. Larken, rector of Burton, wrote to William Monson on 21 October
1856: 'Seely is said to have had a desperate row with Clayton and Shuttleworth – and
the young Keyworths – on account of his dictatorial conduct in respect of politics, and to
have withdrawn from the city in consequence. This is from Mitchinson, but I cannot
vouch for its authenticity.' L.A.O. Monson 25/13/1/25/14.
[5] G. K. Jarvis noted that at nominations there was great noise and confusion during
Heneage's speech, Gervase Sibthorp spoke only like a man, and Palmer, the ultra liberal
candidate, spoke well and had his subjects well up. Jarvis Diary, 25 March 1857.

The working men were becoming more vocal, and they would only support a radical.

As another election approached the liberals were pledged to Palmer, though there was talk of bringing back Seely, who had been defeated at Newport. In 1859 Sibthorp and Heneage held their seats, but Palmer was gaining ground, and he promised to continue as long as he was wanted. The liberals had to decide upon tactics. Some of them hankered after Seely; his partner Clayton urged that Palmer could not win. They decided to be loyal to Palmer, and adopt Seely as second candidate.

Talk about another reform bill was in the air. In 1859 a tory bill and in 1860 a liberal bill proposed a £6 or £7 franchise in boroughs. Robert Toynbee, a liberal agent and lawyer, thought that this would be the end of Heneage in Lincoln, and that he would seek refuge at Grimsby and Lord Worsley be transferred from there to North Lincolnshire. With 1000 new voters even Sibthorp would have a hard fight.[1] Heneage duly announced that he would not stand again; and then, after the failure of the reform effort, that he would.

Sibthorp died in 1861. The tories nominated John Bramley Moore, a Liverpool merchant and shipowner, and former chairman of the Liverpool Dock Company.[2] Palmer, absent abroad, was willing to stand, and Shuttleworth issued a handbill on his behalf. Then Seely jumped in and announced himself; and Palmer's leading supporters deserted him and rallied to the intruder. Palmer, with a patience and courtesy which contrasted vividly with Seely's selfishness, withdrew. The tories, concluding that they could not win at a by-election, withdrew, and Seely at last was returned, and without a fight.[3] The death of Lord Yarborough in 1862 created a vacancy at Grimsby, Worsley being called to the Lords, and Heneage, thinking he would be safe there, in what the *Chronicle* called 'a snuggery of the Houses of Brocklesby and Hainton', resigned his

[1] L.A.O. Monson 25/13/10/12/52, 53. Colonel Tomline was likely to oppose him at Grimsby, no. 61.

[2] Nathaniel Hawthorne, who dined with him in Liverpool, described him as a violent tory and a fanatical churchman of the low church variety, apparently rich, with property in the Brazils. 'He is a moderately bulky and rather round-shouldered man, with a kindly face enough, and seems to be a passably good man; but I hope, on the whole, that he will not ask me to dinner any more – though his dinners are certainly very good.' Julian Hawthorne, *Nathaniel Hawthorne and his Wife* (1885), II, 40–2.

[3] For Garibaldi and Mazzini at Seely's house see *Diaries of John Bright* (1930), pp. 277, 282, where Seely is confused with his son. In 1864 Seely invited Garibaldi to England. Queen Victoria disapproved of the tumultuous public welcome given to the Italian rebel. In 1887 Seely presented an address from the Isle of Wight to the Queen, who said that they had not 22 years ago been in such complete agreement. Seely replied, 'Well, Ma'am, I suppose as we get older we get wiser', and the Queen was amused. J. E. B. Seely, *Adventure* (1930), p. 3.

seat for Lincoln. His move was to cost the liberals two seats: in Lincoln, and at Grimsby, where he was defeated.

For the casual vacancy in Lincoln Moore was nominated by the tories and Palmer by the liberals. Moore was accused of being the owner of 70 slaves in Rio de Janeiro, and of rising in the world by dealing in human flesh. His denial that he had ever owned slaves was not as clear as it might have been,[1] and when he was elected by a majority of 15 over Palmer there were riots, and the county police were called in by the city magistrates. It was felt by some in the city that the county police had behaved with undue violence, and those who felt aggrieved determined on revenge. The windows of the mayor and others were broken. The rioters dispersed on the arrival of troops: the city assembly room became a barracks, and 250 special constables were sworn in. Captain Bicknell, the county chief constable, was besieged in his house at Washing-borough, where he was defended by 30 men. Colonel Amcotts (Weston Cracroft), who was high sheriff, went over to support him. Later he saw Mr Clayton and Mr Shuttleworth, and told them that unless they took very serious steps to stop 'the conspiracy', they and their brother ironmasters, public opinion would not exonerate them in case of anything happening to Bicknell's house or person. They both looked very serious, and agreed to take immediate steps to endeavour to purge themselves of the not unfounded suspicion which attached to the foundrymen at Lincoln.[2] It was no doubt a mob with a political bias; on the other hand, a public meeting about the election riots produced a list of persons indiscriminately injured by the county police. The chairman of the meeting – Joseph Ruston, another ironmaster – said that they had had a constitutional right to complain, and it was agreed to ask the Home Secretary for a commission of inquiry.

There was some feeling against Seely, who had not helped Palmer, and moreover his agent, Tweed, had attempted, though without success, to remove some of the freemen from the electoral roll. On the other hand his sponsorship of the visit of Garibaldi to England aroused enthusiasm, and he was urged to bring him to Lincoln.

As the general election of 1865 approached the electoral tide was running strongly in favour of the liberals. Seely was standing again, and Bramley Moore, and the liberals brought in as a second candidate the

---

[1] It seems that he found it difficult to deny that he once owned slaves, but so, it was said, did the Society for the Propagation of the Gospel.

[2] Cracroft, 17 February 1862. When Ruston was mayor in 1870 the county police were warned against exercising any authority during the visit of the Prince of Wales, as was intended, and the city police were placed under the direction of the mayor.

young Edward Heneage, son of the late member. Cracroft described him in 1869 as very domestic. 'Edward Heneage has a kind heart, and is a thorough gentleman, but wants tact, and has too much of a flippant, jocose, boyish manner, which doesn't become a man of some 28 or 30 and an ex-M.P. He is too precipitate, and does not weigh words, forgetting they have wings. Everyone likes him, and his intimates call him Smike, from his supposed resemblance to that personage.'[1] He stood as a supporter of Palmerston, and favoured any liberal measures for settling the vexed question of church rates, and extension of the franchise. Moore failed to hold his seat, although he had 568 plumpers. There were riots again, (500 special constables having in view of previous experience been sworn in), and troops imported who behaved with moderation.

In 1866, after Palmerston's death, the subject of parliamentary reform was revived by the liberal government under Russell, and Gladstone introduced a reform bill providing for the lowering of the franchise in boroughs from £10 to £7. The total number of electors in Lincoln was 1,713, of whom it was calculated that 765 were mechanics, artisans and manual labourers. There would be added to the register 612 voters, all in this category, making a total of 1,377. On this basis it was clear that the working class would have a majority.[2] A like calculation was made by the tory agent in London; he calculated that the percentage of working-class voters would rise from 45 to 62.[3]

This prospect roused great enthusiasm in the radicals, and when Edward Heneage voted against the government and helped to bring it down there was a public meeting of protest, and a liberal association was formed to do battle. A tory government followed, and after an extraordinary series of parliamentary manoeuvres a new bill was carried incorporating the principle of household suffrage. Gladstone opposed this bill, and some of his followers, including Seely, refused to support him: the rebels were known as 'the tea room party'. There was distrust of Gladstone, and Seely was heard to say that it was better to have the question settled by Disraeli and Derby than by Beales and Potter (the radical pacemakers). A proposal of a week's strike horrified him: industry would be ruined, because there was but one week's consumption of coal above ground.[4]

The new act led to the registration of 4,157 voters in Lincoln. There

---

[1] Cracroft, 18 November 1869. Smike was an inmate of Dotheboys Hall in Dickens' *Nicholas Nickleby.*
[2] *S.M.,* 20 December 1865. *L.C.,* 16 March 1866, gives slightly different figures.
[3] R. D. Baxter, *The New Reform Bill: the Franchise Returns Criticised and Examined.*
[4] Monypenny and Buckle, *Life of Disraeli* (1929 edition), II, 251; F. B. Smith, *The Making of the Second Reform Bill* (1966), p. 175.

could be no doubt of working-class predominance, but it did not follow that they would vote radical. A Lincoln Constitutional Society was formed, at which Henry Chaplin emerged as a future party leader. The county was redivided into three divisions, the tory M.P.s having secured the northern division they wanted, leaving knots of liberal voters to the new Mid-Lincolnshire division.

When the election came in November 1868 the liberals in Lincoln formally adopted Seely and Heneage, in the latter case without enthusiasm. But this was too much for some of the new voters; there was a meeting at the White Swan which decided to put forward Hinde Palmer. Public meetings, first one of a thousand, then another of two thousand, wildly approved. Official liberals said they were committed to Heneage, but they were swept aside. There were rumours that Captain Chaplin, Henry's brother, would come as a tory, but he did not; Heneage angrily withdrew. Seely and Palmer were elected unopposed, Palmer's proposer saying that his election would remove the blot of ingratitude on the city.

Palmer was not present, he had not been consulted, and indeed he had not known about his nomination, and he was returned free of expense. He reported to his father-in-law Tennyson d'Eyncourt:

17 November 1868 Great Northern Hotel, Lincoln. Yesterday morning when I went to St George's Square to go to my chambers I had as much idea of being Archbishop of Canterbury as Member for Lincoln, but, as you have heard perhaps, I was returned *without opposition*.

The working men have done it all. They appointed a chairman and committee from their own body, and raised a fund by subscription to guarantee the Sheriff's expenses, and to make me a *present* of the seat. As soon as I got the telegram in London I came down here, and such a *mass* of people were assembled at the station I never saw before. There was a carriage to take me in procession to the Corn Exchange, with music and flags and thousands of people. I thought I should have been torn to pieces. It made me nervous to see blazing tar barrels rolling about amongst the dense multitudes. When we did get to the Corn Exchange (which was a work of danger) it was crammed, and I made a speech of thanks. It certainly is a flattering glorious result, and I doubt if there will be *another* such spontaneous display of the newly enfranchised voters throughout the country.

Heneage retired before the nomination. I had had *no previous communication* with *any* body at Lincoln, and was taken quite by surprise.[1]

The new voters had done something. There would be no more whigs, and the middle-class liberal leaders had clear notice that the balance of power had shifted. It is not surprising that the rejoicings issued in riots. A vast crowd occupied the centre of the city for hours, and lighted tar

[1] L.A.O. 2 Tennyson d'Eyncourt, H64/61.

barrels rolled about for two nights, the police office and the chief constable's house were wrecked; and magistrates appealed for the enrolment of special constables. Democracy could not achieve maturity in a night.

There was underlying uneasiness at the celebration meeting. Seely did not feel at home, and the Heneage group must have been embarrassed. Shuttleworth, in the chair, urged party union, and gave credit to Heneage for withdrawing. But nothing would be quite the same again.[1]

[1] In the new northern division of the county the parties divided the seats without contest – Cholmeley (liberal) and Winn (tory); similarly in mid-Lincolnshire, Henry Chaplin (tory) and Weston Cracroft Amcotts (liberal), the diarist; in the southern division Welby and Turnor, both tories, defeated the liberal G. H. Packe.

CHAPTER III

REFORM IN LOCAL GOVERNMENT

The old close corporation of Lincoln,[1] recruited by co-option from the ranks of the freemen, in no way conformed with the modern conception of a local authority: indeed the concept was not yet born. The corporation was thought of as a guild, or body of trustees, with general responsibility for the well-being of the city, and applying its revenues to that end. Its responsibility however, was a moral one, not enforceable by law, and it rendered no public account. Its specific powers were small, and as it levied no rates it made little direct impact, save ceremonially, on the lives of the citizens. Their contacts with the parishes were closer: it was the parishes, through their officers chosen at vestry meetings, which collected rates – the poor rate, accounted for to the guardians of the poor, the lighting, watching and paving rate, accounted for to the commissioners appointed by the parishes for that purpose – and met other parish expenses such as the upkeep of roads, or, through a church rate, for the upkeep of the parish church.

The Reform Bill of 1832 was followed by the Municipal Corporations Act of 1835. It brought the old corporation to an end and substituted an elected council, the franchise for which was vested in householders paying rates. The franchise was wider than the new parliamentary franchise, but it was not in practice quite so democratic as it sounded. In Lincoln all houses were rated, though a few rates were excused or not recoverable,[2] but some householders were excluded because the landlord paid the rates and was entered in the ratebook instead of the occupier. It seems likely that most of the working class were so excluded from the franchise. The freemen as such did not get a municipal vote.

Before the first elections under the Act the reformers used smooth words about not making the elections a party matter; but after a secret canvass of the city, being confident of the result, they called a meeting to choose candidates, the real selection having been previously decided upon at a secret party conclave. Thus popular election and the party caucus system began together; and one of the earliest complaints against the new system was that the mayor was chosen in a beershop.

[1] See *G.L.*, ch. x.
[2] The amount not recovered did not average £30 a year; this was thought a strong proof of the condition of the poorer inhabitants. *Report of the Poor Law Commission*, App. A, Part II, p. 132a.

Reformers, whigs or radicals, captured every seat. It was a portent that whereas, in spite of the repeal of the Test and Corporation Acts, the old corporation had remained solidly Anglican to the end, the new council included two Roman Catholics,[1] two Wesleyans[2] and two Unitarians.[3] Only four of the old corporation were elected: Wriglesworth, Robert Fowler, Trotter and Blyth. The victors proceeded to take the spoils of victory. They took all the aldermanic seats, of course chose the mayor – Fowler – and the sheriff (there was only one sheriff now) and ejected some of the officers. The treasurer, John Hayward, was replaced by Charles Arnold the grocer, who, when he died at the end of 1836, was followed by Edward Bell Drury, editor of the *Lincoln Gazette*.[4] James Hitchens, formerly a tailor in Manchester, a Unitarian and a pronounced radical, became coroner, and Henry Wilson town crier, he having been bankrupt and in need of a living. Sir Edward Bromhead resigned office as steward of the courts, and the pliable John Fardell[5] was chosen in his place. W. A. Nicholson the architect was, however, re-elected surveyor in spite of his political views.

Richard Mason, who had been elected town clerk by the old corporation in 1826, was confirmed in office. He had solicited the Lighting and Paving Act of 1828, helped to promote the Lincoln Gas Light and Coke Company in the same year, and the Lincoln and Lindsey Bank in 1833, of which he was later to become chairman. He was a whig, and had been election agent for the Monson family; he was an expert in literary composition, and may be suspected of having composed an 'Ingoldsby Legend' about Sibthorp.[6] When he retired in 1855 he said he thought some members held the view that he had addressed the council oftener than was consistent with his position as a public officer. But he urged them to reflect that the new corporation were total strangers to the duties, habits and privileges of the corporation, and having himself had considerable experience he was anxious to impart to them all the information he could, and to keep them from those projects which all young corporations were too eager to entertain. He thought the council hankered after affairs over which they had no legitimate control. He was undoubtedly right, and their treatment of him on his retirement showed that at least in retrospect they knew it.[7]   The council were not vested with the appointment of magistrates, and the Act of 1835 expressly

[1] Willson and Hill.   [2] Harvey and Wetherell.
[3] Nettleship and Bedford.
[4] He died in 1843.
[5] As to whom see *G.L.*, pp. 233–4.
[6] App. V.
[7] There is a portrait of him in the Guildhall, presented by his grandson Richard Mason.

transferred from them to trustees the municipal charities. The party caucus drew up a list of names for submission to the Home Secretary as magistrates: the names leaked out and the list was revised, the *Chronicle* remarking that some of them would think themselves called to a court of bankruptcy or the bar of the Lion and Snake.[1] The radicals were watching for the slightest deviation from the principle that all public life belonged henceforth to them, and when the names came out the radical Edward Drury wrote:

30 January 1836. We have some miserable trimmers in the new corporation, who seem to hanker after the baubles against which they preached so much. Perhaps it is a wise ordinance, after all, that changes should be tramelled thus, as the transition might be too powerful.

P.S. The Lincoln Town Council have put down seven names of a good sort for magistrates, and the eighth name is that of the most mischievous sinister tory in the kingdom, viz., the Hon. A. Melville! The town is electrified by the discovery of such monstrous folly, and our Blues are already calling out that they may as well take two guineas as be sold themselves! Wriglesworth is left out of the list, because he is too independent of the Jew-ocracy.[2]

When a new commission of the peace was issued in 1842 – the whig government being out of office – the Home Secretary ensured a political balance on the bench.

For charity trustees the council nominated only their own party men, all save one being members of the council. The Lord Chancellor refused to confirm a nomination of more than two-thirds who were council members; though it appears that in the end more of them were. It was quickly pointed out that the trustees found it convenient to distribute charity moneys shortly before the municipal elections. Here again a few tories were added in 1844; this was the result of a petition organised by Robert Swan, diocesan registrar and a leading tory, who dragged out the facts.

As a result of the amendment of the Act of 1835 during its passage through parliament there was some doubt whether the Bail and Close – which had not formed part of the old municipal borough but were part of the county at large – had been brought within the borough or not; and whether four rural parishes which had formerly been part of the county of the city[3] were now within the liberties or in the county. The revising barristers determined that the Bail and Close were now within the borough[4] and the 'four towns' outside it. Instead, however, of dividing

[1] *L.C.*, 12 February 1836.
[2] L.A.O. Tennyson d'Eyncourt, H26/7.
[3] *M.L.*, pp. 281–2.
[4] The duchy of Lancaster did not abandon its right to market tolls in the Bail until 1847, and the duchy steward continued to hold his court leet until 1861.

the city into three wards as the Act contemplated, they divided it in exercise of a discretion given to them, into two. The town clerk said that the reason for their action was that the liberty of the Monks[1] and the commons were not included in the wards, and therefore two were thought enough. Whatever the reason, the division had the effect of attaching the parishes in the Bail and Close, which might be expected to have a tory majority, with a small population and large rateable value, to radical parishes in the city, with a large population and small rateable value. This could hardly fail to be put down to political malice.

Legal doubts as to the area of the borough were removed by an amending Act; but the ward division, although it had never been sanctioned by the privy council, remained until a memorial was sent to them in 1843, praying for a division into three wards, and specifying the division sought. There was much dispute, the radicals fearing that their strength might be too heavily concentrated in a middle ward, the upper ward being probably lost to them, and the lower ward doubtful. A public meeting opposed the suggested division, but seemed to accept the idea of three wards, and eventually the council and the liberal party accepted it too. The division into upper, middle and lower wards was made in 1845, and henceforth there was one ward that the tories might reasonably hope to hold.

The new council's zeal for putting the world right, as Mason said, found expression in petitions against the flogging of soldiers, in favour of the ballot, against slavery in the colonies, and for the penny post.

In their eagerness to have done with ancient abuses, the reformers abolished the small pomp and circumstance of civic life. There was to be no more turtle soup at the public expense; therefore the corporation plate was not needed and must be sold.[2] An attempt was made to sell the insignia, but happily it was defeated; they were, however, put away and ordered not to be used. In consequence the ceremony of proclaiming the accession of Queen Victoria was a drab affair, the dean walking with the mayor, and accompanied by a brass band. Charles Anderson thought it very poor.[3]

Gradually, the tories and whigs having ousted the radicals, ancient ceremonies crept back; and at last, in 1849, the mayor, James Snow, who had twice been mayor of the old corporation, went in procession in blue

[1] Land to the east of the city which had formerly belonged to the Benedictine Abbey of St Mary of York – the Black Monks.

[2] It appears that it realised £240, averaging 9s. an ounce. Several pieces of plate have been recovered in recent times.

[3] L.A.O. Anderson, 5/2/2, p. 237.

gown and gold chain, preceded by officers in three-cornered hats, with sword and mace.[1] Royal visits completed the process. The visit of Prince Albert on his way to Grimsby to open a dock there in 1849 led to the purchase of a new chain for the mayor and robes for the council, there being three dissentients, Andrew, Battle and Gresham. The mayor and aldermen were to wear scarlet, the councillors violet coloured silk, following the custom of London. The Prince received a loyal address at the Corn Exchange, and visited the cathedral. Next, the council went to church in full state.

In 1851 Queen Victoria and Prince Albert and some of the royal children passed through the city by train. Lord John Russell descended from the train and said that the queen would receive an address in the carriage. She stepped to the door, and the mayor, Charles Ward, respectfully kneeling, presented the keys of the city – what keys? – to the queen, who graciously returned them, saying 'They cannot be better than in your keeping, Mr Mayor' and that she would have liked to see more of the city if circumstances had permitted. Anderson, who was high sheriff that year, said that the mayor and corporation looked well in their robes.[2] A gradual return to old ways, prompting the thought that the new corporation were not so very different from the old, strengthened the feelings of disillusion of working-class radicals who had hoped too much of reform. Thomas Cooper the chartist, sitting in gaol, looked back to 1835 and before:

How eloquently abusive was the prevailing Whig strain about 'nests of corruption' and 'rotten lumber' and 'fine pickings' and 'impositions and frauds and dark rogueries of the self-select'. And how the scale has turned since, in the greater share of boroughs, where the poor and labouring classes threw up their hats for joy at 'municipal reform' – and now mutter discontent at the pride of upstarts become insolent oppressors...recreant middle classes whom municipal honours have drawn off from their hot-blooded radicalism, and converted into cold, unfeeling, merciless wielders of magisterial or other local power.[3]

The caucus in the Guildhall had not only to contend with the tories:

[1] Before 1835 the mayor had been used to sending his official ring to the grammar school to give the boys a holiday. *L.C.*, 13 February 1852. It seems that it was about 1852 that the practice of sending it to all schools (other than private schools) was instituted. It was not introduced by Richard Sutton Harvey as stated in *Notes and Queries*, 10th Series, III, 436. In that year John Holton, master of Rosemary Lane Wesleyan School, made the announcement of a holiday an object lesson in the duty of submitting to authority.
[2] *S.M.*, 29 August 1851; Anderson Diary, 27 August 1851. Anderson said that the mayor got into the train in his robes and was taken to Doncaster to dine with the corporation there. Anderson's daughter had presented the queen with a nosegay, and the mayor said afterwards that he saw the Princess Royal 'a-smelling of Miss Anderson's nosegay'.
[3] *Wise Saws and Modern Instances* (1845), II, 11–12.

from the first it had to face internal differences between the moderates and the radicals, and differences of outlook were accentuated by personal quarrels and motives. At first the radicals predominated, and deviation from the party line incurred its own penalty. Thomas Wetherell the tanner criticised some of his colleagues, and was dropped, though he soon came back. W. H. Brook refused a party contribution and he too was dropped. In the following year Wetherell and Alderman Luke Trotter had actually toyed with the idea of a mixed list of tories and whigs. Perhaps this partly accounts for the success of the tories in winning two seats in the upper ward: Robert Swan and Frederick Kent the surgeon. The radical assessor refused to return Kent, on the ground that he was the police surgeon, and returned instead William Dawber. Charles Seely was elected to fill a casual vacancy. Both returns were challenged as irregular, and eventually overruled in the Queen's Bench. Seely came back in another seat, and he and his brother-in-law John Norton proceeded to make things as difficult as possible. Seely was building up a party with a view to higher things, and he organised a club which was derisorily called the 'pie-club' meeting at 'the Pig and Whistle'.

The caucus upset the dissenters by voting £50 to increase the stakes at the next races. An attempt was made, under pressure from the chapels, to rescind the vote, some of the council disliking the grant, but disliking more the council changing their minds. Presently Henry Blyth was dropped, presumably as a scapegoat, though he recovered his seat.

The two tories were defeated, and the fight between whigs and radicals became fiercer. When William Rudgard the maltster, who was virtually leader of the council, retired from the mayoralty in 1840, E. J. Willson was proposed, but opposed on the ground that he had not done his duty at parliamentary elections; also he was a Roman Catholic. Seely was then elected, his seconder remarking that no man was so fit to be mayor as one who had erected chimneys such as those at Seely's mill. Seely had not the decency to attend the usual dinner in honour of the retiring mayor, preferring to be at a municipal reform supper at the Green Dragon: Dr Beaty acidly remarked that he was sorry that merit and dignity seemed now to be measured by the height of chimneys. Mason the town clerk impliedly rebuked Seely for his constant denunciations of the old corporation, because it ought to be remembered that they were fettered by charters and usages, which the new corporation were not. At the end of his year of office Seely retired from the council in readiness for the parliamentary election, but only after a violent altercation with Rudgard.

Divisions within the caucus continued, being aggravated by John

Norton's violence against the agricultural interest and his membership of the Anti-Corn Law League. In 1842 the tories won two seats. In the following year their ticket included four whigs, and they continued to gain ground. When at last the redivision of the wards took effect they had a decisive victory, which gave them the mayoralty for the first time since 1835. They brought James Bruce, for many years a member of the old corporation, on to the council and made him mayor; and unlike their rivals, they allowed the opposition to choose the sheriff. The radicals were set back, and their 'pie-club' wound up. The upper and middle wards were held by tories and whigs, and the lower wards by radicals who were roundly accused of bribery in money and ale. The tories and their whig allies were in control, and there were dire prophecies of a borough rate, which had hitherto been avoided. Feuds and personal enmities broke out in 1855. The noisy and assertive Brogden (elected to the council in 1848), who was the correspondent of the tory *Chronicle*, declared that the tories and the Lord John Russell whigs led by Rudgard on one side were opposed by the liberals and liberal conservatives on the other: by this last group he meant himself and a few satellites. There was talk of 10s. a vote at the election, and the *Mercury* said that no election since 1835 had aroused so much interest. The tory–whig party were successful, and the tory William Cooke Norton was elected mayor against the liberal ironmaster Nathaniel Clayton by 13 votes to 9. Brogden left the *Chronicle* in 1856; besides being an auctioneer, he started the *Lincoln Gazette* in 1859; and his transition to liberalism was complete.

In the following year the tories accepted Nathaniel Clayton the ironmaster as mayor, and in 1858 his partner Joseph Shuttleworth. Rich and respectable liberals had their advantages; they were willing to spend and easy to get on with, and the parties reached an understanding in 1862 which was attacked by the radicals, who denounced 'unprincipled coalition' and 'disgraceful compromise'. The radical John Richard Battle was indiscreet. He said that his contest in the lower ward the previous year cost £150, and nobody need come forward unless he was prepared to spend £30 or £40 in half-crowns or crowns.

Joseph Ruston, another ironmaster, was elected to the council as a liberal in 1865. There were then sixteen conservatives (including all six aldermen) and eight liberals in the council. The latter were growing again, and distinctions were being drawn between the sober and respectable businessmen – Clayton, Shuttleworth, Ruston and Doughty – and the noisy ones, Brogden, Maltby and Shepherd.

In these years the great controversy over underground sewerage[1] had

---

[1] See chs. VIII and IX.

grown fiercer, and when at last the Local Government Act of 1858 was adopted (February 1866) the tories, as the party in power, incurred the odium of a new rate, and the liberals gained a majority in 1867. In that year the tories withdrew from the elections, and after 20 years the liberals were in control. In 1869 the practice by which owners compounding for the rates of their tenants excluded the tenants from the municipal franchise was abolished. This must have helped the liberal party by extending the number of their voters; there followed the Ballot Act in 1872 introducing the secret ballot, and this may well have reduced the pressure of landlords on their tenants.[1]

Many of the elected did not stay long: some were induced to stand in a wave of enthusiasm for reform, and excitement of this kind was soon stilled. Others stayed the course and played the party game. A few emerged as leaders: Rudgard, rough spoken, stubborn and a good hater, whom Charlesworth described as an overbearing ruffian; then Brogden, an ebullient figure who loved the game, enjoyed power, and was more concerned to keep it than to use it. In fairness, however, it must be said that it was not easy to go far ahead of public opinion, and when a town poll was invoked it became impossible. Not only in health matters[2] but in other improvements the council might have gone much further had they not been so stopped.[3] On the other hand, a determined attempt at educating public opinion ought to have been made and might have succeeded. The level of education in the council was not high; by contrast with the others there stand out the doctors, lawyers and architects. R. S. Harvey the surgeon led on the subject of underground drainage; and perhaps the lawyer Richard Carline was the most far-seeing of all. He pioneered the Water Company, the cemetery, the Yarborough Road development and the visit of the Royal Show.

John Thomas Tweed had come to Lincoln as a stranger in 1846 and started in legal practice. He was elected to the council in 1852 and by 1854 he had made his way to such purpose that he was elected mayor. He was lavish in his hospitality, especially during the visit of the Royal Show, which occurred during his mayoral year. According to tradition[4] he spent his limited means in a gamble to establish himself; and the gamble came off when in 1855 he resigned from the council and was elected town clerk. The salary of the office had been £300, and though

---

[1] B. Keith-Lucas, *The English Local Government Franchise* (1952), p. 73.
[2] Ch. VIII.
[3] Cf. the Barton plumber whose poster read 'Vote for Flower and no improvements'. Janet Courtney, *Recollected in Tranquillity* (1926), p. 47.
[4] Passed on to me by the late Richard Mason.

this was reduced to £250 there were in addition fees to be paid by the corporation for legal work, and this of course was in addition to his private practice.

He owed his election to Brogden, and indeed had been called his town clerk. He declared that he would not take part in municipal elections, but he added meaningly that he should not cease to take a deep interest in the success of those who had helped him, and he knew how to distinguish between friends and foes.

It is difficult now to realise that in these years there was no borough rate, and indeed no rate at all that was levied by the corporation. The ancient levy on the inhabitants known as the town scot, which had been exercised down to the sixteenth century, had fallen into disuse, and it was generally accepted that it did not exist. Perhaps this was because new statutory duties relating to highways and the poor had been laid by parliament on parishes both in the country generally and inside the boroughs. By the time that there was need for new local provision for lighting, watching and paving the streets, or for dealing with the poor, the corporation showed no desire to seek new powers for itself, but promoted bills for federating the parishes for these purposes.[1]

The corporate body had its own income from rents, fees, tolls, fines and the like, and out of it had been used to pay its own expenses. These were few; most of the modern functions of a local authority were foreign to them. They were chiefly concerned with those of an ancient market town set in a rural countryside: quarter and petty sessions, the gaol, the markets and fairs, the commons, with their regulated rights of pasture, and to a very limited extent the roads and waterways. Brayford Pool, the inland port, belonged to the city, though through it passed channels under the control of other authorities or owners concerned with the drainage and navigation. They shared with the dean and chapter control of the grammar school.

There being no borough rate, one unfailing way of making the flesh of the new electors creep was to remind them that the reformed council had the power to levy a borough rate for the general purposes of the borough, and indeed that if there were a deficiency in the borough fund it was their duty to do so. Every new impost must be resisted. A rate, however small, would be the thin end of the wedge, and nobody could foresee what it might grow to; which was undeniably true.

The threat began at once. The improvement of the Guildhall for the comfort of the council, the support of the races, even the calling of a

[1] *G.L.*, p. 246.

meeting to raise a subscription for the poor in a hard winter, must not be at the expense of the borough fund. Subscriptions to public institutions were voted a year at a time. The lighting of the town clock was abandoned, and the lights outside the Guildhall reduced in number, even though the Gas Company would pay for two of them.

Members constantly pledged themselves against a borough rate, and although the town clerk warned them that they could not do without one, pride and the fear of odium and defeat were decisive. The council assumed that as before 1835 the borough fund would have a sufficient income to pay its way: there were some unavoidable outgoings, the courts, the police, the gaol, the officers' salaries, and there ought to be a surplus available for emergencies and improvements.[1] Sums were voted for special purposes, such as a sewer to carry off filth from the butchery, or for popular causes like the races, or to encourage the Witham Commissioners or the Fossdyke lessee to spend money.

While the council shrank from the slippery slope of a borough rate there was a new limitation of power which impelled them towards the brink. The corporation could no longer do as it liked with its own, its legally own:[2] it was now taught that it was a trustee for future generations of citizens as well as being the elect of the present generation. This meant that it could not sell corporate property, sweep the proceeds into revenue, and then spend them freely. Capital transactions came under the control of the Treasury or the courts. When therefore compensation moneys were paid for lands taken by the railway companies, they were invested by order of the court in 3% Consols, the dividends being paid into the borough fund.

Such questions came up with increasing frequency. In 1843 the council were able to rebuild the city gaol at a cost of £6,000, to be raised on bond and repaid by annual instalments of £200. If they could not meet the repayments then in the last resort they must make a gaol rate. In 1847 they obtained Treasury permission to sell corporate property to pay off debts incurred before 1835, interest on which had been a burden on the borough fund. Nearly £17,000 was so used, and a balance of £1,000 was cheerfully swept into the borough fund, and spent partly on cattle market and other improvements and partly in paying off accumu-

[1] In 1839–40 there were over 70 boroughs still not levying a borough rate. See Joseph Fletcher, 'Municipal Institutions of English Towns' in *Journal of the Statistical Society*, v, Table x.

[2] It appears that on their part the freemen thought that on a sale of the commons the purchase money might be divided amongst the existing freemen, L.A.O. Town Clerk's Letter Book, 21 November 1850.

lated annual deficits. When in 1851 they had to find their share of the cost
of the new county pauper lunatic asylum at Bracebridge Heath – some
£1,500 – they had either to borrow on mortgage of the rates or to sell
property; and they again obtained leave to sell. Of the surplus the bulk
was invested, and an oddment swept into the borough fund.

At that time the annual borough fund income was about £4,830. The
town clerk pointed out that the asylum charges could be met by a rate;
and if there were a rate there would be a grant from the Treasury for the
maintenance and transportation of prisoners and half the cost of prosecutions. Of this aid the city was deprived because there was no rate. Bold
spirits like Rudgard and Harvey favoured a penny rate, which would
have been enough to secure the grant: it would yield £200, and bring in
a grant of £300, and so avoid the sale of property. But the very idea of a
rate aroused so violent a disturbance in the minds of councillors that they
shrank from it, and a memorial to the Treasury for the sale of property
was carried by 11 votes to 5.

Hitherto the Treasury had been compliant, but in 1855 they refused
an application for leave to sell property to provide funds for purposes
required by law to be provided out of annual income. They pointed out
that the council were both authorised and required to levy a rate for such
purposes. They suggested that yearly income might be increased by
letting land on building leases. The finance committee drew the moral
that if no rate was to be levied to meet a deficiency then a deficiency must
be avoided, as expenditure in anticipation of income was illegal.
Economy measures were therefore sought.

Debts grew nevertheless, and in 1857 another memorial for the sale of
property to pay them was in preparation. Some of the council and some
other householders who felt strongly about this evasion of responsibility
prepared a counter-memorial asking that the sale be approved on
condition that the proceeds be invested and the income only brought into
the borough fund. The council's defence was that since 1841 money had
been spent out of income for capital purposes – buying and building for
the farms belonging to the corporation, for the markets and the police –
and that it was reasonable to meet debt so incurred by resort to capital.
The Treasury found no reason for departing from the rule that a
municipal corporation must not sell property to pay debts incurred since
1835; and they authorised the sale on condition that the proceeds were
invested. The council resolved to sell.

The town clerk warned the council that if a deficiency arose in the
borough fund and they had to face the levy of a rate, they would meet a
difficulty; part of their expenditure, the payment of subscriptions to

charities, was illegal. This point arose when the cost of meeting election riot damage had to be met in 1865. It was about £430. The mayor favoured the levy of a special rate, even though the innocent would be punished as well as the guilty. But the charitable subscriptions haunted them, and no rate was levied.

In these same years the inadequacies of markets in the streets were being increasingly felt. The Lincolnshire Agricultural Association called for an enlarged and improved cattle market, the existing accommodation being not only too small but inconvenient to graziers and inhabitants and injurious to stock; graziers and jobbers were declining to attend the market because of the damage done to stock by standing on the stones of the streets.

The corporation market committee sought a new site, and presently chose four fields north of the Monks lane belonging to the dean and chapter. In spite of opposition from some farmers and cattle dealers to a move from Sheep Square (now St Swithins Square) the corporation held on, fearing that failure to improve would mean that the railways would take the stock to other markets; and they enquired the railway rates for beasts and sheep to London, Rotherham and Wakefield, and whether an alteration of market days would be an improvement. The Agricultural Association approved the new arrangement, and agitation by tradesmen who feared the loss of custom by the removal of the market was countered by memorials from butchers and cattle dealers and 226 citizens.[1] The scheme was complete by 1849.

But the opposition to the removal of the cattle market was as nothing compared with the outcry about the removal of market stalls from the streets.[2] It was proposed to use the Cornhill and land behind it stretching to the new road (Melville Street) for open market and it was opposed by those who feared loss of trade to tradesmen in other parts. The butter market was inadequate, and the streets were half blocked with stalls on market day. The *Chronicle* (then the mouthpiece of Brogden) denounced the interests which opposed the clearing away of butterscotch stalls and cabbage baskets which disgraced the High Street

---

[1] *L.C.*, 8 May 1846.

[2] Alderman Glasier recalled the time when there were no market buildings; 'stalls used to stand down the sides of the streets, corn used to be sold in the open, wet or fine. Sometimes when it was windy, we used to see all the goods blowing down the streets, and the women running after them. Then, nobody cared what they did in those days. I can remember Colonel Sibthorp galloping through the market, upsetting the stalls and smashing the crockery. But he paid for it like a gentleman, and paid well, I expect. Well, some of us started a company to build a market. Everybody laughed at us, and said that nobody would go near it. But look at it today.' *L.L.*, 31 March 1900.

on market day. The small area of shops was no longer adequate for a
growing city: the rents in this area had so risen that the tradesmen there
were obliged to let their frontages to stall-keepers: in the end, only the
landlords benefited. If the tradesmen below High Bridge had the right to
let their frontages, so had those above the bridge, in the Strait and
elsewhere; yet if a tradesman in the upper part of the town placed a
bundle of his own goods outside his own door on a market day, he ran the
risk of being brought up by the surveyor under the Lighting and Paving
Act and fined. The stalls were a nuisance, and might be removed by any
resolute man who would lay an information against the surveyor or the
overseers of the highways. The stalls might be removed to the old sheep
market.

The corporation wished to undertake the project of a market, but as
Seely pointed out, not only had they no surplus income, but they were in
debt. Nobody had the temerity to propose the levying of a rate for the
purpose. The Lighting and Paving Commissioners took legal opinion,
and were advised that they could remove stalls erected on the carriage
roads generally; the roads were for passage and not for stallage. Their
erection could only be justified on market days or fair days by some
franchise reserved by the Lighting and Paving Act. There was none, and
the stalls were ordered to be removed in 1848.

The farmers were accustomed to the buying and selling of corn on the
Cornhill, and as ideas of comfort rose there came a demand for a corn
exchange. By 1845 leading merchants, William Rudgard, Edward Rudgard and Charles Seely were offering to pay for a standing. Others were
sceptical whether enough support would be forthcoming, and the *Chronicle* thought[1] that farmers would not give a farthing for a place to stand
in for a few minutes in a week. Nevertheless the formation of a public
company was resolved on, and all shares were quickly taken. The council
intervened with the idea of undertaking the work itself, but did nothing.
The company therefore proceeded under agreement with the corporation, and the foundation stone of the corn exchange was laid in September 1847. By the following year it was open and the stalls all taken.
After paying no dividend for three years the company began with 4%,
rising to 9% in 1869.

These changes called attention to the deficiencies of the old butter
market. There the rain and sleet blew through the open windows and
open iron gates. Furthermore, the only approach to the city assembly
room upstairs was through the entire length of the butter market.

[1] 6 June 1845.

Stall-holders asked for the glazing of the windows and doors in front of the gates, and they were provided.

The fish market moved from the High Bridge to Witham Street in 1849. It seems that most of the fish had come from London. Carline thought the East Lincolnshire Railway Company expected large returns from the carriage of fish from the Dogger Bank. Whilst farmers had to feed cattle, fish did not need to be fed, yet fish was dearer than meat by quarter or half or more in some cases. He would like to see ten times the amount of fish in fishmongers shops.

All these improvements in the lower city raised complaints from tradesmen uphill. They had not called on the corporation for any improvements since 1842, although about a third of the population lived there. They had had three or four pumps and a couple of walks; that was all.

It was a matter of long standing complaint that corn being brought from villages north of the city still had to pass through Minster Yard and down Lindum Road, which provided the only oblique negotiable descent to the lower town for vehicles; and even then a waggon could not get down without locking a wheel. In 1854 the farseeing Richard Carline submitted to the city council a scheme for a new road 'from the junction of far and near Newland direct to Brickkiln Lane, continuing through the fields below the asylum, Female Penitents Home, and the Union, to the top of the Race Course, and thence under the brow of the hill to Burton Road, between the sixth and seventh sail windmills – for greater certainty marked on Padley's map'. The map has survived, foreshadowing the present Yarborough Road and Carline Road and other connections. The council gave its cordial support to the scheme.[1]

But vested interests were involved. The shopkeepers in the Bail were afraid of the loss of custom if traffic from Burton and the other villages on or below the cliff no longer had to cross the upper city with their waggons and carts to get down the hill on the east side of the city. They had already lost, they said, by the formation of the Manchester Sheffield and Lincolnshire Railway line, along which travelled those who used to pass through the Bail.[2]

Two years later Carline and others were trying to form a commercial company, a 'Land and Local Improvement Association'; and they

[1] The map was given to me by Mr Edward Mason, the road being marked 'new road proposed by Richard Carline and submitted for the approval of the Corporation. July 1854. Length about [   ] yards'. About the same time he initiated a plan to open a way from Castle Hill to Drury Lane.
[2] *S.M.*, 13 October 1854.

approached Lord Monson through E. R. Larken, rector of Burton, pointing out that Monson's estates would be enhanced in value by a west road shortening the distance from Burton to Lincoln, and bringing into the market eligible sites for villa residences.[1] Carline's plan shows a possible layout of streets in the area north of the present West Parade and below the hilltop. He was a generation too early.[2]

The commerce of the city centred upon Brayford Pool whose soil belonged to the corporation as lord of the manor. The earliest prints depict the pool as having no wharves. The water flowed up the walls of houses and warehouses and until the south bank was raised about the beginning of the century it flowed in times of flood freely over the Holmes and the adjoining low lands. Then planks, with trestles placed across the inclined foreshore were used for gangways between the merchants' yards and the vessels to be loaded and unloaded. Gradually wharves were formed along nearly the whole of the east and north sides of the pool, so as to afford a level landing ground between the yards and the decks of vessels. They had been made by different merchants for their own convenience without regard to regularity, and the corporation had made some. But who was to pay for the upkeep of the wharves and the road along them?[3]

The question of repair arose in 1839 and the parishioners of St Martin maintained that as they had never repaired the wharves, the corporation as well as the lessee of the Fossdyke and the frontagers ought to be asked to assist the parish.[4] In 1844 some of the frontagers refused to pay quitrents, contending that having made the wharves they had a right to them; but the town clerk advised them that they had no exclusive right save for landing articles from boats. The wharves were public roads, and if goods were left on them the remedy was to take proceedings for nuisance.

As water traffic increased the nuisance grew, and the merchant Mr Coupland complained to the magistrates, and some kind of promise was given that obstructions on the wharves should be removed. Coupland then represented that persuasion was out of the question. Three thousand quarters of corn weekly more than there were a few years ago were brought to be shipped at the east wharf, and the other day he counted 37 vessels being laden, 32 waggons and 20 carts; and on account of the

[1] L.A.O. Monson 25/13/10/8/28, 29; 22, 23 February 1856.

[2] The plan was in substance adopted later. Below, p. 225.

[3] The Lighting and Paving Commissioners had wanted a macadamised road to bear the pressure of the loaded waggons carrying produce to the warehouses. *L.C.*, 1 November 1833.

[4] *L.C.*, 1 March, 24 May 1839. Later, St Benedict repudiated liability.

wharves being occupied by stones, wood, bricks, ashes etc. the carts in one place stood so thickly that the highway was impassable. Public necessity demanded that the whole of the wharves should be clear for loading and unloading.[1]

The council then took a hand and drafted by-laws for submission to the Secretary of State; and some of the merchants – Rudgard, Huddleston, William Dawber, Charles Ward and Charles Allison – petitioned against them. The by-laws came into force. When he was requested by the wharfmaster to remove some stone slabs from his wharf, Rudgard refused, and a summons was issued against him. Brogden of the *Chronicle* then took a hand.

We are sorry to find a gentleman of Mr Rudgard's position setting the bad example of breaking those laws which he assisted to make; and we cannot understand how parties who thus act can bring poor men before the magistrates for stealing bones, or otherwise violating the laws of the land. Can any casuist inform us of the difference of guilt between two men, the one taking possession of a quantity of bones which were not given to him, and which he never bought; and the other taking possession of a stoneyard which was never given to him, and which he never bought, and yet the one wrongdoer does not at all scruple or blush, to proceed against the other wrongdoer, although perhaps the humbler and more ignorant sinner may have been stimulated to his evil course by the powerful influence of bad example. The corporation are not without blame in this matter, for they ought resolutely to set their faces against the elevation to aldermanic honours of gentlemen with confused notions on the important matters of *meum* and *teum*.[2]

Rudgard brought an action for libel against Brogden, claiming that his father had made the wharf; he admitted having assented to the by-laws, but having since seen in Mr Ellison's lease a provision that persons might make wharves for their own use, had changed his attitude. Verdict was given for the defendant; it was not a libel but merely a strong comment upon the public acts of a public man. The bells of St Mary le Wigford were rung, and the victory celebrated in various public places. Public rights were established; but the real problem of maintenance had to await the taking over of responsibility for highways by the corporation.

The resident freemen had survived to plague a hostile corporation. The Municipal Corporations Act had severed them from the corporate body and deprived them of administrative power, but preserved their parliamentary votes and their rights of property. In Lincoln their only property rights consisted of special rights of pasture in the common lands of the city. There were four commons: the west and the south might be stocked with one head of cattle by householders generally, but a freeman

[1] *L.C.*, 25 November 1853.   [2] *L.C.*, 1 June 1855.

had the right to turn two head of cattle on any of the four commons – the other commons being the Holmes and the Monks Leys – in right of their freedom.

The ruling caucus regarded the freemen as a relic of the bad old days, and anyhow likely to be tories. When therefore the council committee concerned with common lands were told that it was customary for the council to keep the common fences in repair there was no response. When the committee drove the Monks Leys they found a horse, the property of a non-freeman, and properly impounded it and received the customary fine. The offender was however one of their political friends, who threatened to vote pink at the next election; and it was no doubt after party consultations that the chairman of the committee returned the fine. Councillors and others then felt free to turn their cattle on the freemen's commons, thinking no doubt to have done with another ancient privilege.

The freemen were roused, and they called a meeting. Sir Edward Bromhead, in the chair, explained the legal position, which indeed was clear. A resolution in defence of the freemen's rights was carried by a large majority. Edward Drury, a radical spokesman, caused much merriment when he protested that he disliked agitation. The freemen might have the bare law on their side, but it would be better for the public at large if the commons were thrown open. In a few years the freemen would be reduced in numbers, and the commons would then be in the possession of a few rich individuals; but it was pointed out to him that herein he was wrong, for the rights of the freemen passed to their heirs and did not die out.

The council maintained their position, connived at flagrant overstocking, and liberated animals which had been seized and impounded whilst trespassing. When the freemen undertook their own impounding their lock was destroyed and the animals released. The freemen then took proceedings aginst one Fotherby for illegal stocking: his friends tried to raise subscriptions for his defence, but had to tell him that he could have no more than bare costs. Judgment went against him in the sheriff's court. The council took no action and continued to neglect the fences. The freemen therefore took on themselves the guardianship of their rights by impounding and selling an 'illegal' cow, which raised a great outcry. A meeting called by the mayor on requisition asked the mayor to direct the sheriff to attend to the commons; and the town clerk advised that the corporation had no power to command the services of the sheriff, who was no longer a member of the corporation. At last, in 1841, the council took legal opinion. Counsel advised that they had power to

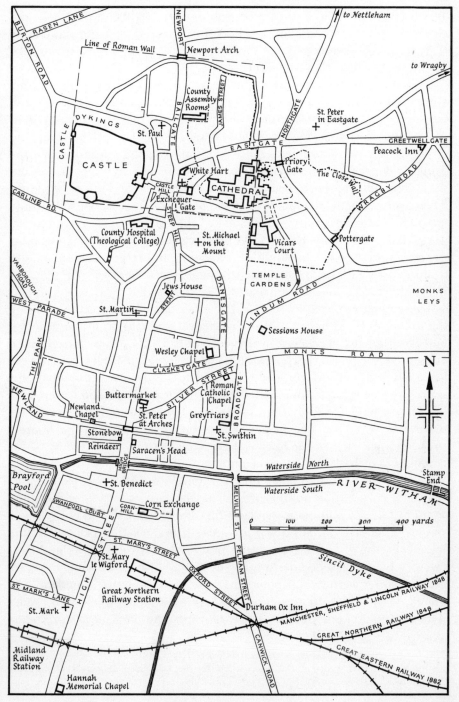

Map 1. Lincoln parishes

appoint an officer to protect the commoners' rights, expenses being charged on the borough fund. The council abandoned the fight, and thereafter the commons and the commoners' rights were given the attention to which they were entitled.

This change of heart was apparent when parts of the Holmes and south commons were taken by the railway. The corporation might have claimed a share of the sale moneys as lords of the manor, but they did not do so, and the moneys were invested for the benefit of the freemen.

There were related subjects of lively discussion: the infection of cattle drinking water from a pool on the common green with dung; horses on the common being 'borrowed' and used by boatmen and others at night. There were bigger issues too. Out of 500 or more freemen, not more than 50 or 60, some of them rich men, stocked the commons; if the commons were sold, all might benefit. As the register of electors grew, the freemen's prestige would diminish, and some future government might disfranchise them. Rights must be strenuously defended on both sides. It was to be long before these matters were disposed of.

There remains the oldest school. The grammar school was the result of the union, effected in 1584, of the cathedral and city grammar schools, and its origin was reflected in divided control. The dean and chapter appointed the master, who must be able to teach Greek and Latin learnedly, and the mayor, recorder and five aldermen appointed the usher, who must have commendable knowledge of Greek and Latin. The master was paid by the chapter, with a supplement from the city, and the usher, who was not under the master, by the city. The school was housed in the chapel – the upper floor – of the Greyfriars.

The school had had its good and bad periods,[1] and at the time of municipal reform it had fallen on a bad one.[2] As might be expected, the reformed corporation addressed itself to the task of reform with gusto. Plain businessmen found it shocking that the chapter should cling to the pattern of education laid down in Tudor times, when Greek and Latin were everything, and a good sound practical education nothing. At an enquiry by a charity commissioner in 1836 Willson and Rudgard, two corporation governors, proposed that the union of 1584 should be dissolved, so that the corporation could adapt their school to modern needs. The chapter representatives, Dean Gordon and Precentor Pretyman,

[1] *T. & S.L.*, pp. 103–4.
[2] *G.L.*, pp. 73, 282. *Charity Commissioners Report 1837*, pp. 349–51; they found that during the last five years of the usher's tenure – he had been dismissed – there had been a fall of half the number of pay boys and three-fourths of the free boys (i.e. sons of freemen).

resisted, and the commissioner ruled that the union could only be dissolved by mutual consent. The corporation took their own measures, dismissing the usher and procuring an English master. The numbers in the lower school at once began to grow, and by 1839 there were 140 boys in it, and about six in the upper school. The master and his pupils were squeezed out of the schoolroom into the school library; and this room not being heated, he retreated to his own house with his pupils, drawing on himself the charge that he was not supervising the whole school.

The young radical Charles Seely said that the original chapter endowment which had once yielded £20 as the master's salary ought now to be yielding more; he darkly suspected that the surplus paid for the turtle soup of the dignitaries. He could hardly think that the conduct of the reverend visitors could be the result of party feeling, for many tory supporters were taking advantage of the cheap education offered at the lower school. He wanted to provide for working-class children; and it ' was suspected that he wanted to graft a government school on the grammar school in order to bring it under the eye of an inspector.

The corporation accepted a compromise proposed by Pretyman; the master should teach English as well as Latin and Greek, and charge £1 1s. a quarter for each scholar; and the visitors might remove boys from the lower foundation to the upper.[1] The compromise failed. In 1843 the corporation visitors found that the master had only five pupils, three of them boarders, one his own son, and a fifth the son of a freeman, so that only the two latter could be said to be on the foundation. The old grammar school system was still pursued, though other subjects were given occasionally. Boys did not pass to the upper school because parents would not let them go.[2] New friction arose in 1847 when it was found that the usher had become a Wesleyan. The chapter, claiming the school as Anglican, tried to remove him. The corporation defended him, commended his service and character, and denounced the master for not removing abuses. They forced him to resign and the bishop gave him a living.

This drastic action led to renewed negotiations. It was agreed that there should be a conference between the visitors before a new master was appointed, and if the chapter did not listen to objections the matter should be referred to the bishop, who would also have the power of summary removal on the petition of either or both parties.[3]

The treaty was signed in 1850. There would be fees for extras, and the

---

[1] *L.C.*, 21 February 1840.
[2] C.M., 17 April 1843.
[3] L.A.O. Cor. B. 5/4/106/7.

usher would be under the master, and would teach such subjects as the visitors should think necessary for a sound moral, religious and liberal education. The corporation were agreeably surprised at the liberal spirit shown by the chapter, especially by the conduct of the dean, whose only desire was to make the school a blessing to the city.[1]

It was at this time that the chancellor, George Pretyman, was being proceeded against in chancery for abuse of the funds of the Spital hospital, of which he was warden. The chapter proposed that part of the endowment should be applied for the improvement of the Greyfriars for the benefit of the grammar school. On their part the city council offered to provide a new house for the schoolmaster on the old sheep market, south of the school, and devote the whole of the Greyfriars, with the land adjoining, to the use of the school. The Court of Chancery approved schemes for the Mere and Spital charities in 1858, providing (*inter alia*) for the enlargement, improvement and endowment of the school. The council, faced with an outburst of indignation at any measure which would eject the Mechanics Institution from some of the rooms at the Greyfriars, began to temporise. The chapter countered sharply. They recalled that the Greyfriars had been conveyed to the mayor and other feoffees in trust for the grammar school, and suggested that any other use of the building was illegal.[2] Only part of the sheep market would be needed for the master's house with room for 25 or 30 boarders, though the larger the number of boarders the better for the school and the city. The council reluctantly complied, though in view of the opposition the schoolmaster's house had to be built uphill. The school took over the lower part of the Greyfriars from the Institution.[3]

The new corporation took over the police from the Lighting and Paving Commission, which had been set up under a local act of 1828, the Commission's rate being thereby reduced.[4] Their new watch committee reported that the average annual cost of the police during the previous five years was £460. The ordinary policemen formerly received about 19s. per week; it was now decided to reduce them in number and pay them 14s. plus a suit of clothes yearly. The sergeant was to have 16s. and the inspector 28s. There would be a total annual saving of £20. A proposal made in 1856 to increase the force from 13 to 16 was not adopted. The stern municipal economist pointed to a low level of crime in the city and hinted that the country gentlemen had only agreed to

[1] *L.C.*, 9 August 1850.
[2] See *T. & S.L.*, pp. 102–3.
[3] T. E. Page and Dr Charles Brook have both left memories of the school in this period.
[4] *G.L.*, p. 212.

saddle themselves and their neighbours with the new county police because they thought the police might put a stop to poaching.

The Lighting and Paving Commissioners – a body consisting of two representatives of each parish with members sent by the council and the dean and chapter – much missed the police who had done various odd jobs for them, such as remedying nuisances and superintending the lighting of street lamps; and they soon came to terms with the council's watch committee on a number of such matters. The Commission's surveyor and the police were jointly to try to prevent cattle from being exposed for sale outside the beast market and Broadgate, except on fair days.

They devoted themselves to many small improvements, removing projecting steps and bow windows, rounding corners and widening streets as opportunity offered. They were advised that they could not compel owners and occupiers of houses to make a footway where there was none before, their powers being limited to existing footways. They had to control the hackney coaches, gigs, sedan chairs and the like; and they drew up by-laws. The struggle to control stalls in the streets – custom died hard – was constant.[1] In 1848 they resolved that as ample provision had been made by the corporation and the new Markets Company for holding markets elsewhere it was desirable that no street stalls be allowed; and orders allowing them were rescinded.[2] The running of perambulators on the footpaths was denounced as a nuisance.

There were constant complaints about the state of the streets, some of them quagmires, especially when there was heavy traffic during the building of the railways, or when the Water Company and the Gas Company were laying mains. Everyone wanted street lighting, but nobody wanted to pay for it. In 1836 a contract was made with the Gas Light and Coke Company. In 1842 twenty-three lamps were proposed, but only fifteen were authorised. The cost of laying mains was £130, and shared with the company. When the short period of lighting was complained of, it was agreed that all lights should be lit for nine months, 1,600 hours for 68s. each, which was an increase of 5s. Presently the magistrates complained that the hours of lighting were insufficient for the security of the public in the winter months, and they asked for lighting from sunset to sunrise; after cutting off an hour at each end of the night this was agreed.

The commissioners welcomed the new Water Company,[3] and opened negotiations with them about fire plugs in water mains. The

[1] *G.L.*, p. 214. [2] Above, pp. 49–50.
[3] Below, p. 161.

corporation sanitary committee suggested the flushing of street channels, and terms were agreed at £3 per week for flushing; but within a few weeks they decided that the cost was too great, and said they had only agreed during the late apprehended approach of cholera. There were successive contracts for flushing with grants from the corporation, with haggling over the price on renewal. Street watering to settle the dust, especially on dirt roads was an amenity which came to be called for, though there was a feeling that it was a pity to spend money for so ephemeral a benefit.

When the Health of Towns Bill was presented in the Commons the commissioners resolved to petition in favour of it; but when the great question of a system of underground sewerage came up they were not to be swept off their feet by the demand for reform, though they made small grants towards underground drainage in some areas.

One of the minor but more enduring activities of the Commission was the naming of many of the streets and lanes which had never been named before, and the numbering of houses. Among the names adopted were Lindum Road (for the then New Road), Bailgate, Steep Hill, and the various parts of the new road to Canwick, Melville Street, Pelham Street and Oxford Street.

Through all the activities of the Commission runs the fear of an increased lighting and paving rate. In 1836 their assessments were compared with parochial rate lists for correcting lists of occupiers; a proposal to revalue the whole city in 1851 was lost, and it was decided to hear individual appeals. The churchwardens of St Mary le Wigford appealed in respect of church property on the ground that there was no church rate, and no other fund out of which to pay the rate. The rate was confirmed, as was that at St Paul's, but St Michael secured a reduction. St Swithin's complained that their increases were out of all proportion to those in other parishes, the increase in their total rate being £440, and that for all the other parishes £315. Their request for a revaluation was refused. In 1856 the rate was still 8d. in the pound, as it had been for many years.

It was becoming increasingly clear that the Lighting and Paving Act was no longer sufficient to meet the needs of the city. Under the Act the frontagers were liable for pavements and the parishes for the carrying out of the highway work, and there were many different standards of maintenance. Only gradually did lime dust and mud as a road surface give way to granite and gravel, 'awkward St Swithin's' leading the way. Furthermore, the extra-parochial places had been held not to be within the Act,[1] and the commission could not therefore repair defective

---

[1] *G.L.*, p. 213.

channels in the Castle dykings, or touch any of the other evils lurking there. Finally, the dean and chapter had a veto on any order affecting the Close: this was reasonable when the Act was passed, for the Close was not then within the municipal borough, but now it was, and it was pointed out that, being much used for bringing in wool and corn to the city markets, Pottergate in particular had become a great nuisance. When in 1866 the Local Government Act of 1858 was adopted, the Commission came to an end, its powers being transferred to the council as the new Local Board of Health.[1]

The parish as a unit of local government was on the decline. The Poor Law Act of 1834 substituted compulsory for voluntary membership of a union of parishes, and the parish's only remaining poor law functions were to elect guardians of the poor, and to collect and pay the rates levied on the parishes. They had the roads until 1866. Some parishes put the repair of their roads out to contract, and some did the work themselves; a rich parish like St Mark could make grants for the purpose out of its own revenues.

There remained the duty of assessment and the collection of the various rates. The duty of assessment lay upon the parish overseers of the poor – now under the supervision of the guardians and the Poor Law Board – and when only land, houses and shops were concerned, common sense and a little experience were enough for the purpose. But to value the gas works was not so simple and the gaspipe passing through the parish might be even more difficult. Then there were the railways; St Mary le Wigford somehow valued them at £800 a mile. There were schools, waterworks and a billiard room; and presently there were the foundries. The time was coming when paid assistant overseers were needed to collect the rates, and experts to fix the assessments. Furthermore, there was gross inequality of parish rating, and there was growing demand for uniformity of standards.

The turnpike roads inside the city had been taken out of the turnpike trust by the Act of 1828, but the trustees were responsible for the approaches to the city, and when an act for the renewal of their powers was sought in 1833 it was proposed to extend the trust powers to the boundary of the county of the city towards Washingborough and Harmston, and also to the entrance to Branston. Still more closely concerned with the city was a proposal to make a road from the swing bridge at the south end of Broadgate (site of the present Thornbridge) to the foot of Canwick Hill, with a branch to St Mary Street. This was important.

[1] For the Inquiry concerning a petition from the Lincoln Local Government Board for the repeal of parts of the Lincoln Lighting and Paving Act of 1828, see L.P.L. L.G. 612.

Through the centuries the long ribbon-built suburb of Wigford had been surrounded by water. At its south end the Sincil Dyke was crossed by the Great and Little Bargate bridges: but the Witham to the west was crossed only by footbridge into the Holmes Common and a private bridge to Boultham. On the east the Sincil Dyke was crossed only by footbridges at the Tentercroft and Sewell's Walk. A new road going south from Broadgate and connecting with St Mary Street would be a startling development. Of course it raised questions of tolls. The scheme was first rejected, but it came up again in 1839, and the difficult questions were compromised. Some of the roads taken from the turnpike and vested in the Lighting and Paving Commissioners were restored to the trustees, as the city council were anxious to ensure that the trust would be liable for the new roads.[1] The new toll bar was placed at the junction of the Branston and Washingborough roads, on Canwick Common; the Great Bargate toll bar was to be removed and placed at Swine Green, with one gate for the Newark Road and one for the Sleaford Road. This important move (for which credit belongs to Carline) meant that the citizens would be able to ride or drive to their own south common without payment of toll. Tolls were never charged on foot passengers.

When the road was opened in 1843, having to be raised above flood level, and the gradient on Canwick Hill lowered, the bells of St Peter's rang, and the Christs Hospital boys and their band accompanied the turnpike trustees in procession from the tollgate to Lincoln, and buns were given to the boys at the new Durham Ox inn, which Mr Fisher had built at the junction of the two branches of the road. A swing bridge had been erected over the river when the navigation was improved and the river walls built; in 1858 a new iron bridge was erected to take the increasing traffic to the factories – Doughty's, Clayton and Shuttleworth's, Duckering's, Proctor and Burton.

By 1870 there were plans for abolishing the toll bars operated by the trustees as the debts of the road were paid off; the bars were abolished, and the trust wound up in 1875, liability for road repair outside the city returning to the parishes.

[1] 4 & 5 Vic. c.cviii, 21 June 1841.

CHAPTER IV

COUNTY INFLUENCE

The death of Charlotte Palmer in 1849 at the age of about 84 prompted Cracroft[1] to reflect that she was the very last of the old county Minster Yard society. The old lady had known the history of all the county families, and she had loved to praise the hospitality and almost grandeur of Cracroft's great-great-uncle Charles Amcotts of Kettlethorpe and Harrington, who died in 1777. She always said 'many people found fault with him for being the main cause of the high road turned through the Minster Yard, which it used to skirt before'.[2] The inhabitants did not like to have their privacy invaded.

Now she was gone, and Cracroft reflected that:

All the residents there now are new, and with the exception of Fred Sutton are not what many would consider very gentle birth. In fact the Lincoln society is completely changed since I first recollect it, and nowadays the younger branches of county families seek homes elsewhere, leaving their places to be filled up by merchants, lawyers and doctors.[3]

This withdrawal from Minster Yard in no way affected the influence of the gentry in the affairs of the city. They still came in on county business and on social occasions. Even the Reform Bill had left virtually unchanged the deference with which they were received by the citizens, and their patronage of the shops, political and social affairs and charities lost nothing in influence and weight.

They were themselves 'the county'. They were a large number of people with roots, deep or shallow, in the soil, of the upper or upper middle classes, with the same social but not necessarily the same political outlook; supporters nearly all, warm or tepid, of the Church of England; living in country mansions and having the wherewithal to support themselves in a proper standard of comfort, derived for preference from land. The class could not be precisely defined, but there was little doubt who was within it: the rest of the world was outside. Friends and equals from Nottinghamshire and Yorkshire were of course welcome in the hunting field or at the ball, but they knew their status as guests, and would not have presumed to interfere in county business.

Precedence in all things belonged to the lord lieutenant John Cust, second Lord Brownlow, who had served in the militia in 1804, had held the office since 1809, and was created an earl in 1815. He took a high

---

[1] Below, p. 70.   [2] *G.L.*, p. 123.   [3] Cracroft, 19–24 April 1849.

view of his rank[1] and his office, and he was a stiff tory with traditional notions of church and state. He was not a clever man, and in a passage of arms with Charles Tennyson about the militia and the Stamford reformers in 1831 was thought to have come off second best. Tennyson later acknowledged that he had since behaved handsomely.[2] He took great care in the appointment of magistrates, pointing out to reluctant gentry like young Bacon Hickman that if persons of status and character refused to act, the result must be the degradation of the Bench by the introduction of an inferior class of men into the commission of the peace. He acknowledged that many of the best were clergymen, but had found it necessary to stipulate that their preferment in the county should be £500 or thereabouts, unless they had property of their own which would give them a qualification. But with all his stiffness and prejudice he was a devoted public servant, and deserved the tribute of Charles Anderson to 'a good Churchman and a man, who, without great talent and no eloquence, fulfilled his duty to the County in a most exemplary manner'.[3]

Brownlow resigned the lieutenancy in 1852, at a moment which put the choice of his successor in the hands of the tory prime minister Lord Derby, who had displeased the high protectionists in his party by refusal to attempt to restore the corn laws; and he took the opportunity of appointing the marquis of Granby, a high tory, who had declined to join the government. Greville commented that the choice might have the effect of stopping his mouth, if it did not remove his discontent.[4] It was generally said that the main purpose was to keep out Lord Yarborough.

Lincolnshire sentiment was offended. Granby belonged to Leicestershire, to which he betook himself in 1857, when he succeeded his father as sixth duke of Rutland and lord lieutenant there.

The prize which had eluded Yarborough fell to him then, when for reasons of health it was too late for him to enjoy it or to do the work well. His family had come into their position of prominence in north Lincolnshire in the latter years of the eighteenth century.[5] Charles Anderson

---

[1] For his determination that his wife should not meet Harriet Mellon the actress, who had become Duchess of St Albans, see *G.L.*, p. 266.

[2] L.A.O. Tennyson d'Eyncourt H122/103, 26 May 1838.

[3] Anderson Letters 1, a note before a group of letters from Lord Brownlow beginning 12 January 1848. Glimpses of him later in life are given in his third wife's memories, *The Eve of Victorianism* (1840). An engraving of his portrait hangs in the Grand Jury Room in Lincoln Castle. Cracroft's comment on him as a landlord is severe. His estates were a by-word for neglect; houses out of repair; undrained land; let his land for little more than half its value, and hence perhaps its deplorable state, the tenants having no motive to exertion. Diary, 26 May 1852.

[4] *Journal of the Reign of Queen Victoria 1837–52* (1895 edition) III, 472.

[5] *G.L.*, pp. 31, 218, 222, 230.

Pelham had been created baron in 1794. Then came the second baron and first earl, who had wanted to go into the navy but was overruled, and represented first Grimsby (1803–7) and then the county (1807–23) in the House of Commons. He indulged his love of the sea, and he became famous as commander of the Royal Yacht Squadron.[1]

The second earl sat for one of his father's four Isle of Wight boroughs[2] in 1830–1, and then for the county of Lincoln in 1831–2, and when the county was divided by the Reform Bill in 1832, for the northern division until 1846, when he succeeded his father. Like his father he was a whig, and was looked to as their leader by the whigs in both divisions even after the division was effected. He became a protectionist, but acquiesced in repeal.[3]

When the promoters of the Manchester and Sheffield Railway sought to extend their line into north Lincolnshire Yarborough became the obvious figurehead, not only as a great landlord, but as chairman of the Grimsby Haven Company, which the railway interest acquired. This enterprise led to the building of new docks instead of enlarging the old dock; had the latter course been taken, Anderson wrote later, a compact town might have grown out of the village that Grimsby had been, instead of which it became a long straggling dirty village three miles long with 12,000 inhabitants. Anderson attributed this result partly to Yarborough's appointment as chairman of the railway company, 'a mere tool in the hands of others, and being given the patronage, which he dispensed in the most foolish way, putting into offices of trust, stations etc., broken down tradesmen or tenants who could not manage their own concerns, and therefore were not likely to manage other people's'.[4] With all his strong political and personal prejudice Anderson admitted – and indeed showed – that Yarborough was a kindly man. Cracroft put it more positively: 'few men in his position are so thoughtful, or recollect old associations as Lord Yarborough'.

By 1857, when he became lord lieutenant, he was suffering from partial paralysis, and Cracroft commented that it was sad indeed to see a young man so infirm.[5] By 1860 it was reported that he was much worse

---

[1] It appears that he gave the name of 'Yarborough' to a hand of bridge in which there is not a single trump (trumps having been called); but that the term properly belongs to a hand in which there is no card higher than a nine. Lord Yarborough used to lay 1,000 to 1 against such an occurrence in any named hand. The actual mathematical odds against are 1,827 to 1. Brewer, *Dictionary of Phrase and Fable*.

[2] His father was a trustee of the Holmes estate which owned the boroughs. It was alleged that he sold them to the Government. A. Aspinall, *Three Early Nineteenth Century Diaries* (1952), p. 90n.   [3] Below, p. 84.

[4] Anderson Diary, 16 April 1849, note apparently added in 1861.

[5] Cracroft, 15 December 1856.

than people imagined, that no one approached him, and that others exercised his patronage.[1] When he died in 1862 he was only 52.

He was succeeded in the earldom but not in the lieutenancy by his son Charles Anderson Pelham, Lord Worsley, who had represented Grimsby since 1857. He was a captain in the militia under Cracroft, who described him as 'nice, unaffected good a little fellow,...but with a very neat figure: I know nothing about his brains, but his disposition is evidently good', with promise of doing well. He looked fat and jovial, and could be happy even without the blandishments of a barrack yard: he once rode back 33 miles after a hard day's hunting. Liquor, said Cracroft, was his besetting sin, though a kinder heart never beat.[2] A correspondent in the Isle of Wight wrote on his accession to the estates that 'he was not fairly dealt with in his early life, being constantly thrown into the society of gamekeepers, huntsmen and grooms, who toadied him out of measure'.[3] He became a lieutenant colonel in the Lincolnshire Rifle Volunteers, and master of hounds, and died in 1875, a young man of 40.

The successor of the second earl in the lieutenancy was Gilbert John Heathcote, who had married Lord Willoughby's daughter and heiress in 1827, and had represented first Boston and then south Lincolnshire in the Commons, transferring to Rutland in 1841. He succeeded his father in the family baronetcy in 1851, being created Lord Aveland in 1856, and appointed colonel of the Royal South Lincolnshire Militia in the following year. He was a whig, and remained lukewarmly so until the 1860s.[4] On his appointment to the lieutenancy Anderson wrote

12 February 1862. I am glad we have got Lord Aveland. He is a gentleman, and we shall have a responsible man.[5]

He died in 1867, and was succeeded by Adelbert, third Earl Brownlow, when he was 23. Elizabeth Wordsworth described him in 1869 as a tall, handsome young man, with delightfully unaffected almost boyish manners, and full of stories about his adventures in foreign parts. 'Having been in the army during his elder brother's lifetime, he had seen a good deal more of the world than if he had been heir-apparent, and it is certainly an advantage.'[6] He was to hold minor office in three tory governments.[7]

When he died in 1921 he was succeeded as lieutenant by Charles fourth Earl of Yarborough, whose step-grandfather the seventh Lord

[1] L.A.O. Daubney iv/3/27.
[2] Cracroft, 11 June 1854, 15 December 1856, 7 February 1875.
[3] Anderson Letters II, from Admiral Love, Yarmouth, 20 January 1862.
[4] Dr Olney's thesis.   [5] L.A.O. Massingberd 4/88.
[6] Note pasted into her diary, lent to me by Mrs Smeeton.
[7] 1885–6, 1887–9, 1889–92.

Monson had brought him up as a liberal. He came of age in 1880. He entered fully into public life, became chairman of Lindsey County Council and quarter sessions, and like his forebears he hunted the Brocklesby. In 1935 he achieved the rare honour of the Garter. It is perhaps symbolic that like other landlords he suffered from the agricultural depression, for 'bad times with farmers mean bad times with all good landlords',[1] and he had to reduce his hunting establishment and sell his dog pack in 1895.

All these grandees lived at a considerable distance from Lincoln. The Monsons were much nearer neighbours at Burton, which lay on Lincoln's northern boundary, and much less grand. The family had long had close associations with it, and during the eighteenth and early nineteenth centuries could generally nominate one of the members of parliament for the city.[2] The long whig connection was broken by the young fifth baron, who was one of the 22 peers who voted against the third reading of the Reform Bill. By his travel, his purchase of Gatton and works of art he impoverished the family; his marriage was an unhappy one, and he died in 1841 at the age of 32.[3]

He was succeeded by his cousin William John, only son of Colonel William Monson,[4] who was the fifth son of the second baron. News that Burton was again to be the residence of the family was received with pleasure, though disappointment followed. The sixth baron found himself so impoverished by the squanderings of his predecessor, and the annuities to three dowagers that he lived there little, though he wrote to his son:

12 July 1855. I like Burton better than any place, but the great drawback is one cannot live there quietly without entertaining, and yet there are others around with much larger incomes who do not do so much.[5]

Nevertheless, he did not seem to like many of his neighbours, having an especial dislike of 'those horrid Andersons', and finding a round of visits to the Atkinsons, Neviles and Jarvises a horrid bore. Most of his letters to his son are dated from Gatton or Chart Lodge near Sevenoaks.

He was devoted to the improvement of his estates, relying on agents whom he expected to deal firmly with farm tenants; a subject on which he had strong views:

19 November 1855. You are perfectly right, they have had their say too much. The Lincolnshire farmers are all like overfed underworked horses. They do not

---

[1] G. E. Collins, *Farming and Foxhunting* (n.d.), p. 122.   [2] *G.L.*, ch. IV.
[3] Anderson Letters 1, a note before a letter from Frederick John Lord Monson, 1 September 1836.   [4] *G.L.*, pp. 220–3; L.A.O. *Annual Report*, 22 (1970–1), pp. 41–4.
[5] L.A.O. Monson 25/10/4/1, no. 63. When it came to subscriptions he wanted to be kept in step with neighbours like Amcotts, Ellison of Boultham or Jarvis, but not to compete with Ellison of Sudbrooke or Yarborough.

know what they would be at, but these days are not such that they can play their tricks. If they kick they now have a chance of being turned out of stall and stable.[1]

His chief interest seems to have been in antiquarian studies, and he was a friend of Willson, Edward Peacock and John Ross, whose family had been Monson tenants at Carlton. He compiled a history of the family, and made notes of the inscriptions in many of the churches in the county which have been published by his grandson.[2] It was his great desire to acquire Ross' splendid manuscript history of the city, and he achieved his ambition after Ross' death.[3]

His son William John, who succeeded him in 1862, was a strong liberal.[4] He was to hold office in several liberal governments, and in 1886 he was created Viscount Oxenbridge of Burton. He married the widow of the second Earl of Yarborough in 1869. He quickly began to take an interest in local affairs, and he managed to hold local office in spite of his constant absence in London.

A few of the gentry call for special mention. One of the most formidable figures, and certainly one of the richest, was Charles Chaplin, the squire of Blankney. He owned property in three counties, and he was an autocratic landlord, though a good one, allowing tenants' widows to remain in their farms. It was said of him that he could return seven members to parliament since good tenants voted as they were told. He applied similar methods when sitting on the bench, where he was a terror to poachers and to others who withstood him. On one occasion a young lawyer from London ventured to criticise one of his pronouncements as not legal, whereupon Chaplin thundered, 'Young man, you are evidently a stranger in these parts, or you would know that my word *is* law.'[5]

Chaplin represented the undivided county in the Commons from 1818 to 1830, being always on the right of the Duke of Newcastle's party, and retired because the life did not suit his active habits.[6] He commanded the yeomanry, calling them out at dates to suit himself, and he took a

---

[1] L.A.O. Monson 25/10/4/1, no. 17.
[2] *Lincolnshire Church Notes made by William John Monson 1828–40* (1936, L.R.S.).
[3] When Ross died in 1870 Monson sought to secure the collection from his nephew the Rev. J. Ross Barker. After some demur by Barker agreement was reached – Monson's solicitor saying that the agreement was 'unusual' – that if through Monson's efforts Barker was presented to a living in the south of England, then the collection was to become Monson's absolute property. Monson offered him Gatton, which he could not accept, as he had accepted a living near Baldock; but when through Monson's efforts Lord Selborne presented him to Evesham, Barker acknowledged that the collection belonged to Monson. Correspondence preserved with Ross Collection in L.P.L.
[4] Above, p. 32.
[5] Lady Londonderry, *Henry Chaplin* (1926), p. 11.   [6] *L.C.*, 27 May 1859.

leading part in the business of gaol sessions. Cracroft noted his conduct one day on the grand jury. A bill was brought against the inhabitants of Sibsey which Cracroft thought a good case. It was, however, thrown out (Cracroft thought) because Chaplin had made up his mind against it before hearing the evidence, his reason being that he fancied that it would be in some way detrimental to the Witham Commissioners (whom he also dominated). He earned the tribute that few men had deserved more of their county, and few had ever done their duty as county gentlemen as well as 'the old Squire': yet he was a narrow-minded man and by no means above a job. To hear his health proposed at public meetings would suggest that he was a little god. A few months later, at gaol sessions, old Humphrey Sibthorp and Gervase Sibthorp sneaked out in the middle, and John Bromhead tried to shirk, but the old Squire caught him *in flagrante delicto*, and made him come back again.[1]

He managed the County Assembly Rooms, and was the principal supporter of the Burton Hunt; and he was an active railway promoter, becoming a director of the Great Northern Railway Company.[2]

The Reverend Sir Charles Anderson, baronet, was, like his father and grandfather, the rector of Lea near Gainsborough. He was a whig, and kin to Lord Denman, the lord chief justice. Thomas Cooper called him 'the beloved and venerated Sir Charles' who was kind to Gainsborough boys.[3] Cracroft, unusually critical for him, said that as vice-chairman of sessions he was a very indifferent performer, slow and without dignity. 'His sentences don't impress, and he often seems lost, which is singular in a man who has had so much experience.' His daughter Emily was at Scawby visiting her sister Lady Nelthorpe:

2 December 1856. I had not seen her since she returned from Miss Nightingale's hospital at Scutari, where she was one of the nurses. She speaks most highly of the medical staff, and say we took away their character most unjustly, that their conduct (from her experience) was beyond praise.[4]

His son Charles soon struck out his own line. At Oxford he was an early Tractarian, and intimate with Samuel Wilberforce, the future bishop of Oxford, whom he entertained at Lea.[5] He became a strong tory. Besides the usual interest in hunting, shooting and fishing, he

[1] Cracroft, 19 July 1848, 27 December 1849.
[2] Below, p. 106. He is commemorated by a portrait in the Grand Jury Room at the castle and a stained glass window in the cathedral. [3] *Life* (1872), pp. 24, 27.
[4] Cracroft, 22 October 1847, 2 December 1856. Emily Anderson went to the Crimea with Miss Stanley's party. See Mrs Woodham Smith, *Florence Nightingale* (1950).
[5] He sent two packets of the bishop's letters to him to the bishop's biographer Canon Ashwell. See David Newsome, *The Parting of Friends* (1966), p. 457. For his attitude to ritualism later, see below, p. 244.

entered fully into public life, serving in the militia and becoming chairman of quarter sessions. He was especially devoted to ecclesiastical affairs (in the high church interest) and to archaeology and architecture, having published several works on these subjects, besides a guide to the county. When allowance is made for his strong prejudices, his diary, volumes of letters and other writings are valuable evidence of affairs in his time.[1]

Weston Cracroft was the son of Lt. Colonel Robert Cracroft by Augusta, daughter and heiress of Sir John Ingilby and of Lady Ingilby-Amcotts. After serving briefly in the 1st Royal Dragoons, he served with the militia and then with the volunteers, as will later appear.[2] He took a leading part in county affairs, becoming vice-chairman of Lindsey quarter sessions and an active member of gaol sessions. In politics he was a moderate liberal, and sat in one parliament for mid-Lincolnshire (1868–74). On the death of his mother in 1855 he took the name of Amcotts by royal licence. His diary, which is much quoted here, shows him to have been a shrewd observer, tolerant and kindly in outlook, eager to understand other people's point of view, and seeking good in everyone. His comments have great historical value. He died in 1883.

The circle of gentry was not a closed circle. Men could settle on an estate, and (if reasonably congenial) be accepted, their origin over-looked, if not in the first generation, at least in the second. The Ellisons, merchants and bankers, had come from Thorne in the East Riding. Money made out of the lease of the Fossdyke navigation was in part invested in Smith Ellison's Bank; and Richard of the third generation had been M.P. for Lincoln, held office as recorder, chairman of the county quarter sessions, colonel of militia, and much else besides. His aspirations to become a knight of the shire, however, were frowned upon by Sir Joseph Banks, who thought a banker a suitable member for a borough, but that a county seat was for his betters.[3]

Ellison died in 1827 without legitimate issue, and his estate at Sud-brooke and his Fossdyke interests passed to his brother Henry Ellison of Thorne, and in 1834 to Henry's son Richard, who had served in the Guards at Walcheren and Corunna. He took little part in public affairs, but was a generous supporter of all good causes, being described by Cracroft as 'the most estimable man and the most thorough Christian I know'.[4] Anderson's note on him reads:

[1] There is a memoir and bibliography in *Lincs. N. & Q.*, III, 1.
[2] Below, pp. 75–6.
[3] *G.L.*, p. 223.
[4] Cracroft, 20 January 1857.

...one of the kindliest of men...He was a real patron of art, especially in water colours, and had fine specimens of Copley Fielding and De Wint. He was also one of the first of Millais' patrons. He left his pictures to the nation. He greatly improved the grounds and made a piece of water at Sudbrooke. He married Miss Terrot, daughter of the Bishop of Edinburgh...He lived a retired life, and did not enter into great society, but few were more hospitable to his friends and acquaintances.[1]

He died in 1859. The elder Richard Ellison had had an illegitimate son Richard, who was born in 1807, and served for 50 years in the militia. When he married in 1830 his father provided for him at Boultham, and on his father's death there came into effect a mutual arrangement by which the Sudbrooke property passed to the son of Ellison of Boultham, the widow of Ellison of Sudbrooke remaining in the property during her life.

Ellison of Boultham acquired the reputation of a good neighbour in the city. During the Crimean War Cracroft, with whom Ellison served in the militia, recalled, sitting at mess, a telegram arriving that announced the death of the Czar of Russia. Ellison especially was pleased because his son Dick was then serving at Sevastopol; and there was a hope that this would end the war.[2] The younger Richard fought at the Alma, and when he returned to Lincoln he was met at the railway station by the mayor and corporation, who took him in an open carriage with four horses to Boultham, where they lunched, and half the town had cheese and ale.[3] His father surrendered Boultham Hall to him in 1881, and died in the following year. In 1907, at the inspection of the Guard, the younger Ellison, then the oldest Yeoman, was knighted.

Christopher Charles Ellison, younger son of the first Ellison of Boultham, took holy orders, crossed the river to Bracebridge as curate in 1862, and became vicar there in 1874. He was also rector of Boultham. He took a leading part in public affairs in the immediate locality, was chairman of the Lincoln Board of Guardians for nearly 30 years, and chaplain at Bracebridge Asylum for 43 years. He was an expert in ivory and metal turning, an angler and a fine shot; but perhaps he became most famous as a rose grower. He laid out four acres of garden, with thousands of roses, and when he opened the garden to the public thousands of Lincoln citizens and others would pay them a visit. It became one of the outstanding events of the Lincoln year.

Alexander Leslie Melville was a new arrival in the county. He had

[1] Anderson Letters 1, a note written after two letters from Richard Ellison, the second dated 7 November 1854. His collection of paintings is at South Kensington.
[2] Cracroft, 2 March 1855.
[3] G. K. Jarvis, Diary 24 July 1855.

married the daughter of Abel Smith the banker, and was sent to manage the Lincoln bank. His origins were unimpeachable, for he was an 'honorable'; but he was still a newcomer, and when he was serving as foreman of the grand jury in 1846 he received an anonymous letter asking him why, though the son of a Scottish earl, he had the impudence to usurp the post of foreman to the exclusion of the old county families like the Trollopes or the Sheffields. Even the kindly Cracroft, admitting his right by virtue of his rank, wondered whether it was wise in him to press his prerogative so often. Later, he noted that opinions differed as to Melville. 'Some like him, some do not. I have always found him kind and agreeble. His countenance is the worst part of him perhaps.'[1]

Mary Fane of Fulbeck had married another banker, Anthony Peacock, a well liked sensible man who had bought Rauceby and had built the hall there, and (again to quote Cracroft) become the first of gentle blood of his race. Mrs Peacock talked freely but not slightingly of her husband's relations. Many of them, she said, 'have just sufficient fortunes to marry, and in the next generation half of the farmers in the neighbourhood of Sleaford will be Peacocks, for they can't afford to bring up their children as gentle people'. Cracroft's own comment on Peacock was that 'he always gives me the idea of being suspicious of detection, and yet I am sure no one would suspect that he never had a grandfather'.[2] He was high sheriff in 1854 and M.P. for south Lincolnshire in 1857–9. In 1851 he inherited estates in Lincoln, and changed his name to Willson.

In 1829 the Doddington estate near Lincoln, once the home of the Husseys and the Delavals,[3] came into the possession of Lt. Colonel George Ralph Payne Jarvis, a cadet of a family of sugar planters in Antigua, then aged 55.[4] He had served in the Peninsular War and at Walcheren, and was never wholly to escape from the Walcheren fever. When he died in 1851 Cracroft commented that he was supposed to have died wealthy; he was once miserably poor, and brought up a family of seven in trying circumstances; and when he became rich he could not find it in his heart to assist his sons to any extent. 'He was an excellent, good brave man, very practical and just, but not very generous.'[5] But his letters clearly show that he was deeply attached to all his family.

He was at once put in the commission of the peace, and anxious to equip himself for his new duties, writing to his eldest son:

[1] Cracroft, 9 March 1846, 5 May 1847.
[2] Cracroft, 21 March 1849.
[3] G.L., pp. 94–9.
[4] R. E. G. Cole, *History of Doddington* (1897), for the history of the family and the estate.
[5] Cracroft, 16 June 1851, Cracroft, brother in law to the sons, had no doubt heard much from them.

7 February 1831. I have been in daily expectation of Burne's *Justice* and Peel's criminal law, and during all this time I am in a kind of fizzle for fear some person should be brought to me, or some one require a warrant or other thing connected with the business...I should be loth to put my foot even with the best intentions into a bog – for these and every other rational reason pray haste the transit of these sapient volumes.[1]

It was with his encouragement that his sons took a large part in public business. The eldest, George Knollis, who succeeded him, was for many years chairman of the Kesteven petty sessional court at Lincoln, Lincoln gaol sessions, and treasurer of the Lincoln County Hospital. He was also a turnpike trustee and a trustee of the Savings Bank. These offices and others were reached by dint of long and regular attendance to business. His diary records the events of his life from day to day, but is devoid of comment. Even the death of his father-in-law the Chancellor Pretyman, on whom his views might have been interesting, merely provides dates of death and burial and particulars of his will in a newspaper cutting.

Of the younger sons of Colonel Jarvis, Charles qualified as a barrister, but abandoned the law, took holy orders and the rectory of Doddington in 1837, and married a daughter of Colonel Cracroft of Hackthorn in 1840. Another son, Edwin, took an M.B. degree at Cambridge, abandoned medicine, married another Cracroft daughter in 1841 and became rector of Hackthorn and Cold Hanworth in 1844. It is perhaps not surprising that their secular rather than their ecclesiastical activities remained the most prominent; Charles as a magistrate, and both as members and vice-chairmen of the Board of Guardians.

The two ironfounding pioneers Nathaniel Clayton and Joseph Shuttleworth were 'received' by the county by virtue of their wealth. They were both of humble origin.[2] After being mayor and appointed a city magistrate Clayton became a county magistrate, in which capacity his services were much valued by Cracroft. He bought the Withcall estate near Louth in 1875, but two years later built and lived in a splendid mansion abovehill in Lincoln called Eastcliffe House. He also had a house in the Isle of Wight, and was elected to the Royal Yacht Squadron. He was high sheriff in 1881. The marriages of his daughters into the established families of Swan and Cockburn helped to secure his social position, and a third daughter kept some of his money in the circle by marriage to Shuttleworth's son Alfred. He died in 1890.[3]

His brother in law and partner, Shuttleworth, also a former mayor,

---

[1] Jarvis Corr.   [2] Below, p. 121.
[3] His house was surrounded by a high wall, still standing on Lindum Terrace, which was raised by the addition of trellis work covered with ivy. A fox had once taken refuge there from the hunt, and the fence was raised to prevent the repetition of such a liberty.

married as his second wife a daughter of Colonel Ellison of Boultham; tried unsuccessfully to buy Newstead, Byron's old home, and then bought land at Hartsholme near Lincoln, and built a house there. At the first dinner party in the house in 1864, the Melvilles, the Trollopes, the Charles Ellisons, the Robert Swans and Jarvis were guests; the drawing room was not finished, but everything was very handsome, there were some nice pictures in the dining room, and the wine was excellent.[1] Shuttleworth bought the Ongley estate at Old Warden in Bedfordshire in 1871, became a magistrate and deputy lieutenant in that county, and high sheriff. Anderson found him a good fellow to deal with;[2] and Cracroft noted that 'Captain Shuttleworth [he was a volunteer] is one of the iron kings or merchant princes of Lincoln, having literally risen from a common labourer. It was thought a misalliance Miss Ellison marrying him, but they seem really happy.'[3] He died in 1883; his son Alfred lived at Hartsholme after him, was high sheriff in 1899, and later lived at Eastgate House in Lincoln.

Their partner Charles Seely, being an aggressive radical, was not so happy in his relations with the county. In 1860, as a Kesteven magistrate, he proposed that the Lincoln Kesteven bench should meet downhill, and weekly instead of fortnightly. This was not likely to suit his colleagues, and it did not. A few months later, Jarvis, persuaded thereto by Cracroft (now become Amcotts), a liberal politician, proposed him for election to the county news room. So sponsored, he was successful, though on a previous occasion his name was withdrawn in face of threatened blackballs.[4]

It was a matter of course that the squires and their eldest sons should be sworn of the commission of the peace; and they were sworn in at an early age. Indeed Frederic Hill, who was an inspector of prisons, recorded about 1850 that on a visit to Lincoln he 'was remarking to Mr Fardell on the youthful appearance of most of the county magistrates at the meeting last week, and was surprised to hear from him that most of them had been put into the Commission of the Peace when they were mere infants; and that till lately this was a common practice, just as children used to have commissions in the army and navy'.[5] Whether this was true of earlier times or not, it seems that young men were often

[1] G. K. Jarvis, Diary 26 February 1864.
[2] L.A.O. Monson, 25/13/8/15/6, 30 January 1859.
[3] Cracroft, 26 December 1862.
[4] G. K. Jarvis, Diary 6 January, 14 December 1860.
[5] Frederic Hill, *An Autobiography of Fifty Years in Times of Reform*, edited with additions by his daughter Constance Hill. (1894). He was the brother of Rowland Hill and Matthew Davenport Hill.

made magistrates when they were in their thirties. Many of them were content to take their share of work at petty sessions, leaving to others the chief burden at quarter sessions and at gaol sessions for the whole county.

When a committee of the three divisions of the county met to choose a plan of work to be done at the castle, Cracroft reflected agreeably that

nothing can be more agreeable than the way business is done by the gentlemen of dear old Lincolnshire. We look like a family party as we sit round the large Grand Jury Room table, and I never remember anything unpleasant taking place at any of these meetings, but on the contrary they are marked by nothing but consideration and goodwill for each other.[1]

The volume of business was growing for the few who would do it. From the gaol sessions came the visiting justices of the county lunatic asylum, established at Bracebridge in 1852, the city also participating. The county police were established under the control of the justices in 1857, there being three forces but only one chief constable. In addition the magistrates were *ex officio* guardians and some took this duty seriously.

In few if any activities did county and city come more closely together than in the militia and later the volunteer movement. All classes, too, were mixed, and Charles Kingsley testified that most of the men preferred to be commanded by men of a rank socially superior to their own, and that goodwill was increased between classes.[2] That ancient force, the militia, had remained in nominal being after Waterloo, but it was not raised by ballot after 1831. It continued as a voluntary force, and the arrival of the troops always caused excitement. There were dances and balls for the officers, and hospitality in the inns for the men. Numbers declined, and after the failure of an attempt at revival, and under the impetus of concern at the activities of the restless Napoleon III in France, the Militia Act of 1852 provided for a general militia organised under a system of voluntary enlistment with the ballot in reserve.

Cracroft has described the resumption of activity. The officers of the old North Lincoln Militia were called up for inspection. Two old captains of about 70 appeared, and the adjutant, Captain Kennedy, in spite of his new wig, could not conceal his Waterloo and Peninsula medals with six clasps. Even Cracroft, at 37, thought he was becoming too old to tramp about Lincoln as a militia captain.

Enrolment went well, and it was expected that the ballot would be avoided. Sibthorp became colonel of the Royal South Lincoln Militia, and George Tomline of Riby, then M.P. for Shrewsbury, of the North Lincolns; he was, said Cracroft, 'an eccentric and uncertain man,

---

[1] Cracroft, 19 July 1848.
[2] *Alton Locke, Tailor and Poet* (1882 edition), p. xciv.

everything by starts and nothing long'. The first thing to be done was to get rid of the lame, the halt and the blind.

After a false start for which Tomline was blamed, resulting in men throwing up work too soon, they assembled in June 1853, fine lusty young fellows looking like navvies and labourers, with ribbands in their caps, and much given to haunting the 'Dolphins' in Eastgate. Cracroft reflected that though he was four years in the Royals he had never done a day's soldiering before. They blamed Tomline also for a shortage of drill sergeants: 'I think as I see him curvetting about Canwick Common what a deal of good it would do him to pay and billet a company of militiamen.' It was all very strenuous, but the citizens enjoyed watching the drill, and the girls all had their squires in the evenings. One lady said all her servants had gone soldiering: her little boy brought her a flower given him by 'Elizabeth's soldier'![1]

The Crimean War, which began in 1853, stimulated recruiting, and in June 1855 the militia assembled for permanent embodiment. The men arrived drunk and shouting, and Major Ellison and Cracroft had trouble in getting them to the railway station for despatch to Dover. It was a blow to the officers when a Government offer to release all who attested before April 1854 resulted in nearly all the 360 men stepping out. The battalion returned to Lincoln in 1856, and was embodied again in 1857. It behaved well during six weeks in Lincoln before going to Portsmouth. It was a matter of pride that only 17 were drunk out of 691, although it was market day and there was many a parting cup. They were absent from Lincoln for three years, returning from Ireland under Ellison in 1860. The militia was merged in the territorial regiments in 1871.

During a later alarm over the plans of Napoleon III a Lincoln rifle corps was formed in 1859, in which Cracroft accepted a captaincy. The Rev. E. R. Larken was chaplain, Nathaniel Clayton treasurer and Richard Hall secretary. Arthur Trollope was a lieutenant, and Richard Carline, one of the first to volunteer, drilled like a youngster. John Swan and John George Williams enrolled. In 1869 a second company was formed. Shuttleworth was a captain and Clayton a lieutenant. They organised a company in the works, and advanced the cost of equipment. There was a band, to which the ladies presented a bugle inscribed 'Ready'. Williams remembered as a private being drilled by Clayton: the company was doing a 'double', and he wanted it to break into a quick march. He forgot the military word of command, and gave that to which he had been accustomed on his steam packet, namely 'slacken speed'.[2]

---

[1] Cracroft, 17 May, 6–8 June 1853, 9 June 1854.
[2] Notes by Colonel J. G. Williams in my possession.

The parades and the annual camps of the volunteers became an important part in the social life of the city, and long remained so, providing for many of the men the only holidays they ever had. A week in the country, at Thornton Abbey, meeting men from other parts of the county, was of great social as well as military value.[1]

But however clamant the calls of public business, and however conscientious his response, the country gentleman still had most of his time at his own disposal. After the affairs of his household and his estate and his parish, sport generally took precedence of other interests. How far this dedication could go is shown by Sir Osbert Sitwell, who described the régime at Blankney, where the Londesborough family were carrying on the Chaplin tradition:

Blankney was, most emphatically, no house in which you were likely to encounter an artist. London existed for parties – and very good after their own fashion they were – and the country was a place in which to kill things, foxes, deer, hares, pheasants, snipe, partridges, woodcock, rabbits, even rats – almost anything you saw except horses and dogs. Horses were enthroned in a state which even Caligula never dreamt of for his favourite, in the temple dedicated to them near by, and dogs were allowed to run about the house itself unmolested: sad, dank Aberdeens, white or peppered.[2]

Hunting was the preserve of the gentry and their tenantry. In 1842 Sir Richard Sutton resigned as master of the Burton Hunt on his moving to the Quorn: there he kept about 100 horses and spent £10,000 a year.[3] Charles Chaplin wrote to Anderson that Frank Foljambe of Osberton (Notts) declined to take the hunt, as he thought the country too extensive:

22 May 1842...but in my opinion, if hunted regularly, without regard to good or bad covers, five days a week, which he does in Nottinghamshire, would show very good sport, though I am ready to doubt that the country is large enough to allow of being hunted oftener. Foljambe thinks Lord Henry Bentinck would like to take the country.[4]

[1] The Volunteers had a drill shed provided for them by Charles Seely, and when this was sold they used part of the Sessions House. There was a long range at Waddington. For some years Colonel Amcotts (Cracroft) commanded the First Lincolnshire Rifle Volunteers, and Colonel Lord Monson the seven companies of the Royal North Lincoln Militia.

Under Cardwell's army reforms, a local brigade was established consisting of the depot of the two battalions of the Tenth Regiment and the North and South Lincoln Militia, to which the several companies of volunteers in the county were affiliated. *L.C.*, 4 October 1878. The new barracks on Burton Road, to the north of the old militia barracks, were built for them. In 1890 the Drill Hall was built by Joseph Ruston for the volunteers.

[2] *Left Hand, Right Hand* (1952), p. 196.

[3] G. K. Jarvis, Diary, 9 February 1849.

[4] Anderson Letters 1.

Bentinck accepted the mastership, being paid £1,900 a year towards expenses, the other costs being interest on land bought at Reepham for the kennels. Ellison of Sudbrooke – 'the king of men' – was the largest subscriber, though he had not followed a hound for twenty years. Bentinck hunted the country six days a week. He first lived at the White Hart[1] and then at the Great Northern Hotel, but often when his father the fourth duke of Portland was alive he lived at Welbeck, and rode from thence to the meet and back in a day, having a hack posted at Dunham Bridge (on the Trent) and another at Lincoln. His horses (80 in 1860) were stabled in the smaller inns of the city until he built a hunting box and stables at Greetwell in 1857.[2]

Cracroft reflected on the social value of the sport: independently of the fine manly dangerous exercise, they would never meet in the county without it. They cemented old friendships and made new ones, and squire and tenant met on even terms for once. Many farmers and yeomen hunted with them, and, rich as they were, not a single one of them wore a scarlet coat.[3]

Things did not go well. There was difficulty in raising the subscription; foxes were sometimes destroyed and gorse covers ploughed up; and Bentinck was so austere in his devotion to the main business of life that after a hard day's sport there were no dinner parties and balls. He retired in 1864, when Henry Chaplin bought the pack, and in the following year he took up the mastership, hunting the county until 1871, when, as the sporting writer Collins said, 'he found that the duties of a member of Parliament sadly interfered with the management of a pack hunted six days a week'.[4] The country was divided, and the Blankney Hunt took over the southern part.

Anderson had taken a gloomy view of the prospects, linking it with the increase of poaching:

13 December (1859?)...our fields (of gentlemen at least) are very small, tho I am glad to see a good sprinkling of farmers ...I expect in another generation hunting

---

[1] Anderson referred to his living at a beastly old inn near the minster where he had two or three small rooms. He had a 'Scottish lassie' as cook who cooked for him only. He had excellent small parties at which he fell asleep, leaving his guests to finish the excellent claret. Anderson Letters II, a note following a letter from Lord Henry Bentinck headed 'Lincoln, Tuesday'.

[2] MS reminiscences of George Nevile of Thorney, given to me by his late daughter-in-law Mrs Annie Nevile. Bentinck and his brothers, Lord Titchfield and Lord George enabled Disraeli to acquire Hughenden, and so to qualify as tory leader by becoming a country gentleman. Disraeli described him as 'with some eccentricities, one of the ablest men and finest characters I have ever met'. Monypenny and Buckle, *Life of Disraeli* (1929 edition), I, 967. He dedicated his life of Lord George Bentinck to him.

[3] Cracroft, 9 December 1848.   [4] In *Lincolnshire in the Twentieth Century* (1908), p. 130.

will be nearly extinct and if we may judge of the signs, shooting too, for these deadly affrays of poachers and keepers must end either in a law which will make people found with game in their possession at unlawful hours amenable to the police, or we shall have the game laws done away and with them the game ...certain I am if game were extinct the poachers would turn sheepstealers and burglars, but it is dreadful to risk one's keepers' lives in the way which must be done now if you preserve at all and the laws remain as they are.[1]

There is much evidence of the increase of poaching, and of poachers entering the city almost every morning bringing the fruits of their nightly exercises to houses which received this sort of traffic. In 1861, when he was high sheriff, Cracroft went to fetch the judges to court. The chief justice said he had seen a sight such as he had never before witnessed. In the middle of the street near Newport Arch about 10.15 a.m. two poachers deliberately poured out the contents of their bags, which contained rabbits and nets, divided the proceeds and went away. He told a city policeman to see where one of them (at least) went, but he stood by looking on and did nothing. The chief justice favoured the game laws, but complained of too much game being preserved in places, and said that the receiving houses were the root of the mischief.[2]

The county was of so great a size that the gentry seldom all met. But they could do so, and at one time did, at the Stuff (or Color) Ball, the greatest of the social occasions of the year.[3] A well attended ball might muster 300. As times changed it declined. Local habits and feelings were dying away before the railroads, and when folk went every day and everywhere, a county ball which had reunited friends who would otherwise never have met at all, lost its special purpose. The southern part of the county was falling away; and Anderson wrote in 1872 that Lincoln was not a county centre like York, and north and south Lincolnshire were in many respects more like different counties.[4]

Some of the gentry also patronised the Dispensary Ball, held the day after the Stuff Ball, in aid of the city institution. It was held in the city assembly room over the cold and draughty buttermarket. Ladies in white satin shoes had to walk along the cold stones from which they were only protected by a sprinkling of sawdust.

The Cake Ball, also a city function, and a copy of the Stuff Ball, was held over the buttermarket until 1860, when it was transferred to the county assembly rooms, a momentous step towards bridging the gap between county and city. It is tempting to surmise that this revolutionary change was made possible by the death of Charles Chaplin.

---

[1] L.A.O. Monson 25/13/10/12/30.   [2] Cracroft, 13 March 1861.
[3] *G.L.*, pp. 266-7, 272.
[4] Anderson Letters II, has note on the back of a letter from Brownlow. January 1872.

It was still a small world, and hobbies meant more than they do today. It might be roses or rhododendrons, or a special breed of pigs or poultry. Holidays abroad in France or Italy stimulated an interest in Roman pottery or coins. Arthur Trollope had a valuable collection, and Edwin Jarvis made a useful record of local discoveries. Local societies came into being. The visit of the Archaeological Institute to Lincoln in 1848 encouraged such studies, and the restoration in particular of Stow church. These occasions did not need to be taken too seriously. Crabb Robinson came in 1848, attending a public dinner of 240 and a capital cold collation at Anderson's: 'I confess to all I meet, I make these journeys merely on account of the social pleasure I receive; and I perceive that it is because I give as well as take in this respect, that I am well received, though certainly one of the least learned Archaeologians who attend these meetings.[1]

Cracroft added that he had never seen so many county people in Lincoln, and 'I must say they excited a great deal of interest even amongst people not much given to antiquarian study. They seemed earnest in pursuit of the ancient, and mixed much less humbug with their proceedings than I expected would be the case.[2]

[1] *Diary etc. of Henry Crabb Robinson* (1872 edition), ii, 294–5.
[2] Cracroft, 26 July 1848.

CHAPTER V

HIGH FARMING

The bad times for agriculture that followed Waterloo and the peace came to an end, of course with ups and downs, in the 1830s. Cobbett gave a glowing account of the Lincolnshire market for horses, sheep and cattle. What had been a great oat county was turning over to wheat, the amount of wheat sold in Lincoln market having more than trebled between 1825 and 1834.[1] In 1837 there were from 25,000 to 30,000 sheep at Lincoln fair, and nearly 1,000 horses could not find stable room. A year later it was reported that corn and cattle were higher in price than they had been for some years, and farmers were warned not to drive prices too high, lest the operation of the corn laws should permit the dreaded influx of foreign wheat before harvest.[2] There were 40,000 sheep at the fair in 1849 and about 70,000 in 1857; and in 1862 the fair was described as one of the largest and finest for many years, with 45,000 fleeces.

Philip Pusey, a leading agriculturalist, declared in 1843 that Lincoln heath, which had been without cultivation or even a road, had become like a sheep market. All Lincolnshire was one new enclosure.[3] This was of course an exaggeration, but it made a point. A like point was made by the chairman of the Northern and Eastern Railway Company at its first general meeting in 1836. He said that the agricultural district of the county was in fact more densely populated than other such districts, because the whole of it might be called artificial land – clearly he was referring to the low lands – and required a comparatively large number of persons to maintain the embankments and improvements, by means of which the district had been converted from almost a barren waste to a highly productive county. Ten years later a visitor to the Wolds referred to the wise liberality of landlords and the skill and industry of tenants, which had converted them from wild moorlands into farms. Like the heath, they had long remained open moors covered with gorse and fern, harbouring only game and a few wild half-starved sheep for centuries after the low lands had been cultivated.[4]

In the years before and after 1846, the year of legislative change, men's

---

[1] *G.L.*, p. 195 and references there cited.
[2] If the price of wheat reached 80s. a quarter, calculated according to the law, the ports were opened to foreign wheat.
[3] *Journal of the Royal Agricultural Society of England*, IV (1843), 287–316.
[4] Samuel Sidney, *Railways and Agriculture in North Lincolnshire* (1848), pp. 32–3.

minds were filled by fears and hopes about the corn laws. Farmers and most landlords thought that their repeal and the free influx of foreign corn must mean ruin. Charles Anderson wrote to Monson in 1843 that the propaganda of the Anti-Corn Law League was causing great alarm, and he feared that as the prices of produce fell rents must follow. Pamphlets were flying about Lincoln to show the labourers that the farmers were tyrannising over them. This was bad at a time when numbers of labourers were out of work, and robberies and pillage more frequent than he had ever known. A farmer had been murdered at Saxilby on his way to an evening lecture, and an old farmer and his wife tied in their beds while their house was ransacked.[1]

Bulwer recalled a few years later that in 1846 he had predicted to the Lincolnshire agriculturalist:

that he, above most cultivators, would suffer, and that his suffering would tell quickly upon the labouring population, where in other counties, the distress of the farmer would be slow in reaching the labourer. 'It is', I then said, 'in proportion to the cost upon the soil, and not to the quality of the produce grown upon it, that the farmer will suffer by a fall in prices below profits. You, who produce such crops by artificial manures, who consume so much upon guano and bones, you will be the first to find how small and minute would be the benefit of any reduction in rent compared to your great cost in cultivating. And as free competition must affect the gross profit of your land, so the larger the expenses in proportion to the profits, why, the greater you must be the sufferers in any great fall in prices.'

Surely, he said, one could not say to the cultivators of the Lothians, Norfolk and Lincolnshire, when they were cultivating at a loss and expected ruin, 'Gentlemen, go home and farm high'. They were farming high already.[2]

When repeal was followed by several bad years, it was naturally assumed by protectionists that repeal was the cause. G. K. Jarvis was urged in January 1849 not to go to Dover to collect his rents, as in consequence of panic from the ports opening on 1 February for the admission of corn duty free, prices were so low.[3] The tory *Chronicle* reported in November 1847 that two large mills were standing idle, and the importation of American flour was feared; and the *Mercury* retorted that the city was feeling triflingly the effects of the general monetary

[1] L.A.O. Monson 25/13/7/7/4, 31 January 1843.
[2] 'Letters to John Bull Esq.', reprinted in *Pamphlets and Sketches* (1875), p. 131. The most reputable economists were substantially agreed that while investments in industry were inherently capable of reducing the unit costs of production, investments in agriculture would inevitably increase these unit costs. D. C. Moore in *Ideas and Institutions of Victorian Britain* (1967), p. 50.
[3] Jarvis Diary, 26 January 1849. He said he would wait until mid-March.

depression.[1] In the following July the *Chronicle* said that property was falling in value; and in December it went on:

The progress of free trade principles, and the carrying out of measures connected therewith, are, as prognosticated, beginning to tell fearfully upon the trade and property of Lincoln. The price which farmers are now obtaining for their corn is so low that they are compelled to exercise the most rigid economy, and, as a consequence, the tradesmen are not taking as much weekly as will meet their expenses. Mechanics and labourers are deprived of work, and there are now no less than 280 inmates of the workhouse, whereas about seven years ago there were only 130.

During the past week there had been several serious failures, and the utmost alarm and want of confidence universally prevailed.[2] Labourers in town and country were out of work; shopkeepers were failing; Lincoln was infested with vagrants and wandering Irish, and hundreds of navvies were out of work. Deposits in the Lincoln Savings Bank fell; Lincoln and Lindsey Bank shares dropped 20% in value; and shares in the Lincoln Corn Exchange and Market Company and the Lincoln Waterworks Company had no market at all. But 1848 was a bad year in the normal trade cycle; certainly some of these things could not be attributed to free trade, the bad effects of which a tory newspaper would naturally be disposed to magnify.

Weston Cracroft, the wise and sober young squire of Hackthorn, noted the reactions of some of his neighbours. Luard of Blyborough thought free trade would ruin all the people of small property like himself. Charles Anderson expected rents to go down 25%. Melville the banker said that one of the largest millers in Lincoln had turned protectionist, and in his opinion a 5s. duty would be laid on foreign corn; public opinion, he thought, was turning.

There were many rent reductions.[3] Cracroft's father gave 10%, Lord

---

[1] *L.C.*, 26 November 1847; *S.M.*, 10 December 1847.

[2] *L.C.*, 7 July, 15 December 1848.

[3] On 14 June 1835 Edward Smith Godfrey of Newark, agent to Colonel Jarvis, wrote to him recommending revaluation of the estate at Doddington, 'for the great difficulty in deciding upon the real situation of tenants arises from their almost universal neglect of keeping any accounts by which they could demonstrate their actual loss or profit...If farmers would do this, how much more forcible their appeal to their landlords must be instead of a vague statement or rather a *guess* of their losses'. He did not think their condition was as bad as superficially appeared, nor that the price of wheat was a correct criterion, especially as it was admitted that the quantum of produce of this grain for the last few years had exceeded the usual average, and the price of barley, wool and stock had been comparatively better than the price of wheat, and the labour had been obtained for less money. Jarvis replied agreeing to a valuation, adding that wheat having been used as a criterion of rent during its very high price, had been so continued without any good reason. Jarvis Corr.

Monson gave first 5% and then 10%, Sibthorp 15%, Lord Scarbrough
not a farthing. Cracroft though it hard that the tenants should have all
the advantages of high prices when they prevailed, and should come on
landlords for returns in seasons of depression. The state of mind of the
Hackthorn tenants was indicated by a petition for remission, not only in
consequence of low prices, but *in consequence of all hope for the future being
taken away.* The agricultural mind was prostrated by repeal. Cracroft
consulted Woolley the valuer on the question whether remission of rent
was necessary. His reply was, 'Men's minds are as unsettled as prices: no
one knows exactly what to do. I have not adjusted any landlord's rents
yet: yet at the same time I don't think prices will ever be much higher
than they are now.'[1]

Cracroft discussed the depression with the Rev. C. J. Barnard, the
rector of Bigby, who hunted with the Brocklesby for many years, and
who said that rents were higher in the Midlands than in Lincoln as 6 to 5.
He said that Lord Yarborough's tenants – always thought of as an
aristocracy among farmers – were not the men of huge capital they were
thought to be. They had lived too high; their farms were well done and
well stocked, but they had no capital. The first Lord Yarborough used to
be angry with his tenants if they did not come out hunting, as perhaps
some of their successors rued.[2] Lord Henry Bentinck reported to Disraeli:

I hear that Lord Yarborough's great wealthy tenants are cracking – one is
already gone, and rumours are very rife about several others...I expect a few
more such failures in the best farmed land in England will settle Free Trade.[3]

The Willoughby agent at Spilsby wrote in 1850 that the majority for
free trade in the House of Lords was a great discouragement to agriculturalists: 'when we find a Minister of the Crown backed by so many
large landlords that they will hear no complaints till the workhouses are
full, and labourers thrown out of employment, and farms uncultivated,
we know what to expect'.[4] In 1851 the Yarborough tenants were angry
with the second earl because having been (though a whig) a protectionist
M.P. for Lindsey, he had become a free trader in the Lords. His reply
would of course have been that he was a realist, and recognised that free
trade had come to stay.

The other view is represented in letters to Lord Monson from his
friend Samuel Ball:

[1] Cracroft, 12 July 1850; for Woolley's remark, 22 October 1851.
[2] Cracroft, 11 December 1849. For Barnard see G. E. Collins, *Farming and Fox-Hunting*
(n.d.), p. 354.
[3] Hughenden (Disraeli) MSS B/xxi/B/354, I am indebted to Dr R. J. Olney for this
reference.   [4] L.A.O. 3 Ancaster 7/23/58/12.

17 December 1849. I fear rents must come down, but in what degree no one can say. But it seems to me the farmer must seek relief by other means than reduction of rent. Nothing but increased capital laid out on the land, thereby rendering it more productive, can afford him relief – and that is what the present race of farmers have to contend with. I fear many have not capital enough, or farm too much for their capital. Many would do better on smaller farms.

But is there any limit to a fall in prices? I think there is. Has America the power of inundating us with corn? I think not...the remedy seems to be an increased quantity per acre to compensate for loss of price.

On a longer view he thought that only an entire alteration of the then slow system of farming could redeem the farmers, which might be impossible with the existing race of tenants. The abolition of protection was doing wonders in improving the land, and he looked to a general plan for drainage and improvement such as a highly competent man could make. In recommending a rent reduction, he recommended also a refusal to convert more land from grass to arable, and a willingness to do more drainage work.[1] The improvements related in particular to the growing practice of field drainage, made possible by the application of mass production methods to the manufacture of clay drain pipes.[2] In 1851 the Lincoln corporation adopted a system of a corn rent for their farm tenants; it effected a reduction of $14\frac{1}{2}\%$ in their payments:[3] Monson wanted to do the same in 1854, but his tenants would not have it.

Within a short time the corn laws, though the issue remained alive in politics, ceased to affect men's minds in their day-to-day affairs. Cracroft, who as a free trader found this easy, noted many improvements, one of them being the immense amount of drainage in Stallingborough and Riby in 1848. A greater project concerned the sandy wilderness between Caistor and Market Rasen: Mr Robinson, the vicar of Faldingworth, recalled that he had shown it to Thomas Malthus, who was rector of Walesby, and who said, 'Well, if I had not known I had been in Lincolnshire, I should have thought I had been in the deserts of Arabia.'[4] Thousands of loads of clay were being spread, Mr Robinson remarking:

> When the sand comes to the clay
> Alas! for England, well a day!
> When the clay comes to the sand,
> All is well in old England.

This enterprise was described to Caird by Dixon of Holton le Moor. When he came into possession of the estate 22 years earlier there were

---

[1] L.A.O. Monson 25/13/7/19/63.
[2] F. M. L. Thompson, *English Landed Society in the Nineteenth Century* (1963), p. 248. J. D. Chambers and G. E. Mingay, *The Agricultural Revolution 1750–1880* (1966), pp. 170ff.
[3] *L.C.*, 3 January 1851.   [4] Cf. *T. & S.L.*, pp. 4–5.

500 acres of rabbit warren, which the tenant refused to hold at a rent of £50. He took it into his own hands, covered it with clay, and by underdraining, he considered the land worth 16s. an acre, or £400 a year.[1]

In 1850 Cracroft noticed that Fiskerton, Barlings and Newball were being drained and ploughed up, though Wragby woodlands were still wild, and there were hundreds of acres awaiting attention. In the following summer he saw the land looking better than ever, with fresh areas breaking up, and wondered again whether the farmers really needed the rent remissions they were getting. Improvement was going on from Kettlethorpe to Hackthorn, and corn was lying uncut for want of labourers. Even so, he reflected, there was still a great deal to do.

After 1852 a fall in the import of wheat flour supported the free trade argument, and between 1851 and 1853 Lincoln long wool rose by more than 22% in price, and the price of wheat was rising.[2] In the latter year the area of wheat sown in the county largely exceeded that of previous years, and farmers were again applying part of their profits to improvement by underdraining. The custom of tenant right ensured that they would receive on quitting the unexpired value of their improvements.[3] In 1854 the amount of money expended in sewerage, tile-draining, quicking, building and miscellaneous works in the county was computed at not less than £10,000,000, and tenants' capital at quite £7,000,000.[4] In these same years there was a slow improvement in the breed of Lincoln Red Shorthorn cattle, and the Lincoln–Leicester crossbreed of sheep was taking high place among the long-woolled breeds on account of both the weight of its carcase and the quality of its fleece.

On the initiative of Richard Carline (Melville being given the credit) the city council invited the Royal Agricultural Society to hold its annual show in Lincoln, and it did so in 1854. It was a great success, being attended, it was said, by 38,000 people, and it gave a powerful stimulus to farming in the county and the new industry of agricultural implement making, Clayton and Shuttleworth of Lincoln and Richard Hornsby and Son of Grantham being prominent exhibitors. At the dinner Melville the

---

[1] J. Caird, *English Agriculture in 1850 and 1851* (1852), p. 186.

[2] J. H. Clapham, *Economic History of Modern Britain* (1952), II, 2–4, 7.

[3] *G.L.*, p. 195. This was in spite of their lack of legal security of tenure. When legislation was sought to put the custom on a legal basis the landlords preferred to adhere to the custom, and so not to abandon that 'quasi-feudal domination over tenants so dear to the English landowner', and a private way of opposing the Tenant Right Bill of 1847 was sought. *Journal of Statistical Society*, XXIX (1866), 614, quoting *The Economist*; J. Huggins to R. A. Christopher, Lord George Bentinck Papers, Nottingham University Library; *L.C.*, 26 March 1847.

[4] *L.C.*, 30 June 1854, quoting *A Farming Tour; or Handbook of the Farming of Lincolnshire*.

banker gave his answer to the question why the county was so pre-eminent in agriculture.

The first point to which they must attribute this was, that there was found in the county so great a variety of soils; they had their fen land, their wold land and their heath land. They were at present on the border of one; they were, more-over in the midst of the heath; and on going on Friday to the station of the Great Northern Railway at Stixwould, they would there see the engine which had been prepared to exhibit the operations connected with their drainage, and to show how they pumped out the water. Although he had been told that they might be carried into other districts, and shown an agriculture superior to their own...let them put together the tillage, the cattle, the sheep and the horses, and they there-by would find the true secret of the pre-eminence of Lincoln. Their real profit lay in the mixture of these different classes of agriculture; the amalgamation of one thing with the other brought out the true merits of each individual part.[1]

It seems to be generally agreed that mixed farming was the secret of the prosperity of the farmers at this period. It meant:

essentially the integration of livestock and crop husbandry on the same farm to their mutual advantage. A greater proportion of the farm was put under the plough, but much of the new arable was devoted to fodder crops. The root break gave the land a rest from grains and allowed weeding to be carried out, but it also provided a feed for sheep, who in their turn manured the land and helped consolidate the lighter soils.[2]

The dreaded influx of foreign corn had not materialised; there was no European surplus waiting to come in; and the American surplus could only come a generation later when railways and steamships could carry it cheaply across the prairie and the ocean.

When it did come, prices tumbled, and rents with them, and much of the money invested in the land, new farmhouses and fine new ranges of farm buildings, showed no return to the investor. Some landlords were highly sceptical from the beginning: as witness Lord Monson, who wrote to his son

22 November 1851. What an infernal bore is landed property. No certain income can be reckoned upon. I hope your future wife will have Consols or some such ballast, I think it is worth half as much again as what land is reckoned at.[3]

And when G. K. Jarvis was in consultation with the trustees of his marriage settlement about the investment of settled funds he expressed a preference for Consols, which paid interest regularly without deduction for building or bad seasons.[4]

[1] *L.C.*, 21 July 1854. The president elect (Mr Miles, M.P.) recollected 20 or 30 years ago seeing the first cargo of bones ever landed at Hull, and the Customs House officers not knowing what duty to charge. In point of fact no duty was charged. The Lincolnshire Agricultural Society was formed in 1869 by union of the northern and southern societies of the county.   [2] David Grigg, *Agricultural Revolution in South Lincolnshire* (1966), p. 144.
[3] L.A.O. Monson 25/10/3/1/19; and see Thompson, *English Landed Society*, p. 290.
[4] 19 March 1862. G. K. Jarvis Letter Book, 1458.

The social and political value of land continued for a long time, but its economic foundations were already being undermined.

Meanwhile the farming community flourished. It was probably Philip Pusey again who said in 1855 that the Lincolnshire tenant farmer was very different from his humble brother in Berkshire and elsewhere:

He belongs to the aristocracy of his race. He can give, if he chooses, a university education to his sons, he rides a well bred horse, and finds time to keep a flower garden, a shrubbery and a greenhouse, and to turn the brook which winds below his house into a tiny lake.[1]

Janet Courtney, daughter of the parson of Barton on Humber, thought the farmers were encroaching on their betters:

The farming society was freer and more open in its intercourse – perhaps because in the hunting field and on county matters it mixed with what was left of the squirearchy. But that was a small remnant. Most of the pretty old Georgian halls and manor houses of North Lincolnshire were in the occupation of farmers whose social ambitions had been awakened during the days of prosperity which followed on the American Civil War. Lincolnshire is essentially a county of high farming.

She remembered also the end of it:

When bad times came and wheat had fallen to 43s. or less, they were slow to reduce their style of living. They still wanted to enjoy themselves and to employ bailiffs to do the overseeing, which the more thrifty and sober-living Scottish and northern farmers did for themselves. Their one cry was for protection, and every measure intended to raise the position and wages of their labourers they strenuously opposed.[2]

Caird had noted in 1850 that increase of rent since Arthur Young's time had been accompanied by the increasing wealth of the tenants. The transition had been perhaps more startling than in any other county, and he thought the Lincolnshire agricultural reputation was due more to the strides it had made in a given time than to any real pre-eminence above the best farmed counties.[3]

The city of Lincoln could not fail to participate in the prosperity of the countryside. The shopkeepers, the builders, the makers of agricultural implements, the charities all benefited. The condition of the farm labourer also closely concerned the city, not only because the labourer spent money in the shops and at the fairs, but because the levels of wages in town and country were closely related. Country lads came in as apprentices and labourers, and country girls as domestic servants, who were a very numerous class. Unemployment in the villages, and a shortage of cottages there, brought a drift to the town, and made

[1] *Fraser's Magazine*, LI, 175.   [2] *Recollected in Tranquillity* (1926), pp. 53–4.
[3] Caird, *English Agriculture*, p. 193.

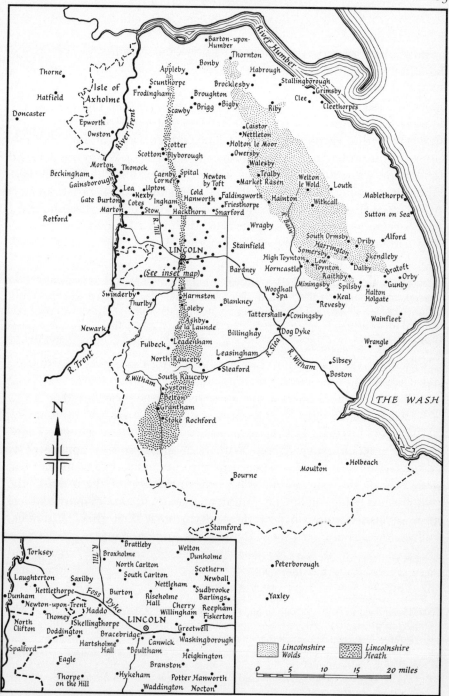

Map 2. Lincolnshire, showing places mentioned in the text.

difficulties of housing and public health even worse than they would have been without the influx.

Pusey had said in 1843 that he knew of no county in which the labourer was better provided for. His wages varied from 12s. to 15s. a week; he obtained a great deal of task work, for more labour was thus paid for than elsewhere, such as filling dung carts at 2d. the load, or the harvest waggon at 1s. an acre, with the usual stimulus to activity. Good hands were thus earning 15s. to 18s. The cottage was neat and cheerful; many labourers had allotments, and some had cows.[1] When the demand for labour was stationary, wages would be low, but the Lincolnshire labourer, being among new enclosures when the plough broke up new fields, was well paid, clothed, lodged and fed, sometimes with fresh meat.[2]

It was no doubt the same observer who said in 1855 that the Lincolnshire labourers' wages were almost uniformly good, and

though we cannot look for any very high average either of intelligence or morality in a class who end their education at ten or eleven, and from fifteen to sixteen are exposed to the trials and temptations of farm service, yet the Wold labourer is a fair specimen of the agricultural peasantry of England, and has none of the crushed, helpless, serf-like bearing which meets the eye in some parts of our island.[3]

The writer was comparing Lincolnshire with the southern counties, especially Berkshire, and by such a standard his judgment may well be justified. In 18 southern counties the average wage was 8s. 5d.[4]

Cracroft too thought the labourer was well off. He was thinking in particular of his own (or rather his father's) men. Cottage rents were low, gardens excellent, wages good. With flour at 1s. 10d. a stone, weekly earnings were 12s., and for superior men 1s. 6d. more. The waggoner was paid 15s. all the year round. The benevolent side of the quasi-feudal relationship came out in the comment that their four employees were more or less infirm, and how they got through their time he did not know. Wives could earn more by washing and charring.

[1] Some of the labourers kept cows and most of them a pig. *S.M.*, 20 May 1836, quoting the *Select Committee on Agricultural Distress*.
[2] *Journal of Royal Agricultural Society of England*, IV, 287–316.
[3] *Fraser's Magazine* LI, 175. In 1843 there appeared the reports of Special Assistant Poor Law Commissioners on the employment of women and children in agriculture. One witness told them that labourers were generally better fixed in Lincolnshire than in any other county in England; though this was almost certainly untrue, at least there was more meat and more milk in the diet than in Norfolk and Suffolk. John Burnett, *Plenty and Want* (Pelican edition 1968), p. 44. For a summary of the evidence given to the Commission on Childrens', Young Persons' and Women's Employment in Agriculture, 1867–70, see W. Hasbach, *History of the English Agricultural Labourer* (1908), appendix VI, p. 407.
[4] J. H. Clapham, *Economic History of Modern Britain* (1930), I, 466.

Clubs for mutual insurance, like the pig club at Nettleham which had 50 members in 1840,[1] and the cow club that started in Lincoln following a Doncaster example,[2] encouraged attempts to supplement the family budget. Joseph Ashby of Tysoe testified that although a pig was essential if a labourer's family were to have a fair diet, it was an undertaking to save out of the wage to buy even a small pig and a bag of meal; but a man who would turn sulky at a hint about his family duties would halve his visits to the Peacock once he grew fond of his pig.[3]

When the price of meat rose in 1853 Charles Anderson raised his labourers' wages to 13s. to take account of the rise. In 1855 many farmers raised wages from 2s. 6d. to 2s. 9d. per day. The *Lincoln Times* optimistically declared in 1854 that there was no unemployed labour. Without exception able men had 15s. a week, and many 18s. at contract work. It thought the agricultural labourer was rapidly progressing both mentally and morally, owing mainly to his attention having been roused by the operation of free trade and emigration, the establishment of friendly societies, and the increased interest taken by his employer in his welfare.[4]

There was talk of reduction of wages in 1857, which was a bad year. Public reaction was significant and interesting. The tory *Chronicle* denounced the move, and a correspondent added that it was monstrous to lower wages with wheat at 60s. a quarter and mutton at 7½d. per pound for shoulders; and he would like to know how a labourer with 13s. 6d. a week and a wife and three children could ever taste meat. Unless this screwing received the attention of every considerate landlord the new rural police would soon have enough work on their hands.[5] Later it was reported that there would be no reduction at Canwick; in Branston the owner had ruled in favour of the labourers against some of the farmers; at Potterhanworth Mr Battle and the farmers generally had set their faces against reduction; similarly at Nocton. Where the reduction had taken place the landlords and tenants were the wealthiest of their class. It pleaded for the children:

It is but of little avail that the labourer has for his children better schools and instructors than formerly if the labourers' wages are so inadequate that he is compelled to press into the service of earning a subsistence the little children, who, as bird-tenters, and in other kindred occupations, have to bring home their 6d. a day to enable the family to live.[6]

[1] *L.C.*, 11 December 1840. An Adam and Eve pig club occurs in 1861, and in 1868 the Waggon and Horses pig club had nearly 90 at supper.
[2] *S.M.*, 4 December 1840. In 1866 a Mutual Cattle Insurance Association had 4329 head of cattle insured. *L.C.*, 18 May 1866.
[3] M. K. Ashby, *Joseph Ashby of Tysoe 1859–1919* (1961), pp. 115–16.
[4] *L.C.*, 6 July 1854, quoting *Lincoln Times*.
[5] *L.C.*, 24 April 1857.   [6] *L.C.*, 8 May 1857.

The rector of Burton (Larken) had his own comments about the labourer's children. He said it was no use worrying about farmers employing boys of school age; they always had and always would. No farmer would pay a man's wage if a boy could do it. Moreover he considered farm work just as much a part of a boy's education as reading and writing. In those hard times, parents were glad enough of their children's wages to help clothe them. Even the Sunday school suffered because boys must work at certain seasons on Sundays as well as weekdays. He wished this manual working of the village boys could be combined with more mental training, 'but I cannot see my way to that at present'. There was a general scarcity of boys at Burton, either for schooling or for labour.[1] These views are the more striking because of the known sympathies of the rector with movements for the benefit of the working class.[2]

The *Chronicle* proceeded to castigate the farmer.

Farmers, whose fathers came to market with their wives behind them on pillions, and who drank beer at the same dinner table with their men now keep their hunters, can treat their friends to princely entertainments, and come to market in their comfortable gig or dog-cart. They have risen in the social scale, and we rejoice at the fact. The landowner has doubled his income from the work of the labourer and the skill and capital of his tenant, and we rejoice at his prosperity; but we deeply deplore that the condition of the class who have given the increased wealth to the social ranks above them should not only have no means of improving their condition but that some of the very men who have been made what they are by their hewers of wood and drawers of water, should be the first to turn upon the substratum of their prosperity in order to squeeze out a little more superfluous wealth for themselves.[3]

Within a few weeks the *Mercury* announced that the rural wages question in the districts around Lincoln was settled. Except in one village the masters had agreed to continue to pay 2s. 6d. a day. Settlement had been reached by the labourers going in a body to their masters, like cool practical men, to talk the matter over.[4]

It was reported in 1861 that in the Lincoln and adjoining poor law unions wages were 12s. in winter and 14s. or 15s. in summer. Children began to have a money value as soon as they could shout loudly enough to scare a crow, or could endure exposure to the weather in watching cows in the lane. At the age of 8 they could earn 6d. a day or more, and, at 11 to 12, a shilling.[5] By 1872, as Cracroft noted, the labourers were

---

[1] L.A.O. Monson 25/13/10/7/7, 5 February 1855.
[2] Below, p. 150.   [3] *L.C.*, 8 May 1857.   [4] *S.M.*, 29 May 1857.
[5] *Report of Asst. Commissioners appointed to enquire into the state of popular education in England,* 1861, xxii, part ii, 147. Dakeyne had said in 1844 that boys had an inducement to leave school when they could earn 10d. to 1s. a day in gathering potatoes and other field labour. There were evening schools at Hackthorn and Cold Hanworth, and Cracroft visited and taught at them.

having a meeting to ask for a rise to 18s. Mr Garfit told him he need not trouble, because his payment of 3s. a day for cleaning out the pond had been the talk of the neighbourhood.

Unlike other labourers, who were hired by the day, farm servants were hired by the year at the annual Mayday hiring statutes. From an early hour carriers' carts, private carts and railway trains brought in shoals of ploughmen and waggoners in their light blue gowns, and girls with their ribbons flying, to celebrate the end of a year of service, to buy clothes, and all too often to squander their wages in public houses, to be swindled by thimble riggers, or to have their pockets picked. Their appearance was beginning to improve: the gown was supplanted by broad cloth, and the shapeless straw or felt hat by a trim beaver. Behaviour was improving, and substantial sums were being paid into the savings bank.

The hiring of men and women, especially the latter, by inspection, was beginning to be thought of as savouring of the slave market. Massingberd urged that if members of agricultural societies would give a written character to their servants, and require them of those they hired, hiring statutes would not be needed. Holidays could be given at different times, perhaps on the occasion of village feasts, when they might meet their own friends at their own homes. Dangers of drunkenness and immorality were being taken more seriously.

In 1858 there was a meeting of clergy and gentry to discuss the establishment of registration offices: when the word 'registration' frightened the farmers it was abandoned, and the Lincolnshire Servants' Amelioration Society was formed, with district offices for registration. Soon the statutes survived only as a holiday, and by 1861 opinions were being expressed that the new law of settlement, more general education, and a better system of cottages would tend greatly to improve the condition of the labouring classes.[1]

As a humane landlord Cracroft realised that one of the great hardships of the labourers was the shortage of cottages. This was partly due to the natural increase of population; building did not keep in step with it. It was partly due also to the poor law, which required each parish to maintain its own poor. It tended therefore to confine the labourer to his own parish, but it encouraged landlords to defeat it by not building cottages, or even pulling them down, so that labourers must live elsewhere, and when unemployed become chargeable to the poor rate elsewhere too.[2] This could happen where proprietors were sufficiently few in number to act together, or where one owner owned the whole

[1] L.A.O. Cor. B. 95/9/10; *L.C.*, 5 September 1856; 22 January 1858; 15 February 1861.
[2] Chambers and Mingay, *The Agricultural Revolution*, p. 143.

parish. At Hackthorn the parish's supply of labourers was not adequate to the wants of the farmers, and hence labourers came into the parish to work from Dunholme, Welton and Scothern. Cracroft's father was averse to building cottages, but neither he nor his neighbour Mr Mainwaring ever pulled one down without building it up again. Cracroft himself built a few when he succeeded to the estate.

He often referred in his diary to the subject of open and closed parishes. The curate of Sudbrooke told him (5 March 1850) that Scothern was a village supported by the bounty of Richard Ellison: it was full of the most ungrateful set of blackguards he ever met in his life. There were many freeholders in the village, and everyone who could, built a cottage in order to participate in this too indiscriminate charity. The result was that the population and the poor rate had both increased. (Its population was 497 in 1831 and 572 in 1851.) He noted at a meeting of the poor law guardians the case of an able-bodied man who walked from Nettleham to work at North Carlton (5 miles as the crow flies). The population had grown 1831–51 from 714 to 944, while that of North Carlton had dropped from 180 to 147. This latter village was Lord Monson's. In his South Carlton the population had dropped from 204 to 183, but at Burton – also his – had risen from 177 to 204. Some of them may have walked into Lincoln to work, as did some from Nettleham. Cracroft commented on 'a great social question', how far each parish ought to provide cottages for those who tilled its soil; many parishes could not hold a quarter of the number who came in to do the work.[1]

Ingham, he noted, had been one of the most forlorn and desolate villages possible. It was an open parish, filled with labourers belonging to adjacent parishes, Hackthorn among them. (Population in 1831, 361; in 1851, 612.) There was no resident squire or parson and everybody and everything was neglected. There were many dissenters. The building of a new vicarage-house in place of an old thatched mud-and-stud cottage might be the beginning of better things (21 May 1856). Dunholme too was a neglected open parish (21 May 1862): in the same period its population had grown from 237 to 411. Cracroft did, however, note occasionally as he went about the county that some cottages were being built. His uncle Sir William Ingilby had rebuilt his cottages at Laughterton out of the produce of the woods. Though they were substantially built, he thought they should have had a third chamber.

Mr Goddard, a Lincoln architect, had drawn plans for cottages, and received many applications for them. The Rev. C. Nevile of Thorney

---

[1] Cracroft, 23 October 1850.

wrote that two of his workmen were willing to build cottages at £170 a pair, exclusive of leading, and to find all materials and fixtures.[1]

What could happen in the absence of authority is illustrated by an appeal on behalf of the Sunday school at Welton le Wold, where there were many children, because the lordship being a matter of dispute it had been found impossible to prevent the waste land from being built upon by young married people from the surrounding villages. When the agent had to find a tenant for a cottage and a bit of land at Toynton, the guardians warned him against letting any fresh labourers and bairns into the parish.[2]

Shortage of cottages meant overcrowding. The Rev. W. F. J. Kaye, the future archdeacon, wrote to Monson that it was a great temptation to cottagers to supplement their meagre earnings by taking in as lodgers farm labourers glad to find accommodation in South Carlton and so save themselves a long walk to and from work. He was worried about the strain on moral standards when sleeping accommodation was so short. He added that despite crowded conditions behaviour was generally good.[3]

The rural housing problem was described generally by Caird. In some localities men paid very high rents for their cottages, being swept out of close parishes, and obliged to compete with each other for possession of the limited number of cottages which speculators, naturally taking advantage of their necessities, ran up in open parishes for their accommodation. This abuse of the rights of property was then (1850) giving way, and landlords were beginning to build good cottages to be let at moderate rents to well conducted men. The system of boarding farm servants in the farmer's house was again coming into practice, and likely to continue if provisions were moderate in price.[4]

The root cause of the closed parish was removed by a change in the poor law in 1865, when the poor law union rather than the individual parish became the unit for purposes of chargeability to the poor rate.

It was reported in 1844 that 50 houses were being built in Lincoln for the poor coming in from the country, some of them, perhaps, still working in close parishes near the city. The census returns of 1851 give a total of 379 male farm workers in Lincoln; as might be expected, they lived in the parishes nearest to the country, St Botolph, St Martin, St Nicholas and St John. In 1861, when a soup kitchen was opened in Lincoln to relieve distress, the rector of Burton subscribed to it on the

[1] L.C., 27 August 1869.
[2] L.A.O. 3 Ancaster 7/23/38, nos. 20–1; 7/23/61, no. 55.
[3] L.A.O. Monson 25/13/10/10/46–8, 13–28 July 1858.
[4] Caird, *English Agriculture*, p. 197.

ground that Burton labourers living in Lincoln might benefit. So closely were town and country interlocked.

Town and country had another common interest in the protection of the low lands from flooding, for part of the lower city lay in the danger area. It was not merely a matter of maintaining embankments. The Witham Commissioners of Drainage had only made a start at their task under the Witham Act of 1812, and the work was still incomplete at the end of the century. This being so, the proprietors of low lands adjoining the river below Lincoln resolved to resort to steam pumps to lift the water in the internal drains into the main waterways. The Commissioners were alarmed about possible damage to their river banks, and sought an injunction to restrain the proprietors. The application was dismissed by Lord Brougham on the ground that the injury was problematical.[1]

There were severe floods in February 1840, when the river was so high that even unladen vessels could not get through the High Bridge at Lincoln. In consequence the resort to steam pumping was extended. Major Ellison put in a pump at Boultham, there was another at Haddo to lift the Till water into the Fossdyke, and Canwick and Washingborough followed suit. Thousands of acres of land were thus brought into cultivation, especially on the south side of the river.[2]

Lincoln was affected again in 1846, when the flood waters were held up by the Lincoln bridges, and houses on the Waterside had to be approached in boats, the tenants living above the water upstairs. It happened again in November 1848, when the floods were the highest for many years. The whole of the low lands were under water. Cracroft noted that a broad river, more like a lake, filled the valley below Canwick, and covered everything except the two lines of railroad and the towing path at Saxilby.[3] In 1852 the lower part of Clayton and Shuttleworth's works was under water, and workmen were paid off.

It was not only the Witham; the Trent was a standing threat to the Lincoln area. Cracroft had seen the new wheel at Torksey, which drove the water by main force through the floodgates into the cut out of the Trent. In the first winter of its being used, both the engine and the banks had been severely tested, the Trent being unusually high. In November 1852 he witnessed a fearful scene from Newton Cliff: the whole country to the south and west was a huge lake. Dunham was half submerged, and the bridge over the river there inaccessible on both sides except by boat. A break of the Trent bank at Dunham on the Nottinghamshire side of

[1] W. H. Wheeler, *Fens of South Lincolnshire* (second edition, n.d.), p. 388.
[2] *L.C.*, 14 August 1840, 19 August 1842, 20 October 1845.
[3] Cracroft, 28 October 1848.

the river probably saved the Lincolnshire side. Spalford bank, always a danger spot, was threatened, and 150 men were working there day and night. The Kettlethorpe engine, Cracroft thought, was like Dame Partington and the Atlantic. Fears for Spalford bank produced the prophecy from Nevile of Thorney that if it broke there would not be a head of cattle or a corn stack between Lincoln and the Trent that would not be swept away.[1] The Court of Sewers of Lincoln and Nottingham decided that the bank must be repaired at the cost of the owners of land liable to flood.[2]

Witham floods continued to occur. In 1857 the losses were so great that it was surmised that they would have been sufficient to improve the outfall at Boston and effect a perfect drainage. The waters of the lower Witham were pent up, the waters of the upper Witham (above Lincoln) could not get away, and occupiers there and on the Fossdyke suffered with the rest. The fields being underdrained, and the land drains emptying into the river, the evil was increased.[3] Flooding became an annual event, and the Commissioners sought the advice of John Hawkshaw the engineer. The refusal of other trusts concerned with the outfall to join drove him upon the second best, and he made proposals for lowering the height of the water in the channel, and so improving the drainage without hindering the navigation, and for strengthening the banks.[4] The Commissioners obtained a new Act in 1865, vesting them with new powers, but the works proved practically useless, no provision having been made for the discharge of water at the outfall to the sea.[5] The folly of improving the upper Witham before the outfall through the city and Boston was improved was brought home to them by one of the worst of floods in 1869, when the lower part of Lincoln was flooded, and the banks of the Fossdyke, and the river banks at Heighington, Bardney and Branston gave way; and also at Stixwould; and the water backed up to Lincoln.[6]

The city not only complained of the failure of the works, and the dictatorial attitude of the chairman of the Commissioners, Banks Stanhope; they complained that the river between Lincoln and Bardney locks had been kept so low that the steam packets – a great boon to the

[1] Cracroft, 21 November 1852; *L.C.*, 23 November 1855.
[2] Lincoln Court of Sewers, 4 June 1857.
[3] *L.C.*, 24 April 1857.
[4] Wheeler, *Fens of South Lincolnshire*, p. 172. The south delph broke at Branston in 1862. Lincoln Court of Sewers, 3 April, 17 July 1862.
[5] Wheeler, *Fens of South Lincolnshire*, p. 173.
[6] *C.M.*, 1 December 1869, 17 January 1870; Wheeler, *Fens of South Lincolnshire*, p. 173; *L.C.*, 8 January 1869.

humbler classes – could hardly get through at all, some often being stuck there for hours.[1] They suspected the Commissioners of wanting to abandon the navigation and treat the river as a drainage stream only.[2] In the eyes of the city there could be no greater heresy.

[1] *L.C.*, 20 May 1853.
[2] *L.C.*, 11 February 1865. C.M., 11, 17 March 1865.

CHAPTER VI

TRANSPORT AND INDUSTRY

Steam, which had come to the river packets,[1] now came to the mills. For centuries the windmills on the cliff had been a prominent and picturesque feature of the scene. Speed filled in corners with them in his map of 1610. More precisely, Padley in his map of 1842 showed a row of eight mills on the cliff towards Burton, and east of the city three more. He also showed several below hill.[2] Ann Seely had bought land between High Street and the Upper Witham in 1824, and built on it a five-sailed corn windmill.[3] By 1833 her son Charles Seely had one of the Burton Road mills and a steam mill on Brayford wharf. In 1819 Thomas Michael Keyworth, whose father had been managing clerk in Smith Ellison's Bank, had bought some mill premises and goodwill for £2,800. He and Seely went into partnership, and in 1835 proposed to build a steam flour mill on the site of a coalyard and granaries on Brayford wharf, which might cost £6,000, and they sought accommodation at the bank.[4] The project prospered; that year, according to Charlesworth, they paid £35 to their sackmaker and bought 1,000 quarters of corn every week.[5] Getting round the corn markets before the railways was a strenuous business. Seely went regularly to Boston weekly market. He left Lincoln on his own horse, hiring relays at Bardney and Tattershall, did his business at Boston, and returned home by the same stages on the same day. By 1849 it was reported that they had taken a corn mill at Peterborough.

Tall chimneys, perhaps 100 feet high, quickly became a familiar sight on Brayford and the Waterside. William Rudgard had gone over to steam. William Foster of Potterhanworth had an interest in a mill at Brayford head, and Doughty and Son pulled down the old county hospital buildings on Waterside South[6] and built an oil and cake mill; they advertised as dealers in crushed bones, linseed and rape cake, clover and other seeds, oil blubber, lamp oil and coal, having taken over the business of Mr Drury, formerly Wriglesworth.[7] And there were other mills.

[1] Above, p. 6; below, p. 116.
[2] In 1830 the constable of St Nicholas tried to prevent the millers from using Sunday's wind to grind their corn; they replied that they could find nothing in the Commandments to prevent mills from working on the Sabbath.
[3] Deeds in the possession of Henry LeTall Ltd.   [4] Smith Ellison Papers.
[5] Bromhead MSS., 2 September 1835.   [6] *G.L.*, p. 71.
[7] When J. G. Doughty succeeded to the business in 1843 they did well to sell 100 tons of crushed bones in a year. In 1891 they could manufacture 10,000 tons of artificial manure and 16,000 tons of linseed cake. *S.M.*, 25 December 1891.

Their raw materials and their products were either bought from, or sold to, the farmers, with whom they had a common interest in getting produce to distant markets. Transport by road was long and bad; sheep and cattle travelling on the hoof lost weight and value; and heavy waggons were slow, too slow for perishable goods. Waterways, where they were available, were the best, and continued to be so until the advent of railways.

Lincoln stood 35 miles up the the modest river Witham from Boston. The river was under the control of commissioners appointed by an Act of 1812, and in the years that followed they were slowly and painfully trying to improve the river. By 1814 steam packets were beginning to supersede the old horse-drawn packets; they were first concerned with passenger traffic. Then boats plied between Lincoln and London with groceries and light goods. John Shuttleworth of Dogdyke, who had been building steam packets, moved to a new dry dock at Lincoln near the locks to develop his trade: in 1835 one of his new schooners with 300 on board capsized, 50 of his passengers being thrown into the water and two of them drowned. In 1837 there was launched a new enterprise to carry fatstock by water to London: its prospectus stated that 18,000 head of beast and 230,000 head of sheep were sent yearly from the Lincolnshire marshes and adjacent parts to London markets.[1] The Witham Commissioners were alarmed at the effects of traffic travelling at so fast a rate as 8 miles an hour upon the river banks, but they had for a time to abandon their attempts to regulate the steam navigation.

But the major interest of the city was in the Fossdyke, a cut of Roman origin connecting the Witham to the Trent at Torksey, giving access by way of the Trent, the Humber and the Yorkshire rivers to the great corn and wool markets of the West Riding and thence by canal to Manchester. The Lincoln corporation, by virtue of an Act of 1671, were undertakers of the canal, and in 1741 had granted a lease for 999 years to Richard Ellison of Thorne. A second Richard Ellison had developed the navigation to the benefit of the city and his own great gain. The navigation had been vested in his successors and became involved in a family settlement, under which a tenant for life had small interest in spending money in capital outlay. The volume of traffic seeking to use the waterway increased as its condition declined, and attempts at negotiation between Henry Ellison and his son-in-law Humphrey Sibthorp, who acted for him, and the corporation were impeded by a long Chancery suit instituted by merchants and traders which ended in 1839 in Ellison's favour.[2]

[1] *G.L.*, p. 198.   [2] *Ibid.*, ch. v.

There had long been complaints about the canal. In December 1836 it was said that the voyage from Hull by Humber, Trent and Fossdyke to Lincoln had of late taken as much time as was required by ships from America to England: three weeks. The bridge at Torksey was the chief impediment, for vessels could not get under it when the Trent was high. The canal channel was too shallow, and shoals near Saxilby meant that vessels with half a cargo had to discharge into lighters to get to Lincoln. Between 30 and 40 vessels were detained at one moment by shallow water, and in consequence linseed cake and coal were scarce in Lincoln, and coal went up in price, with great hardship to the poor. By the time the channel was navigable again there were great stocks of flour malt and ale, Lincoln's chief products, waiting there, and not enough boats to carry them.

As soon as the litigation was ended Ellison, alarmed at the threat to his interests by the railways, was as eager to negotiate as the citizens. That same summer he offered to sell his lease for £160,000. He was prepared to show by annual receipts that after deducting £1,000 for repairs, salaries and other outgoings there remained a surplus income of £1,600 per annum. He would not only be giving up this sum: he would be relinquishing all the prospective benefits accruing from the increase of trade which must follow the increase of population. On this offer a public meeting voted in favour of management by the corporation on the principle that they should derive no benefit from the tolls other than a return on their capital outlay. The city council did not proceed on those lines: it resolved that, with the strongest conviction that the defective and inadequate state of the navigation was detrimental to trade, and with the most earnest desire to meet the wishes of the public, the price was too large to afford reasonable expectation that the corporation could adopt the undertaking on these terms with prudence or with advantage to the public. Press comment added that a railway to Gainsborough could be built for less.[1]

The negotiation ended, a new Richard Ellison (fourth of the name and grandson of the second) set about improvement, his father Henry having died in 1837. He drained off the Fossdyke in order to survey the channel, and widened it from Drinsey Nook to Torksey, prior to bringing in a dredging machine to deepen it and remove the need for lighters. It was increasingly recognised that the delays to vessels in the Hull and Yorkshire trade were not due solely to the Fossdyke: the shoals in the Trent were also an obstacle; sloops and keels from Hull had sometimes to wait

[1] C.M., 28 September 1839; the £1,600 must be a mistake, perhaps for £6,000. See G.L., appendix II. S.M., 27 September 1839, said the net yield was £8,000.

for four or five successive tides, each carrying them past a single shoal, and ebbing before the vessel could reach the next. It was no wonder that thoughts turned eagerly to the miracles that railways might effect.

Compared with these vital questions of goods traffic, the convenience of passenger travel was relatively unimportant. Yet progress had been made. Daily coaches plied to and from London, Hull, Nottingham and Manchester, the Snake Pass road from Sheffield to Manchester having been opened in 1821. By 1835 London could be reached in thirteen hours (the fare being for outside passengers 16s. and inside 30s.), and three years later the London coach had only to reach Denbigh Hall on the Holyroad road between Fenny and Stony Stratford in order there to join the railway to London.

In 1842 the banks between Brayford head and High Bridge, a distance of 160 yards, were in disrepair as they so often were, and the channel was choked with silt and rubbish; and the corporation proposed to Ellison that a joint opinion should be taken as to the liability for repair. Ellison declined, but while denying liability he agreed to repair the banks but not the public footpath along them, the maintenance of which could not belong to him. He was, however, as a member of the public prepared to subscribe towards the cost of protecting the path. To a suggestion for the improvement of the waterway through the High Bridge by an inverted arch, the corporation offered to give £60 if the Witham Navigation Company and the Fossdyke lessee would give the remainder. No action seems to have been taken.[1]

The last recorded communication from Ellison to the corporation on the subject of the Fossdyke was dated 7 November 1843. He had been asked by the Witham Company and various owners of vessels to allow a drawback on coal passing through the Fossdyke and going down the Witham to Boston. He made no objection, but said he had no power to alter the toll without the consent of the corporation. He sought leave to diminish or increase the toll (but not beyond the existing amount) from time to time on such articles as he might think fit. His only object, he declared, was the hope of benefiting the trade of Lincoln. The council agreed, limiting the period of consent to seven years. Before the period had expired Ellison had succeeded in divesting himself of his declining asset.[2]

---

[1] It was complained in 1840 that owing to a strong current in the Witham unladen vessels could hardly get through the High Bridge even with 7 or 8 horses. There were 30 cargoes for the Trent waiting for abatement of current, and improvement of the drainage was much needed.

[2] Below, p. 113.

The importance of the Fossdyke to Lincoln was summed up in an anonymous address to the tradesmen and inhabitants. It was the city's means of communication with the rest of the world. It brought 40,000 tons of coal yearly, almost entirely from the coalfield between Nottingham and Leeds; it carried wheat, barley and flour on their way to Manchester; cattle to Rotherham, and, more important, to Manchester; wool to the clothiers of Huddersfield, Barnsley, Manchester, Halifax and Leeds. Besides coal, it brought back lime for farmers' manure from kilns between Swinton and Doncaster; hardware and earthenware from Sheffield, Rotherham, Birmingham, Staffordshire, Derbyshire and south Yorkshire, cotton goods from Manchester, linen from Barnsley, and woollens from the West Riding towns: timber, linseed cake and oil from Hull and Gainsborough.[1] But its greatest days were over; and a railway was not only to lie along its banks, but actually to acquire its control.

Early railway schemes had seemed very remote in Lincoln; yet in 1825, four years after the passing of the act authorising the Stockton and Darlington Railway, a line from London to Cambridge, later to be extended to Lincoln and York, was proposed though abandoned. Promoters became active again in 1833, when there were three schemes, each of which would have put Lincoln on the main line to the north. Henry Handley, M.P. for South Lincolnshire, heading one of the committees, said that the counties of Lincoln and Cambridge were stated to supply 8,000 sheep and 500 bullocks weekly to the London market alone; that sheep lost 8 pounds in weight in driving to London in eight days, and the loss on a bullock was 25 or 30 shillings. The principal portion of the corn grown in the country came from the counties of Lincoln, Cambridge and York.[2]

A Lincoln committee, under the chairmanship of Thomas Norton, the last mayor of the old corporation, reported on the alternative routes in March 1835. The realisation of a line from Leeds to Selby encouraged the idea of connecting the Yorkshire manufacturing towns with London; this took Lincolnshire by surprise, it there being assumed that so ambitious a project might be half a century in the future. More serious attention was given to the north–south lines. A midland advocate urged that it would be cheaper to take advantage of the line then in progress from London to Rugby (the Birmingham line), and connect it to Nottingham and Lincoln. This would be a much smaller undertaking than the 180 miles from London to York, and would connect with the

---

[1] *To the Tradesmen and Inhabitants of Lincoln*, from 'A Lincoln Tradesman'. *c.* 1844.
[2] *Report of Directors of the Northern and Eastern Railway Company*, First General Meeting, 5 August 1836.

midland manufacturing towns instead of running through agricultural districts of small population and little potential traffic.

The Lincoln committee was not misled. It wanted a direct line from London to the north. The cost would be low, as almost all the way from Cambridge to Selby it could run upon a level at an estimated cost of £8,000 per mile (compared with £32,000 over Chat Moss between Manchester and Liverpool). The wool and retail manufacturers of Leeds and Sheffield would reach London quickly, whereas they would be handicapped *vis à vis* Warwickshire if they had to travel via the west midlands. There were, it was true, intermediate districts not offering much traffic, but so there were on the London–Birmingham and other lines. The Lincolnshire view was thus stated:

What therefore may not be expected if the manageable and rich corn districts of Lincolnshire become assisted by means of intercourse between the greatest of markets and the greatest accumulation of manure, to be exchanged with all the facility that a farmer possesses in transporting the fodder from his fields to his crew yards, and returning it in the shape of manure to his fields...why should not a northern railway supersede the use of fly waggons and caravans that now carry the prime parts of meat from the several market towns of Lincolnshire? It is only because meat is a more perishable article than *scissors* or *knives* that the demand is limited: give but the means of speedy transit, without risk of injury, and with cheapness, speed and safety; and it may be safely conjectured that not all the tons of manufactured goods can outnumber the *tons* of food, of which no inconsiderable weight, even in the present limited degree, passes on the line by the costly and tardy means of waggons and vans.[1]

In the next few years much eager thought was given to the prospective advantage of railway communication. Carriage of goods would be cheaper, and prices would fall and thereafter be steadier. Distant markets would be brought within range, especially for perishables like vegetables, dairy produce and meat. Distant and waste lands could be brought into cultivation. Merchants would not need to carry such large stocks of goods; animals would not lose weight by walking on roads; coal would come down in price; and dependence on canals stopped by drought or frost would be eliminated. The number of horses needed would be reduced; it was Adam Smith who said that each horse required for its support as much land as would support eight men.[2]

Of the bills that came before parliament in 1836, one project was rejected, one cut down to end at Cambridge, and communication between London and York was secured by the circuitous midland route, providing a branch to Nottingham and Lincoln.

[1] *Report of the Committee appointed at Lincoln to examine the Proposals for a Northern Railway, 1835.*
[2] See W. T. Jackman, *Development of Transportation in Modern England* (1962 edition), p. 485 *et seq.*

Other projects appeared. In 1837 there was promoted a Manchester South Union railway, and the city council passed a resolution that if it came into effect it would furnish easy transit for the corn, flour and malt grown and made in the city and county to their principal markets, the Staffordshire potteries, the manufacturing towns of Cheshire, and Manchester and Liverpool. The projectors of a Hull and Nottingham line were in touch with the Witham Navigation and other local interests in 1840, and a local board was formed with Thomas Wetherell as secretary. In that year confidential visits were paid in Lincoln to measure the local interest in a line to connect with the midland system.

There followed a lull in railway promotion, but railways remained in the forefront of public discussion, and a commission of the Board of Trade on communications with Scotland favoured a line through Cambridge and Lincoln rather than through Derbyshire and Rotherham; and thought that ere long a new line would be needed to serve the highly productive district east of the midland route; they also thought, however, that as that line had not overwhelming traffic it was not yet expedient to proceed.

By the time that railway activity was resumed in 1843 the midland network had gone further. From its London connection at Rugby it reached Derby, with a branch to Nottingham, and on through Rotherham (with branch to Sheffield), by Swinton to Normanton near Wakefield (where it connected with the Manchester and Leeds) to Leeds, York and Hull, with a line crossing it from Leeds to Selby.[1] It was therefore possible, however inconvenient, for traffic from Lincoln, getting by coach or waggon or on hoof or by water to Rotherham or Nottingham, to proceed by railway to Leeds, Manchester, Liverpool or London. Up to that moment it was the only line of any use to Lincoln. East of this network there was still virtually nothing save the Northern and Eastern line which had reached Hertford, and the Eastern Counties from London to Colchester, with plans to continue to Norwich and Yarmouth. The area from Ouse to Humber lay open.

Schemes for filling the void now came thick and fast.[2] A Cambridge-

[1] E. G. Barnes, *Rise of the Midland Railway, 1844–1874* (1966), p. 37, giving timetable for London, Leicester, Nottingham, Sheffield, Leeds, York and Hull (5 different companies) in 1840. There is a map of the railway system in 1843 in R. S. Lambert, *The Railway King, 1800–1871* (1934), p. 91.
[2] In 1845 a Lincoln, Horncastle, Spilsby and Wainfleet Haven Company was projected; among its promoters were the mayor of Lincoln, Dr Charlesworth, W. H. Brook and Henry Blyth. W. R. Collett, M.P., was on the committee for the Birmingham, Nottingham, Gainsborough and Hull Railway. There was a Birmingham and Boston project, with a branch to Grantham. In a Lincoln and Retford Junction Railway proposal many Lincoln citizens took part. The East Lincolnshire Railway was supported by an impres-

York project, formerly cut down to end at Cambridge, was supported by Charles Chaplin and other Lincolnshire gentry, who furnished two-thirds of the provisional committee. The Eastern Counties Railway proposed to seek power to extend their line through Lynn, Wisbech, Spalding and Boston to Lincoln. There was the midland plan for a line from Nottingham, which was to undercut the Fossdyke tolls and make coal cheaper; it had already had the effect of making the navigation lower its charges on coal. (Collett M.P. was pushing this line; it was understood that he was to be one of the directors.)

A line from Lincoln to Gainsborough formed part of plans both for the north to York, and west to the clothing towns and Manchester. One of the latter, the Wakefield line, proposed to go from Lincoln to Gains-borough, Doncaster and Wakefield, which was declared to be the principal corn and cattle market for the manufacturing populations of Yorkshire and Lancashire. The circuitous route hitherto available had handicapped Lincoln in competition with foreign grain; a direct route would bring coal, coke, lime, stone and salt to Lincoln cheaply, and salt and lime especially mattered for agricultural purposes. The cost might well come down by 50%. To counter this proposal the midland interest produced a plan for a line from the North Midland Railway at Swinton to Doncaster, Gainsborough and Lincoln, providing direct communication with Rotherham, Sheffield and Manchester. It had powerful county support, and George Hudson, the midlands champion, told a Gains-borough meeting that it would be linked with the Nottingham–Lincoln line, providing a way to the south. (Adam Stark said that the plan originated with the people of Gainsborough, and not with the directors of the North Midland.)

This latter route had Charles Seely's support. He said that compared with Wakefield the Swinton connection would save 14 miles to Manchester, 30 to Sheffield, 30 to Rotherham. From 1 October to 1 April 59,000 quarters of wheat were sold in Lincoln market, of which quantity the five wholesale millers bought 43,000 quarters, the greater part of which they converted into flour and sent to Manchester, Stockport, Stalybridge and Ashton. The greater part also of barley and malt went to Manchester, 5,500 quarters going there as against 80 to Wakefield. He was of course a miller.

sive array, including Lord Yarborough, Charles Tennyson d'Eyncourt, Richard Ellison of Sudbrooke, Humphrey Sibthorp (not deterred by his brother's hatred of railways) and Thomas Wetherell of Lincoln. (Particulars from the Bromhead Collection of Railway Broadsheets, now in the British Museum, B.M. 1855 b.9.) Railway fever in Lincoln continued to mount through 1845, several brokers' offices being opened, and it only abated as the cost of defunct schemes began to fall on their unhappy promoters.

'By the middle of April' [1844] writes the historian of the Great Northern Railway;

there were four north and south and three east and west lines in the field, every one of which proposed to enter Lincolnshire; and thus 'threatened', as a contemporary writer put it, 'with no less than seven different lines of railroad, with all the infernal machinery connected therewith', it was no wonder that the people of Lincoln became excited and full of party feeling on behalf of one or other of the projects.[1]

Railways were indeed the chief topic of conversation in Lincoln; which line to back; whether to invest in it; and where the station should be. On requisition the mayor called a public meeting, fixing it for 5 o'clock so that their agricultural friends could be present. The Wakefield and Swinton lines had their champions, and a case was put for a Sheffield line, though there was a doubt when the Manchester–Sheffield line could be finished, because it had to cope with the Woodhead tunnel, three miles long. It was a point for Wakefield that it had aroused the Eastern Counties to propose an extension from Boston to Lincoln.

Melville told the meeting that before any of the six or seven projected railways to Lincoln had been brought before the public, a gentleman had called on him and asked his opinion as to a railway from Gainsborough to Peterborough by Lincoln. He had replied that it must bring with it the great traffic which had formerly gone along the great north road. The promoters in London accepted this, and prepared the York–Cambridge line: it had gained the support of the four M.P.s for the county and of the gentry. Now strangers came in with speculations as to which was the best road to Manchester; and to London they would have to go round by Derby and Rugby. Why were they thus interfered with? He had told a Nottingham deputation that he would give them his support provided that they did not interfere with his going to London by the nearest way of Peterborough. Then another set of gentlemen proposed to come from the midland line at Swinton by Gainsborough to Lincoln, connecting to Nottingham. His objection to this was that they sought to pick out the plum from the York–Cambridge line, namely the Lincoln–Gainsborough stretch of 20 miles, leaving the rest of York–Cambridge to be made how and when it could. He gave examples of delay and inconvenience resulting in transfers from one line to another, as he had found at Rugby.[2]

[1] C. H. Grinling, *History of the Great Northern Railway 1845–1895* (1898), p. 14.
[2] Herein Melville invited the criticism, which was forthcoming, that he was not so much interested in commercial as he was in passenger traffic, and an anonymous pamphleteer suggested that he was chiefly concerned to be able to visit his aristocratic friends in London or his noble relatives in Scotland. *Rival Railways and their Advocates* by Zeta. L.P.L.

The other speakers were chiefly concerned with the routes to the west. Thomas Greetham of Stainfield preferred a line from Boston through Lincoln to Wakefield. There would be 60,000 sheep penned in the following week at Lincoln fair, and 60,000 more at Caistor fair. They then cost 3s. to 5s. a head to get to Yorkshire markets, but they could be conveyed by rail at 10d. A bullock cost 10s. on foot; by rail, 4s. 6d. He was indifferent about the north–south line.

A Leeds speaker, Mr Waddingham, said the Swinton line would give a choice of Rotherham and Sheffield, and three routes to Manchester. There were better prices at Manchester than at Wakefield, which was only a place of transit, and from it there was no coal or lime for the return journey, though both abounded round Swinton. Mr Booth of Wakefield put the opposite view. Wakefield was a depot for a vast body of consumers. He thought that Lincolnshire produced 1,000,000 tods of wool per year: a quarter of it was consigned to Wakefield, an eighth of it going through his hands, the remainder going to Leeds, Bradford, and Halifax. Swinton did not carry them into that market. The quantity of wheat sold in Wakefield during the past three years exceeded the quantity sold in London. Nor was it contemptible in cattle: the average at the fortnightly market was 6,000 sheep and 300 oxen. Good coal could be had at Flockton and High Moor at 2s. 6d. a ton and brought to Lincoln for 3s., making 5s. 6d. a ton. Hudson promised, if the Wakefield line was not continued beyond Lincoln to Boston, to make a separate and independent line; and a spokesman for the North Eastern Railway said they intended to continue to Boston and Lincoln, though whether in conjunction with Wakefield or in opposition to it he could not say.

Charles Seely asked what was the agreement between the Wakefield promoters and the Witham Company and the Fossdyke lessee? This was a subject of which much more was to be heard.

The meeting agreed that a railway committee be set up, consisting half of members of the city council and half of members of the public, to examine all the relevant railway proposals and report to another public meeting.[1]

The new committee went over all the ground again at length. It emerged that Ellison, the Fossdyke lessee, and the Witham Company had come to terms with the Wakefield promoters: they were to buy the Fossdyke, guarantee a permanent dividend of 6% to the Witham shareholders, and reduce the tolls on both waterways. The railway would be built on the banks of both streams.[2]

[1] *L.C.*, 26 April 1844.
[2] British Transport Commission, G.N. 1/4B. Minute Book, London and York Railway, 1844–6, pp. 147, 152, 157, 159, 308. Ellison and Humphrey Sibthorp had evidently become directors.

Ellison had had good cause for alarm, for he knew railway competition would ruin his navigation. He issued a letter to the owners, masters of vessels and boatmen navigating the Fossdyke, pointing out that the tolls could not be increased by the new owners: any railway must injure it, but it was better that it should come as a friend than as a foe. If the two went hand in hand the canal would keep part of the carrying trade, and the railway would carry the goods requiring speed. He had secured in all seasons five feet of water for navigation, and he was supporting the line which he believed likely to do them the least injury and give the public the greatest advantage.[1]

The deal raised a storm of protest against the dangers of monopoly. Charles Seely spoke up for the Swinton line, urging that it would give the best connections with the midland coalfield, in which he had interests. He said Lincoln received more and cheaper coal from the Swinton and Barnsley district than from the Wakefield district; and brought Mr Wetherell, the Lincoln director of the Wakefield line, to promise that a branch should be made from the Wakefield line to the Barnsley district.

Wrangling at the railway committee meetings brought the city council to withdraw the corporation members from what the mayor called 'the Procrastination Committee'. The Cambridge–York party amalgamated with the London–York party, and its strong Lincolnshire following went with it, the gentry being powerfully represented on the new provisional committee. Anxious questions then arose as to the route the line would follow, and its engineer proposed to take it through Beckingham (with a branch $4\frac{1}{2}$ miles to Newark) and Doddington, with a branch $4\frac{1}{2}$ miles to Lincoln. An objection by Colonel Jarvis of Doddington helped to push the line westwards to Newark. This was called the 'towns line', linking Grantham, Newark, Retford and Doncaster, in preference to the 'fens line' through Lincoln.[2] This upset some of its supporters, who seceded and revived the Cambridge–Lincoln project. A Direct Northern scheme also took the field. On the other side the London–Yorkers gathered up the Wakefield party, with a loop from Wakefield to Lincoln and Boston, linking with the main north–south line at Peterborough. So came together north–south and east–west interests. A stormy Lincoln meeting, said to have been packed with the tenants of gentlemen interested in the two navigations, resolved in favour of the London–York line, and the

[1] Later he wrote privately that if the London and York Bill (that company had taken over the Wakefield project) was lost he would not be able to live at Sudbrooke, and rather than jeopardise Smith Ellison's Bank he would retire from the partnership. Smith Ellison papers.

[2] Grinling, *History of the Great Northern Railway*, p. 21, for Denison's determination to have the shortest distance between London and York.

residue of the Lincoln railway committee was dissolved.[1] On 19 September 1844 the city council aproved the projected united lines, London–York and Wakefield–Lincoln–Boston, as likely to be highly advantageous to the county and city of Lincoln, and said that the distance to Doddington would not be productive of such prejudicial effects as to call for opposition. A central station would be required as a depot for engines, and their construction and repair, and they recommended that every effort should be made to have such a station at Lincoln, and promised that every facility for securing a proper site should be offered to the company. They also favoured a short and direct Gainsborough–Sheffield–Chesterfield line, which would unite with the Wakefield line near Gainsborough; and they approved a Nottingham–Lincoln project. They dissented from seven other proposals.

Meanwhile the Board of Trade – known as the Five Kings[2] – reported in favour of the Cambridge–Lincoln line (supported on negative grounds by the midland interest) against London–York, and the rival interests in Lincolnshire prepared for battle. The London–York party had lost ground by taking their line west of Lincoln and by the unpopular deal with the navigations. A committee of citizens denounced the London–York supporters for hiring hordes of labourers at 2s. each to attend the impending county meeting and hold up their hands at the proper moment. The great county meeting was held at the castle, and the high sheriff with some difficulty declared that the London–Yorkers had a majority over Cambridge–Lincoln.[3] A resolution in favour of Gainsborough–Grimsby was carried unanimously.

A few days later the mayor (William Rudgard) presided over a city meeting of at least 3,000 people in the beast market. Excitement had been increased by a long delay in complying with a requisition for the meeting, and by news of the London–York tactics at the county meeting. It was at once pointed out that many agricultural labourers were present at what ought to be a town meeting. The mayor gave leave for Richard Ellison to speak, but the crowd refused to hear him, and at last he retired. When the mayor declared a vote in favour of London–York there was great disorder: the Cambridge party charged him with partiality and stones flew thick and fast. After the mayor had left the chair and the Cambridge party had cleared the ground of their opponents, Charles

---

[1] S.M., 27 September 1844. The minutes of the Lincoln Railway Committee are in B.M. 1855, b.9.

[2] Colonel Sibthorp said they had undertaken a duty which five angels could not have performed satisfactorily if they had come down from heaven and sat four hours a day as a board.

[3] S.M., 4 April 1845.

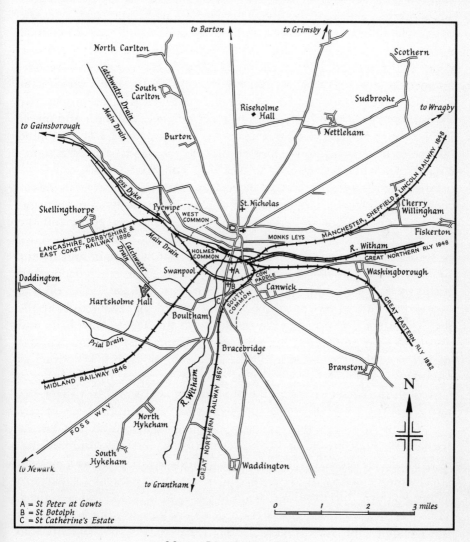

Map 3. Lincolnshire railways.

Seely spoke in favour of the Cambridge line, and a resolution was passed and forwarded to the mayor by Brogden, who was Hudson's agent, to the effect that the meeting thought the lines recommended by the Board of Trade would prove more conducive to farming, river, merchant, trading and public interests generally than the York line; and that as the council was a representative body and undoubtedly desirous of representing the interests and wishes of their constituents, they were respectfully required, by petition to parliament or otherwise, to give all the effect possible to the decision of the meeting. A vote of censure was passed on the mayor.[1] Rudgard and Seely were to meet in battle again.

On receipt of these resolutions the city council passed a vote of confidence in the mayor, and expressed indignation at the improper interference of 'certain parties' at the meeting. The mayor had dissolved it before Brogden's resolution was passed, and it was, moreover, in direct contradiction to the determination of the question by the meeting.

The London–York committee proceeded with their parliamentary bill, fortified by the support of the city council, the Lincoln Lighting and Paving Commissioners, and the Master and Governors of Lincoln Christ's Hospital, the lords of the manor of Potterhanworth. The hearing before the select committee of the Commons lasted 70 days. The bill was opposed by all the rival interests. It was claimed that one advantage of the Cambridge line was that it would pass at the heads of the principal drains and navigable cuts in the fens; but it appeared that the line did not intersect them at points at which they were navigable. When it was pointed out that the London–York line (the loop line by Boston) was placed on the eastern bank of the Witham, which would be convenient for contact with the drains on the west side, the Cambridge engineer declared that the Witham was an impetuous torrent which could not be crossed; the boats would be swamped in crossing the river. Counsel had no difficulty in disposing of this imputation on a placid fenland stream. He had also to defend the deal with the Navigation Company, which was again denounced as a sinister monopoly.[2]

At last the chairman of the Commons committee[3] announced that the London and York preamble was proved, but the branches to Wakefield and Sheffield were omitted for the present. Hudson, however, was successful in obstructing the passage of the bill in 1845. Meanwhile he had secured powers for his line from Nottingham to Lincoln. His attempt at a settlement with the London–York committee failed: the

---

[1] *S.M.*, 4 April 1845.
[2] *Report of the Select Committee of the House of Commons on the London and York Railway Bill*, 24 April 1845.   [3] Rejecting the Board of Trade report.

latter came to terms with the Direct Northern committee to form the
Great Northern Railway, and their bill became law on 26 June 1846, the
day of the repeal of the corn laws. On 21 December of that year Ellison
granted a sublease to the company of his Fossdyke undertaking at a rent
equal to his net revenue plus 5%, namely £9,570. The company was to
pay to the Witham Company an amount equal to 5% in the navigation
capital, i.e. £10,545. Humphrey Sibthorp entertained the leading
Witham proprietors and supporters of London–York on a steam packet
to Boston, leaving Lincoln at 7 a.m. with a splendid breakfast, returning
after dinner and speeches near midnight. Ellison sang a song of his own
composition which went

> The great Mr Hudson is knocked off his perch,
> Derry down, derry down etc.[1]

The great Mr Hudson's purpose of defeating an independent trunk
line from London to the north had failed, but he determined to show that
he 'could provide Lincolnshire with a railway before other people had
done talking about it'. He pushed rapidly on with his line from Nottingham. In June 1846 a steam engine arrived in Lincoln from Collingham,
crossing a wooden bridge over the river laid only that day, amidst a great
concourse of citizens – the first railway locomotive ever to visit the city –
and on 3 August the line was opened. Hudson attended a grand dinner
at the National School to celebrate the occasion; and the Travellers'
Handbook for the Lincoln and Nottingham Railway described the
journey from the handsome brick and stone structure which was the
Lincoln station, over the Witham, by the neat little Gothic building
which was the Boultham lodge, and so to Nottingham.[2]

Another project was about to affect the city. The Manchester–Sheffield line, which was coping with the Woodhead tunnel under the
Pennines, was to extend eastwards; and some of the Sheffield promoters
enlisted the support of Lord Yarborough in promoting a company to
extend it to Grimsby and absorb the docks there;[3] and in 1845

---

[1] Anderson Diary, 10 August 1846. The Witham was the only fenland river to come under
railway control. J. H. Clapham, *Economic History of Modern Britain*, II (1932), 199.
[2] *Travellers Handbook for the Lincoln and Nottingham Railway*, Drury, 1847. The perils of
railway travel came home to people when a van, part of a train, caught fire between
Lincoln and Thorpe-on-the-Hill. The next carriage was scorched, and the passengers
being locked in could not have escaped if the train had not stopped at Thorpe. Jarvis
Diary, 10 June 1848.
[3] Leslie Melville commended the scheme to Charles Tennyson d'Eyncourt as the probable
means of communication to Manchester, which was the market for a very great
proportion of Lincolnshire produce; it would also carry manufactured goods in large
quantity to Grimsby. He thought Coupland of the firm of Keyworth and Seely would
probably be a good witness, as his was the largest firm sending flour to Manchester.
L.A.O. 2 Tennyson d'Eyncourt, H41/46 23 June 1845.

procured an act empowering them to extend their line from Market Rasen to Lincoln. The several parts of the line almost at once became the Manchester, Sheffield and Lincolnshire Railway. This company proposed that their line should cross the High Street from the east and run into the Midland terminus on the west side of the street. About the same time the city council asked the Great Northern to form the main and loop lines from Peterborough to Bawtry at the same time as the other parts of the line. This also raised the question of a level crossing over High Street. The prospect of two crossings 200 yards apart caused dismay, and the council declared that they had understood an arrangement to have been made that if the Great Northern Bill passed the Rasen line should not have another crossing. The most urgent representations were made, and the town clerk was sent to London to pursue them. There he was assured that the city's apprehensions were exaggerated, and he was advised to go to Canterbury to form a judgment upon the degree of inconvenience caused by a level crossing over a street. There the mayor and a bench of magistrates affirmed to him that the crossing of their High Street caused not the slightest inconvenience; it had not nearly so great an effect as a turnpike gate would cause in the same situation, and they would as lief it were there as not. His own impressions confirmed this opinion; 18 trains a day, each taking two minutes to cross, was a tolerable burden. So reassured, the city council took no further action, with results that afflict the city to this day.

The great debate about routes was ended, leaving Lincoln with branch lines only. The loop line from Peterborough by Boston to Lincoln was opened on 17 October 1848, and the line was extended to Gainsborough in the following spring. The direct line from London to Peterborough was opened in 1850, and in the previous year the Manchester, Sheffield and Lincolnshire Railway, connecting Lancashire and the West Riding with Lincoln, Boston and the eastern counties had been completed. It was not until 1867 that the direct main line from Peterborough to Doncaster, with the branch from Grantham to Lincoln, was opened.[1] Until then, the journey from Lincoln to London by Boston had taken five hours; the Grantham route cut the time to $3\frac{1}{2}$ hours. The Midland line was no longer able to compete for the Lincoln–London traffic; it had maintained so sharp a competition that first-class fares were cut to 4s. 6d. and second-class to 2s. 6d.[2] The more direct line at once increased the number of visitors to Lincoln market.

[1] In the same year the company completed extensive sidings along the edge of Brayford Pool, where grain could be loaded direct into railway trucks.
[2] G. K. Jarvis Diary, 25 February 1856.

Railway works in Lincoln caused a great upheaval. In February 1847 seven vessels laden with pig iron came into Boston for the Great Northern, to be brought to Lincoln to be wrought into chairs in the company's foundry near the Durham Ox inn, and thence distributed along the line. Twenty men by day and twenty by night were engaged. A further 60,000 tons of iron and immense cargoes of timber were expected in Boston forthwith. There was a great shortage of houses and lodgings needed to accommodate the navvies who came to work, and rents were rising. Houses were cleared away to make room for the railway stations and lines. Perhaps the most dramatic event was the building of the great railway embankment below Stamp End for the Manchester, Sheffield and Lincolnshire line; it was built from ballast taken from the Greetwell cutting, a process watched by many people who directed their walks through the Greetwell fields.[1]

The railways inflicted on the city one appalling handicap, namely the level crossings of the streets, two of them of High Street. A first complaint was that engines went snorting over so quickly that horses were alarmed, and the safety of riders and drivers endangered. This was only a temporary problem, and horses on the road and cattle on the south common were soon educated to the new conditions. But complaints of nuisance grew rapidly as both road and rail traffic increased; and threats

[1] In many towns not served by a main-line railway the blame for its absence is laid on a local landowner. In Lincoln the blame is commonly laid on Sibthorp, though he would have called it credit. Canon Maddison wrote in his privately printed *Account of the Sibthorp Family* (1896) that 'it is certain that his opposition, combined with that of Mr Chaplin of Blankney, prevented the Great Northern coming direct from London to Lincoln' (p. 83). Though it is impossible to prove a negative, it is difficult to believe that he had much influence on the course of events. The violent language in which he denounced railways gave scope to *Punch*, which depicted him arresting a railway engine. John Francis, who published his *History of the English Railway* in 1851, merely quoted him as the most extreme opponent of railways (II, 36), in spite of whom legislation took its course.

Sibthorp knew that his brother Humphrey was busy on behalf of his father-in-law Richard Ellison, the lessee of the Fossdyke, and also, as a shareholder in the Witham navigation, was involved in negotiations with the railway interests, and indeed appeared on the provisional committee of one of the railway companies. He referred to his brother in the Commons: 'He never travelled by railroad – he hated the very name of a railroad – he hated it as he hated the devil. There was at present a railway in contemplation between the City of London and the city which he had the honour to represent; and if he thought that such a railway would benefit that city, or the county with which he was connected, or the line of country through which it was to pass, there was no Member of that House who would be more ready to contribute to aid in the undertaking by his labour or by his money. He had a brother who embarked in the speculation, but who had withdrawn his name from it within the last few days – second thoughts were always best' (*P.D.* 3rd. Ser., LXXVI, 515. 8 July 1844). No doubt Humphrey, who managed his brother's elections, felt he could not withstand his brother publicly, and so he withdrew publicly. His interest and his conduct were not otherwise affected.

of legal proceedings to prevent illegal shunting from time to time produced some attempt at mitigation. The building of the high level line[1] and the provision of foot bridges gave some relief; but the nuisance was not seriously reduced until the opening of the Pelham Bridge in 1958.

In spite of the railways the river and the canal still mattered. The dangers of monopoly that were foreseen when the railway promoters came to terms with the Witham and the Fossdyke proprietors were soon realised. The railway company put halfpenny a mile trains of fourth-class carriages on the Boston line in 1849 with a view to destroying the competition of coaches and steam packets. They were not at once successful, as the carriages were open and without seats, and did not yield much revenue. But even though they reduced their fares the packets could not hold out long, and after reducing to three days a week they had vanished in 1852. Furthermore, it was to the advantage of the railways to save money by neglecting the waterways, and forcing traffic on to the rail: so taking advantage of their own wrong. When the packets had gone, the cheap trains could disappear.

The city had constantly to press for repair of the navigation. The Torksey engine on the Fossdyke was said in 1854 never to have been in operation since the takeover of the canal: the channel was filling up with mud, and the company had raised the price of coal by 2s. a ton; for it was itself selling coal when the rivers were open, and when they were closed by frost prices were so high that the poor could not buy it at all. Coal brought by the Trent to Torksey had to be carted to the station there and brought by train. The channels were choked with mud and filth, and one boat-owner wished the company directors and the corporation might be compelled to swallow the weeds. Another, carrying 40 tons of coal to Boston, spent six hours in dragging his boat from Pyewipe Inn to Keyworth's wharf (a little over a mile) with two horses and four men. Then it stuck again, and he was selling coal cheap to lighten the boat. A third owner, bringing grain from Hull, reached Torksey, and had to hire lighters and unload part of the cargo. He then reached Carholme corner and stuck again; dragged half a mile with ropes and windlass in four hours, achieving another few yards in two hours.[2]

The corporation took up the matter with the railway directors, and argued that the lowness of the water in the river was not (as was suggested) due to drought, but to the defective state of the lock gates at Boston, through which the water was escaping. A meeting with three of the railway directors, Charles Chaplin, Hussey. Packe and Thomas

---

Wetherell, issued in agreement on a joint cleaning of Brayford, the proper handling of the sluice gates at Boston, improvement of the shunting nuisance, and the opening of a path to Skellingthorpe. (As a result of the cleaning of Brayford, 100 tons of mud were put into the swampy southern part of the west common.) Two years later the complaints were as loud as ever.

The vessel owners and watermen in the Yorkshire trade complained of delays. During neap tides vessels with coal lay idle for eight or ten days, and when the spring tides came in the water was run off to 4 feet 8 or 9 inches, though the Fossdyke should be 5 feet. There were about 22 lighters lying at Torksey, most of them penned in the Trent even when the tides made 7 or 8 feet of water into the lock, to the great waste of the water in the Fossdyke, which was also sadly clogged with weeds; these boats were let out to lighten the cargoes of vessels that could not get up to Lincoln with full cargoes.[1] In August 1858 six or eight vessels lay 4 miles from Lincoln, and with canvas, horses and ponies to boot it would take all night to reach the city.[2]

In 1865 the city council resolved that it was most important that the navigations of the Witham, the Bain and the Slea and their tributaries should be kept up, and that any measure having its for object the closing of such rivers for navigation or lessening their usefulness for that purpose, and turning them into mere arteries for drainage would be detrimental to the trading interests of the city; and that any clauses in railway bills to that end should be resisted.[3]

Like the river packets the coaches had quickly succumbed to the railways. The Horncastle and Louth coach ceased in 1847; in 1848 the TallyHo to Stamford went off, and the Lincoln and Hull coach came in dressed in sable and the horses with plumes, to mark its demise; and after a giant fight, the owner working 18 hours a day, the Gainsborough coach ended in the same year. The last survivor was the daily coach between Lincoln and Grantham, which ceased in 1853 and was replaced by a horse mail-cart.

Diversion of traffic from road to rail reduced the yield of the turnpike tolls which were let as a whole. When the Nottingham line was opened the lessee of the tolls at once sought a reduction in his rent, because of the effect on the Newark road traffic. He obtained an abatement of £330 on his rent of £2,470; on renewal of his lease in 1847 the rent dropped to £2,100, with a proviso for further reduction when the Gainsborough line opened. By 1856 the rent was down to £1,800, though it crept up again

[1] *S.M.*, 4 June 1858.   [2] *S.M.*, 13 August 1858.
[3] *L.C.*, 17 March 1865.

and by 1868 was £1,950. The lessee of the Gainsborough bridge
tolls refused to renew in 1849 without a clause enabling him to end his
lease on the opening of the Manchester, Sheffield and Lincolnshire
Railway over the Trent. Thereafter the rent fell from £895 to £530 by
1857, after which the tolls were not let again but managed by the bridge
company.

The railways gave an impetus to trade, and the Lincoln enterprises
continued to grow. William Rudgard first enlarged his steam mill, and
then rebuilt it in 1856. He was primarily a maltster, having succeeded to
a business started by his father before the turn of the century. By 1861
he was paying £10,000 annually to the Great Northern Railway and
other railways for the carriage of goods alone, being not only a large
seller to the home market, but an exporter on a considerable scale to
distant parts of the world, including New Zealand and South America.
His products were chiefly pale ale and stout.[1] Dawber the brewer
planned a corn mill on his premises at Brayford; he was already
established as a manufacturer of family ales, which went to all parts of
England, and by 1857 had converted the old military depot into a
brewery and storehouses. It was said in 1836 that Lincoln had over 40
maltkilns, sending three-quarters of their produce to Manchester, and
bringing in over £40,000 a year.[2] Doughty and Son took a new
partner in W. W. Richardson, and by 1864 had a manure store on the
Fossdyke at Burton Lane end.

New enterprises were appearing. Most of the men who promoted them
were immigrants, either from the adjoining countryside or from further
afield. All the new undertakings were in some way related to agriculture,
though in rather specialised ways. John Jekyll was a veterinary surgeon
and an able agricultural chemist; his grandfather was Sir Joseph Jekyll,
F.R.S., and his father a farrier who came to Lincoln late in life. In the
early sixties he joined Mr Singleton, who had a ropery in the east end of
the city; they established a chemical manure business, and were later
joined by a third partner, William Gresham. As they prospered in
chemical manures they dropped the ropery; and after Gresham's death
and Singleton's withdrawal, Jekyll was joined by Charles Pratt and
George Glasier. Jekyll also farmed at Coleby and under Lord Monson.
Glasier, who was the son of a farmer at South Hykeham, had previously
had a business of his own, which he had given up for reasons of health.
He was for 38 years chairman of the Lincoln Corn Exchange Company.

Bernard Cannon had founded a business as a leather dresser and glue

[1] Meason, *Official Illustrated Guide to the Great Northern Railway*, 1861.
[2] *Lincolnshire in 1836*, p. 79.

manufacturer in Dublin, and he opened a small branch in Lincoln, where he came to live in 1863, having bought a small skinyard on the upper Witham. In 1874 he leased land on the west of the river from Colonel Ellison, obtaining leave from the Court of Sewers to put a bridge over the river, thereby running into trouble with the West Drainage Trustees for putting foundations into their bank.[1]

In 1873 Toynbee and Larken proposed a company to take over a chemical manufacturing business near Saxilby. They asked Monson if he would be a partner.[2] This apparently was the Lindsey and Kesteven Chemical Manure Company Limited, which was formed in 1874.

In the second quarter of the century the English iron trade vastly increased its output, and so too did the coal industry: and this happened at the very time when railways, by providing cheap and rapid transport, opened up new markets for the heavy products of these developing industries. Cheap coal and iron penetrated to the agricultural districts, and made it easy for men of small capital to turn smithies into something more like factories. Several pioneers of ingenuity but no great technical skill were engaged in harnessing steam to agriculture, and improving implements for which there was a market at their doors. Lincoln and Boston were fortunate in finding men thus to provide the springs of enterprise.

William Howden opened a foundry at Boston in 1803. He had been apprenticed to John Rennie. As his first venture in engine building he built an engine for a steam packet, and by 1839 he had built a portable engine. He showed it at Wrangle in 1841; it was for many years to drive a scoop wheel pump in a nearby fen. William Tuxford, of a family of flour dealers and bakers in Boston, had also started a foundry business, and by 1842 had completed a prototype thrasher and portable engine. The first steam portable thrashing machine to be exhibited at a Royal Agricultural Show was shown by Ransomes of Ipswich at Bristol in the same year. Key, ironfounder, claimed to have made the first engine boiler in Lincoln: it was for Edward Rudgard's porter brewery.[3]

The new industry seemed to grow quite naturally out of agriculture, both relying on water transport. William Rainforth, who had bought a fleet of keels to ply between Lincoln and Hull, bought Michael Penistan's foundry. Penistan formerly made thrashing machines for driving by horse power; he had turned over to steam-engine making, but failed in the process. Rainforth began to make screens and agricultural implements.

---

[1] L.A.O. Monson 25/13/18, 5 July 1874.
[2] L.A.O. Monson 25/13/16–17.
[3] Isaac Wilson also claimed that honour. *S.M.*, 18 August, 1 September 1843.

John Cooke was born at Eagle in 1821. He served an apprenticeship to a wheelwright, and he began as a blacksmith and maker of agricultural implements. He invented a plough, and moved with it to Lincoln in 1857. His plough was an instant success. It suited all soils, and he sold 2,000 in a single year. By 1870 he had on the market a double-furrowed plough which could be worked with three horses and one man instead of four horses and two men.[1] In 1887 when he died he was employing 70 men.

Another firm was founded by Robert Robey, a Nottingham man, in 1854, who traded under various names. He incorporated the company in 1864, and then changed it back into a partnership in 1865. By then he was employing 114 men and boys. His brother, William Robey, joined him. The firm began with the production of portable steam engines and thrashing machines; to which were added traction engines and steam ploughs, followed later by mining machinery and the drop valve engine. They found markets in Australia and South America, taking medals at Santiago in 1864. Towards the end of the century they were pioneers in electrical work.[2]

During the Crimean War William Foster was a flour miller on the Witham bank; in 1856 he set up his foundry and rapidly built up a manufactory of steam engines and thrashing machines. He had 44 men in 1861; 200 in 1885. Richard Duckering, a Retford man, began to make farm implements and kitchen ranges in 1845, and Clarke's Crank and Forge Company began in 1859.[3]

Frederick Henry Harrison was a versatile man. His father was a miller and baker at Boston. He himself worked in a solicitor's office first at Boston and then at Lincoln; he then built a cotton mill at Carlton near Nottingham, and sold out. In 1874 he took over premises in St Mark's lane, Lincoln, late of John Tye, millwright, and started the

---

[1] J. G. Williams recorded another instance of ingenuity, which was told to him by the Rev Mr Hill, vicar of Cherry Willingham. One day a working man walked into a blacksmith's shop in Grantham and asked for a job. The blacksmith asked him if he could turn a grindstone, and set him to turn one for half an hour. The man set to work, and at the end of the half hour the blacksmith, seeing that he was a man of determination, gave him work in the shop. One day he told him to put a set of harrows in the cart and deliver them to a customer. On his return the man said, 'Why can't you put wheels on the harrow and a lever to raise and lower them as required?' The master was struck by the suggestion and adopted it; and he took the man with ideas into partnership. The man was Richard Hornsby, the founder of Hornsbys of Grantham. The story is also told in Bernard Newman, *One Hundred Years of Good Company* (1957), pp. 61–2.

[2] Information supplied to J. G. Williams by W. T. Bell, managing director, in 1920.

[3] Ronald H. Clark, *Steam Engine Builders of Lincolnshire*, Norwich, 1955; *Handbook of Mechanical Engineering Meeting*, 1920.

Lincoln Malleable Iron and Steel Alloy Works, which later became a company.[1]

There were three men who more than any others contributed to the transformation of a market town, based on agriculture, into an industrial town whose interests lay far afield and were largely divorced from most of the surrounding countryside. The change was effected in half a century. The fortunes of two of the three, Clayton and Shuttleworth, were tied together.

Nathaniel Clayton, whose father had once plied a horse-drawn packet on the Witham between Boston and Lincoln, later worked for his mother Mary Clayton as a packet captain at a wage of 30s. a week plus a share of the profits.[2] He became proprietor of the steam packet *Celerity*. All his interests lay on the river, and he and his mother lived on the Waterside. But he had begun work at the Butterley Ironworks, and so was likely to keep an interest in the iron trade. Naturally he became acquainted with William Howden at Boston; and perhaps it was by way of discouraging competition that Howden told him that there could not be more than 40 engines needed in all England.

In 1842 his sister married Joseph Shuttleworth, whose father was a boatbuilder at Dogdyke in the parish of Coningsby on the Witham where the river is joined by the little tributaries Bain and Slea.[3] In the same year Joseph became a partner in the boat-building firm of Shuttleworth and Godwin at Stamp End, next to a foundry which Clayton had started. The romantic story was told long after that once when one of Clayton's packets broke down he and Shuttleworth, who was a passenger, spent the night at the inn at Tattershall, and that they then decided on their joint venture.[4]

They began in partnership in 1842, taking 1½ acres on Waterside South, of which half an acre was always under water, and the rest covered in times of flood, and which they had to raise by carting soil. They began with 12 men, 2 forges and a lathe; and they made pipes, built bridges and did railway work, and made small products like fire grates. Their first large contract was to supply pipes for the Boston waterworks at Miningsby. Then they applied themselves to the portable engine, and produced one rated at 8 horsepower. By 1848 they turned out the first engine having a single horizontal engine in the firebox. It

[1] *L.L.*, 24 September 1910.
[2] *G.L.*, p. 197n.
[3] There are various Shuttleworth entries in the parish registers of Coningsby and St Swithin, Lincoln.
[4] The story was recorded by J. G. Williams; it was also told to me by Richard Mason, whose father became a director of Clayton and Shuttleworth Ltd.

was claimed to save 25% on the common horse-thrashing machine; and they announced with pride that their engines were used not only in Lincolnshire, but in other counties. By this time they employed 100 men, and were short of capital, and they sought help. They entered into partnership with Messrs Coupland, Keyworth and Seely, the millers, who contributed, not cash, but a bank guarantee.[1]

In 1849 the firm began to exhibit at agricultural shows, and took the first of many prizes at Norwich. They came to the fore at the Great Exhibition in 1851, where they showed a six horse-power portable steam engine, a grinding mill and a thrashing machine. At the Lewes meeting in 1852 they took the prize for a movable thrashing machine not exceeding 6 horse-power with shaker and riddle to be driven by steam, in the face of formidable competition from Garrats, Tuxford, Hornsby and Ransomes.[2] They were of course prominent when the Royal Show visited Lincoln in 1854, by which time they employed 520 men and 80 boys.[3] They all worked 'time and a quarter', and average earnings were about £1 a week.

They published their first catalogue in 1850, with German and French translations for the Paris International Exhibition in 1855. Steam engines were sent to the Crimea for the war against Russia. They were penetrating the corn-growing districts of Austria, Hungary and Turkey, and branches were opened at Vienna (with 200 hands), Pesth, Prague, Cracow and Lemberg. By 1858, the war over, the Russian market was developing. The *Mercury* noted that large quantities of Clayton products were seen passing through Berlin on their way to Vienna for Hungarian grandees and landowners.[4] New fields opened in Canada, the United States, Australia, Egypt and South America. By 1870 they employed 1,200 men, and made 1,000 engines and 900 thrashing machines a year.[5]

As the number of employees and the number of workshops increased, the overseers – 'collar and tie gents', wearing top hats – were given horses to carry them on their rounds. As times changed it was remembered that in earlier days the works seemed like a family affair, fathers,

[1] This was to cause trouble later; see p. 189. The late G. L. Haslehurst told me that Clayton and Shuttleworth had previously approached Richard Carline, who declined.
[2] Sir William Tritton in *Lincolnshire Magazine*, II (1934–6), 'The Origin of the Thrashing Machine'.
[3] G. K. Jarvis noted that they employed 570 men and paid £500 weekly in wages. *Diary*, 28 October 1853.
[4] *S.M.*, 20 June 1856.
[5] *L.C.*, Supplement 1854; *Illustrated London News*, 7 August 1869, reprint from *Engineering*, 1870. They also built engines for use on railways in the fens, first taking six days to make one, then turning out four in a day. Their rating assessment was more than doubled in 1862.

sons and grandsons employed at the same time, and the masters knowing every man by name. On their part they all knew 'Natty' Clayton.

John Burton of Waterside South had carried on business as a brass and iron founder since about 1835; in 1843 his administrator, perhaps his son, was Theophilus Burton, a blacksmith. James Toyne Proctor of Waterside was a millwright. By 1849, starting with a man and a boy, they were in partnership as millwrights and general smiths, agricultural implement and machine makers, on the Waterside. They were sub-tenants of Lincoln corporation and were given credit for raising the level of the land and putting up buildings. Joseph Broadberry, the first working man magistrate in Lincoln, recalled fifty years later that he had worked for them for a year; they had no engine, but kept a blind man to turn the wheel. It was hard work then to bore cylinders and turn cranks.[1]

They presently needed a third partner, and they found him in Joseph Ruston. Ruston was the second son of Robert Ruston of Chatteris in the Isle of Ely, a farmer of 600 acres employing 28 labourers.[2] The father was a well known Wesleyan local preacher; he died in 1851 when Joseph was 16. The son went to school at Wesley College, Sheffield, and later was apprenticed at Wolstenholme's cutlery works there. In 1856, as soon as he was of age and out of his time, he entered into negotiations with Burton and Proctor, and references were exchanged. He joined the firm on 1 January 1857, and first lived in two rooms at the corner of Norman Street and Sincil Street.

He was then 22. The firm announced to their customers that they would carry on business under the name of 'Ruston, Burton and Proctor', thus telling the world who would take the lead. The original partners were each to draw salaries of £100 per annum, Ruston £150 rising to £200, profits being shared equally. Ruston was to bring in capital as required until his investment was the same as that of the others.[3] Burton quickly became alarmed at Ruston's methods, which he thought portended ruin, and he sold out for £855 in 1859, retiring to farm at Morton near Gainsborough, where he served as a waywarden and poor law guardian, dying in 1898.

Ruston and Proctor then employed about 50 hands, but they still had no draughtsman. Proctor was the working partner, going to work in his shirt sleeves; he had a garden between the works and Sincil Dyke, and he could be seen going to it before 6 a.m. An old employee, Charles Hopewell, remembered him as a 'kind, humble-minded Christian gentle-

---

[1] *L.L.*, 22 July 1899.
[2] Details from census returns.
[3] The partnership deed is among the firm's records.

man'.[1] Ruston looked after the business, and was never easy unless he was looking for work. An old workman recalled that once when there was no work in portable engines they made lawn mowers.[2]

By 1861 the firm employed 135 men and boys. Ruston's energy became too much for Proctor, as it had been for Burton. At one show Ruston took an order for four engines, and Proctor thought it impossible to get them out; and in 1865 he sold out to Ruston at the price of £8,000. The story told later was that a year after Ruston had been to the continent securing an order for a small corn mill with French burr stones, Proctor still had not designed it, and one day he walked into Ruston's office with a few wire nails in his hand which a man had dropped in the yard, and said, 'This, Mr Ruston, is where your profits are going.' Ruston then felt it was time that they parted.[3]

They continued to need more land for building new workshops; having been tenants of the corporation they sought to buy the freehold because by reason of the boggy nature of the soil the workshops had become dilapidated and needed to be rebuilt; they succeeded in 1876, having then lately taken a lease of the corporation's ironstone and iron ore on their Canwick farm. They built locomotives for the Great Eastern Railway, and by 1876 were making steam excavators, road rollers and tractors.

In the census of 1851 only 62 persons were given as employed in iron manufacture, though there were 98 blacksmiths, no doubt mostly of the old-fashioned sort. By 1870 there were about 2,500 men and youths employed in the industry, and by the end of the century that number had doubled.

Increasing industry and increasing population involved a large increase in the building industry. In 1851 the census gave a total of 596 men plus 102 under 20, which was more than twice the figure for 1831. Twenty-four builders were named as employers, ranging from one builder working with one man, or a man and a boy, to the larger firms: John and Thomas Foster, the only notable family in St Botolph, had 27 men; and Charles Ward had 125.

In a building boom in 1857 there was a shortage of bricks, and the

---

[1] *L.C.*, 4 June 1910.
[2] *L.C.*, 11 September 1909. George Alderson called on Ruston late one Sunday night. Ruston put his head out of the window, refused to come down, and told the caller he would be at the office in the morning. 'But I've come from Egypt to do business, with £400 in my pocket', said the caller; whereupon Ruston said 'Why didn't you say that before? I'll come down.' B. Newman, *One Hundred Years of Good Company* (1957), p. 13.
[3] In this account I have relied chiefly on notes made by J. G. Williams, who knew Ruston; they were annotated for me by G. R. Sharpley, later managing director of the company, who was Ruston's nephew.

Lincoln brickmakers were denounced for lack of enterprise and energy. It was found that bricks could be bought from Nottingham more cheaply. New brickyards had been opened in 1845 north of the race course; Charles Ward went into the business himself; Robert Toynbee financed another brickyard and in 1875 F. J. Clarke promoted new enterprises at Bracebridge. Four small firms at Waddington, Bracebridge, West Cliff and Cross Cliff Hill were amalgamated in 1889 into the Lincoln Brick Company. Timber too was in demand; and in 1856 Henry Newsum, a young man not quite 22, arrived by road from Rotherham to set up a steam sawmill on the site of the future Drill Hall, and offered to saw any timber that was brought to him. The builders were also customers for the iron foundries, because of the large quantity of cast iron used in buildings.

CHAPTER VII

ECONOMIC AND SOCIAL CHANGE: I

The most striking fact about the city at this period is not so much the growth of population as the rapid rate of its growth. In the four decades 1831–71 the population of the city grew by 150%; in the seven decades to the end of the century it had quadrupled. This rate of expansion was unprecedented; all earlier growth had been very gradual. It was the more striking because in the four decades the population of the county had grown only by about a third, and by the end of the century by two-thirds. But the natural increase in the county – that is to say, the excess of births over deaths – had been much greater than this actual increase. The difference is accounted for by migration. In the decade 1851–61, 93% of the natural increase migrated beyond the county; in the following decade, 59%.[1] There was a further migration from the villages into Lincoln, and others came to the city from other counties. It is a striking fact that in 1851, out of a total of 9,801 people in Lincoln of 20 years of age or more, 6,779 had been born outside the city, and of that number 2,811 outside the county. It was to be expected that a higher proportion of those under 20 would be born in Lincoln, the migrants being many of them young, and having their families after settlement: there were 7,735 people in Lincoln under 20 in that year, and of them 5,147 were born in the city, 1,470 elsewhere in the county, and 1,118 outside the county.[2]

The movement into Lincoln was mostly of short range, from villages near by, which provided numbers from 8 to 25; towns like Boston, Gainsborough, Louth, Horncastle and Sleaford from 20 to 50; and the movement from outside the county came chiefly from Nottinghamshire and Yorkshire, no doubt largely from the West Riding. Similarly much of the movement outwards was to neighbouring counties.[3]

It had long been the custom for farmers to send their sons and daughters to towns for the girls to learn millinery and dressmaking, and the boys to see something of business on the wharves and in the

[1] John Saville, *Rural Depopulation in England and Wales 1851–1951* (1957), p. 43, and table IVb.

[2] *Population Tables II*, I, civ; II, 602, 605. In almost all the great towns the migrants from elsewhere outnumbered the people born in the town. The father of a family in a declining trade would in the last resort move to the nearest adjoining town. A. Redford, *Labour Migration in England 1800–1850* (1926), pp. 19, 186, Appendix I.

[3] The places of birth are given in the census returns of 1851.

warehouses and shops. Poorer boys were bound as apprentices, and poorer girls put out to domestic service. There was increasing scope for domestic servants, male and female, as the middle class grew and prospered, and wages were so low that some working-class households, perhaps where everyone went out to work, also had servants.

But more was happening than this. Agriculture could not, or at least did not, absorb the natural increase of the country population; and so young men, unable to find work or house or both in their villages, went off to take their chance in neighbouring country towns, or in the mines or the mills of the industrial areas. Furthermore, the poor law provided an incentive to parish overseers to drive the surplus poor away so as to limit the parish poor rate; and in close parishes[1] the number and perhaps the quality of cottages was sometimes severely controlled. Village guardians and overseers would give paupers a trifle and post them to city parishes; and in some cases the city parishes took the paupers rather than dispute the settlement at law. The inhabitants of the north district of the Lincoln Union were driving their poor into the city.[2] Even if the village was not rid of the man it was rid of his children, and the burden of supporting them in sickness or destitution evaded.

The most obvious and clamant problem resulting from this unwelcome influx was a shortage of houses. The cheapest sites for building were provided by gaps in existing streets, and by building in yards, where no roads need be made. There were gradual increases of population in the Wigford parishes. In St Botolph, for example, Sarah Abraham lived in one of four houses in Abraham's Passage, no doubt built by her or her husband; there were ten houses in Gadsby's Row, probably built by a member of the Gadsby family, who also gave their name to twelve houses in Gadsby's Court in St Swithin. The two Waterside parishes, St Martin and St Swithin, had begun to grow earlier;[3] Thomas Holland the bricklayer lived in Holland's Row, which in 1841 comprised 15 occupied houses and one vacant, with 68 inhabitants, and in 1851 20 houses with 107 inhabitants. Housing began to thicken on the steep hillside in St Michael, but the most spectacular increase in the same decade was in St Nicholas in Newport, houses being built on the main road with courts behind them; here the number of houses grew from 122 to 234.[4]

In the following decade the land south of the Witham and east of the Sincil Dyke, lately drained by the Witham Commissioners, and opened up by the great project of the turnpike trustees of a road from the south end of Broadgate to Canwick[5] came into the market, as the Reverend

---

[1] See above, pp. 93–4.   [2] *S.M.*, 4 May 1849, 30 November 1849.
[3] *G.L.*, p. 206.   [4] See Appendix II.   [5] Above, p. 61.

Francis Swan and others, buyers of corporate land,[1] realised on their investments. Houses in St Martin were spreading westward: William Rudgard was building in his paddock in Far Newland, leaving his name on one of the lanes. The abovehill parishes of St Paul and St Peter in Eastgate were filling up.

Most of these houses were small and poor, and all the worse because of the absence of a good supply of water and other measures of public health,[2] but at least Lincoln did not suffer like the great industrial towns from having vast areas of little houses jostling one another, nor did it suffer from the same degree of overcrowding.[3]

Some better houses were being built as early as the 1840s. In the new areas, like Melville Street, along the new road to Canwick, houses of a superior kind were going up in which a Clayton or a Shuttleworth, in days of mounting prosperity, would be willing to live. Charles Ward the builder was erecting good middle-class houses – notably a handsome terrace on Newland – and better working-class houses of the £10 to £12 class were beginning to appear. The *Mercury*, noting the contrast with slightly older ones, gave warning that when an inevitable change in the poor law enabled the labouring classes to return to their own parishes instead of residing in the nearest market town, rents would fall, and owners of these small houses might suffer great loss. It looked forward to the time when those who had thrown up mere dogholes would have their just punishment in not being able to get tenants for their miserable kennels.[4] Yet bad building went on: the Primitive Methodist minister was accused of building fever-holes near his chapel;[5] and houses in Canwick Square were built in a swamp.

The land monopoly was breaking up, and problems of building became easier as more land came into the market. A very high proportion of land in the city had belonged to two great corporate owners, the city corporation and the dean and chapter. The corporation had owned many plots of land and buildings, some of which had come to them as escheats under their charter powers,[6] and it had enclosed and let large areas of waste, notably the Bargate closes lying in the angle east of Sincil Dyke and south of the river. Some of this property had been enfranchised on the eve of the Municipal Corporations Act of 1835, in favour of

[1] Below, p. 129.
[2] Below, ch. VIII.
[3] Below, p. 290.
[4] *S.M.*, 25 October 1844, 1 August 1856.
[5] *S.M.*, 19 September 1856; *L.C.*, 5 and 12 December 1856.
[6] *M.L.* pp. 148, 242.

tenants holding under constantly renewed leases at rents which had become nominal with the fall in the value of money.[1] Other parts were sold in the years following for the payment of corporate debt and the financing of new capital expenditure.[2] In 1848, for example, the Reverend Francis Swan bought the Tenter Croft in St Mark's parish, and in 1852 part of the Bargate closes; by 1856 he was bringing land into the market, and laying out new roads between High Street and the new Canwick Road; this was the beginning of St Andrew's parish.

The problem of the chapter lands was more complicated. They were administered on a system whereby a lease was renewable on payment of a fine; and the fact that if the tenant carried out improvements the fine was accordingly increased effectively prevented improvement altogether. As early as 1837 church lessees in Lincoln were considering how to obtain a grant in perpetuity of their property without prejudice to the rights of the Church. There were repeated attempts at legislation, which failed, and it was asserted in Lincoln that minster leasehold had become unsaleable. At last in 1851 an act was passed empowering chapters to sell. The Lincoln chapter did not move. Individual members of the chapter had their vested interests, for they took the fines which became payable when they were in residence, and as might be expected the chancellor and the precentor, the two Pretymans, were standing out.[3] In 1859 a meeting of church lessees declared that the dean and chapter of Lincoln were almost the last ecclesiastical corporation to stand out, their objection being stated to be that under the Act any surplus proceeds went to a common fund in London instead of being applied for the benefit of the diocese. Things, however, began to move, though slowly, because the Ecclesiastical Commissioners were slow in action and set their terms high. Lincoln, declared the *Mercury*, was remarkable for its wretched buildings, and in no part of the city were they worse than in Minster Yard, where the dean and chapter did nothing to keep them from falling into decay.[4]

By 1870 the bulk of their property had been transferred from the chapter to the commissioners (though not the Minster Yard houses), and it was hoped that large quantities of it would be released.

Besides these great corporate owners there were private owners of large holdings, such as the Black Monks and the St Catherine's estates, secularised at the Reformation, who were willing to sell as the demand

[1] *G.L.*, pp. 254–6.
[2] Above, p. 47.
[3] *S.M.*, 13 August 1858; and see below, p. 257.
[4] 20 June 1862.

increased and prices with it; and others who had invested as opportunity offered. Thomas Winn the brewer is an example. When his estate came into the market in 1857, it was offered in 250 lots.

Middle-class purchasers of houses generally had no difficulty in borrowing on mortgage, but for the smaller of them and the artisans, something more was needed. In 1839 there had been a scheme for a society, to have say 500 members, each paying 6d. a week, to buy and sell land in small lots, in order to give some independence to the poor. The first of a long series of terminating building societies began in 1847, with E. R. Larken as first chairman;[1] they helped a large number of middle- and working-class citizens to acquire their own houses. A Lincoln and Lincolnshire Freehold Land Society followed in 1849 and the Conservative Land Society in 1853; two years later it bought $5\frac{1}{2}$ acres of the St Catherine's estate, and sold land at less than 1s. 6d. a yard, including the cost of roads. Previously, purchasers had had to pay 5s. to 10s. a yard, and make their own roads. Other societies followed, and there grew up a strong tradition of owner-occuticipership in Lincoln.[2]

The influx of people from the country at a rate faster than could be absorbed by trade and industry meant that not only the number but the proportion of the population who were regularly or from time to time in distress greatly increased. It was reported in 1841 that the number of prowling thieves and beggars was worse than ever, and sheep were being slaughtered and stolen. Distressed Irishmen drifted across England, and some of them established themselves in pockets in the worst alleys and in overcrowded conditions. Vagrants who could not get into the workhouse broke windows and gave themselves up to the police, and when no one appeared to prosecute before the magistrates, were discharged. Honest men went on tramp, and swelled the ranks of the beggars, and householders were intimidated as they went about their business. Crime, gambling, drunkenness and vice went hand in hand.

Wages were low. Men raising stones in quarries for road work were paid 9d. a day. Others were working for 12s. a week, and after paying rent there was perhaps 2s. a head for food and clothing; they worked on bread with sometimes a morsel of bacon and cheese. This was at a time when, according to Thomas Miller of Gainsborough, it cost a family of six 7s. 6d. a week just to keep alive – rent, clothes, bread, coal, candle and soap, small beer and potatoes, flour lard and milk; and another 7s. for common necessities extra – meat, tea and coffee,

---

[1] John Norton was a trustee, and George Boole and the Rev. John Craps, Baptist minister, were directors.
[2] Below, p. 290.

sugar, butter and cheese, more potatoes bread and beer, and more clothes.[1]

Conditions were aggravated by a rapid influx of mechanics and labourers employed on railway work. Trade flourished for a time, and building went on quickly, but when the railway works ceased, families who had expected to settle permanently were stranded without work. Outbreaks of fever made matters worse.

It was in such conditions that the Board of Guardians, constituted under the new Poor Law of 1834, had to begin work. The whig government had found serious abuses to be reformed, especially in the southern counties, where wages were sometimes subsidised out of the poor rate; but the rate was felt to be too heavy everywhere, and the new law could be represented as a measure of agricultural relief. The law was based on two principles: first, that outdoor relief must not be given to the able-bodied, who might be deterred from applying for relief if they knew they would have to enter the workhouse; and secondly, that conditions inside the workhouse must be such as to deter the lower classes from entering it willingly – that is to say, the standard of living in the house must be lower than that of the lowest paid worker outside. This was known as the principle of less eligibility.[2]

It was all so rational, but so harsh in operation. An estate agent in Newark wrote to Colonel Jarvis of Doddington on the new system, and no doubt spoke for many observers:

23 October 1837. I hope you will have no trouble in the regulation of the poor rates. I have a favourable opinion of the new law prospectively, but I should not have liked to be one of its *executioners* – they must have had their feelings painfully affected often. I am very well acquainted with Captain Nicholls, who is a very humane religious man, but very intrepid and of a businesslike mind. They had to overturn a system founded upon a most benevolent principle, but it had outlived its usefulness and had become a great nuisance, especially from its being administered unequally according to the feelings and not the understanding of those who acted under it.[3]

New unions of parishes were set up which overrode existing local government boundaries, on the ground that the board of guardians would be more distant and impartial, less open to suspicion, and less

---

[1] *Pictures of Country Life* (1847), p. 139.

[2] In *Oliver Twist*, begun in 1837, Dickens branded it for all time, as the rule 'that all poor people should have the alternative (for they would compel nobody, no, not they) of being starved by a gradual process in the house or by a quick one out of it'.

[3] Jarvis Corr. He added that it was fortunate that the poor had improved and were improving in their intellectual and moral conduct and their religious inclination. Captain George Nicholls was one of the Poor Law Commission. He had won success at sea, in banking, and as a reformer of the poor law at Southwell. David Roberts, *Victorian Origins of the British Welfare State* (1969 edition), p. 151.

likely to excite revengeful feelings in dealing with the poor than the executive of a single parish. There was rigid central control by the poor law commissioners in London, the smallest item of expenditure requiring their consent. Even the minute book, with specimen minutes, was supplied from London.

The Lincoln Union, constituted on 28 November 1836, consisted of the parishes of the city and 63 country parishes,[1] each parish electing a guardian of the poor, rated occupiers and landowners both having votes from one to twelve in number according to the value of the property owned or occupied; and magistrates were *ex officio* members of the board.[2] The Lincoln board was an unwieldy body, having more than 100 members, and power inevitably fell into the hands of a small number.

When the first guardians were elected many of the leading citizens took their places, John Coupland for St Botolph, Dr Charlesworth for St Margaret, Henry Blyth for St Peter at Arches, John Stevenson for St Peter in Eastgate, Thomas Wetherell for St Peter at Gowts, John Willson for St Paul. In 1839 new members included Edward Drury for St Peter at Arches and Dr Cookson for St Peter in Eastgate.

At the first meeting an assistant commissioner, Edward Gulson,[3] took the chair to instruct the guardians and to supervise the election of officers. There was to be no nonsense; no snap decisions, reversing policy already defined. No minute, once passed, might be rescinded without two weeks' notice, and notice to the assistant commissioner, and without a two-thirds majority. The gentry were installed in office. Melville the banker was elected permanent chairman; he held office until 1870. Humphrey Sibthorp was vice-chairman. Richard Ellison, a partner in the bank, was elected treasurer, and when he resigned in protest against the use of force against paupers Melville took over the treasurership. Although reports of meetings leaked into the press, reporters were not allowed to attend the meetings until 1850. Cracroft said that this was because kindly guardians might be frightened and stay away. It was even proposed that district assistant overseers should be appointed who would in effect supersede the parish overseers, and would reinforce the central bureaucracy. But the proposal was rejected by a large majority: the ratepayers could manage their own affairs, and would not submit to the dictates of any stranger who might be sent to

---

[1] Extra-parochial places were brought in under an Act of 1857 – the Castle Dykings, Monks Liberty, Cold Bath House, the Holmes Common and South Common.
[2] George Nicholls, *History of the English Poor Law* (1854), II, 301.
[3] He had been a fellmonger at Coventry, and was a Quaker. David Roberts, *Victorian Origins of the British Welfare State*, p. 154, and see p. 289.

control parish affairs. Besides, they would have added to the burden of the rate.[1]

Governor and matron, schoolmaster and chaplain, were appointed for the workhouse, and the standard required for the schoolmaster is suggested by the grant of a testimonial to a porter on his applying for a schoolmaster's post at Sleaford workhouse. The union area was divided into districts for which there were relieving officers. The House of Industry was rented from the directors of that house, which belonged to a voluntary union of parishes, now superseded, and its fittings taken over.[2] The building of a new workhouse on an adjoining site was put in hand, W. A. Nicholson being the architect. It was complete by 1839.[3] It was a general mixed workhouse, men, women, the sick, and the children being all housed within it. Contracts for supplies were placed; for a pauper funeral, including the coffin, 16s. was allowed.

Conditions in the 'House' were rigidly prescribed by the commissioners, to whom the weekly diet table had to be submitted. Dr Charlesworth wanted four meat days, and the guardians agreed. But the commissioners rejected the fourth meat day, 'giving', said Charlesworth, 'a dumpling day instead, forgetting the cheese given up…Themselves are evidently unsound both in heart and *head*'.[4] The guardians occasionally sought to make additions to the diet table, but they could not include more meat instead of cheese, or transfer Friday's broth to Saturday without leave from London. Visitors, whose visits were strictly regulated, were not allowed to take food to the inmates. But humanity crept in at Christmas and on a few other occasions. As no money could be spent without permission, the chairman's fund, raised by collections at guardians' meetings, was instituted to pay for extras, or alleviate special hardship; and treats, particularly for the children, were provided by kindly people.

Vagrancy was one of the most serious problems, and in 1838 vagrant tickets were issued, entitling a beggar to a night's lodging, supper and breakfast, and cleansing in the House, in exchange for work adequate to strength, as a test of willingness: two hours' work was required. For them, as for other able-bodied inmates, the tasks provided included grinding corn by handmill, picking oakum, breaking stones in the quarry, and emptying cess-pools, for men; and picking oakum for women. The rate for out relief was fixed subject to approval from London. In the hard year 1846 the amount allowed was discussed, and

---

[1] *L.C.*, 15 February 1839.　　　　[2] *G.L.*, p. 247.
[3] Its gaunt walls continued to stand until 1965.
[4] Bromhead MSS, 4 May 1837.

Charles Jarvis wanted an increase of 10%; 6d. extra was allowed for adults and 3d. for children. In the following year the rate was 2s. 6d. for adults, and 1s. 6d. for children, which was a reduction. In 1848 Cracroft, a new guardian, asked an old hand, Mr Hood of Nettleham, if the increase of expenditure throughout the union was in his opinion the result of increasing pauperism or increasing liberality; Hood said the latter, which pleased him.[1]

The guardians did from time to time stand up to the commission. In 1837 sixty of them signed a petition to the House of Commons against the commissioners' order preventing out relief from being given to paupers not residing in the parish to which they belonged, and it was sent to Lord Worsley for presentation. In 1840 Nassau Senior, one of the commissioners, sent out a circular on the matter. Whatever it may have said, the guardians resolved to make no change in their practice, and in 1841 they petitioned again, though they expressed approval of the general principles of the law, which they believed tended much to check the progress of demoralisation which the former law had introduced.

One of these principles was of course the refusal of outdoor relief to the able-bodied, which the commissioners had applied to Lincoln (having a discretion as to the date when it should take effect in each union), though they could relax it in case of exceptional distress. In the bad winter of 1838 some Lincolnshire unions sought exception from the rule, but the Lincoln union was not one of them. In 1840, not for the first time, the city guardians tried to persuade their country colleagues to join in giving temporary relief to beggars, but failed; and St Mary Magdalene asked for outdoor relief for sick and disabled labourers with families in distress during a stoppage of their daily earnings, but there was fear of any relaxation in the harshness of the rule, for the number of prowling thieves and beggars was greater than ever.

Nevertheless it appears that in some respect the guardians went beyond the book, for though the official records are silent, the *Mercury* said:

Men of Lincoln...have preferred the law of humanity to the law of England...you are every day breaking the poor laws, and you may be made to pay for your kindness to the poor, yet what care you? You have defied and defy the Bashaws of Somerset House. The gallant spirit of 1835 lives yet...

The assistant commissioner attended a meeting and laid down the rule again: no outdoor relief to able-bodied people.[2]

[1] Cracroft, 29 March 1848.   [2] *S.M.*, 12 January 1849.

The new system provided many instances which appealed to what has been called 'the sentimental philanthropy of the upper classes'.[1] It has been noted why Ellison resigned. In 1841 the Reverend Richard Garvey, of St Mary Magdalene, complained that the wife and family of Joseph Swift, a coal porter then in the county hospital, had been refused out relief. They were in great distress and without food, and would have had to sell their horse if a miller had not taken him to use. The family could not appeal for ten days. Garvey had given a certificate of the facts to the relieving officer, as he often did in such cases; and he complained to the commissioners of the indescribable hardship to which the poor were continually subject for want of prompt assistance in need. The board said that Garvey was wrong as to the facts; the wife was not refused relief. She was offered the House.

In another case Humphrey Sibthorp complained through the press on behalf of two Washingborough widows, sisters, who had lived there for many years, each receiving from the Lincoln union a 6d. loaf and 2s. in money per week, with nothing but charity in addition. One died at 79, and the other aged 76, paralysed, nearly blind and almost bedridden, was told by the relieving officer that a fly was being sent to take her to the House. The fly did not arrive and relief was forgotten. When renewal of relief was sought on her behalf, it was refused, and she was offered the House. She wanted to die at home, and so she was left to starve. A move to compel aged women, living alone and receiving out relief, to live two in a house was defeated in 1847. It was no wonder that there was strong revulsion of feeling against the whigs, and a passionate hatred of the 'Bastilles' they had set up.

Pauper children were treated a little more kindly, though the conditions of living were harsh enough. When they went out to service, if of good character, they were given a Bible and prayer book, were fitted out, the contracts of service were approved, and track of them was kept if possible. The officers of the chargeable parishes were asked to help to find them work. Boys in the House were allowed an occasional bathe in the river, and they were sent for their walks in the fields and not in the streets. They were taught by their own schoolmaster, and there was an annual examination, often by a local clergyman, followed by buns and tea. Kindly residents paid for them to go to exhibitions and circuses, or for a trip on the river, and an inspector of schools presented a magic lantern. The number of children in the House varied; in 1867 there had been 24, but the next year there were only four boys and two girls

[1] Redlich and Hirst, *Local Government in England* (1903), I, 110.

above the age of 12. Presently there began an attempt to board them out.[1]

In 1850 a poor law inspector said that the rates had gradually increased by about £1,000 a year in his district, and he called on the guardians to carry the law more stringently into execution. He said that the vagrants had been reduced from 23,000 to 4,000 merely by washing them; but Finlay the governor said that had nothing to do with it, as they had not had a bath, the reason being merely that they had been refused admission.[2] It appears that the inspector privately signified his approval of the Lincoln union, the board being well attended by gentlemen: 'it's a good county'.[3] Certainly they gave little trouble to authority, and throughout the period there was little public interest in their proceedings or their elections. In 1852, for example, in the 86 parishes of the union, there was not a single contested election. St Swithin even sent the Roman Catholic priest, and several parishes made no election at all, and the old guardians continued to sit.

The records of the board throw some light on the volume of distress. Early in 1842 weekly payments of out relief in the home district – which included the city and a number of rural parishes – were about £70; in 1843 they ranged from £375 to £450; by 1847–8 they topped £700. Between 1840 and 1849 the number of applicants for relief in the home district rose from 306 to 915. The Poor Law Commissioners were told in 1843 that the increase of both in and out door relief was due to the depression of the time, the fall in agricultural wages and the small number employed. The agricultural interest predominated in the ranks of the guardians, and in 1854 they actually told the inspector that there was no scarcity of employment in the union area, where the average wage was 15s.[4]

They did not show much concern for vagrants, with many of whom it must have been difficult to sympathise. By 1847 there was difficulty in housing them all in the workhouse, and the next year they were behaving so violently that the workhouse master was empowered to get extra help in keeping order and discipline. In 1857 the problem of vagrancy was worse than ever. Beggar lads were said to be making 4s. or 5s. a day and spending it in smoking and drinking, and women in the lower parishes regularly let out their infants to beggars standing in the streets for 8d. a day.[5] Numbers were still worse in 1862.

---

[1] Below, pp. 294–5.   [2] Jarvis Diary, 27 February 1850.
[3] Cracroft, 20 March 1850.
[4] In 1855, owing to high prices, the outdoor allowance was increased to 3s. for adults and 1s. 9d. for children. The lower figures were restored in 1863.
[5] S.M., 13 February 1857.

The vagrants were of two classes: there were the distressed unemployed who would beg rather than go to the workhouse, and who were said in the county police report for 1866 to be comparatively few in number; and the majority who were born of tramp parents.[1]

Along with attempts by the public authorities to cope with destitution, vagrancy and crime went campaigns, the impetus to which came almost wholly from the churches, against two great moral and social evils.

Perhaps the graver problem was presented by the houses of ill-fame, concentrated in particular in the Castle Dykings, an extra-parochial place where there were no parish constables or other authorities to intervene. Already in 1830 there was a scheme for a charitable institution for the reformation of prostitutes. It was complained in 1836 that several tenements were being built for brothels, and that magistrates ought to stop them. Then in 1841 Mr Garvey appealed against immorality, and said that the victims were being prepared for the brothel and the prison. The magistrates directed the indictment of a number of brothel-keepers with a view to stemming the torrent of vice and crime that poured upon the city. Girls were being lured there at so much a week; when they lost their uses they were kicked out. The mayor even observed that there was more debauchery in Lincoln than in any other town of its size in the kingdom.[2] Press comment continued until in January 1846 the grand jury at the city quarter sessions called the attention of the city authorities to the state of the Castle Dyke, which was a sink of iniquity propagating vice and crime throughout the city; it was known that for some time the greater proportion of the crime committed in the city had originated there (though this was later denied) and they recommended that occupiers should be indicted. The recorder appealed to the town clerk, who said the misfortune was that the dyke being extra-parochial there was no person whose duty it was to originate proceedings.[3] The city council joined in condemnation, and directed the police to watch and bring offenders to justice: the council could not themselves prosecute, but any party proceeding by information and indictment would get costs awarded by the court.[4] In 2½ years 13 females from there had been taken into the workhouse in a diseased state, their average age being 18, and one of them 13. The road passing it now was entirely deserted by decent persons. Women died on an average in four years, and half became inmates of lunatic asylums and parish paupers.[5] In a prosecu-

[1] L.A.O., Foster Library, County Constabulary Report for 1866.
[2] S.M., 29 April 1842.   [3] S.M., 16 January 1846.
[4] C.M., 1836–47, pp. 678, 708, 779.
[5] S.M., 6 February 1846.

tion in 1848 William Andrew the solicitor said it was notorious that these houses were built for brothels, and had always been let for immoral purposes. One man had been murdered there, and Gardiner Hill the surgeon was ready to verify that he was continually being called in to girls who took poison.[1] In 1855 the dean and chapter took the initiative in putting down an infamous den of iniquity in Bullring Terrace, for the first time for many years freed from a nuisance which had demoralised the youth of the district and deteriorated the value of property.[2]

The magnitude of the evil prompted a movement among women, led by Mrs Carlisle. 'We were aware', said the *Mercury*, 'that the appearance of a bold and determined woman was only requisite to break down the prejudices of her sex, and kindle up those warm and zealous sympathies which must be productive of good.'[3] Evangelicals and dissenters and liberals supported her, and a meeting was called. It then emerged that in some Anglican circles the initiative was not welcome unless it came from the right source and the movement was in the right hands. It was announced that 'some friends of the undertaking who were of the communion of the Church of England, shortly afterwards felt themselves in a position to announce that the subject had been taken up by some of the clergy, that information, statistical and otherwise, was being collected, and that a plan would shortly be produced which, under the auspices of the Bishop of the Diocese and the Lord Lieutenant of the County should provide for the establishment of a Penitentiary on a scale adequate to the requirements, not of the City alone, but of the County at large'. The project thus pompously announced did not go well, nor did it succeed in defeating the smaller plan. After a first meeting at Newland chapel a public meeting was held in the city assembly room; it was supported by Lord Yarborough and Lord Monson, liberal peers, a few clergy and a number of dissenting ministers. In spite of attempts at discouragement by the dean and J. S. Gibney, the plan went on; the bishop was elected president, and the co-operation of the dean and his friends was invited.[4]

The first house taken was not large enough, and a home was built. The committee were scrupulously anxious not to offend religious susceptibilities, and emphasised in an annual report religious impartiality and toleration, family worship in the home; and attendance at church or chapel.[5]

---

[1] *S.M.*, 29 September 1848.   [2] *L.C.*, 5 October 1855.

[3] 25 December 1846.

[4] George Boole and E. R. Larken took an active part.

[5] See *Annual Reports* in L.P.L.

Though the home had success in individual cases the social problem remained. In 1865 Dr Richardson wrote in the *Medical Times* that there were 58 prostitutes in Lincoln who plied their calling in an open way and were all known to the police; but that in addition there was a large amount of secret prostitution. There were 22 brothels and 10 common lodging houses. At last in 1878 the city council adopted by-laws to enable their officers to take steps to suppress disorderly houses.

The other great social evil was drunkenness, an obstacle to progress and a rise in the standard of living. Sir Joseph Banks had said that if the necessaries of life were cheaper, the greater would be the indulgence in liquor insisted upon by workmen.[1] The problem was aggravated by the Sale of Beer Act of 1830, which established free trade in beershops and beer, it being argued that it would promote the sale of malt and hops, cheapen the poor man's beer, and lessen the sale of spirits. Its results were disastrous. There began a national campaign against a great national evil: and when a move was made in Lincoln in 1833 to form a temperance society it was hailed by the *Mercury* as one of the most important movements of the time. It was not only beer: dram drinking was rapidly on the increase, especially among women.[2] The large number of public houses was due in part to the large fairs and important weekly markets.[3] Evangelicals and dissenters worked together; and Mr Quilter the rector of Canwick and Mr Bergne the Independent minister, invoking the aid of Sir Edward Bromhead, launched the society. It was formed on the basis of voluntary agreement to abstain entirely from the use of distilled spirits, except for medicinal purposes, and to discourage intemperance of any kind. Frederick Kent the surgeon tried without success to include wine, on the ground that the rich ought to set an example.[4]

A temperance hotel was opened, and much propaganda was carried on, especially in the chapels; and to such an effect that some of the dram shops agreed to close on Sundays, and the beershops were exhorted to follow their example. For the purpose of providing an alternative to the public house a temperance hall was opened in Grantham Street to hold 700–1,000, in which zealous workers carried on an unending series of concerts and lectures. In 1863 there was a plan for a working men's hall

[1] *G.L.*, p. 190. The Willoughby agent said in 1857 that hard drinking was making fearful havoc in several tradesmen's families at Spilsby, as he supposed it did in all towns. L.A.O. 3 Ancaster 7/23/73, no. 77.
[2] 12 July 1833; *L.C.*, 23 August 1833.
[3] L.A.O. Cor. B. 5/9/10, report 14 May 1844, p. 36. At least there was no pawnshop (1844).
[4] *L.C.*, 13 September 1833.

for recreation and amusement – something between the Mechanics Institution and the public house. It was soon established, and many youths and young men frequented the coffee room, where a bagatelle board, chess and draughts were provided.[1] Yet the number of houses for the sale of beer and spirits grew from 150 in that year to 183 in 1869, which was one for every 25 families.[2] A lecturer from London declared that on an average a working man spent 5s. a week out of 20s. in beer and spirits. Nevertheless a meeting of the city council failed to get the necessary two-thirds majority in favour of the Early Closing Act of 1864.[3] The reformers were divided between those who advocated total abstinence from alcohol and those who advocated temperance; and the former did not always understand that the public house was the poor man's club, where he sought congenial company away from an overcrowded home and unpleasant surroundings.[4] But there could be no doubt about the gravity of the drink evil.

The greatest of all voluntary efforts at improvement of social conditions was in the schools, and the impetus came wholly from church and chapel. The public elementary school of the nineteenth century had grown out of the Sunday school, and secular instruction came second in importance both to religious instruction and to moral teaching to fit children for the place in life to which God had evidently called them. Sunday schools in Lincoln seem to have owed their origin to Dean Kaye, who planned four of them in 1785.[5] The next seems to have been a Methodist school opened perhaps in 1802–3, certainly by 1806.[6] About 1820 Matthew Turton, a wine merchant, opened a Sunday school, which in 1831 was granted part of the playground of the grammar school, and which at once had 120 scholars.[7] He added classes for writing and arithmetic on Wednesdays, and on Sunday evenings took the children to St Peter at Arches church. It was his custom to visit the parents and ask reasons for absence, and the evidence that he cared had its reward in the support that they gave him. Commendation of this school enabled the *Chronicle* to snipe at the parishes of St Botolph and St Peter at Gowts, the inhabitants of which, it said, 'have ever been noted for their slow progress in civilisation, and are yet far behind the other parishes in Lincoln', in spite of the efforts of the devoted curate, the Reverend William Brome-

---

[1] *S.M.*, 10 June 1864.   [2] *L.C.*, 1 May 1863, 2 April 1869.
[3] *C.M.*, 14 February 1870.
[4] This matter has been put into perspective by Brian Harrison, *Drink and the Victorians* (1971).
[5] *G.L.*, p. 71.
[6] G. Barratt, *Recollections of Methodism and Methodists in the City of Lincoln* (1866), p. 38.
[7] *S.M.*, 12 August 1831, 24 February 1832.

head, who had opened a Sunday school there some months before.[1] The Reverend William Bagge, curate of St Peter in Eastgate, opened a Sunday school there; when he left the parish Miss Cookson carried it on, turning it into a day school. In 1852 a pretty little Gothic schoolhouse was built for her by W. A. Nicholson, which is still in use.

The National School had been founded in Lincoln in 1812–13. The movement was conceived and wholly controlled by the Church of England; the catechism was taught and church attendance strictly enforced. Dissenters' children were admitted, but must observe the rules, though they might go with their parents to other places of worship at other times.[2] The clergy did not give much help, and may well have said, with H. V. Bayley, the archdeacon of Stow, that they saw positive danger in any attempt to take the minds of the poor from the manual employment and necessary labour which went with their occupations in life.[3] The registrar of the diocese complained to the bishop on the same point in 1839. After saying that they needed a better schoolmaster if they were to compete with other schools, raising his salary from £60 (and a house) to perhaps £100, he went on:

there has, I fear, been great neglect of late years in the superintendence by the clergy of the school. A friend mentioned to me a fact that on a Wednesday he met at the Dean's table 28 clergymen at the rent day. Mr Apthorpe the Secretary was the only one who met the Dean at the committee of the National School. I mention this fact to show to your Lordship the great want of attention to this school and in other matters which pervades the clergy of this place. If your Lordship could conveniently attend a meeting of the committee of the National School...it would, I am sure, have a good effect in producing more energy. But it is not only in attending the committees of the National School, but it is likewise as Visitors of the School...I am quite sure that if your Lordship should think fit to intimate to them the propriety of a cordial co-operation in an energetic superintendence it would be cheerfully complied with.[4]

To the competition of a number of private schools was added that of dissenting schools. About 1841 the Methodists grafted day and industrial schools on their Sunday schools. The bishop's inspector was much impressed by what he saw there, especially by the school library,

---

[1] *S.M.*, 10 February 1832; *L.C.*, 18 October 1833.
[2] *G.L.*, p. 283. The school was revived and reported on in 1835, it being emphasised that learning was subordinate to moral and religious improvement. Although there was a great need of Sunday schools such as Bromehead's, as a day school it was sufficient. *L.C.*, 26 June 1835.
[3] *Charge delivered to the Clergy of the Archdeaconry of Stow, 1826*, p. 12. Perhaps they remembered the saying that it was books that started the French Revolution.
[4] L.A.O. Cor. B. 5/4/150/6/1. Charlesworth confirmed that the clergy disliked the National School and thought the bishop would feel obliged to patronise it. Bromhead MSS, 16 June 1842.

and the avidity with which the children took the books. The buildings were soon found to be too small, and new schools were opened in Rosemary Lane in 1860 for 600 children. They were opened with 400 scholars, and were quickly filled, children being turned away.

When the Independents moved from Tanner's Lane and built a chapel in Newland in 1840 they decided to establish a school on the principles of the British and Foreign Schools Society, which did for dissenters what the National Society did for the Anglicans, save that its religious teaching was undenominational. It at once exceeded the National School in numbers, although it charged 2d. or 3d. a week instead of a penny. The Baptists opened another British School in Mint Lane.

A little earlier, in 1837 the Reverend J. O'Brien, priest of the Roman Catholic chapel in Silver Street, aided by subscribers, founded a school in Mint Lane, giving instruction irrespective of creed or religious opinion. The master, David Sampson, was a converted Jew, who had not had the advantage of having seen the working of a normal or training school, and moreover had to teach boys and girls in a crowded room.

About 1850 Benjamin Wilcox the chimney sweep started a Ragged School in his own house, which the *Chronicle* hailed as urgently necessary, especially in the wretched courts and alleys of St Botolph and St Peter at Gowts; Brogden, with unwonted humility, said of Wilcox, that he could never pass that humble yet noble-minded man without feeling dwarfed in his own estimation.[1] Wilcox was helped by others; and in 1858 Clayton and Shuttleworth lent their messroom for evening classes, beginning with Ragged School children, the intention being to extend the classes to foundry youths. After finding various homes the school planned a new building in Sparrow Lane, the prime movers being the archdeacon Kaye and two dissenting ministers (Goodwin and Metcalfe). It was opened by the bishop in 1866.

By 1841 there were also in being the Victoria Infant School in St Botolph's Green and the St Swithin's Infant School. In that year the city council had a survey made of all the day schools, giving their numbers, curriculum and accommodation, no doubt with a view to grants from the corporate funds.[2] In 1844 the bishop's inspector reported on the schools, having been allowed to include the non-Anglican schools. He estimated that there should be 1,800 children in school. There were then, adding 150 for schools he had not visited, 1,575. Allowing for those educated elsewhere, or ill, or in dames' schools, the number who were

---

[1] *L.C.*, 10 February 1860. Wilcox died in 1860, and a fund was raised for the erection of a monument.

[2] *C.M.*, 18 May 1841.

and the number who ought to be under instruction was not much different. As to quality, the broad results were gratifying, but wages were good, and were a great inducement to leave school, and it would be good if adult classes (like Mr Turton's) could be formed in the Sunday schools. He added that at the dames' schools the instruction was of the lowest description, pupils being sent rather to be kept out of the way at home and to learn to sew, rather than to acquire any mental cultivation.[1]

In these years the whig government made the first move to intervene in elementary education. In 1833 they procured a grant to the two school societies. Large areas of the country were left untouched, and of the grant the lion's share went to the National Society. Thereafter successive whig and tory governments were involved in battles between the church and dissent, the result of which was a kind of stalemate; and so in 1846 the privy council increased the parliamentary grant, with provision for the training of teachers. Some of the dissenters refused to accept the grant, preferring independence – among them the British school in Newland – and the Anglicans continued to receive the greater part of the money.[2]

In pursuance of a national Anglican scheme a Lincoln Diocesan Board of Education was set up, plans made for establishing a school for training masters, for bringing into union all the Anglican schools in the diocese and for collecting information with a view to extending education for the middle classes in connection with the Established Church. There was no enthusiasm for the training school in the diocese generally: Lincoln was too remote to interest those concerned with their own parish needs.[3]

The training school was built on a site in Newport, Lincoln, and a school for 200 boys planned to go with it. By 1841 the Reverend F. R. Crowther was appointed master, and besides all the obvious problems of a new school there were other questions. Were the boys to go to St Nicholas church for morning prayer by the master? The vicar was willing. But the master was against. He thought that some of the day scholars, children of dissenters, who did not object to the prayers used at the school and the instruction given there, might be removed if attendance at church was required. The proposal was abandoned. The school

---

[1] L.A.O. Cor. B. 5/9/10, report 14 May 1844, pp. 32–42.
[2] See Norman Gash, *Reaction and Reconstruction in English Politics 1832–52* (1965), chs. III and IV.
[3] An anonymous letter, printed in 1839, to the local board of management, assumed that the intention of the school to be started in connection with the training school was to provide for the children of professional men, the leading agriculturalists (who were treading closely on the heels of the country gentlemen) and the superior tradesmen, and suggested that a classical education would be best adapted for the purpose. L.A.O. Cor. B. 5/4/150, 8/1, 6/2–7, 7/1–4.

prospered, and quickly had 40 boarders and 34 day boys, and room was kept for five adults to be trained as teachers. By 1846 the little Gothic 'Diocesan Training School' was built.

High churchmen like Anderson were not satisfied. He noted at an examination that the church catechism and the principles embodied in it were not as prominent as they ought to have been. Obedience to the 'powers that be' was taught in history, but doctrines impugned by dissenters – baptismal regeneration[1] for one – ought to be brought forward. He was suspicious of the phrase in the school advertisements, that the business of the day began and ended with 'prayers and readings of the Holy Scripture'. This might mean church prayers and the lessons of the day, but it might mean extempore prayers and an exposition. He hoped that the so-called liberal systems of divinity would not be introduced for the sake of popularity.[2]

The bishop agreed with him that though the middle school had answered, the training school had failed. The former was closed and the training school converted into a training school for women.[3]

The Diocesan Board had to face the fact that dissenters had made enormous strides in the 1840s, in both chapels and schools; and the *Chronicle*, a candid friend, told them that in these years when dissenters had built many schoolhouses, the church remained in almost the same position as before, the numbers in the Diocesan School or in the private schools of churchmen not having made up for the decrease of more than one half in the numbers attending the National Schools. There they had dropped from 500 to 250 nominally, 160 or 170 attending. From figures given by the masters six months earlier, it said that of about 4,000 children in school, there were 2,990 in Anglican or dissenters' schools, the Anglicans having 1,442, and dissenters 1,548, of whom 57 were in the Roman Catholic school, It exhorted the church to give and do more, cheaply and better, than the dissenters.[4]

The board knew the challenge. It had a programme to provide seven

---

[1] This was a reference to the Gorham case. The doctrine was that the infant was regenerated by baptism; evangelicals said that baptism was a conditional sign of future regeneration.

[2] L.A.O. Cor. B. 5/4/150/7/2.

[3] Long afterwards archdeacon Kaye said that the school had failed as a training college for masters because young men thought that if they were to become masters of National Schools they must be trained in London: but it did not fail either as a school for the sons of gentlemen in the middle class of life or others who were not prepared to bear the expense of large public schools. He thought that the success of the women's training college was largely due to the personal influence of Bishop Jackson. *L.D.M.*, xvii (1901), 115. It is now the Grosseteste College. See D. H. J. Zebedee, *Lincoln Training College 1862–1962* (1962).   [4] *L.C.*, 14 September 1849.

schools in Lincoln, three above and three below hill, with an infant school added to the National School.[1] As a first step the bishop was trying to get a teacher for a school in St Paul's parish. Mr Richter, the rector, objected to having the sole superintendence, and wished the ministers of other parishes to be on the committee. The school was to be called the Lincoln North District National Schools, to serve the uphill parishes, and to give religious and secular instruction to boys, girls and infants. In drawing up the inscription to be placed on the building Richter took care to avoid offence; as it was desired to catch some of the dissenters they must not be scared. They had to have 'National School', as it involved a principle, but a bit of Latin would impress the parents, and enshroud it in that mystery which was always attractive with the uninstructed. The school was opened in 1852.[2]

The two groups of schools continued to exist side by side, raising their income partly by fees, and in some cases by government grants, but largely by voluntary giving, bazaars and the like. Edward Peacock, a sympathetic but detached observer, reviewed the scene about 1857:

...whether the high caste education which is now supplied by our National Schools be calculated to improve the tone of society in the next generation is a problem which time only can solve. Some entertain a sanguine anticipation of the most essential benefits, while others have very serious doubts whether it is not calculated to do more harm than good...

In addition however to the provision made for this purpose by our church establishment, the Roman Catholics, the Independents, the Baptists, the Wesleyan and Primitive Methodists and the Unitarians have each of them schools for effecting the same end; and there are also two schools for infants. The institutions, in the aggregate, cannot fail to effect a certain amount of good; and always open on the Sabbath day, the youth of all sects and parties are trained to habits of regularity and discipline, and taught their duty to God and man.

He turned then to the grammar school, and

the numerous seminaries of an independent nature for the board and education of youth of both sexes whose parents are able to give their children advantages of a superior character, communicate to their pupils classical, mathematical and scientific knowledge, and the more refined accomplishments of music, dancing, drawing, and the living languages, which enable them to move gracefully in the higher grades of society, and dignify and adorn the sphere, whatever it may be, in which they are destined to move in after life.[3]

Between the two spheres there was a great gulf fixed, which was assumed to be impassable.

Fresh impetus was given to the movement for more schools by the long

[1] *L.C.*, 30 April 1852.   [2] L.A.O. Cor. B. 4/100/4.
[3] MS in my possession, p. 128.

argument about extension of the franchise which ended in the Reform Bill of 1867. William Rudgard told a parish meeting of St Martin that there was property belonging to Wilkinson's trustees which formerly supplied a school for the Bail and Newport, but which had long ceased to exist. Application was made to the Charity Commissioners for leave to sell it and devote a portion of the funds for the benefit of St Martin. The commissioners granted £1,200 on condition that St Michael could participate; and plans for a new school for 500–600 children were put in hand.

The new buildings were opened by Bishop Jackson in January 1868. He said that there were at the primary church schools in Lincoln (including the Victoria and Bluecoat schools) 1,266 children; at non-church schools (including the Ragged School) 1,037; at private schools, day schools and some of the higher class schools 677; making in all 2,980 children at the various schools in the city. Assuming that the population was 24,000 and that one-sixth of it should be at school, there ought to be 3,840 (*sic*) at school; there was therefore a deficiency of about 900 to be provided for. He admitted that the nonconformists, especially the Wesleyan Methodists, had done more than their share in educating the poor, and they fully deserved the acknowledgment of the people of Lincoln; but the church was not relieved from doing its fair share of the work. As to St Martin, the population of the parish was 4,000; there ought to be 400 at the Church school, instead of the existing 100. He was not surprised that the government inspector had stated that in no town he had visited had so little been done by the church towards educating the people as in Lincoln; a statement he had found to be correct. He thought the reason was partly that there were so many small parishes. It would be better that each parish should have its own schools, but many of them in Lincoln were too small to do this, and they were obliged to combine, in which system there were many evils.[1]

The other swollen parish was St Swithin, and here a site was given for a school at Stamp End by Coningsby Sibthorp, and fund raising began. The *Chronicle* extolled the work done by voluntary effort in the schools:

The school question has not been taken up in Lincoln as a mere hobby horse. Young as the colt may be, it promises to take a foremost position in the popular education race. But to do this it must be given its head, and not ridden by a Government jockey from the Board of Education.[2]

The race was already doomed to be lost.

Apart from the schools, a young man of promise and determination

---

[1] *L.C.*, 10 January 1868.   [2] *L.C.*, 6 January 1871.

could find a well disposed citizen to give him a hand. The few men of lively mind to be found in the city seized upon the opening provided by the formation of a Mechanics Institute. This was part of a movement for the education of working men which had spread rapidly throughout the country, largely through the restless energy of Henry Brougham.

A first attempt to form one in Lincoln failed because it was thought that it would degenerate into a political debating society, and certainly the most active promoters were well known radicals, led by W. S. Northhouse. Their efforts were successful in 1833; part of the Jersey school, on the ground floor of the Greyfriars, was secured as premises, and the New Permanent Library, a lately established lending library, agreed to merge in the institution. Lord Yarborough became patron, Sir Edward Bromhead president, and Northhouse secretary, presently to be succeeded by James Hitchens. The committee stood firmly by the rule excluding politics and controversial divinity from its activities. Bromhead was careful to say at the foundation meeting that 'here we are, whigs, tories and I believe radicals, all agreeing and combining to set the Witham on fire', though it was evident that the Sibthorps and other tory houses, and most of the clergy, were conspicuous by their absence.

John Boole the cobbler for a time acted as honorary curator, his son George taught there, and was joined by Dr Cookson, W. A. Nicholson the architect, and Cooper. Boole senior was soon to protest against the sacrifice of utility to the frivolities of light reading and conversation meetings. But facts for their own sake were a dreary and arid fare: the emblems of 'literature and science' to be carried in procession on the celebration of the coronation were a picture of Sir Isaac Newton, a geological map, globe, electrifying machine, steam engine, telescope, galvanic battery, and chart of the kings and queens of England accompanied by a banner with the motto 'Wisdom is the principal thing'.

Too much was expected of working men after a day's work. The forthright Charlesworth was not surprised that the results did not come up to expectation. He wrote:

14 June 1836. Hunt is surprised at the apathy of the Mechanics, under such efforts to please and excite them. I tell him that bodies of (really) working people can not be simultaneously roused except under the stimulus of opposition, or excited vanity, or politics, or religion, or I might have added by offering such special endeavours to attract the females of their families.[1]

Some years later he wrote of a visit to the Institute:

*29 July 1859...*where I at this moment find a display of more confusion, dinginess and dirtiness than I ever remember to have witnessed in one single room in my whole life.

[1] Bromhead MSS.

The books were dirty, there was a stifling smell, the ceiling was black with smoke and there was no fresh air.[1] About the same time Cooper, who had long left Lincoln, wrote that the Institutes were confessed by their best and worthiest supporters to have failed in their purpose.[2] Nevertheless they did good as night schools at an elementary level.

Socially Sir Edward Bromhead, baronet of Thurlby near Lincoln, belonged to the gentry. His interests were elsewhere. He was a scholar by nature, a considerable mathematician, a botanist and an antiquary; he took a close interest in social problems, helping friendly societies to find solvency by regulation of subscriptions and benefits, and promoting the temperance society. Perhaps it is not surprising that some at least of the gentry regarded him as a busybody, and a few wrote him off as crazy.[3]

Dr Edward Parker Charlesworth was a staunch whig, though caring more, Cracroft thought,[4] for the Pelham and Monson families than for the principle itself. Certainly he was a faithful satellite of Bromhead, who was a conservative.[5]

Thomas Cooper belongs chiefly to the history of Chartism, though his Chartist period was a small part of his life. He had been apprenticed to a cobbler, and moved to Lincoln from Gainsborough in 1833, setting up a school. For a time he was Lincoln correspondent of the *Stamford Mercury*. Later he lived in Leicester, and became a leader of the Chartists there, being imprisoned for two years for complicity in riots in the Potteries. He made a great impression on Charles Kingsley, who used him as the model of his hero in *Alton Locke*. There is an interesting comment on him from his wife's cousin George Boole:

15 January 1847. I am afraid that in my account of Cooper (judging from the impression it produced in your mind) I scarcely did him justice. It is true that he is vain and perhaps pedantic, but after all he has a good deal that might justify vanity, if anything could in such creatures as we are, and then he is so honest and sincere and open that perhaps his vanity may not be greater than that of many who are not thought to be at all conspicuous for that quality, but only more exposed to view.[6]

His later years were spent in Lincoln. When the General Baptists there decided to build a new chapel in 1884 he was the first subscriber, and it was partly in recognition of his service to the chapel that the building was named after him.[7]

[1] *Ibid.*
[2] *Cooper's Journal*, I, 1. The minutes of the Institute are in L.P.L. MS 5108–13.
[3] See *G.L.*, index.   [4] Cracroft, 23 February 1853.
[5] See *G.L.*, pp. 277–81.
[6] Letter from Boole to E. R. Larken, from a copy kindly lent to me by the late A. P. Rollett.
[7] See his autobiography, *Life of Thomas Cooper* (1872), and *Thoughts at Fourscore* (1885); R. J. Conklin, *Thomas Cooper the Chartist* (Manila, 1935); *Annual Register* (1892). The late

George Boole belongs to the history of mathematics. He took part in the founding of the Mechanics Institute, and the desire to provide leisure for study led to his joining in the movement for the earlier closing of shops. He had been to an elementary school; he was taught Latin, according to one account, by William Brooke, the bookseller, and according to another at Thomas Bainbridge's private school; and he taught himself Greek, French and German. He acquired such a reputation as a mathematical writer that in spite of the lack of a degree he was appointed professor of mathematics at the newly founded Queen's College, Cork, in 1849. He died in 1864, and is commemorated by a window in Lincoln cathedral.[1]

Boole's friend, William Brooke the bookseller, had succeeded his father in the business, where he had a circulating library of 2,000 volumes; he had worked in the British Museum and the Bodleian Library, and gave some of the results of his work in local history in *Tracts and Miscellanies*, and a number of other pamphlets which occasionally occur bound up together. He was for some years correspondent of the *Mercury*, being an ardent liberal.

Another member of the circle was Edward James Willson, architect and antiquary, and the best helper John Britton could get in drawing up his accounts of the cathedral. Britton wrote of him in an obituary notice:

When in his teens, and working for his father, who was a respectable builder in Lincoln, I met him in the cathedral of his native city, where he was occupied in carving some of the fine stall work, which first awakened his young fancy, and admiration for that species of beauty.

They became friends for life, and did much work together.[2] Willson was a Roman Catholic and a friend of Pugin, but he was on friendly terms with the dean (Gordon) and Archdeacon Bayley recommended him to direct some work at the minster, and he became architect and surveyor to the county.[3]

In 1843 the Reverend Edmund Roberts Larken was presented to the living of Burton by his brother-in-law the sixth Lord Monson. He was active in Oxford affairs, proclaiming himself a disciple of Richard

Cecil Radford passed on to me the memory that by reason of deafness Cooper would sit on the pulpit steps during the sermon, and make audible comment on the doctrine handed down from above.

[1] *British Quarterly Review*, LXXXVII, 2 July 1866; and an article by his grandson Sir Geoffrey Taylor F.R.S. in *Proceedings of the Royal Irish Academy* LVII, 66–73. Mr Rollett was engaged upon a biography of Boole when he died. It is hoped that his son will complete the work.

[2] *The Builder*, XIII, 4–5, 6 January 1855.

[3] He died in 1854. H. M. Colvin, *Biographical Dictionary of English Architects, 1660–1840* (1954), *sub nom. G.L.*, p. xii. His son Thomas John Willson, also an architect, accompanied Francis Penrose to Athens for the purpose of measuring the Parthenon.

Whateley, who had been professor of political economy there before he became archbishop of Dublin. He later aspired to a chair in that subject himself, first at Oxford and then at Lausanne. These ambitions were not realised; but he threw himself into the campaign for Christian socialism, especially in the co-operative movement. He took a leading part in the Leeds Redemption Society – to enable the working classes to work out their own redemption by union amongst themselves. It threw off many branches, but the parent society at Leeds was wound up in 1855. He was secretary of a scheme for self-supporting villages.[1] In Lincoln he had Brooke print for him a pamphlet on the Ten Hours Question in 1846; he was a promoter of the Penitent Females Home: and he was president of the first co-operative flour mill in Lincoln, taking inspiration from a like venture at Hull. It was said that there were 15,000 shareholders with shares of £1, paid by instalments. Ten years later the project failed, owing, it was said, to mismanagement, lack of skill, and want of unity of purpose.[2]

He acted as representative in Lincoln of the absent Monson, especially in politics. He often sought preferment, but without success; he was no doubt thought dangerous. Though he dropped out of public affairs, he led a full life. On Sundays he would take four or five services: for the volunteers, whose chaplain he was, at the barracks at 9; at Burton at 11 and 3; and then in Lincoln at the penitentiary and the asylum.[3]

The ignorant and sluggish majority found no use for newsrooms. The City Newsroom (started for war news in 1793) was sold up in 1843; a People's Newsroom ran for a short time at the City Assembly Rooms. Uphill the County Newsroom fared better. It came through a great battle about Sunday opening in 1838, acquired new premises on Castle Hill in 1843, and was closed and advertised for sale in 1851 though it succeeded in re-opening, offering the new amenity of hot and cold baths. For ten years there was a newsroom at the Corn Exchange, but it closed for lack of support in 1861.

There had been several literary societies, and in 1814 the Lincoln Library had been formed, which by 1827 had 270 members, among them gentry, clergy, merchants and tradesmen, and the library acquired

---

[1] W. H. G. Armytage, *Heavens Below* (1961), pp. 211–18; L.A.O. *Annual Report*, 22 (1970–1), p. 43.

[2] *S.M.*, 24 July 1857.

[3] He died in 1895 at the age of 85. *L.C.*, 2 March 1895; Publications of the Thoresby Society, Monograph III, 'James Hull and Social Reform in Leeds' (1954). According to Holyoake, Larken was the first clergyman to wear a beard in the pulpit, though he wore it only below the chin. The innovation was thought to be serious, indicating laxity in theological principles. G. J. Holyoake, *Sixty Years of an Agitator's Life* (1893), I, 237.

1   The Brayford Pool and Lincoln Cathedral (1838) by James Wilson Carmichael

2 City of Lincoln, south view from Canwick, _c._ 1870

3   Protectionist meeting in the Corn Exchange, January 1850

4 Great Protectionist meeting in the Castle Yard, February 1850

5 Agricultural meeting at Lincoln: Messrs Clayton and Shuttleworth's works and the show yard, August 1869

6   Lincoln Horse Fair, May 1870

7a   The floods in January 1871 – view from Bracebridge

7b   A street in Lincoln during the floods of 1871

8 Catching a poacher! Cobden and Sibthorp by H.B. (1845)

6,000 books. Though it was frequently rent by dissension it served a most valuable purpose, and continued until 1909. Music flourished for a time; at one subscription concert Paganini appeared, and sacred music was said to be nobly supported.[1] But societies, the Choral Society, the Harmonic Society, and the Sons of Vulcan, which was a glee club, came and went rather quickly.

In these years the county hospital, then on Steep Hill,[2] was struggling with fearful difficulties. Its water supply had been condemned, though the Waterworks Company had been able to provide a fresh one. It was too small and overcrowded, its air space half what it should be, and the medical men said the building could never be made fit. With the aid of an appeal for funds it had been able to add thirty beds and an operating room and it joined with the Lawn (mental) Hospital in sharing a sewer which discharged into Brayford. On an average there was one nurse to twelve patients, but the nursing system was deplorable:

The night nurses are old women living in the city, who often have been at work all day before they come to the Hospital – worn out before their most important labours commence; their night duties are performed with the most scrupulous observance of the rules laid down by that most eminent authority, Mrs Gamp – that is to say, they sleep as much as they can, and leave the sick as long as is possible to the care of their useful sister, Nature. In cases where the patients are seriously ill, or where special watching has to be maintained, the House Surgeon is in the habit of visiting the wards at all hours of the night. That he may not find his weird watchers slumbering, they strew cinders along the passages, that he may crunch them on his way, and use other and similar tricks to raise the necessary alarm and report who is coming.

This was written in 1864.[3]

Reform was not easy. Although the Hospital's constitution was complicated, with its weekly board which any subscriber of £2 2s. could attend, real control was in the quarterly board which was in the hands of gentry and clergy, the presence of the mayor being sufficient to represent the city at the meetings that mattered. The doctors were constantly quarrelling, and the meetings notoriously stormy, as Cracroft noted in 1849. On that occasion, he said, there was a religious dispute between professing Christians, many of them clergy. The business was the election of a matron, who must be a member of the Church of England. Miss Kirkby was supported by the church and landed interest; Miss Howitt

---

[1] *G.L.*, pp. 279–81, 291. See *Lincs. N. & Q.*, XII (1912), 97–106. *Reminiscences and Biographical Sketches of Eminent Musicians*, composed and compiled by R. Charlton, Lincoln, 1836. Bromhead Tracts in Exley Collection in L.P.L.

[2] *G.L.*, pp. 70, 281. The building now houses the Lincoln Theological College.

[3] Thomas Sympson, *Short Account of the Old and the New Lincoln County Hospitals* (1878), p. 18. For Mrs Gamp, see *Martin Chuzzlewit*, ch. xxv.

by Dr Charlesworth, Captain Wright, Richard Mason the town clerk, James Snow, the rector of Brattleby (Carr), and, by proxy, Lady Yarborough and Mr Chaplin. She was also supported by the dissenters. It was said that Miss Howitt had been a member of an Independent congregation, but had taken the sacrament in the Church of England several times, and had a certificate of membership. Naturally it was alleged that she had become an Anglican to qualify for the post. Nevertheless Miss Howitt was elected, and Carr told Cracroft that the bishop would have voted for her.[1] She was, however, discharged for incompetence the next year, and her competitor, Miss Kirkby, appointed, giving rise to corresponding suspicions on the other side.

The radical and dissenting party was creating faggot votes by taking up governorships at £2 2s. and a reporter got in at the price. The country governors often did not attend the weekly meetings, which meant that on small matters the townsmen might get their way. There followed a demand that church tracts should not be distributed to Roman Catholics or dissenters. The matter went to the quarterly board, and the arguments of some of the clergy that the church should not give way in what was claimed as a church institution was defeated on Charlesworth's motion: the bishop supported him, saying that Roman Catholic subscribers recommended patients of their own church, and they had a right not to have their beliefs intererefed with.[2]

There were also troubles about nursing, and Miss Anderson, sister of Sir Charles, who had been out in the Crimea, offered to take charge of the nursing; but as her religious principles were objected to, the bishop withdrew her offer. Then the head nurse gave notice, and it was resolved to try to do without one.

In 1864 Mrs Annie Bromhead, daughter of Colonel Jarvis of Doddington, assisted by a committee of ladies, offered to institute a better system of nursing, and its management was handed over to them. A head nurse and eight others were to be employed. There followed rows between the matron, the head nurse and the house surgeon. The head nurse resigned and her resignation was put on the file, and they were all told to go on quietly. Another head nurse entered the board room, called the chancellor a liar and a hypocrite, and threatened to bring actions against everybody. She was ordered to leave that day.

By 1866 Mrs Bromhead had had enough. She wrote that:

Different causes, to which it is unnecessary now to allude, have deprived me of the assistance of head nurses one after another, and the combined opposition I

[1] Cracroft, 6 February 1849.
[2] L.A.O. Cor. B. 5/4/106/6.

have met with in the Hospital convinces me that it is hopeless to expect that we can any longer administer the funds committed to our charge with benefit to the nursing in the Hospital.

The committee of the Nursing Fund accordingly gave notice to resign their connection with the hospital and the quarterly board decided to have nothing more to do with the ladies' meeting. The quarrel was clearly with the doctors. When the matter was discussed the chancellor said he did not want to go back to the bad old days. Melville recalled the quarrels of the past 30 years, and cited a letter from Florence Nightingale saying that the worst hospitals were those where the doctors had control; and the doctors ought to have nothing to do with the weekly board. The bishop said that the new system had not been fully tried.[1] Later Alderman Harvey, a doctor, said they now saw the result of giving power to ladies of delicate rearing and health, who would not make the sort of nurse they needed. An attempt to make a lady superintendent the principal authority was defeated.[2]

There was no room for two autocracies in the hospital. Mrs Bromhead then founded the Institution for Trained Nurses, which was the origin of the Bromhead Nursing Home. At one time several of her nurses worked among the sick poor at the workhouse, until she withdrew them owing to the regulations of the Local Government Board. She died in 1883.[3]

The hospital still suffered from the inadequacies of the building, and at last the governors resolved that they must start on a new site. Plans were prepared for a hospital of 120 beds, and Brownlow was asked as lord lieutenant to lay the foundation stone. On this he wrote to Monson:

5 May 1876. I am also somewhat deterred by the feeling that the county has not taken up the new hospital very warmly, and the town of Lincoln has, and therefore I am not sure that it would be quite civil of me to take a leading part in the affair as representing the county, and in a sort of way cutting out the town, which has done so much.[4]

He did in fact lay the stone, and the new building was opened in 1878. There at once began the great Hospital Saturday collections in the works and from house to house which continued until the end of the voluntary hospital system.

This was the great age of voluntary effort for the improvement of social conditions. Much of the impetus came from the upper and middle classes for the benefit of the poorer classes. But with some help the latter did

[1] *L.C.*, 19 October 1866.   [2] *L.C.*, 18 January 1867.
[3] Lady Robertson, 'A Victorian Venture' in *Lincolnshire Magazine*, II (1934), no. 2. Mrs Bromhead was succeeded as superintendent of the institution by her daughter Henrietta Bromhead, who held office until her death in 1907.
[4] L.A.O. Monson 25/13/2/10/9.

much for themselves. The friendly society movements made great prog-ress after the Reform Bill campaign. The Lincoln General Friendly Institution came into being in 1829, and helped to support its members during illness. The energetic James Hitchens formed the Russell Lodge of Oddfellows: it enrolled many distinguished honorary members, and its annual procession exceeded in number, respectability and imposing appearance anything of the kind seen before in Lincoln.

Long afterwards Charles Keyworth recalled that about 1836 a few working men, tanners by trade, knowing apparently the excellent prin-ciples of Oddfellowship, induced a few others to join with them to form the City of Lincoln Lodge, under dispensation from the Hull district. It had 24 members and met at a public house in an obscure part of the city. It was looked upon with scorn and he too had laughed; but he had later been proud to join.[1]

By 1859 there were five lodges of the Manchester Unity of Oddfellows in Lincoln: there was a weekly benefit of 10s. during sickness, and £1 10s. funeral benefit. There was a widows' and orphans' provident fund.[2]

In these early days it is hardly possible to distinguish trade unions from friendly societies. Tradition says that a branch of the Mechanics Union was formed in 1848. There was industrial action at Claytons in 1851, when 60 engine fitters struck, choosing a time when there was a great demand for engines. It was said that their earnings ranged from 26s. to £2 a week, but the men alleged that their average was below 32s., which was less than the average in other towns. They wanted a reduction of hours from $59\frac{1}{2}$ per week, to the usual $57\frac{1}{2}$, to cut out systematic overtime, it being paid when necessary at the rate of time and a quarter. They were against piece-work, and they sought dismissal of men who had not been apprenticed, with a limitation of one apprentice to four men. The men on strike received 10s. a week from the club, they picketed the works and railway stations and when men came by train to seek work they were taken to public houses, regaled, and packed off again. They succeeded in getting concessions: a $58\frac{1}{2}$ hour week was agreed, and 2 hours overtime was to count as $2\frac{1}{2}$ hours. The men were told by their delegates that they must accept the terms or leave the club.

In 1859, under the influence of the London builders' strike, the operative stone masons proposed that they be allowed to leave work at 4 o'clock on Saturdays. The masters agreed, though they objected on principle to combinations of workmen. In 1864 the masters, finding trade

---

[1] L.C., 27 April 1860. This became the Lincoln district of the Manchester Unity of Oddfellows. L.P.L. U.P. 480.
[2] L.C., 5 August 1859.

bad, wanted to reduce the daily wage by 6d. which would have left the weekly wage at 24s. It was settled at 25s. In 1867 the bricklayers struck for a rise from 4s. 6d. to 4s. 8d. per day, with a Saturday half holiday. The Saturday claim was abandoned, but wages were increased to 27s. a week. Some of the other trades were less successful. In 1868 the tailors struck against a revision of the tariff; the masters refused to take them on again, and non-society men were employed.[1] There were fluctuations in wages owing to trade conditions, but on the whole they crept up slightly.

The members of the Boilermakers Society, a lodge of Oddfellows, and the Lincoln branch of the Amalgamated Society of Engineers all celebrated in 1857, the engineers drinking to the health of the Lincoln firms. The friendly societies grew rapidly. In 1868, 4,000 members attended service at the cathedral, and in 1869 the Lincoln district of Oddfellows (Manchester Unity) had 24 lodges, over 2,490 members and a capital of £1,200; they attributed their improved finances to the Friendly Societies Act, the growing intelligence of members and the discarding of expensive mummeries.[2]

The hours of work in shops were being gradually reduced. In 1839, drapers, whose assistants were in the shops from 12 to 14 hours a day, began to close at 8 o'clock. An early closing movement had little immediate success; but in 1853 grocers' assistants asked the mayor to persuade their masters to close at 8 o'clock instead of 9, and succeeded. Solicitors began to close at 2 o'clock on Saturdays. By 1859 drapers were closing at 7 o'clock and grocers followed suit in 1867 except on market days and Saturdays. With the provision of even a little leisure, organised sport was becoming possible.

---

[1] *S.M.*, 9 December 1864, 3 May 1867, 14 February 1868.
[2] *S.M.*, 15 January 1869.

CHAPTER VIII

PROBLEMS OF PUBLIC HEALTH

Most of the new population lived in new houses, small and poor and packed tightly together in courts and alleys. The kind common to the area was described in 1842 as consisting of a common sitting room of from 12 to 14 feet square, with a small kitchen and pantry, with one or two sleeping rooms on the first floor. The common cost of building such a house was about £50, and the average cost of repair from 5s. to 10s. a year. In the country there would be a garden; with it, the rent might be from £3 10s. to £4 a year; without it, and without even accommodation for a pig, it would be from 30s. to £2 10s. An unmarried lodger might pay 6d. to 1s. a week for a single room.[1]

Rents in Lincoln were higher than this. The *Mercury* said these houses would let at rents of from £5 to £6 per year, the cost of 'these worse than Indian wigwams' being only £25 each. House room was so scarce that in two small rooms in St Swithin there were 20 persons lodging.[2] In 1841 the average number of persons per house for the whole city was 4.75, and it varied hardly at all in the next half century. In the bad areas it must have been much higher.

Even when these houses were building there was denunciation by enlightened opinion. Hainworth the surgeon read a paper to the Lincoln Topographical Society in 1844 on the dwellings of the poor and labouring classes in the city, with ideas for its complete drainage. The increase of tenants within ten years he stated to be 1,000, and the demand for houses had outrun the supply. The badness of the site of some dwellings at Stamp End was said to be such that the inmates were driven to occupy the upstairs rooms for a fortnight together, the filth from the swampy ground on which they stood rising as high as the first step, and sending up the most pestiferous exhalations. Uphill, the refuse water, running into the fissures of the rock, found its way under the thin upper layer, and sent up perpetual damp to the houses above: three years after some new houses thus situated had been erected they became little less than a fever hospital, and in one small row there were 22 persons ill of fever during one season.

[1] *Sanitary Inquiry – England. Local Reports on the Sanitary Condition of the Labouring Population of England*, 1842, p. 153. The inspector thought that the exemption of cottages from rating was injurious to the labouring class, because it made the worst description of cottage property the most remunerative to the owners. He thought the owners should be rated.
[2] *S.M.*, 25 June 1847, 12 May 1848.

The mixture of houses, cowsheds, pigsties and dunghills in the small squares of Newport could not fail to endanger the health of the population.

Hainworth said that being in attendance on a female who lived in the Castle Dyke, he saw that the walls of the house were damp and filthy, and found that at the back were cowsheds and pigsties: the husband was warned of the probable consequences of dwelling amid such a pestilence, but he would take no heed. Next year he himself, his wife and one of the children were carried off by the fever, and the remainder of the family were left to be brought up by the parish.[1]

The 'little landlords' who put up these houses were to become a grave obstruction to public health measures when the latter became practicable, but at the time of building Hainworth's attack was more an indictment of the lack of water and sewerage than of the builder. Sir John Clapham has pointed out that at least the jerry-builder was not responsible for the lack of planning, paving and draining. The water-closet and the iron water main were barely invented, and a cheap method of making earthenware drainpipes was unknown.[2]

Certainly these houses were better than the mud and stud and thatched cottages which were still being built in the villages: in 1849 an estate agent wrote of the rebuilding of cottages that 'the *mud walls* is getting more in favour with me. For £20 a good sized cottage may be built, to last 80 years, which is better than a high-rented one for the labourer.'[3]

It is not surprising that in these circumstances a cholera alarm in 1831 started a long campaign for the improvement of these conditions in the city. The Lincoln Board of Health,[4] a voluntary body without powers, tried to find places in which to put patients if the cholera broke out, the city council refusing them both the racecourse stand and the Jersey School, the latter being too near the grammar school. When the panic subsided subscriptions fell off, and the board continued to exist only in name. An application from a society for establishing public baths for a site for the erection of warm baths was similarly refused.

There was all manner of public complaint, notably of the liquid filth pumped into the gutter from the butchery, for which the council felt obliged to provide a sewer, whereafter the filth appeared on the surface of the river. The practical difficulty in which individuals found themselves is illustrated by the plight of Mr Moss, of the Lion and Snake inn, who was fined for putting noisome fluids into the street channels. His yard was lower than the street; in it was a well for the reception of

[1] *S.M.*, 22 March 1844.   [2] *Economic History of Modern Britain*, 1 (1926), 164–5.
[3] L.A.O. 3 Ancester 7/23/55, no. 39.   [4] *G.L.*, pp. 216–17.

rainwater, but he could not deepen it without putting stagnant water into fresh water wells on both sides, which were used for drinking. What was he to do?[1]

The problems of public health in Lincoln were reviewed by the Lincoln registrar in reply to the queries of the Registrar General in 1843. There was, he said, a factory building in St Botolph which had for years past been converted into lodging houses or rooms for tramps; during the prevalence of cholera it was the only parish which was attacked and two only died. Courts and alleys made the parish more unhealthy. Deaths had increased in St Martin and St Michael owing to the increase of small houses. The former Board of Health had found new St Swithin the most unhealthy, and procured a new tunnel, working some improvement. Places on the hillside were bad, though the fall of the hill and the presence of a river ought to make drainage easy. His description of conditions generally is of special interest:

The labouring population is not very large; their occupations are as millers, watermen, coal-porters and artisans occupied in building. Several small houses have of late been erected in the outskirts of the city, rendered necessary from the pulling down of the 'harbour houses' of the adjoining country parishes, and to which agricultural labourers repair. Wages are tolerably good, and the food comprises bread and potatoes, and, perhaps one day in the week, meat. The habits of the poor are generally temperate, and comparatively little drunkenness prevails. The drink is generally ale; very little alcohol is taken. Coals are tolerably moderate in price, and with the eleemosinary channels, public and private, little want of firing is felt. Our main streets are wide – generally 40 feet; and the outskirts of the city border on cultivated lands, which I consider one great means of health.

He thought the provision of footpaths and surface channels would encourage cleanliness: efforts to that end were being made.[2]

As typhus and smallpox continued to recur, definition of existing powers was sought. The Lighting and Paving Commissioners could make channels, and their surveyor could take steps to prevent nuisances; and the council agreed with them to experiment in the appointment of an inspector of nuisances. On their part the council's sanitary committee suggested that the commissioners should make arrangements with the Waterworks Company for the flushing of gutters with the company's water; but another alarm having gone by, this was thought too expensive. The council also approached owners of steam chimneys and asked them to adopt some efficient apparatus for consumption of smoke. A Nuisances Removal Act of 1860 gave the guardians some public health powers.

[1] *S.M.*, 18 December 1840.   [2] *S.M.*, 11 August 1843.

An observer of actual conditions could hardly have been aware of the existence of these various powers. It was said in 1848 that chandling houses annoyed the occupants of every street, and skinyards, places for boiling dead horses, pigsties and crowded stables formed the chief subject of complaint. Some of the churchyards were so full as to be an abomination, and neighbours had to keep their windows shut. The number of deaths continued to rise. The number for the quarter ending 30 September 1848 in the guardians' home district (the city and a number of country parishes) was 123; five or six years earlier the average had been about 80; of the increase 36 were due to causes which were remediable. 'But', said the *Mercury*, 'let an alderman be struck to death, and the whole city will be horror-struck.'[1] Measures to remove pigsties were at once denounced as an attack on the poor man's pig.

It was true that the churchyards, each under the control of a vicar and churchwardens, had become hopelessly inadequate. Complaints were first heard about St Peter at Arches, where in 1834 burials were said to be not two feet underground; dogs scratched up the mounds, and lads defaced the tombstones. There were mounting complaints of overcrowding and stench, and in 1847 there occurred an incident which set the subject ablaze. A gravedigger was digging a grave in St Benedict's churchyard, and came upon the coffin of a man who had died ten years earlier; his name and the date of his death were plainly visible on the coffin-plate. The coffin was broken to pieces, and the human remains thrown out. The widow was passing, and actually saw the bones of her late husband.[2]

There ensued a discussion of the need for a general cemetery, but it was said that this would require the consent of the bishop and all the parochial clergy, and also that of all parties living near the proposed site. After some havering the council began to enquire about a site, no doubt stimulated thereto by the Public Health Act 1848, and impending legislation which would empower the closing of cemeteries by order. As matters moved slowly St Swithin provided itself with a new cemetery in Rosemary Lane. The council then issued a public appeal for funds, saying that if two-thirds of the parishes concurred, it would subscribe towards expenses.

Procrastination came to an end with the announcement of a visit by an official from the Central Board of Health. By October 1854 it was known that all the city burial grounds would be closed except the new St Swithin. There followed a meeting of a committee for the formation of a

---

[1] *S.M.*, 6 October 1848.
[2] *L.C.*, 24 September 1847.

burial board. Separate boards were formed for St Nicholas and St John (Newport), and for St Peter in Eastgate with St Margaret. St Swithin was provided for. All the other parishes joined together. The Rev. J. S. Gibney became chairman and the solicitor William Andrew, who had campaigned for a cemetery for some years, joint clerk. The board bought 20 acres of land on Canwick Road from the council, thus severing the cowpaddle from the south common.[1]

The cemetery became a battle ground between church and chapel. Part of it must be consecrated, for Anglicans, and part left unconsecrated, for dissenters; but when a plan was produced for two chapels, each costing £500, Gibney protested. The majority of the burials would be in the consecrated portion, and the greater part of the money would come out of the pockets of churchmen, for dissenters were the poorer part of the population. For the dissenters Mr Freshney objected to a plan that would put the Anglican chapel on the hill, while the dissenters' chapel was put in the valley and their burials in the low ground, which was more likely to flood. Lengthy argument ended with the chapels side by side, though there was only one bell, and that on the episcopalian part of the building.

One of the greatest needs of the city was an adequate supply of good water, not only for flushing street channels, but still more for domestic purposes. In the sixteenth century the city had obtained a grant of the water supply of the Grey Friars, who had been given leave to lay their pipeline from the Monks lands through the city's common land, and the water was led to a conduit which still stands in front of St Mary le Wigford's church.[2] This supply cannot ever have served the whole city, which must always have been partly dependent on wells, some public and some private.

Murmurings about water shortage broke into the press and the council records in 1844. Pumps above the public wells were demanded. There were special complaints in Newport, where the two public wells – one held to be public only after enquiry – were totally inadequate, even though there were 57 wells in the vicinity, a large number of them sunk in the previous 20 years. Pumps were ordered, and another for St Michael's well at the foot of Steep Hill. The poor of Newport complained that they had to pay 2d. a day for water from private wells, carrying it a great distance; others that water was fetched in soas[3] from the conduits,

[1] In 1877 St Swithin's vestry decided to appoint a burial board consisting of the vicar, 4 churchmen and 4 dissenters. In 1899, their new cemetery being full, they bought land adjoining the general cemetery.
[2] *T. & S.L.*, p. 64.
[3] *Soa* is a local word for a tub carried on a pole.

exhausting the daily flow early in the morning with the result that in one day 28 people were disappointed of water for their tea; it was clear therefore that something must be done.

A petition having been presented in favour of public waterworks, the town clerk advised that the corporation could not establish a company. Robert Dawber said in the council that except for gentlemen uphill, the inhabitants were deprived of the luxury of baths; and he thought they should not be denied to mechanics and tradesmen. The council set up a committee to enquire into the formation of a water company.

Citizens were found to undertake the enterprise, with Richard Carline in the lead. It was thought that there was reasonable prospect of a return on capital invested. Initial enquiry led them to suppose that the water in Prial Brook (Boultham) was suitable, and a public meeting was held to show its purity in comparison with water from other sources. The amount of lime contained in the water used in Lincoln astonished everyone. In a small bottle containing half a teacup of water there was shown to be, in water from various places in the city, at least half a teaspoonful of lime. Next to distilled water and rainwater, the Prial Brook supply was the best: this was explained as due to its rising out of and flowing through beds of gravel which acted as a huge natural filter. Other waters came through limestone beds. Water from the old well at the county hospital was so unwholesome and bad that the governors had, at great expense, sunk a new well.

Carline said that the company would provide against the probability of water failing at a dry time by making a reservoir capable of containing an 87 days' supply for a population of 30,000. If by reason of extraordinary drought even this reserve failed they would resort to the neighbouring catchwater drain, which was nearly as good as the Prial Brook. The sample bottles were put on show, so that, as the *Chronicle* said, the public could speculate on the number of limestone rocks which a moderate family must have swallowed in the course of 20 years.[1]

The company obtained its Act of Parliament, and began work with a capital of £18,000 in £25 shares.[2] By 1848 water was being laid on in the houses, at what was held to be a moderate cost; it was of a quality good for all culinary purposes and for washing, but above all for the making of tea. One six-cup man said 'We can now have a cup of real stingo at a small cost.' Another great advantage was that it abolished the

---

[1] *L.C.*, 20 February 1846.
[2] 9 and 10 Vic. c.cxi, 22 June 1846. T. M. Keyworth was chairman, R. S. Harvey, W. H. Brook, G. Calder, Rev. H. W. Sibthorp, F. Straw of Skellingthorpe, R. Whitton, W. H. Johnson and J. Middleton directors, and Carline secretary.

necessity of sending servant girls out at night to fetch water from the
conduits: a practice which had probably produced more profligacy than
any other.[1]

But the company's supply was inadequate in some parts of the city,
and not all houses had water installed; and the council were still
concerned with the conduit supply. Too much of it was being used for
flushing purposes, and there was water running to waste – 250 gallons an
hour, it was said, at St Mary's. The conduit was extended to St Peter at
Gowts, one placed in Baggeholme Road, and there were plans for other
extensions if the consent of the owner of the Monks estate could be
obtained. It came as a sharp shock in 1867 when the conduit water was
condemned by two doctors as being unfit to drink, one saying that it was
the worst he had ever analysed except that from a London well.[2]

In spite of this progress in the matter of water and a cemetery there
was no general advance. The Public Health Act of 1848 (virtually a
permissive act) started new discussions. The council directed a sanitary
committee, under the chairmanship of Robert Swan, to obtain a plan for
a general underground sewerage of the city, with estimates of cost, and to
consider whether the effluent could be used for agricultural and other
purposes. By September 1849 the expert, George Giles, had reported.
The cost of a complete system of underground sewerage was estimated at
£29,388, involving a rate of $8\frac{1}{2}$d. for 30 years. As the death rate was 24
per thousand, and the Act could be brought into operation if it exceeded
23, the council decided that the scheme was desirable, and directed the
holding of a public meeting. Opposition appeared at once. Parish
meetings were held to organise resistance. The Lighting and Paving
Commissioners said that they, the guardians and the council had power
enough to abate nuisances without this expensive scheme. The sanitary
committee had just reported on the city's good health, and deaths had
slightly decreased. At the town meeting Charlesworth and Brogden were
in favour of the plan, and Tweed and Nettleship against. Charles Seely
wanted to sell the commons to pay for it, and was howled down. The
meeting broke up in disorder, and after the mayor had left the chair
Nettleship took over, and a hostile resolution was carried. The first round
was over.[3]

Halfhearted measures went on. A contract with the Water Company
for the flushing of gutters was abandoned on the ground that the benefit

---

[1] *L.C.*, 21 April 1848.
[2] *S.M.*, 24 May, 28 June 1867.
[3] At this stage serious and sober men like E. J. Willson and R. S. Harvey thought
underground sewerage unnecessary.

was not adequate to the expense, though a cholera alarm brought a change of heart. Brayford and the river were denounced as a danger to health. The trouble there was that the lock gates could not be opened until the water reached a certain height, and until then the water was stagnant. The medical men in particular continued to press for action. In two years 600 cases of nuisance had been brought, but most of the nuisances were soon recreated. The rector of St Peter at Arches denounced the disgraceful state of the city from his pulpit.

The position was temperately reviewed in the Dispensary report for 1856. Much had been done to improve the condition of the humbler classes during the last few years, though much remained to be done. Their dwellings had increased in number, and were now seldom occupied by more than one family, as they had been 15 or 20 years ago. They were more substantially built. Yet they still had many defects:

First, they are much too small for the large families of many of the occupiers, if they are to enjoy health, decency and comfort, in many cases there being only one sleeping room for a family consisting of two parents and six or eight children; secondly, all proper means for ventilation seem to be neglected; and thirdly, the solitary privy appropriated to several cottages (with perhaps an open cesspool or ashpit) is permitted to remain uncleansed for months, or even years, exhaling constantly a noxious effluvium, and polluting still further the confined atmosphere of the dwellings.

Water had been led into every court and alley, and strengthened resistance to disease. The chief remaining cause of disease was the want of an efficient drainage.

Surprising is it that habitations are allowed to be yearly built in this corporate city without any provision being required by the authorities to carry away the dirt and filth which necessarily collect around any habitation. In too many instances the surface water even is unable to make its escape, and, therefore, collects close to the cottage, becomes loaded with suds, urine and dung, as well as decayed vegetable and animal matter, and sends forth the seeds of disease.

Until there were sewers filth would percolate into the adjoining well, or kitchen, or cellar.

The coroner Hitchens denounced all the authorities: 'in Lincoln we have a corporation, and typhus fever; a Board of Lighting Paving and Cleansing, and scarlet fever; a Sanitary Board and diarrhoea; all more prevalent than has been known for years. We have also a Water Company, and streets stinking in our nostrils for want of flushing the channels.'[1]

The question of action came up again because of the passing of an amending but still permissive Public Health Act of 1858, the execution of

[1] *L.C.*, 30 October 1857.

which was vested in the corporate body of every borough. Two-thirds of the council might adopt the Act on a requisition from 20 ratepayers, but if a twentieth of the whole number of ratepayers objected by memorial the Home Secretary must issue a commission of enquiry.

That autumn there was fever again. The sanitary committee of the council, with the mayor, Carline, in the chair, supported by Clayton, Broadbent the surgeon and Mortimer the architect, resolved:

that the present state of mortality and sickness in Lincoln calls upon the authorities to take some measures to ascertain its real cause, and it being proved to this committee that the drainage of the city is in a very imperfect and unsatisfactory state, which tends materially to greater fever and epidemics, it recommends to the council that the Health of Towns Act should be adopted and put in force in the city of Lincoln.

It also invited the opinions of the medical men.[1]

The council, having heard the medical men, lamely decided to tell the Lighting and Paving Commissioners that the city was suffering materially in consequence of the filthy state of the channels, and asking that they be flushed continuously. The commissioners had already decided that rather than flush the gutters they would employ labourers to sweep them, but they agreed to comply as far as possible. The council then considered whether to adopt the new Act, and resolved by 13 votes to 9 not to do so. They were in no doubt that the ratepayers would have refused to support them had they decided otherwise. Indeed, a petition against adoption, presented by Charles Ward, bore 2,550 names, which was more than the number of all the registered burgesses in the city.

Meanwhile the commissioners were considering how to remedy the evil state of the river, which was detrimental to health in summer; and they suggested an experiment to the directors of the Great Northern Railway, which then controlled the river. During the dry seasons a temporary dam might be made at Brayford head, water let off by driving clews at the lock at night, and then on removal of the dam in the morning the rush of water would flush the whole of the walled part of the river. The engine at the Torksey end of the Fossdyke might be worked occasionally. Charles Chaplin, a railway director, replied that the Torksey engine was out of repair, but the company would give facilities if they were indemnified against damage. In the end a little money was spent in dredging. In 1863 the corporation threw 50 tons of lime into the river in order to correct its putrid state.

In 1864 the subject was resumed in the press. The *Mercury* declared that:

[1] 9 September 1858.

already, year by year, the victims of this stinking receptacle for the filth of the town (to wit, the river) can be numbered by the score, as well as in too many cases the health of nearly 1000 workmen is broken or lowered, so that the masters of the funds of the various charities and clubs are drained of their resources to a serious extent. Let those in authority reflect, and then we apprehend that their foolish fear of giving offence to the lower classes and the housebuilders will give way before the solemn duty of preserving the life and health of their fellow citizens, very many of whom are both willing and able to pay for the requisite amount of sewerage.[1]

That November R. S. Harvey, doctor and sanitary reformer, was elected mayor for the third time. He made a speech at the council which fell dead. The *Mercury* commented that when the subject was agitated several years ago the Conservatives were the obstructives, but they had been converted since then, and would now gladly consent to a well-matured scheme for ridding the town of its filth.[2] It little thought that the liberals would run away when they came to power.

The council, solemnly thanking the commissioners for directing their attention to the sanitary condition of the city, which was well worthy of their consideration and that of the citizens at large, hoped that as the citizens at a large public meeting had previously opposed and stopped the council from adopting the Local Government Act they would now themselves request the mayor to convene a public meeting of the inhabitants to consider the sanitary condition of the city if they deemed it worthy of their notice.[3]

This ironical invitation produced an instant response. The doctors led in letters to the press. Dr Sympson, taking the number of recorded deaths in the preceding two years, and the proportion of deaths to attacks, argued that there must have been in that time 245 attacks of typhus, 510 of bronchitis and pneumonia, over 3,000 of scarlet fever, and 630 of measles; there were 44 deaths from smallpox and 119 from consumption. Dr Garnham of the Dispensary described conditions in some of the worst districts of the city: Sincil Street, with its courts within courts; High Bridge houses which were more filthy rabbit warrens than human habitations; and Witham South Bank, a conglomerate mass of ill-built dwellings, stables and slaughter houses. Sickness was increasing and the death rate unusually high. Drury, the corporation surveyor, gave particulars of a number of underground drains serving limited areas. They were fed from open drains scarcely ever free from rotten and sickening filth. The hillside was dotted with cesspools, the contents of which helped

---

[1] 26 August 1864.
[2] 23 December 1864.
[3] 19 September 1865.

to supply wells and pumps. Belowhill cellars were apt to flood, and in consequence of the contaminated state of the subsoil water, at every flood pernicious gases and miasmatic effluvia were pumped up into the houses. On a new calculation he thought that a complete drainage system could be installed at the cost of a 3d. rate. The reports of the Registrar General had to be searched to find a death rate as great as that of Lincoln, and only in large towns was it exceeded.[1] W. J. Mantle, the proprietor of a private school in Northgate, said that there was typhoid fever within 100 yards of his house, and that in one house the wife was dead and the husband and six children in the last stages of the disease. Parents for 20 miles round were refusing to send their children to school.[2]

A memorial to the mayor to call a sanitary meeting bore 600 signatures, including all the medical men but two. At the meeting the mayor said he hoped they had come in a better spirit than they did at the meeting thirteen years ago. Nathaniel Clayton said that those citizens who had the means could move about, but the working population were tied to the place where they earned their living, and their health was their capital and stock in trade. He moved a general resolution about the state of the city which was seconded by Rudgard. When it was put the mayor was uncertain whether it was carried or not. W. B. Maltby, a chemist and a councillor, then moved an amendment that the increased mortality was not due to preventible causes. He attributed the death rate to the mysterious workings of a Superior Power, and argued for temperance, proper food, ventilation and better houses. Mr Clapham, a working man, found the opposition among the little landlords who wanted their 12 or 14% for their dirty houses. Eventually the first resolution was carried by a small majority. Mr Dickinson then moved to prevent the corporation from adopting the Local Government Act; and although the town clerk pointed out that this would prevent the corporation from adopting the only measure for effecting the desired improvement, it was carried. Not more than 500–600 persons were present when the vote was taken, and not more than 300 voted against adopting the Act, and about 250 in favour. If only two-thirds of the requisitionists had attended the result would have been different.

This disgraceful exhibition stimulated the council to the necessary action, and on 30 January 1866 it was resolved by 16 members, being upwards of two-thirds of the 22 present, to adopt the Act of 1858 (as

---

[1] Dr Garnham's press cutting book, lent to me by Mr H. J. J. Griffith. Lincoln was one of 18 districts in which the death rate had risen. A. P. Stewart and E. Jenkins, *Medical and Legal Aspects of Sanitary Reform* (1867), p. 48.

[2] *L.C.*, 15 September 1865.

amended in 1861). Several liberals helped to provide the necessary majority. There were howls of rage. Members of the majority were beset by threatening letters; Alderman Charles Ward, once an opponent but converted to reform, was told that his coffin was ordered; R. S. Harvey, under threat to murder him, resigned from the sanitary committee; but the more robust Robert Seely said that anyone who wanted to take his life would find him at home any morning at 9 o'clock.

The council became the local board under the Act. By-laws were made[1] and Dr Harrison was appointed medical officer of health, though at first only for three months. In a contest for the clerkship T. G. Dale, who had been clerk to the Lighting and Paving Commissioners for many years, was defeated by Henry Kirke Hebb, who had been a member of the city council since 1863 and a determined sanitarian; he resigned from the council.

There was a strong practical defence of the adoption. It did not in itself increase expenditure. Highways would be repaired uniformly throughout the city instead of varying according to different parish standards; the layout of new streets would be controlled; scavenging and the emptying of privies would be done at the public expense; all properties would be chargeable to rates, and assessments would be standardised instead of being at the discretion of the Lighting and Paving Commissioners. This latter body came to an end. It had been constituted chiefly by the parishes, and its disappearance marked another stage in the decline of the parish.

But so far as concerned the sewerage question the change made no difference. The council as the local board declined an offer by the Water Company to sell its undertaking. It examined the drainage question afresh; and it agreed with only one dissentient that as the scientific authorities were at issue upon the best mode of getting rid of and using sewage it would be wise to postpone action. Clearly they were afraid of the public outcry.

The public attitude was described by W. J. Mantle in evidence he gave to the Royal Sanitary Commission in 1870. He was asked if there was among the ratepayers a feeling of odium towards any person who reported nuisances. He replied:

A man is looked upon as an informer, and the lower class are so misguided by their landlords that they are apt to believe that the man has some bad motive in view, rather than give him credit for a good intention towards them. The upper class of Lincoln are desirous that the Act should be put into force, but the lower class are not, being misled by the political party and the middle-class men.

---

[1] Confirmed by the Local Government Supplemental Act 1866, *Accounts and Papers*, 1866, III, 441. The Lighting and Paving Act was amended and partially repealed.

He described the station in life of people of that 'party':

They are landlords of houses, men who have raised themselves by trade to some degree of independence, and have built a lot of cottages. But before this Act came into force they could build up without any regard to the comforts with which they ought to supply the poor, and we have a great number of them in Lincoln; they are retired tradesmen generally.

They were afraid of the expense. When he was asked if this feeling was peculiar to Lincoln or general in cathedral towns, he replied that things were similar in Chichester, which he knew. In both towns the cathedral authorities were in favour of reform; the archdeacon of Lincoln had preached a sanitary sermon a few months ago. He took a poor view of the guardians, most of whom were tenant farmers, concerned to keep down the rates.[1]

Complaints of course continued, and the conduit water was denounced as the worst outside London ever known. A memorial from owners and ratepayers to the Home Office to enquire into the sanitary condition of the city brought down an inspector in 1870, and the council in its corporate capacity authorised the town clerk 'to take such measures as he may deem necessary to give full effect to the opinion of the vast majority of the citizens upon this question'.[2] This was a cowardly way of opposing reform.

At the enquiry Dr Lowe and Dr Sympson gave evidence of increasing cesspool contamination, and Mr Shuttleworth said that as the railways took traffic off the river the locks were not opened so often, and the water was more stagnant. The river water opposite his works was so foul that it could not be used for engine purposes; and his manager said that men working in the enginehouse were made sick by the stench. The council reply was that the city was in a healthy state, and that the condition of the river was due to an exceptionally dry season: in such a season, quantities of liquid tar and other chemicals were thrown in to neutralise the smell. It was admitted that some sewage flowed into the river, but a supply of pure water from the Trent would render further complaint impossible. The council put on an air of levity, and Brogden – once a sanitary reformer, but now in power – was defiantly fighting a losing battle, and had the effrontery to say that the council would not carry out a scheme of general drainage even if so ordered by the government: for which subversive utterance he was reproved by the inspector.

The inspector found that the river was a foul stagnant sewer, and

---

[1] *Royal Sanitary Commission* 1869–71, vol. 3, part 1, minutes of evidence 1869–70, c.281, II, p. 144. I am indebted to Mr Owen Hartley for this reference.

[2] 4 October 1870. 2560 inhabitants signed a memorial against underground drainage.

concluded that 'there is not a town in England which offers a more
flagrant instance of the dereliction of this duty than the city of Lincoln'.
The Secretary of State concurred in this finding, and gave the city three
months in which to decide what to do. — *gov. intervention only — provoked action*

Submission, at least in principle, was inevitable; the council fell to
considering how to finance the operation; and thoughts turned to the
profits of the Water Company. Its water, furthermore, might flush
the river, and might make public baths possible. It happened that the
company was then proposing to apply to parliament for powers to
increase its works and supply the needs of a population which had nearly
doubled since the company was formed: shortage of water was especially
complained of in the upper part of the town, as the mains in High Street
were tapped so often. The local board opposed the company's bill, and
reached agreement for purchase of the undertaking in 1871. They
obtained a Lincoln Waterworks Act giving them powers to use the water
of the Witham, and to take into the water district the parishes of
Canwick and Greetwell.[1]

While these matters were in treaty smallpox broke out, and the
guardians were asked to allow the workhouse infirmary to be used for the
patients. The guardians were favourable, but the Poor Law Board in
London refused permission, and the local board enquired about the cost
of a hospital tent. A great increase in the number of patients at the
Dispensary prompted the house surgeons there to send to the council a
report, which was dismissed as utopian. The Dispensary then resolved
that all sufferers from smallpox should cease to be Dispensary patients.
The infirmary was refused again in 1871, and a room in Temperance
Hall was taken as a vaccination station.

The council were still justifying delay when the Public Health Act of
1872 transferred the powers of the local board to the council in a new
capacity as an urban sanitary authority. The new authority took some
first steps. They bought land for irrigation purposes in 1873, and
instructed a consultant to draw up plans for underground drainage but
they did not commit themselves further. On 8 March 1875 the new
authority was ordered to commence drainage works within four months:
it procured a short delay. There was great debate in the council: Akrill,
Ruston and Williams, all liberals, favouring drainage, the liberal majority resisting it, and Brogden denying the truth of the surveyor's

---

[1] 34 and 35 Vic. c. cxlix, 24 July 1871. Bracebridge, Boultham and Skellingthorpe were
already included. With an eye to profits, there was a proposal also to take over the Gas
Company's undertaking, but the council were daunted by the cost of purchase, and the
subject lay in abeyance.

evidence. While they were still arguing about alternative methods of doing the work and sending deputations to London they heard of proceedings for a *mandamus* in the High Court to compel them to proceed. After the proceedings the mayor told the council that 'One of the justices – I think it was Justice Blackburn – said distinctly that it quite depended on the zeal, industry and energy of the corporation what the amount of the fine should be, and what should be the future attitude to the city...the three judges were dead set against us.' The mayor had therefore instructed the engineer, Mansergh, to complete his plans. The liberals, yielding to force, took credit with the ratepayers for their delaying action. Cottingham claimed that by pausing to ascertain the best or cheapest method of doing the job they had saved at least £30,000.

The contract for the work was signed in September 1876. The cost was to be £63,605, or a shilling rate for 50 years. Street excavation became a familiar sight. When it was suggested to Mansergh that private connections to houses be put into the sewer as the work progressed he at once refused: he was too busy. By 1881 nearly all the houses were connected to the main sewer, and pumping began.[1]

By then the new Waterworks Committee of the urban sanitary authority had inspected the upper Witham and other sources of water supply. Between Hykeham and Bracebridge there was a junction with Hykeham brook, which took Hykeham sewage; but in its course of about three miles the whole was taken up by absorption and evaporation. At Bracebridge the drain from the county asylum sewage farm joined the river; it was similarly disposed of. The sewage from several houses in Bracebridge would at times if not prevented run into the river. The committee recommended a diversion of the drain and the removal of a sheep-washing pit used annually. The new work that the company had lately completed for taking water from the Pike Drain was in a very satisfactory state; and they were satisfied with that drain, Prial Brook, Skellingthorpe reservoir and the catchwater as sources of supply. They were easily pleased. Meanwhile warnings were issued about the quality of water in the public pumps.

Henceforth the council was to operate in two distinct capacities: as a municipal corporation, and as an urban sanitary authority under the Public Health Acts, first of 1872 and then of 1875. In this second capacity it would levy a general district rate, which would take the place of the local board rate and before that of the lighting and paving rate. There

---

[1] Quicksands were met in High Street at 19 or 20 feet, and pumping was carried on day and night. In Anchor Street house foundations gave way; doors would not shut, and windows were cracked.

was not the same psychological resistance to this as to the idea of a borough rate; and as most of the necessary expenditure was to be incurred for improvements under the Public Health Acts it was easier to postpone the evil day when a borough rate must be made. H. K. Hebb became clerk to the urban sanitary authority and deputy town clerk, Tweed of course remaining town clerk. By the end of the century, when a borough rate was being made, the district rate was ten times as large, and most of the work was done in the deputy town clerk's office. Separate minute books were kept, until the office of town clerk and clerk to the urban sanitary authority were united in W. T. Page, but separate borough and district rates continued to be levied until 1925.

Hebb was a Lincoln man. During his tenure of the clerkship from 1866 to 1899 the authority bought the waterworks, the gasworks, inaugurated the sewerage scheme, and launched the electricity undertaking. He had an extensive private practice, was a director of several private companies, and after the death of J. W. Danby became chairman of the Lincoln and Lindsey Bank. He built Coldbath House, at the north-east corner of the Arboretum, providing a large room in which he could entertain the council.[1] He died in 1902, having used his great private influence in the faithful service of the city.

[1] The house was bombed during the Second World War, and its site and garden are now incorporated in the Arboretum.

CHAPTER IX

CHURCH AND CHAPEL: I

John Kaye had been translated from Bristol to the see of Lincoln in 1827 by Lord Liverpool, who, according to Sydney Smith, intended to promote him to Canterbury if a vacancy occurred while he was in office.[1] Physically he was a little thin spare man. He was a senior wrangler,[2] and had been Master of Christ's College and regius professor of divinity at Cambridge. He was respected and liked in his diocese: 'Loved,' said Cracroft, who added 'I never met a man with more anecdotes or a more charming, unaffected way of communicating his multifarious information: He deserved a Boswell to hand him down to Posterity.' He could hold his own in any society.[3] In matters of policy he had supported the repeal of the Test and Corporation Acts in 1828 for the relief of protestant dissenters, but in the following year had opposed Catholic Emancipation. In some quarters – especially among the new high churchmen[4] – he was disliked because he was not a party man: he opposed the revival of Convocation, upheld the Gorham judgment in which doctrine was defined by a secular court (the judicial committee of the privy council), and concurred in the judgment against the high church Philpotts, the bishop of Exeter.[5] Cracroft's only criticism of him was that he was too gentle and kind, and not firm enough: 'over and over again I have heard it said "It's no good writing to the Bishop, he is sure to refuse you; go and see him yourself, and he'll allow you to do anything".'[6]

[1] *Letters of Sydney Smith*, ed. Nowell C. Smith (1953), II, 760n. He was also proposed for York in 1847. Owen Chadwick, *The Victorian Church*, I (1966), 237n. A portrait of Kaye by Sir Thomas Lawrence in his son's home showed him wearing a wig: the portrait at the Bishop's House has no wig. Bishop Edward Hicks remarked to the archdeacon that his father outlived his wig; to which the reply was 'Oh yes; he had to give it up, but he made the change by degrees.' Hicks wondered how he managed to do this. E. L. Hicks Diary, 26 August 1911.

[2] George Boole wished to dedicate a book, probably his *Mathematical Analysis of Logic*, to him, as a tribute to his scholarship and character. Boole to E. R. Larken, 13 September 1847 (per Mr A. P. Rollett).

[3] Diary, 23 February 1853. He liked meeting laymen at dinner, objecting to a host of 'crows' on these occasions, 16 February 1850.

[4] For the opinion of Charles Anderson, see *G.L.*, p. 300.

[5] In discussing the matter with the assize judges, Lord Campbell and Baron Parke, who had been on the judicial committee, he said, 'I think my brother of Exeter would have made a good Attorney-General.' Cracroft, 11 March 1850.

[6] 23 February 1853.

Kaye found large scope for reform in his diocese, and his vision and opportunities were enlarged when Sir Robert Peel appointed him to the new Ecclesiastical Committee, which was charged with the reform of abuses. His task was eased in 1840 when his vast see, which had stretched into Buckinghamshire, was reduced in size to include only the counties of Lincoln and Nottingham.[1] As the chief episcopal residence at Buckden in Huntingdonshire was then no longer in the diocese a house at Riseholme, two miles north of Lincoln, was built for him by the Commission.[2]

There were great evils facing him in the diocese. Absenteeism and the holding of livings in plurality were widespread. There were persons who had become utterly unfit for reasons of health: for example, the rector of Scotton who had become a harmless driveller who did not know what Good Friday meant;[3] or the old clergyman, for forty years (on a stipend of £65) the poor paralytic parson of Torksey and Newton, two of the most neglected parishes in the county, swarming with dissenters, poachers and depraved people.[4] There were those who wilfully neglected or scamped their duties, like King of Ashby, who, in the shooting season, consistently shot his way to Sir Henry Nelthorpe's on the Monday and went back to Ashby on the Saturday.[5] Galloping parsons would hold curacies in parishes far apart.[6]

Cracroft noted two stories that ought not to be lost. Carr, the rector of Brattleby, told him of his introduction to the parish in 1838. He went straight from Balliol, full of orthodoxy, theology and logic, and met a gentleman in the lane who said, 'I am Mr Pulley, the curate of Brattleby, and you, Sir, I presume, are the man from the College.' They walked to Pulley's lodgings, and after a good dinner Carr said, 'Mr Pulley, I can't go away without asking you what your theological opinions are.' 'Sir,' said the curate, 'You'll find me perfectly orthodox. I never hunt except someone gives me a mount, and as for shooting, Sir, I shoot a great deal

[1] The counties of Huntingdon and Bedford were transferred to Ely, Buckingham to Oxford, Leicester to Peterborough; Nottingham was transferred from the province of York to that of Canterbury and to the see of Lincoln. For Kaye see *D.N.B.*; a tribute by one of his clergy in *Life of Rev. C. S. Bird* (1864), pp. 226–9; and an unpublished thesis by the Rev. R. Foskett in Nottingham University Library. For his charges and letters on public subjects, see *Works of Bishop Kaye* (1888), VII.
[2] Anderson urged that the old palace at Lincoln should be made into a residence. Wilberforce MSS, d.25, fol. 141. Charles Mainwaring was lessee of the old palace. Perhaps it was not wholly an accident that in 1838 he was busy improving the place, pulling down old stables and disclosing the ruins of the hall. *L.C.*, 27 April 1838, 11 January 1839.
[3] W. B. Stonehouse, *A Stow Visitation*, ed. N. S. Harding (1940), pp. 65–6.
[4] Cracroft, 26 May 1852.   [5] L.A.O. Cor. B. 5/29/38.
[6] See, e.g., L.A.O. Cor..B. 5/29/19, 34. For a survey of 75 parishes around Lincoln see *P.D.*, 3rd Series, 98, 1078.

– in fact, a brace of partridges given to the farmers every now and then does a great deal of good and keeps us all friends.' Carr came away wondering what his Oxford friends would make of it. Later he stopped a duel between squire and curate, the latter saying that he did not see why he should be insulted because he was a clergyman.[1]

Charles Anderson's uncle, Mr Vevers, was vicar of Marton, and did duty at Cotes once a month. The church stood close by the only farmhouse in the parish. The farmer was an old drunkard, and when he returned from Gainsborough market he always unsaddled his old grey mare and turned her loose to graze. One morning after market day the mare could not be found. The next Sunday three weeks the clerk came to the church and found her lying dead in the aisle. No one had ever thought of looking there for her. Thither she had strayed, the wind had closed the door, and after eating the hassocks, communion cloth and prayer books she had died of starvation.[2]

The parson's freehold made him virtually irremovable, and reform often had to wait for death or resignation, and even then was hampered by the rights of patrons. Otherwise there remained exhortation and example.

There was a like sad record of the ill-use of church fabrics. Archdeacons were among the worst offenders. Dr Cayley Illingworth, archdeacon of Stow, was pilloried by Anderson as:

a great, fat, redfaced parson, a justice of the peace, and a great bully of churchwardens. He did as much harm as anyone during the time of his office, in pulling down aisles and chancels, putting on barn roofs, and disfiguring and half ruining the churches in his archdeaconry. Nor did Dr Bayley, who succeeded him, do much better. The mischief these two ignorant men (of their office and its details) did is irreparable, but they were only specimens of what was very general in those days. Now the opposite extreme is more common of over-restoration, i.e. pulling down unnecessarily in order to rebuild new.[3]

Bishop Kaye appointed H. K. Bonney archdeacon of Lincoln in 1845 and W. B. Stonehouse archdeacon of Stow in 1844. Both carried out visitations, and were no doubt an improvement on their predecessors, but they were still too ruthless for later taste. Stonehouse threatened to have the splendid St Paul tombs at Snarford removed on the ground that

---

[1] Cracroft, 22 February 1850. Carr wrote out the registration of his own death on the morning of his death and desired it to be sent to the registrar, but it was held not to be legal, not being subscribed by a witness. 14 January 1861.

[2] Cracroft, 28 October 1852.

[3] L.A.O. Anderson 5/2/2, p. 29. For Illingworth see Stonehouse, *A Stow Visitation*, p. 74. As a magistrate he cleared the county of vagrants – no gipsy had been seen in Lincoln for 30 years – and he knew nothing of the Reform Bill. For E. J. Willson on archdeacon Goddard, see L.A.O. Massingberd 1/75.

they were dangerous; Cracroft said that the county rose on him, and he gave up his barbaric intentions.[1]

It was in these years that Tractarianism, the new Oxford high church movement, was arousing in English breasts the ancient fear and hatred of Rome. It was, after all, not until 1858 that the gunpowder plot service was removed from the Book of Common Prayer, and hard faced parish overseers had been accustomed to grant money from parish funds for the parish bonfire on the fifth of November.[2] Individual conversions to the Roman Catholic Church might be the beginning of a great secession. Richard Sibthorp, brother of the colonel, once noted as an evangelical preacher (mixing with Methodists at Waddington), was admitted to the Roman Church in 1841. His wax candles on the altar, three reading desks at which he read different parts of the service, and his custom of prostrating himself before the altar when reading the Litany caused alarm; and one observer thought that he 'was a little cracked, he looked so wild and haggard'.[3] He was not a Tractarian; Newman did not go over to Rome until 1845, by which time Sibthorp had returned to Anglicanism and was planning the almshouses which Pugin was to build for him in Lincoln. Kaye treated him with consideration, and on his return to Lincoln in 1847 he recovered his old popularity with the citizens, taking morning duty at St Peter at Arches and evening service at St Martin; it was the only parish church evening service. As he grew older he became unsettled again and returned to the Roman Church.[4]

Parallel with the Oxford movement a society was formed at Cambridge, the Cambridge Camden Society, for the study of Gothic architecture and ecclesiastical antiquities. Its romanising tendencies brought

[1] Cracroft, 25 November 1850. Stonehouse's *Stow Visitation* and Bonney's *Church Notes* (1937) were edited and published by the late Canon N. S. Harding, who did much on his own initiative and at his own expense for the repair of several churches in the diocese.
[2] The celebration of Guy Fawkes Day was extinct in Lincoln. *S.M.*, 10 November 1858.
[3] *Letters and Papers of the Cholmeleys from Wainfleet 1813–53* (L.R.S.) edited by G. H. Cholmeley (1964), p. 71. Cracroft thought he looked more like a monk than a man. Diary 14 October 1846.
[4] Lytton Strachey gibed at him in his *Eminent Victorians*; for a sympathetic study see Christopher Sykes, *Two Studies in Virtue* (1943). There is a biography by R. W. Fowler, based on a memoir by Sibthorp's Oxford friend Dr Bloxam. Canon Cooper Scott, who knew him well, said he was good and true, and only wanted perfection too soon. *Things that Were* (1923), p. 43. Cracroft wrote: 'what an agreeable fellow he is...he is a genuine Christian, whatever the forms may be under which he has worshipped.' Diary, 4 December 1849. After a visit to Canwick in 1857 Anderson wrote: 'it is quite delightful to see how the young Sibthorps revere their Uncle Richard, and the pleasant terms they are on. He is quite charming.' Wilberforce MSS, 8 November 1857. For a tribute by Mr Gladstone see L.A.O. *Annual Report* (1970–1), p. 48. For Bernard Smith, the Romanising rector of Leadenham, see R. D. Middleton, *Magdalen Studies* (1936), pp. 232–42; S. L. Ollard, *Short History of the Oxford Movement* (1915), p. 168.

about the resignation of some of its episcopal members, including Kaye. A society was formed in Lincolnshire on the same lines in 1844, on which Kaye, who became its president, kept a kindly but cautious eye, supervising its rules and annual reports. Country clergy were the backbone of the society. It was slow to establish itself in Lincoln, and the dean and chapter had no part in the movement.[1]

All these things could only strengthen the fears and suspicions of those willing to see a pope in every candle. In one church he visited Cracroft noted a screen before the chancel 'just as if the mummeries of Rome were still in force'.[2] The stern unbending evangelical was typified by W. F. J. Kaye – 'grave' and 'quiet' were the adjectives used of him – who after the death of his father the bishop was, to the regret of high churchmen, appointed archdeacon of Lincoln. He was perpetual curate of South Carlton, a parish of which Lord Monson was proprietor and John Ross the antiquary a native. Kaye wanted to remove the screen in the church, as its retention was likely to result in the form of service being tilted in the direction of Rome. Monson wanted to keep it, not fearing any new-fangled introductions into the service; adding that if he did he would sacrifice the screen, having strong feelings on that subject.[3]

The evangelicals worked especially through societies, in some of which, the Bible Society, the Ragged Sunday School, the Penitent Females' Home, they worked with dissenters; but they depended chiefly on a few country clergy, some gentry and some devoted laymen in the city. When their Church Missionary Society sought to have services at the cathedral they were refused permission, and took refuge at St Peter in Eastgate. The *Mercury* commented that there were few clergy present: 'between the orthodox clergy and the evangelical body who are the supporters of this society there seems an impassable gulf, as the former invariably abstain from countenancing it by taking part in the proceedings'.[4] Kaye was careful, though in 1848 he presided for them at a meeting.[5]

For fervour, high church or low, there was no place in the thirteen

---

[1] It was the Architectural and Archaeological Society, whose precise title varied from time to time. See my 'Early Days of a Society' in *Lincolnshire History and Archaeology*, 1 (1966), 57.

[2] Cracroft, 29 August 1850.

[3] L.A.O. Monson 25/13/10/12/151–3, Ross Letter Books, 12 May, 13 August 1860; *Monson Church Notes* (L.R.S. 1936), p. xiii.

[4] *S.M.*, 27 March 1846.

[5] At the Society's Jubilee he took the chair at a meeting in the Corn Exchange, though he never before took part in its public affairs; he said that public meetings were not congenial to his feelings, though he acknowledged that they acted as a stimulus upon the public mind.

parish churches in the city. Seven of the livings were held by four vicars choral who lived in Vicars Court in Minster Yard, who also did duty at the cathedral and in three parishes outside the city.[1] The chapter, said Stonehouse, usually bestowed a few of their small livings on their priest vicars, with the result that no one resided or looked after them: the glebe had been lost and the vicarage house let fall into ruins. The priest vicars almost had to be pluralists because they were so poor, their corporate estates having been let on lease. Stonehouse thought this state of things had done more harm to the church in the city and neighbourhood than could easily be imagined.[2] One of the vicars, Gibney, said in 1849 that besides his minor canonry he held the perpetual curacy of St Michael on the Mount and the sequestration of St Mark, with a total average income of £235. He had the cure of nearly 2,000 souls, took three services every Sunday and four on every fourth Sunday, besides attending to his parochial school without any help. He had hoped the cathedral would help, but it did not.[3]

The growth of population of Lincoln presented Kaye with one of his many difficult problems. A survey of the position, which uses the population figures of 1831, was made for him.[4] The proportion of the inhabitants who could be accommodated in church was 25%; including the cathedral, computed to provide for 300, it was 28%. The uphill parishes made the worst showing. St John and St Nicholas had no church, and this part of the city was described later as a nest of profligacy which it would take the utmost pains to eradicate.[5] The middle group of parishes made a slightly better showing, because the corporation church, St Peter at Arches, seated 550 people, the parish population being 534. But St Swithin, seating 300, had a parish which had grown in 30 years from 940 to 2,202. Things were a little better in the southern parishes.

A proposal to unite St Nicholas and St John with St Paul was forestalled by a move, prompted by the ardent young layman, Charles Anderson, and taken up by the dean and clergy generally, to build a new church at St Nicholas. The architect chosen was George Gilbert Scott,

---

[1] St Botolph and St Peter at Gowts were held by the Rev. George Jepson, who also held Boultham; St Mark and St Mary Magdalene by the Rev. John Nelson, who also held Nettleham and Sudbrooke, St Paul by the Rev. William Hett, St Nicholas and St John by the Rev. Samuel Martin. Pluralities had been much worse a few years earlier. *G.L.*, pp. 296–7.

[2] *A Stow Visitation*, pp. 70–1.

[3] L.A.O. Cor. B. 5/4/106/9.

[4] See Appendix III.

[5] Wilberforce MSS, d.27, fol. 149.

who had theretofore been known for his workhouses. It was his first church. Like some of his other early churches it had no regular and proper chancel, his idea being that the feature was obsolete. Presently he was convinced of his error by the new high church doctrine on the subject.[1]

The building movement was the outward and visible sign of reviving life in the parish churches. Every change was watched and criticised by the vigilant ecclesiologists. In enlarging St Peter at Gowts the traces of the Romanesque north aisle and the Norman chancel arch disappeared, and the removal of the latter caused censure.[2] Mr Teulon's plans to replace the little barnlike St Michael incurred both praise and blame. The gothicisation of St Mary Magdalene was approved as judicious and tasteful. Other churches were repaired and renewed, and gas installed; and more services were held, Sunday evening lectures being started by several incumbents.

The greatest activity was at St Peter at Arches, which in some ways served as the parish church of the whole lower city. About 1840 a committee was formed for supporting Sunday afternoon and weekday evening services, the purpose being not for parishioners exclusively or chiefly, but for the inhabitants generally, and particularly for the poorer classes, many of whom, it was rightly feared, never attended a place of worship, and for whose accommodation the church, from its central position and size, was well calculated.[3] In 1852 the rector proposed, in pursuance of a memorial from nearly all the communicants and regular churchgoers who were the heads of the families in the parish, to discontinue the Sunday afternoon service. It was his duty to provide two full services, and he thought the second should be in the evening rather than in the afternoon. He proposed that the Wednesday evening service should be left at the disposal of the committee. The latter acquiesced, acknowledging the courtesy they had received.[4] No doubt this return to the normal parish pattern was welcomed – perhaps prompted by – the other parishes.

Mr Teulon was called in to overhaul the building. It was classical, having been completed in 1724 probably by one of the Smiths of Warwick,[5]

[1] He also commented later on the meagre construction, contemptible fittings and plaster mouldings of his earlier churches. *Personal and Professional Recollections* (1879), pp. 85–9. The new church was begun in 1839.
[2] *A.A.S.R. passim; Ecclesiologist*, xv, 64.
[3] *L.C.*(21 April 1848) referred to the time when the bulk of the population used to parade the High Street from teatime until suppertime every Sunday when weather permitted.
[4] L.A.O. Cor. B. 5/4/100/7. The parish of St Benedict was united with St Peter in 1854.
[5] *G.L.*, p. 64.

and hence was little thought of by current fashion. The *Ecclesiologist* spoke scathingly of 'a miserable pseudo classical apsidal church'. A chancel, formed out of the eastern bay of the nave, and arranged stall-wise with new woodwork of a Jacobean air, and other changes, enabled the architect to improve it considerably.[1] The Lincoln Architectural and Archaeological Society said that the application of colour to the church had shown that buildings that were in themselves unattractive, might be rendered not only cheerful, but pleasant to the eye and churchlike in effect.[2] It was long before this Gothic obsession passed. Even in 1930 the Society abandoned St Peters though they had helped to save the medieval St Benedict.

The operations set in motion by Kaye were continued after his death in 1853 by his successor John Jackson, appointed by Lord Aberdeen. He was a genial soul who hated formality – he was to be seen riding into Lincoln on horseback – and who, though a low churchman himself, sought to support the objects of both high and low church.[3] He called attention to the continuing lack of church accommodation in Lincoln, and by the time that he was translated to London by Disraeli in 1868 he could claim great progress in building churches and schools, in the foundation of the Lincoln Training college for schoolmistresses, and in the more regular holding of church services. High churchmen found his episcopate disappointing; Anderson said he was a timid man and hardly knew his own mind on some theological questions of the day.[4] However, they thought, no doubt rightly, that they had made progress in the diocese.

At his primary visitation Jackson said that the diocese was one of those in which dissent was strongest, and he thought it an act of justice to their nonconformist brethren

[1] *Ecclesiologist*, xvii, 78.
[2] *A.A.S.R.*, ix, part i (1867), p. xiii.
[3] *Edinburgh Review*, xcviii (1853), 333. For a tribute see *Fraser's Magazine*, li, February 1855; and see also Janet Courtney, *Recollected in Tranquillity* (1926), p. 83. The dean hoped he would live at the old palace, and Anderson suggested that Riseholme would make a training college for clergy. On his translation to London an address in the bishop's honour was presented by clergy and laity. Banks Stanhope opposed, saying 'every stationmaster gets one', but he was put down.
[4] Wilberforce MSS, d. 30, fol. 174. Jackson employed an artist to enlarge a portrait of himself as rector at St James Piccadilly, and then gave him a commission to copy portraits of early bishops of Lincoln, the originals of which were said to be in the halls of Brasenose and Lincoln Colleges and Christ Church, Oxford. Jackson, having an unbroken succession of daughters, was comforted by Bishop Blomfield with the words 'Never mind, Jackson: perhaps you will have all the nine Muses, and then Apollo at last.' E. L. Hicks' Diary, 22 September 1912, and letter dated 22 September 1911 from Archdeacon Kaye to the Bishop, pasted in at 27 December 1915. See also *Lady Knightley's Journals*, ed. Julius Cartwright (1874), p. 263.

to acknowledge the service they have rendered to religion by stepping into the void which the retreating vigour and discipline of the Church had left, and keeping alive the flame of piety which might have been extinguished in the damp of indifference and neglect.[1]

Edward Peacock too thought Anglicans ought to be obliged to those who at great personal and pecuniary sacrifice had provided places of Christian worship.[2]

Nonconformity had made great strides since the beginnings of political reform. The repeal of the Test and Corporation Acts removed some of the disabilities of dissenters and made them eligible for some public offices. The Reform Bill gave more of them the parliamentary vote, and municipal reform opened the town councils to them. Civil registration of births marriages and deaths in 1835 and the Marriage Act of 1836 relieved them of unwelcome dependence on Anglican clergy;[3] by 1847 cemeteries could be divided into consecrated and unconsecrated parts, and by 1852 the division became obligatory.[4]

These measures they owed to the whigs, and it was to the whigs that they looked for the removal of remaining disabilities. They had therefore a strong political bias in favour first of the whigs and later of the liberals, and political nonconformity remained a force until the echoes of Balfour's Education Act of 1902 died away. Whig and radical politicians knew the importance of their support (though they did not want to pay for it), and local leaders subscribed to their building funds. Even the Sibthorps, who would not give to their building funds, would give to their charities. Their attacks upon the Church of England threw that cause upon the tory party, and the line of division between politico-religious groupings grew sharp, and Anglican recovery and the rise of the new High Church party was to make it sharper still. The division broadly corresponded also to a social distinction, the dissenters at first being mostly of the lower middle or the working class – as generally were their ministers – and the Anglicans looking to the leadership of the gentry and the well-to-do middle class. Cracroft confided to his diary that he was really a dissenter, but that he wanted to live with his own social class and among gentlemen.[5]

The Wesleyans had become a great force in the county, and although they were separated from the Church of England they were not hostile to

---

[1] *Charge at the Primary Visitation of Bishop Jackson*, 1855. L.P.L., U.P. 285.

[2] MS in my possession.

[3] But in Lincoln civil marriages were performed at the workhouse until at the request of the Lincoln Evangelical Free Church Council they were transferred to the Guardians' clerk's office in Bank Street in 1897.

[4] For the abolition of church rates see below, p. 188, and for the Burial Act, p. 241.

[5] Cracroft, 29 September 1851.

it as the older dissenting bodies were. Some of them went to church more or less regularly, and some to communion. Cracroft noted that Keal Cotes school feast was organised at the Wesleyan school, though most of the children went to the parish church. Harry Ingilby the rector stayed away, but he had played his cards with so much judgment that all active opposition amongst the dissenters to the church had died away. Cracroft thought that they all would go back to church if it were warm and comfortable instead of damp and cold, though they would still attend the chapel too.[1]

This modest degree of tolerance was a great advance on the hostility and contempt with which dissenters were met generally half a century earlier, depending in the village largely on the attitude of squire and parson. In Lincoln there was not the difficulty sometimes found in a village of acquiring a site for a chapel: but on the other hand there was the chilling presence of the higher clergy, mostly patrons of the city incumbents, and there was the enmity of an ignorant mob. For example, when the Wesleyans went to their meeting-house on the Waterside South – opened in 1789 – they had to run the gauntlet of men and boys on the other side of the river who pelted them with missiles and abuse.

Perhaps the most impressive evidence of the early growth of the movement in Lincoln was in the emergence of leaders. It was only gradually that the full-time itinerant preachers became differentiated from the lay local preachers, and grew into a formal ministry which through the Methodist conference was to exercise dictatorial powers. From the Lincoln community there emerged preachers who took a prominent part in the national movement. By 1829 Watmough, a local writer, could name ten members who had become itinerant preachers. Richard Watson, president of the conference in 1826, had been apprenticed to a Lincoln joiner. He preached his first sermon at the age of 15; he was refused registration under the Toleration Act by the Lincoln magistrates on the ground that he was still an apprentice, but he was registered at Newark, and he became an itinerant minister. John Hannah, who became secretary and was twice president of conference, and first theological tutor of the first Methodist theological college, was the son of a maltster and corn merchant on the Waterside in Lincoln;[2] he began to

---

[1] Cracroft, 22 September 1853. Later on a visit to Upton he noted that, though the vicar only reckoned some 6 or 7 church families in his population of some 560 in Upton and Kexby, every soul of whatever form of dissent had given in either money, leadings or labour to the building of the church; and at that moment the labourers were building the churchyard wall, Kexby labourers taking one half, Upton the other. 'But then Mr Vaughan (the vicar) knows how to conciliate and win men.' 27 March 1875. For the attitude of nonconformists at Barton on Humber, see Janet Courtney, *Recollected in Tranquillity*, pp. 38–9.   [2] According to *D.N.B.* a small coal dealer.

preach at the age of 19. John Bedford became an itinerant preacher, and after some years returned to Lincoln and became a local preacher.[1] Others there were who with them were celebrated by Thomas Cooper in his verses on the *Wesleyan Chiefs* (published by subscription in 1833) bringing himself in with them in the lines:

> All hail! my brothers of the local band
> Proudly I see myself enrolled with you.

A Methodist layman, Thomas Bainbridge, opened a successful private school in Michaelgate which no doubt helped to keep the society together; and a social element began with the introduction of tea meetings, first for Sunday school teachers and their friends, and then for a wider circle. As they were introduced by Mr Dalby after the departure of the more austere Mr Isaac, who disapproved of junketings giving licence to scandal, they can be dated about 1818. The fact that they provided good cheer, were useful for raising money, and gave opportunity for speaking for mutual benefit did not prevent the older brethren from frowning upon them: William Mawer remarked that 'it would be no hard work to collect of this sort'.[2]

The society grew so rapidly that a new chapel opened in 1815 soon proved inadequate, and in 1836 Wesley Chapel, built to hold 1,400 people, was opened. It was a good austere brick building with an Ionic front, designed by W. A. Nicholson. At the opening ceremony 3,000 people were present, and Dr Charlesworth reported to Bromhead:

Sunday evening, 1 July 1836. The concourse at the Methodist Chapel today has been immense, the whole collection £140. Whitehead attended last week, Wayland, the Mayor and the Melvilles. All the people appear to be well dressed.[3]

The question whether organs were permissible was one of much controversy in the connection, and Wesley Chapel had to manage without one for 20 years. There were lots of anniversaries. In 1838, 496 sat down to tea, with addresses to follow; and the next day, tea and ale for 300 poor.[4] They also had their own benevolent society.

---

[1] His son John became vicar of Brighton and archdeacon of Lewes.

[2] For the early history of Methodism in Lincoln see T. Jackson, *Memoirs of the Life and Writings of the Rev. Richard Watson* (1834); James Everitt, *The Polemic Divine: or the Memoirs of the Life, Writings and Opinions of the Rev. Daniel Isaac* (1839); A. Watmough, *History of Methodism in the neighbourhood and city of Lincoln* (1829); G. Barratt, *Recollections of Methodism and Methodists in the City of Lincoln* (1866), and now William Leary, *Methodism in the City of Lincoln* (1969).

[3] Bromhead MSS. The foundation stone of a new Wesleyan Sunday school was laid in 1839, and two houses were built near by for ministers in 1842. Wesley Chapel was demolished in 1967.

[4] *L.C.*, 16 February 1838.

Growth did not end there. In 1831 they bought a little meeting house in the Bail which had been built by the General Baptists, moving to a larger one in 1842. But they were to suffer much from secessions, and the results of one of them showed in 1818, with a twelve-hour assembly on Castle Hill, interrupted by stone throwing and a goat sent into the assembly by scoffers. These were the Primitive Methodists or 'Ranters', and it seems that their first meeting house was in Hungate. They continued to hold camp meetings on Canwick common or elsewhere, lasting most of the day, followed by a 'love feast'; these became an annual institution. By 1839, this gathering of the poor, 'despised', said the *Mercury*, 'by their opulent Wesleyan brethren', began to build in Portland Place on a site now covered by the central railway station; their fervency in chapel was described by the hostile *Chronicle* as sounding like a public house fight.[1] A period of depression followed for them, but by 1854 the chapel was enlarged to seat 500; even that was not large enough, and a larger one was built on the site in 1874. Like the Wesleyans, the Primitives founded chapels in other parts of the city.

Methodist dissension in 1837 did not affect the Lincoln Wesleyan circuit, and it was later said that for at least a generation the Lincolnshire preachers had been a proverb of simplicity and fervour, and of hardy, plodding earnestness.[2] But ministers of a dissident party later expelled from the central Conference for seeking a more democratic form of church government visited Lincoln in 1849. There were unseemly scenes at Wesley Chapel and in the Corn Exchange. Members were expelled from the parent body without trial or ceremony. At Wesley Chapel Mr Bulman, who should have preached, did not appear. Mr Bacon, the superintendent minister, entered the chapel early, took possession of the pulpit, opened the service and then handed over to a stranger from Boston and retired. Mr Battle and an ex-policeman attended at the door, presumably to keep out 'improper characters'. The tory *Chronicle* strenuously defended the Wesleyans against the 'Chartist Wesleyans', whom it described as a band of demagogues and an ignorant mob.[3] In consequence of this split the Wesleyans lost in membership, and reduced their circuit staff of ministers from three to two; but they soon recovered from this setback, and went on to greater numbers.

The Wesleyan Reformers met in rooms or in the Corn Exchange until in 1854 they bought Zion Chapel in Silver Street, built by Calvinistic Methodists. They were another gathering of the poor. Their early

---

[1] *S.M.*, 16 August 1839; *L.C.*, 12 May 1843.
[2] B. Gregory, *Sidelights on the Conflict of Methodism* (1898), p. 247.
[3] *L.C.*, 14 February 1851.

minutes are written in crude hands with errors of spelling. Clearly they were determined not to fall under ministerial domination as the Wesleyan connection had. Laymen occupied the chair at meetings; ministers were not mentioned by name; the title of 'reverend' was not accorded to those who had not received it previously; and all office holders were to be elected annually. The brethren were addressed as 'Brother'. Precautions were taken against the entry of undesirables to their love feasts; only authorised brethren might give notes to applicants, and the notes must be given up at the door to brethren duly appointed. Spiritual discipline was enforced; an inveterate habit of smoking called for remonstrance; the death of a brother was to be improved for the edification of the brethren; a printed card was placed in the pulpit adjuring preachers to start the service punctually.

The last service was held in Zion Chapel in 1864, and at the opening of a new chapel on the site a tea meeting was held at which more than 1,000 people sat down. Soon afterwards the minister begins to appear in the chair at meetings, and is given the title of 'reverend'. The minutes are well kept. An organ is thought desirable. Respectability has crept in. The latest burst of Methodist fervour moves, like its predecessors, from the turbulent to the sedate.

The Zion Chapel already mentioned had been built by the Methodists who followed Whitefield and became the Countess of Huntingdon's Connexion; but the missionary fervour which had marked their origins had long died out. An unkind Wesleyan wrote of them that 'they had a humble good man, as harmless as a sheep, for a minister, and, for a while, a respectable congregation used to assemble, but it soon became a dwindling affair, going down lower and lower, till the wheels of this Gospel chariot finally stood still'.[1]

Until the impetus given them by Methodism the older dissenting communities had shown little zeal, and indeed one or two of them existed in little more than name. The Presbyterian meeting house[2] had been borrowed by the Whitefield Methodists before they built Zion, but the older body, now become explicitly Unitarian, resumed in 1837. The Quakers held only quarterly meetings in their meeting house, built about 1690. The General Baptist chapel in St Benedict Square had been closed, and was for a time borrowed by the Independents, but they too made a fresh start. The Particular Baptists built a chapel in Mint Lane in 1818 and a larger one in 1871; by 1851 they had 118 members. A small Roman Catholic chapel was built in Silver Street in 1799 and rebuilt in 1854.

---

[1] Barratt, *Recollections of Methodism*, p. 85.
[2] *G.L.*, pp. 68, 296.

In 1819 a few of the congregation at Zion Chapel seceded, borrowed the General Baptist chapel, and procured a minister from the dissenting academy at Hoxton. It was regularly organised as an Independent church practising infant baptism, and built a chapel in Tanner's Lane in St Peter at Gowts parish. Its membership grew, the chapel being enlarged three times, and though an attempt at union with Zion Chapel failed, its progress no doubt contributed to the latter's decline. It exercised strict discipline over the lives of its members. Although the Independents did not have a centrally organised system of itinerant ministers as the Methodists did, their ministers came and went from time to time, and hence it is that in accounts of them as of other dissenters there is not the same emphasis upon individuals as there is in accounts of the Church of England. One of the Independent ministers, the Reverend Samuel Brodribb Bergne, does, however, stand out. Thomas Cooper wrote of him in the *Mercury* that he was undoubtedly the most talented of the non-established clergy in Lincoln, though he was not a great preacher. He was discreet enough not to take a prominent part in the agitation for the abolition of church rates, though he was of course against them. He may well have been embarrassed to be elected a guardian at a vestry meeting at St Peter at Gowts in 1842, and he resigned two years later. He took part in the work of the Mechanics Institution.

A wealthy baronet, Sir Culling Eardley Smith, who had property at Nettleton, passes over the scene. Anderson recorded:

16 June 1830. Culling Smith passed through Lincoln whilst we were there. He is I suppose going to spend the summer in the county. He will be no acquisition, for he is always meddling. He has just presented the Independents of Lincoln with a tent to preach in in the open air, or at least to assist their camp meetings. I fear the Dissenters are in the increase hereabouts.[1]

He was the founder of the Evangelical Alliance, and friend of the persecuted in many countries. Maria Edgeworth, with whom he and his wife toured Connemara, wrote of him as 'of old family, large fortune and great philanthropy, extending to poor little Ireland and her bogs'.[2]

On one occasion Bergne had 1,000 hearers at an open-air meeting; and on that or another Smith, then high sheriff, was present with his chaplain. He was reported to have said at a dissenting tea meeting that he wished the day would soon come when all dissenting ministers would be called to preach in the cathedral. When it became known that the Independents were coming out of Tanners Lane to build in a more prominent place in Newland, the rumour spread that Culling Smith

[1] Wilberforce MSS, d.24, fol. 142.
[2] A. J. C. Hare, *Life and Letters of Maria Edgeworth* (1894). II, 204. I owe this reference to Miss Joan Gibbons. See also *D.N.B.*

would lay the first stone of the new chapel, and Yarborough the first stone of the new school. But rumour had gone too far: the whig notables would subscribe, but did not usually grace the gatherings personally. Yet Smith was a law unto himself. At St Peter in Eastgate, when he attended officially, he followed the vicar into the vestry, and asked him to subscribe to a dissenting school, to which Mr Bagge replied that he would subscribe to no school that did not support the church. The sheriff said 'You may as well subscribe to support the devil'.[1] He subscribed to the new Independent chapel, as did Lord Yarborough and Sir William Ingilby. The architect was Fenton of Chelmsford, described as 'an architect of great respectability and celebrity in chapel building'.[2]

Comparisons were being made between the relative strengths of Anglicans and dissenters. Edward Horsman, a crotchety whig who had served in Palmerston's first government,[3] was a hostile critic of the Church of England, and he had clerical correspondents in the Lincoln neighbourhood. He told the Commons that he held it to the discredit of the dean and chapter, who shared the patronage of the parish churches in Lincoln, that the 13 parish churches, miserable, decayed and dilapidated, were ill served by ten ill-paid incumbents, of whom six had other clerical duties (the highest stipend being £150 and the lowest £68) and their total income £1,444, less than a third of the income of one member of the chapter. He had had a return of attendances at churches and chapels in Lincoln on the same Sunday. Of the 13 churches 9 only were open for morning service, 3 for afternoon service, and 7 for evening service, and in all of them only 19 services were performed. There were present at the morning services 1,013; at the afternoon 175; at the evening 1,075, making a total of 2,263, out of a population of 13,000 inhabitants. This did not include the cathedral. On the same day the attendances at the dissenting chapels were: morning, 2,565, and evening 3,102, making a total of 5,667 in ten dissenting chapels, which had 21 services. The greatest number attending dissenting chapels was therefore three times that of the greatest number at the parish churches.[4]

---

[1] *L.C.*, 21 December 1838. It added 'yet he would not dine with the Judges on Sunday, as it would be a desecration of the Sabbath'. In 1860 the Newland chapel had 160 members, 250 Sunday school scholars and 28 teachers. The Tanner's Lane chapel had 82 members, 300 scholars and 30 teachers. J. T. Barker, *Congregationalism in Lincolnshire* (1860). The old chapel had continued.

[2] H. M. Colvin, *Dictionary of British Architects 1660–1845* (1954), p. 204.

[3] It was of him that Bright said that he had retired into his political cave of Adullam, and had called about him everyone that was in distress and everyone that was discontented. According to *Sir Wilfred Lawson, A Memoir* (ed. G. W. E. Russell, 1909), p. 30, he was a regular and successful panic monger.

[4] *P.D.* 3rd Ser. 98, 1076; reprinted in *Five Speeches on Ecclesiastical Affairs* (1848).

No doubt this evidence was dismissed as coming from a prejudiced source. Yet broad confirmation came from the religious census of 1851. The number of attendances on the appointed Sunday at the thirteen parish churches plus the cathedral was 4,242; at the eleven dissenting chapels 5,670; at the Roman Catholic chapel 374. There were probably more 'twicers' among the dissenters than among the Anglicans, and there is no sure way of translating the number of attendances into the number of adherents. But it was evident that something like half the worshipping population were dissenters, and henceforth it would not be possible for the legislature to assume that the National Church was the church of the whole nation, or that church and state were coterminous. The other startling conclusion was that at least a third, perhaps a half, of the population did not attend religious worship at all.[1]

Many of the battles of the dissenters for the removal of disabilities were fought in parliament, and some were fought by individuals against individual clergy. Church rates were fought in the parish vestries. They were a levy on the ratepayers of the parish for the upkeep of the fabric and the services of the parish church, and payment was enforceable by law. This was not unreasonable when church and state were assumed to be different aspects of the same community and everyone was deemed to belong to both. But this was no longer tenable, and dissenters, who had to pay for the building and the repair of their own chapels and support their own ministers, naturally objected to the impost. They were supported by others who disliked the Church of England on political grounds, and perhaps by still more because they disliked rates and taxes in general. The dissenters therefore had numerous allies.

The battle did not arise in all parishes: some of them had income enough without a church rate, and in others, as at St Margaret and St Mary Magdalene, where there were few if any dissenters, the rate was paid without objection. In some parishes there was no church at all.[2]

The grant or refusal of a rate had frequently to be decided on a poll of

---

[1] See Appendix IV. The census reporter, Horace Mann, used a method of estimating attenders (taking the whole morning attendance plus half the afternoon plus one third of the evening) designed to favour the Church of England, where the most popular service was in the morning, as against the non-Anglicans, whose largest services were held in the evening. On any other method, such as two-thirds attendance, the non-Anglicans retain the majority, H. Perkin, *Origins of Modern English Society 1780–1880* (1969), p. 199n. The printed returns are given by poor law unions. *Census of Great Britain, 1851, Religious Worship, England and Wales.* (1853), pp. 83, 428.

It was pointed out at the time that numbers might be pushed up on the appointed day by pressure to attend, and that figures would not necessarily represent the normal attendance.

[2] *Accounts and Papers*, 1845, xli, Abstract of Returns relative to Church rates.

the parish. There were violent arguments, with charges of bad faith. Refusal of a rate led in one case to a threat to close the church, in another to stop the church clock; on one occasion it was announced that there would be no sacrament, as there was no money to buy wine. 'Awkward St Swithin' was the most turbulent: not only parish affairs, but everything done in the parish meeting was liable to challenge. It was alleged that an agreement about assessment of the Gas Company's undertaking had been improperly altered after signature. The long-suffering incumbent, who wrote the minutes, added, 'the most remarkable mare's nest to be found in the parish annals'.

The old method of raising income for parish church purposes had ceased to be practicable in face of opposition, and could not fail to poison the relations of clergy and part of their people, and it is not surprising that by 1858 W. F. J. Kaye, then archdeacon's deputy, was advising parish officers that where a rate could not be obtained without arousing hostility it should not be pursued. When church rates were abolished by law most parishes petitioned against the bill, but by then it was not necessary for the abolitionists to attend.[1]

----

[1] Most of the vestry minutes are now in L.A.O.

CHAPTER X

POLITICS, 1868-1914

At the time of the election of 1868 Seely was 65. For more than ten years he had lived in the Isle of Wight. The men with and against whom he had fought as a young man were dead, including his former partner in the mill, T. M. Keyworth. Clayton and Shuttleworth, his partners in the foundry, had been his most influential supporters, but he had exhausted their goodwill. He had never invested a penny in the foundry, but he had become a partner – a sleeping partner – in exchange for guaranteeing a bank overdraft twenty years earlier. As the years passed and the profits grew, and with them Seely's share, the active partners became more and more restive, and after much acrimony brought matters to a head. Seely was only willing to be bought out for the full value of his share, and the dispute went to arbitration. The works were closed for stocktaking in April 1869, and 1,000 men were out of work for a week: these things could not be done in a corner, and everybody knew. So Seely lost the 'foundry influence'.[1]

Seely gave a dinner in 1870 which neither Clayton nor Shuttleworth attended; they told both the mayor and Seely that they would oppose him tooth and nail, and that if no other candidate could be found one of them would stand against him. 'This,' said Francis Larken to Monson, 'would be a bad lookout for Seely, for he has hitherto ridden in on the backs of the foundries, and is far from popular in the city.'[2]

Sir Henry Lucy has described Seely in his later years:

A mild, softly spoken, precise gentleman of the old school, is Seely, who walks about with disproportionately long strides and vaguely conveys the impression that he wears snow-shoes. It seems a peculiarly happy indication of the fitness of things that he should represent Lincoln, of which one (who really knows nothing about it) has the impression that it is a dapper, clean-looking, highly respectable, but decidedly slow cathedral city, which years ago was stranded somewhere on the east coast, out of the main highway, and has lived very happily there ever since.

Seely contents himself with one speech a year: but what a speech it is! You cannot hear it all, for though his spirit truly is willing, his voice is weak. But – though this impression also is vague and indefinable – your feeling is that he is

---

[1] Gossip at the time said that after costly adjournments during the arbitration proceedings Clayton leaned over the table and said 'Seely, how much will satisfy you?' When a round sum was named, Clayton drew and handed him a cheque for it, saying, 'Now you need never speak to me again.' J. G. Williams' notes in my possession. The late Richard Mason confirmed this account.

[2] L.A.O. Monson 25/13/16-17, 8 August 1870.

framing a tremendous and unanswerable indictment. There is no mistaking the way in which he carries his glasses to his eyes after having made an inaudible remark. You know by the severe expression of his mouth, the flash of the inflexible eye, and the unyielding grip on the *pince-nez*, that somebody has been hit, and hit hard too.

Then when Seely has finished his speech, and sits listening with judicial air to the criticism of honourable and right honourable gentlemen, he has an impressive way of taking notes which is perfectly overpowering...In the course of the debate to-night, Seely took more notes than he could possibly have read out in an hour, and in replying did not refer to one in a hundred. It was enough that he had noted them down. The presumptuous disputants were answered.[1]

The speech was probably about Admiralty expenditure, of which Seely, watching the dockyard near his home, was a stern critic.[2] Spy in *Vanity Fair* (1875) added to his cartoon the note:

he addressed himself to those small economies in which the salvation of a nation is to be found, when the graver matters are delivered over to wrack and ruin...a few years ago Mr Seely's pigs were as widely known as he himself is now widely forgotten.

A much more colourful personality had emerged from the ranks of the tory squirearchy. Henry Chaplin had succeeded his redoubtable uncle Charles[3] at Blankney in 1859, and came of age in 1862. He was owner of 25,000 acres of land with a rent roll of perhaps £40,000, and besides Blankney Hall, which with the village his uncle rebuilt,[4] he had a lease of Burghersh Chantry in Lincoln, where he was to entertain the Prince of Wales. He spent his patrimony with a reckless lavishness which eventually ruined him. He hunted the Burton, and for him the Blankney Hunt country was carved out of the Burton country. He kept a racing stable, out of which, at the age of 26, he won the Derby with Hermit in 1867.[5] In the following year he was returned to parliament for the Mid-Lincolnshire division, and he held it and its successor the Sleaford division until 1906. He was described by a foreign observer in 1885:

He appears to take as his model the late Lord George Bentinck, who was the champion of the Protectionist party in Parliament when Free Trade was being pressed forward, and who was also a mighty patron of the turf. There is a

---

[1] *Diary of Two Parliaments*, I, 193, 7 March 1877.
[2] *Letters and other Writings of the late Edward Denison M.P. for Newark* (1872), p. 95.
[3] Above, p. 68.   [4] The architect was W. A. Nicholson.
[5] The odds were 66 to 1 against him at starting. Chaplin was said to have won £150,000, and Captain Marshall his partner £60,000. G. K. Jarvis, Diary, 22 May 1867. A tremendous sensation had been caused when he was jilted by his fiancée, a few days before the date fixed for the wedding, in favour of the Marquis of Hastings. The latter lost heavily in betting against Chaplin's Derby winner, and Chaplain treated him with magnanimity. See the biography by his daughter the Marchioness of Londonderry, *Henry Chaplin, a Memoir* (1926).

mixture in Mr Chaplin's bearing of geniality and pomposity which will be found by no means unpleasant. He has had his crosses, vexations, even his serious troubles in life. But his disappointments and his suffering, deep as they have been, have not permanently embittered him. He denounces his political opponents in Parliament, but there is no malignity in his invective. His oratorical manner is heavy, his voice sonorous, his sentences rotund. He reminds one alternately of a schoolboy declaiming his theme and an evangelical clergyman proclaiming the doom of the scarlet lady from his pulpit. He has all the instincts, and takes interest in all the avocations, of the country gentleman. Of practical politics he is ignorant: he calls himself a Tory.[1]

Another observer shrewdly remarked that after a sensational début in an attack on Gladstone, he settled down to the reputation of a country squire rather than a statesman. For a whole generation or more he was 'the Squire'.[2] His reputation as a sportsman brought him a great following not only in the county but among the working men in Lincoln, and the *Mercury* remarked that they would have voted for his footman had he so wished it.

Chaplin and some other representatives of the landed interest were never really reconciled to the repeal of the corn laws, though for long it was imprudent to say so and thus rouse the battle cry of 'cheap food in danger'. References to the sufferings of agriculture owing to foreign competition led by stages to a more explicit declaration of policy. In 1879 he moved for a Royal Commission to enquire into the depressed condition of agriculture, disclaiming that he advocated a return to protection: a following speaker accepted the assurance, adding that a more powerful speech in favour of protection he had never heard.[3] Presently industrialists crying out against foreign tariff walls were to become allies, and the full-blooded policy was to be proclaimed by Joseph Chamberlain.

For the election of 1874 the Lincoln tories adopted Chaplin's younger brother, Colonel Edward Chaplin, as their candidate. He was a great hunting man; for years he was mounted six days a week in the season by Lord Henry Bentinck, and for a time he hunted the Blankney. He was also a big game hunter, and perhaps his greatest day came in Zulu country in 1867, when one morning before breakfast he killed three lions, and rounded off the day by adding to his bag a large crocodile and three antelopes.

He stood in Lincoln against Seely and Palmer, whose prospects were improved by the growth in the number of householders on the register as a result of the second Reform Bill – there were over 4,000 – while the

---

[1] *Society in London*, by a Foreign Resident (Tauchnitz edition, 1885), p. 112.
[2] T. Wemyss Reid, *Politicians of To-day* (1880), II, 217–31.
[3] *P.D.*, 3rd Series, 247, 1425, 1476.

number of freemen (545) was declining; the Ballot Act of 1872 affected both sides by reducing the scope for corruption.

Excitement was intense, and it was said to have been the most fiercely contested election in memory. Though Edward Chaplin 'can't speak a bit'[1] he and his brother brought up voters in splendid four-in-hand drags, supported by the handsome waggonette of Coningsby Sibthorp. There were riots, the military (brought in as a precaution and hidden) were called out, the Riot Act having been read by the mayor, and great damage was done. Chaplin headed the poll with 2,107 votes, and Seely secured the second seat with 1,907. Palmer polled 1,784, though he had more than three times the number of Seely's plumpers, having strong support from the working men. It had been noted that the liberal joint committee did not contain the names of Rudgard, Clayton and Shuttleworth. Seely had been in danger of losing his principal support among the foundry workmen, and he persuaded his agent, Tweed, the town clerk, to intercede with Clayton. The latter generously responded, and at the last moment announced that he would vote for Seely. This may well have saved him.

The election of 1874 gave Disraeli his greatest triumph, one striking feature of which was the eclipse of the politically minded whig gentry. As the economic and ultimately the social position of the gentry began to decline, the whigs in their ranks became more uncomfortable in a liberal party increasingly influenced by its radical wing. This trend was especially noticeable in Lincolnshire. It happened that the liberal Cholmeley who had sat for North Lincolnshire died only a few days before the election, and the liberals made no attempt to hold the seat. There was no contest. Rowland Winn,[2] who had first been returned in 1868, was elected with Sir John Astley in place of Cholmeley. Astley was no politician.[3]

In the Mid-Lincolnshire division Amcotts withdrew: his heart was not in politics, and he told his wife he was too old. The promising young Edward Stanhope, a cousin of Banks Stanhope,[4] was brought in with Chaplin. In the Southern division William Earle Welby and Edmund Turnor, both tories, were returned. The *Chronicle* exultantly remarked that

---

[1] Stanhope (Chevening) MSS., bdle 533,29/1/74. I owe this reference to Dr Richard Olney.
[2] Winn, who was the son of Charles Winn of Nostell Priory near Wakefield, lived at Appleby near Brigg. By 1868 he had developed the ironstone mines at Frodingham and built a railway to serve them.
[3] *Recollected in Tranquillity* (1926), p. 46. See Astley's *Fifty Years of my Life* (1895), p. 258.
[4] Stanhope early achieved office, though he did his party disastrous service in 1885 by describing the radical policy as 'promising to every labourer three acres and a cow'. This became a catchword which helped the liberals in the counties. J. L. Garvin, *Life of Joseph Chamberlain*, II, 79. Stanhope died in 1893. According to Lord Frederick Hamilton his life was shortened by staying long hours on the Treasury Bench.

the great hereditary whig families could not find either among themselves or elsewhere a single candidate for the representation of the county.[1]

The loss of a seat prompted Lincoln liberals to a new activity, and they organised an association on the successful Birmingham model. There were rumours that the mild whigs and the upper crust of tories would be content to continue to share the seats between the parties, but the Liberals would have none of it. Nonconformists in particular were roused by the Turkish atrocities and the burials question, and the temperance movement was more active. Seely and Palmer were both put forward again, as was Edward Chaplin. Henry Chaplin was calling attention to the industrialists who were asking for protection against foreign competition, and pointing out that their prediction made at the repeal of the corn laws that other countries would follow our example had proved untrue.[2] Chaplin walked warily; he proposed to repeal the malt tax, and suggested a tax on beer, but he would not tax wheat without absolute necessity.

On election day the foundries were closed, and the men sported their bright blue ribbons. Lighted tar barrels were as usual rolled up to the Saracen's Head gates, and the mob had to be dispersed by the police. Seely (3,401) and Palmer (3,128) were returned, Chaplin polling only 2,190. Henry Chaplin attributed his brother's defeat to the big battalions of his opponents, then united, as they had not been at the previous election; and there were charges that the liberals, having their committee rooms at public houses, had indulged in wholesale bribery.

The death of Palmer[3] on 2 June 1884 caused a by-election. The tories had adopted Richard Hall, a much respected citizen and supporter of philanthropic causes: the liberals looked for a leading engineer. First they invited Nathaniel Clayton to stand, and, when he declined on grounds of age and health, Joseph Ruston. He accepted, and he won the election.[4]

Soon afterwards there was a great demonstration in support of parliamentary reform. A thousand men marched to the South common, all the trade societies with their pageants. The boilermakers had a huge boiler, lent by Ruston and Proctor, with the legend:

> We zealous toilers
> Who make these boilers,
> We'll be the foilers
> Of the Peers.

There were eleven bands, and an audience of 25,000 people, including

---

[1] *L.C.*, 6 February 1874.   [2] *L.C.*, 7 March 1879.
[3] He gave his name to the Married Women's Property Act 1882, promoted by him.
[4] *L.C.*, 25 July 1884, described his style of oratory as clear, forcible and natural.

deputations from most of the towns of north and mid-Lincolnshire. Ruston was in the chair, supported by Edward Heneage, Francis Otter[1] and other candidates.

A dispute between the liberal majority in the Commons and the House of Lords about reform having been compromised, the Redistribution Act which accompanied the Reform Bill of 1885[2] deprived Lincoln of one parliamentary seat, and brought Bracebridge into the constituency. Liberals were in a difficulty: they had two members. Seely had been steadily losing ground. His name was often absent from division lists, and when in 1882 he had made a speech in Lincoln 'bristling with Conservative ideas and sentiments', the *Mercury* asked why, if he could not support Mr Gladstone's government, he did not resign.[3] He was 82. But he wanted to end his days in harness. His son sat for Nottingham, and his grandson was standing for a Derbyshire seat, and the thought of three generations in the House together appealed to his vanity. Ruston belonged to a later generation; he was at his most active, and his views were acceptable to the party; he was a nonconformist with active sympathies with the temperance movement. It was urged that he, as the junior, should stand down, and fight the Sleaford division. Both members were asked whether they would abide by the decision of the liberal association; both knew what it would be, and Ruston agreed while Seely declined. Ruston was chosen, and Seely unwillingly withdrew. It was the end of a long Lincoln connection for him, though not for his family.

A tory candidate, F. H. Kerans, was chosen on the initiative of the working men of the party: he was only 36, and a London barrister. Ruston soon got into trouble with the Anglicans. He advocated disestablishment of the Church of England, but denied having spoken in favour of its disendowment also; though it was ferreted out that he had seconded a resolution in favour of both at a meeting of the Congregational Union. When the election came in 1885 Ruston was returned with 3,726 votes against Kerans' 2,701. There had been riots as usual, and when no prosecutions followed the question was asked 'Are the Watch Committee all liberals?'

---

[1] He won the Louth division in 1885. He was a barrister, a pupil of Arnold of Rugby and brother-in-law to George Eliot. His home was at Ranby. See *George Eliot Letters*, vi, 116n, vii, 318–21.

[2] The three Lincolnshire divisions were redistributed in six, all single-member constituencies. Boston, Grantham and Lincoln each lost one member. Stamford had lost one in 1867, and in 1885 was merged in the Stamford division of the county. Grimsby had lost one member in 1832. The age of the carpet bagger had arrived, and henceforth a member of parliament, however successful at Westminster, would play a lesser part on the local scene.

[3] 17 November 1882.

Within a year Ruston was in further trouble. Gladstone introduced his Irish Home Rule Bill, and local liberals sent Ruston a telegram earnestly desiring him to vote for the second reading. He voted against it, and there was instant speculation what would happen next: would Seely reappear? Ruston met his supporters, explained his attitude, declined to stand again, and left the room. Many maintained that he had pursued a fair and manly course, and the meeting turned to the choice of a new candidate. Eventually they chose William Crosfield, a Liverpool merchant and a Congregationalist, who had contested Warrington at the last election. One of his supporters afterwards wrote of him:

He was one of the best of men, but not the best of candidates. He had rather a gruff voice, and he was prone to be dull and prosy in his speaking. He was not specially prepossessing in his appearance either. I had great difficulty in persuading certain fierce temperance people that Mr Crosfield was a teetotaler. 'Water', they said, 'never gave him that nose.'[1]

When the next election came in 1886 Ruston stood aloof. The dissentient liberals who, like him, were opposed to Irish Home Rule rallied formidable support to Kerans, who stood again: Clayton, among engineers and business men Thomas Bell, Henry Newsum and John Jekyll, all Congregationalists, among clergy Chancellor Leeke, and the one-time Chartist Thomas Cooper. Feeling ran so high that they could not get a hearing. Nevertheless the action of the liberal unionists was decisive, and Kerans was returned. Lincolnshire, which at the previous election had returned seven liberals and four conservatives, now returned nine conservatives, one liberal, and a liberal unionist, Edward Heneage, at Grimsby.[2]

The agricultural depression deepened. At a county meeting held in November 1886 Henry Chaplin dwelt on the troubles of the growers of corn. He would not impose a duty on imported wheat without the consent of the people; but the proceeds of a duty on foreign manufactured articles applied to the encouragement of wheat-growing would improve both trade and agriculture. In 1889 he became president of the Board of Agriculture in Lord Salisbury's government, but he was not able to implement his favourite policy.[3]

Kerans was hampered by local feuds at the election of 1892. He had offended the liberal unionists, he was believed to have been drunk at a public dinner, and he alienated other supporters; and he was defeated by

---

[1] J. D. Jones, *Three Score Years and Ten* (1940), p. 51.
[2] For his negotiations with the Irish leader Parnell, see J. L. Garvin, *Life of Joseph Chamberlain*, I (1932), 614.
[3] He turned to bimetallism in the belief that it would help agriculture.

Crosfield, who, said the *Chronicle*, was supported by all the faddists in the city.[1] A liberal club was opened in that year, and many speeches in denunciation of alcohol resounded in a building which owed its foundation and continued existence to malt liquor.

Kerans died in 1894, and Charles Seely's son, Colonel Charles Seely, then M.P. for West Nottingham, was invited to stand as a conservative candidate. He accepted and then withdrew, but not before making a handsome gift to the new public library[2] and promising to build a unionist club. His son Charles Hilton Seely, who had been a wrangler at Cambridge and had fought two elections, was chosen in his place, and received the support of the liberal unionists. Crosfield's strength lay in the engineering works; and during the election campaign of 1895 an unfortunate reference to his supporters as 'the unwashed mob' did Crosfield great harm: a body of 500 or 600 men marched from Stamp End and polled *en masse*, and Seely was returned.[3]

In October 1899 war broke out in South Africa. Though there were many people who thought that it could and should have been avoided, and held the tory government responsible, nevertheless the vast majority held decidedly that now that war had come it must be fought and won. There was great popular fervour. The second battalion of the Lincolnshire Regiment – until 1881 the North Lincolnshires, the Tenth Foot – was ordered to the front, and sailed in January. (The first battalion was in India.) A few weeks later men of the Lincolnshire Rifle Volunteer Companies were sworn in and sailed, and they were followed by others. A county meeting for a Lincolnshire Yeomanry ran into difficulties. Applications to join were not enough for a squadron: some men from the county had already joined the Sherwood Foresters, who would not release them, but offered to form a Lincolnshire squadron as a separate unit. It was, however, decided to wait for a reorganisation of the yeomanry as mounted infantry; by May 1902 the Lincolnshire Yeomanry were in being, and holding their first annual training at Belton. The Lincoln squadron had 175 men plus 55 not yet mounted.

The Lincolnshire Volunteers so grew that the first battalion, comprising the companies north of the Witham, was divided. J. G. Williams retained command of the first battalion, the third battalion being placed under J. M. Warrener. The second battalion comprised the companies south of the Witham; and the Lincoln companies of the first battalion

[1] 9 July 1892.
[2] Below, pp. 227–9.
[3] *S.M.*, 19 July 1895.

later became the fourth battalion, by which name it became memorable in Lincoln. On their return from South Africa, the city volunteers were individually admitted to the honorary freedom of the city.

There was a general election in 1900. It became known as the khaki election, because it was dominated by patriotic fervour, favouring the tory party, the more because the liberals were divided on the issue of the war. In Lincoln Crosfield's defeat in 1895 had given the liberals the chance to choose a new candidate, and they chose Charles Henry Roberts, who had been a Fellow of Exeter College, Oxford. He had already fought an election on the issue of popular control of the liquor traffic. Throughout his career this traffic was to be one of his chief concerns: moreover he had married a daughter of the redoubtable Countess of Carlisle, who was popularly believed to have poured the contents of the wine cellar at Castle Howard into the lake. Hence Roberts made a special appeal to nonconformists and blue ribbon campaigners, though at the same time he may have alienated others. He took up residence in Lincoln in March 1900.[1]

Seely held the seat by a narrow majority.[2] In his manifesto Roberts had used the Union Jack and the portrait of the other Roberts, the hero of the war, on his manifesto, but this was no doubt due to the zeal of his agent J. G. Williams. Perhaps the most remarkable fact about the contest was that Williams, then mayor, was liberal agent, and Tweed, the town clerk, was tory agent.

Seely was soon to upset his followers. He was one of two tory members to vote against a revival of the duty on corn. This was an issue which led to the formation of a protectionist group in the House, supported of course by Chaplin. Then the cabinet agreed to the importation of indentured Chinese coolies into the Transvaal to work in the mines. Seely opposed the measure, and read from a white paper the objection of the Chinese Minister, who sought to prevent his countrymen from being 'mere chattels or implements of husbandry'.[3]

Both issues echoed in Lincoln. The heads of the engineering firms were divided on the question whether protection would benefit the city's trade: but it was argued that as their products had been driven out of some countries by tariff walls, they should develop colonial trade by giving the colonies a preference. This was of course a form of protection. The Conservative Association, after hearing Seely's defence, declared

---

[1] For the wine story see Dorothy Henley, *Rosalind Howard Countess of Carlisle* (1959), pp. 109–11.

[2] By 4,002 to 3,935.

[3] J. E. B. Seely, *Adventure* (1930), p. 105.

that they could not support him at the next election, though one section remained loyal to him.

The leader of the protectionist cause in the country, Joseph Chamberlain, was in touch with Chaplin – it was 'my dear Joe' and 'my dear Harry', a degree of intimacy which Chamberlain neither gave to nor received from anyone else on the unionist side – and it was agreed to send Henry Page Croft to contest Lincoln as a protectionist. Chamberlain knew that in a three-cornered fight the liberal would probably win, but he declared that he would prefer an open enemy as member for Lincoln to a professing friend who would stab him in the back. Croft was adopted, fighting on the effect of the new German tariff on agricultural implements, and giving warning that if Lincoln's markets in South America were lost to the United States, a third of Lincoln's workmen would be on the streets. He partially undermined Seely by capturing the Constitutional Club, whose building, ironically enough, had been built at the expense of Seely's father.[1]

On his part Roberts had the support of the city council majority and the Free Church Council. When the election came in 1906 the liberal tide rose higher than it had ever risen before or ever would again, and Roberts won with a clear majority over both the other candidates.[2] The floodtide swept Chaplin out of the Sleaford division. The strong liberal vote in the rural divisions of the eastern counties was due in part to the small size of holdings and in part to the strength of nonconformity and the hostility of nonconformists and low churchmen to the spread of ritualism among the Anglican clergy.[3]

Neither the Seelyites nor the protectionists would withdraw from the Lincoln field, and manoeuvres continued. The latter produced Sir Robert Filmer, a soldier who had served in the Sudan and South Africa and was master of the Blankney Hunt, as their candidate. Seely stood again, and Roberts, who declared in favour of votes for women. When the contest came in January 1910 Roberts held the seat by a majority of 37. Filmer came second, having nearly trebled the protectionist vote of 1906, largely at the expense of the unionist free trader. By then the liberal tide had ebbed, and the tories had won the Sleaford and Louth divisions. During the year notable local liberals – Lord Monson, H. J. Torr, Edwin Pratt, A. C. Newsum – seceded to the tories – and Seely unwil-

---

[1] Julian Amery, *Life of Joseph Chamberlain*, VI (1948). 639, 753, 774; Lord Croft, *My Life of Strife* (1948), pp. 43–4. Croft sat for Christchurch, 1910–18, and Bournemouth, 1918–40. He became a peer, and died in 1947.
[2] Roberts 5,110, Seely 3,718, Croft 1,163.
[3] H. Pelling, *Social Geography of British Elections* (1967), pp. 226–7.

lingly withdrew. At the election in December of the same year, Winston Churchill having spoken on election day in support of Roberts, causing tremendous excitement, Roberts won with a majority of 606.[1]

Chaplin, having lost his seat at Sleaford in 1906, was returned in 1907 for Wimbledon, which he continued to represent until he went to the House of Lords as Viscount Chaplin in 1916.[2] His extravagance had brought him into serious financial difficulties, and by 1897 Blankney had finally passed into the hands of Lord Londesborough. The accidents of life, however, did not displace Chaplin from the hearts of hosts of Lincolnshire people. A. G. Gardiner painted a not unkindly portrait of him as representing

the calm, ineradicable conviction of the governing class, the *ancien régime*. He is a statesman not by virtue of so dangerous and democratic a thing as intellect; but by divine right, by right of blood and race...It is this portentous gravity and detachment from the reality that makes him, if not witty himself, the cause of wit in other men...What moment, for example, ever rivalled the hilarity that shook the House when, speaking on the Old Age Pensions Bill, he declaimed, his left hand upon his heart, his right uplifted to the heavenly witness: 'It has ever been the purpose of my life to do nothing that would sap the foundations of thrift among the poor'? He paused, puzzled by the hurricane of laughter, for his mind moves with bucolic leisure, and it did not occur to him that his noble sentiment had any application to himself – he, a gentleman of blood and birth, whose career was a legend of splendid lavishness, and who, in his old age, honoured the State by receiving from it a trifling pension of £1200 a year, a mere bagatelle, a thankoffering, as it were, from a grateful public, almost, indeed, in the nature of conscience money.

And he recorded a story which is still told in various forms in his home county:

a friend of his tells how he was once staying with him at a country house, and in the midst of conversation Mr Chaplin excused himself on the ground of work. And later the friend, while wandering in the pastures, heard from the other side of the hedge a sonorous voice delivering itself thus: 'Mr Speaker – Sir – Little did I think, when I came down to the House this afternoon, that I should feel it incumbent upon me, in pursuance of my duty to the country, and, Mr Speaker,

---

[1] The number of electors on the register had risen from 1043 in 1832 to 4,151 in 1868, and 11,577 in 1910. Austen Chamberlain commented that Seely was one of Lord Cromer's followers, and like Cromer having done all the mischief he could for several years, rallied at the last moment because the Referendum satisfied him. 'What was the value of his support? The liberal polled more votes than ever, and had a majority of over 600.' *Politics from Inside* (1936), p. 309. Seely later emerged as a liberal.

[2] Having to choose supporters for his coat of arms he said he would have his Derby winner Hermit, and was indignant when the Heralds' College produced something between a dragon and a dachshund. He found for them an old picture of the horse. E. F. Benson, *As We Were* (1930), p. 302.

may I add to myself, to address the House upon – ' and the friend fled from the august recital.[1]

Shortly before the outbreak of war in 1914 Roberts was appointed to minor office in the Asquith government, but he was displaced when the coalition was formed in 1915. As an adherent of Asquith he was denied the Lloyd George coupon at the election of 1918, and he was unseated.[2] He might have gone much further, but his political career was virtually ended, He was a man of integrity and great ability but no small talk. He was elected for Derby in 1922 but lost the seat in 1923, and thereafter served as chairman of the Cumberland County Council from 1938 to 1958, dying in 1959.

[1] *Prophets, Priests and Kings* (1907 edition), pp. 212–17. Lord Oxford said he would have formed an admirable model for a character part in one of Disraeli's novels. *Memories and Reflections* (1928), I, 174.
[2] It is remarkable that he and Bishop Hicks saw the coalition victory as a triumph for their favourite hates, Drink and Tariff Reform. Diary of E. L. Hicks, 29 December 1918.

CHAPTER XI

INDUSTRY AND AGRICULTURE, 1870-1914

Trade was good and the city was growing fast as the third quarter of the century neared its end. The city council had declared in 1865 that:

there are now established in the city of Lincoln many large manufactories of agricultural engines, machines and other implements of chemical and other manures, of oil and linseed cakes, besides maltkilns breweries and various other trades in which an extensive business is carried on, that the rise of these manufactures has been rapid, and that they contribute very materially to the prosperity of the city.[1]

In 1873 the directors of the Lincoln and Lindsey Bank reported that Lincoln was attaining a position of considerable business importance and that Lindsey with its ironstone discoveries and extending railways was opening new fields for enterprise. The reference was to the industrial beginnings of Scunthorpe, described as a second Middlesborough, where, between Doncaster and Gainsborough on Rowland Winn's estate, there would soon be nineteen blast furnaces. Almost at the same time part of the Monks estate at Greetwell on the Lincoln boundary was let to a firm of ironsmelters at Frodingham for ironstone workings.[2]

Ruston followed by testing for ironstone on Canwick common and towards Washingborough. It was found at Bracebridge; and press correspondence suggested that stone overlaying the iron was suitable to burn for lime and the shale of the upper lias underneath it for bricks; and water might be tapped to supply the lower city. But another Scunthorpe did not materialise, and only the Greetwell workings continued. Coal was bored for at Swinderby, but it was found too deep to be economically workable.[3]

But engineering was much more successful. Cooke had produced his successful double-furrow plough. At Robeys, in 1875, Robert Robey, Thomas Bell and John Richardson[4] were joined in partnership by several farmers and professional men, with loans from others;[5] they were making a patent road steamer for the War Office, and their

[1] C.M., 24 February 1865.
[2] L.C., 2 August 1872; S.M., 23 May 1873. Lord Yarborough planned to bore for ironstone at Claxby in 1869. L.A.O. Daubney iv/3/38.
[3] Christopher Nevile wrote in 1874 that the coal under Thorney had been valued at £400 an acre. He did not seem to take it seriously. L.A.O. Jarvis vii/A/12.
[4] Richardson was a skilled engineer who patented many improvements in engine construction. He was a Methodist, a temperance reformer and a magistrate, and a radical with strong socialist sympathies. [5] L.A.O. Misc. Don., 268.

plough could plough one acre in an hour at a cost of 2s. 9d. They were soon to turn to electrical equipment. Clayton and Shuttleworth had introduced threshing machines and straw elevators into eastern Europe.

Ruston and Proctor were building steam navvies which were used in making the Manchester Ship Canal, which was the first large civil engineering scheme to use excavators in large numbers;[1] Ruston was later to claim that his steam navvies were the most successful yet introduced as a substitute for pick and shovel in the large excavations constantly being made for railways, docks and canals. In 1889, when the business was taken over by a limited company, there were 1,600 employees, and by the end of the century about 2,000, and the works covered about 1,700 acres.

Ruston remained chairman of the company until his death in 1897. In his earlier years he had travelled incessantly, night and day, spending perhaps only three nights a week in bed. By his personal efforts he had built up trade with eastern Europe, Australia and South America, especially the Argentine. There were branches at Milan, Budapest and elsewhere, and agencies all over the globe. His prescription for success was a truly Victorian one, and would have pleased Samuel Smiles: all attention to work, no hobbies, giving everyone full value, and making his customer his friend.[2]

Other firms, Rainforths, Penneys and Clarkes, were becoming established in cornscreens, harrows, potato diggers and crank shafts. Ruston said in 1873 that there were 3,000 men employed in the engineering industry in Lincoln, representing 9,000 to 10,000 people supported by it, and from £4,000 to £5,000 was paid weekly in wages.

Within a few years Lincoln and Lindsey Bank shares rose in price from £120 to £300; a third bank, the Midland Banking Company, opened about 1861, followed by the Stamford Spalding and Boston Bank in 1882. Agriculture was doing well. The Lincoln and Lincolnshire Hide Skin Fat and Wool Company was formed, and at its first annual meeting in 1876 declared a dividend of 10%. Farmers were paying higher wages: a farmer of 560 acres in mid-Lincolnshire said his wage bill had risen from £725 in 1861 to £1,224 in 1874.[3] A new and larger corn exchange was built over the old open market and opened in 1880. The *East Anglian Times* was reported as saying that Lincoln corn market was perhaps the most important that had been opened up to merchants in the eastern counties: 330 merchants frequented the exchange, and 250 farmers were

---

[1] See W. Barnes in *Lincolnshire Magazine*, I, (1934), 370.
[2] E.g. *L.C.*, 25 July 1884.   [3] *L.C.*, 14 April 1876.

regular subscribers. The average weekly number admitted was close on 500. It was twice the size of the Ipswich market.[1]

The annual sheep fair, moved to the west common, had 30,000 sheep in 1878. The horse fair no longer consisted mainly of horses bred in the county; they were being brought from distant parts of the kingdom, perhaps 2,000 by rail and several hundreds by road. Some came from Prussia, but the best were from Ireland or were of Irish breed, and many Irish dealers were present and willing to buy. Other buyers came from the War Department, the railway companies, London brewers, and from France and Germany.[2]

Presently a shadow began to fall across the trade of the city. The Lincoln Co-operative Society (formed in 1861), which had just opened its central store, found its sales falling in 1875. The *Mercury* wrote in 1878 that trade was in a curious state. The foundries were full of work, and there had never been so many engines sent away in so short a time. Building was going on, and there was full employment, yet there were scores of houses to let. There were weekly failures in business, for the city depended on the agriculturalists within a radius of twenty miles. Farmers had had three bad years; they paid their rents with difficulty, and took long credit from merchant and tradesman. Corn being deficient in quantity and low in price, their bullocks and sheep were forced into the market, and there was much less livestock on the farms than there had been four years earlier.[3] By the end of the year the bankers began to press their customers, the shares of local companies fell heavily and shares in unlimited banking companies were forced into the market.[4] Towards the end of 1879 some of the larger foundries were putting their men on short time and discharging younger men. There were signs of improvement in 1880, and the horse and sheep fairs recovered, but things were bad again by 1884, and rents came down sharply.

The fears of the defenders of the corn laws that free trade in corn would ruin agriculture had not been realised at the time,[5] but they were being realised a generation later, as American railways and British cargo steamers brought prairie corn into the home market. In 1881 Mr Druce, an assistant commissioner, told the Royal Commission on Agriculture that in Lincolnshire farmers had been first to feel the depression, followed by labourers and landlords and the tradesmen who depended on the custom of the farming classes. He attributed the depression first to

[1] *L.C.*, 6 October 1882.
[2] *Illustrated London News*, 7 May 1870, and local newspapers.
[3] *S.M.*, 5 July 1878.   [4] *S.M.*, 13 December 1878.
[5] Above, p. 87.

the several bad seasons, and secondly to foreign competition, especially from the immense quantity of corn and cattle from America. The price of homegrown produce was being determined by foreign harvests, and had become more hazardous than in the days when a bad harvest often paid better than a good one because of the increased price. A third cause was the increased cost of production, the small amount of work done by labourers, higher wages, and the removal of boy labour from the market by the Education Act. He said in 1882 that the farmers of the county were asking for a protective duty to save the amount paid for local charges, but not so high as to raise the price of bread.[1]

The position was not seen so clearly by many experienced and intelligent people. Robert Toynbee, the Lincoln solicitor, kept his friend and client the seventh Lord Monson fully informed of conditions on the Burton estate, and his comments are especially interesting. As lately as 1876 Monson had bought back the North Carlton estate, sold by a predecessor, for £95,000; Sibthorp land was selling well at Wainfleet, and indeed land prices were good generally; and the prospects for farmers were brighter than they were a little earlier.[2] Three years later he found it impossible to deny the severity of the depression. He did not believe in its permanence, but at the same time he thought good tenants should be encouraged to hold on to their farms, and that a return in money would be much more gratefully received than a present of artificial manure.[3] After harvest he said that many large owners had numerous farms on their hands, and that Lord Scarbrough and others had reduced their rents to half. But 'notwithstanding all that is said of the competition with America I cannot doubt that two or three good harvests would restore the previous state of things, for even now prices would not be unsatisfactory if the yield and condition of the corn were at all up to an average'.[4] He thought the division of holdings might bring higher rents and more competition, but it would involve the expense of additional buildings.[5]

Conditions in 1880 were made worse by heavy rain and floods. Thousands of acres of corn were not worth gathering. Weston Cracroft noted in his diary:

13 October 1880. It is impossible to exaggerate the calamitous period we are going through, Squire and farmer. This (in the poor Midland counties) is the fifth bad harvest owing to rains, such as never fell so continuously, or so heavily,

---

[1] *Royal Commission on Agriculture,* 1881, xvi, 371–2; xvii, 2–5; 1882, digest of further evidence.
[2] 2 July 1876.
[3] 6 July 1879.
[4] 23 September 1879.
[5] 20 November 1879.

in man's memory. At this moment all below Canwick is one wide spreading sea – the little meres are out between the Far Lodge and Lincoln, the springs too in the Park. Not a farmer can get on any land to clean or sow, and the question put, when friends meet, is 'have you any farms given up?'...farms, chiefly clay, are thrown up all over the country. Such evils days I never remember, nor anything approaching them.

Two years later Toynbee was still saying that he agreed with Henry Chaplin in thinking that the bugbear of American competition had been much exaggerated, and that at that time it had nothing whatever to do with agricultural depression.[1]

Chaplin, always a protectionist at heart, was recalling the fears of 1850, but acknowledging that no government could act against public opinion, which had to be educated.[2] Writing privately to Disraeli, he could be more forthright:

15 August 1879. There is a large district in my own county, commencing with the Isle of Axholme, and extending pretty well all through the Marshes from the Humber to the Wash, where many old estates have been sold and broken up, and are now replaced by an infinite number of small holdings and an incredible number of small freeholds, with no game, no resident proprietor, no large places, or estates, in fact where Mr Bright's 'beau ideal' is in existence already. I have had it partly surveyed on my own account already, and the result of my private enquiries, which are not yet quite completed, lead me to believe the system to have utterly broken down...hundreds of them must fail and be broken up this year.[3]

But the time for talking of protection was not yet.

Woeful reports continued of tenants having exhausted their resources, farms being thrown up, and rents being dropped in the hope that the landlord would not have to raise capital to farm the land himself. Lord Ripon's best farm, all heath land, was let at 12s. an acre in 1885, presenting all tenant farmers with a new talking point. Chaplin had 3,000 acres given up on the heath. Towards the end of a long series of accounts of distress, however, Toynbee could yet tell Monson that 'we are still very far from there being nothing for the landlord out of your Lincolnshire estate'.[4]

In 1884 the low price of corn brought down the price of bread and flour, and American and Australian beef and mutton brought down the price of butcher's meat. Two years later a writer in the *Yorkshire Post* said that, except for a farmer with some knowledge of chemistry who wanted more scientific farming, the Lincolnshire answer to the question 'What is the

[1] 28 July 1882.
[2] *L.C.*, 13 November 1886.
[3] Hughenden (Disraeli) MSS B/xxi/c/155. I owe this reference to Dr R. J. Olney.
[4] 12 December 1893.

remedy for agricultural depression?' was 'Protection'. The West Riding had been the great market for wool and mutton; but changes in fashion and the vast increases in imports had brought about a great fall in the value of the Lincolnshire fleece. The value of wool had declined in five years by more than half, and within two years cattle had dropped by £6 to £8 per head. Fall in demand for agricultural implements meant that in Lincoln from 1,200 to 1,500 hands had been discharged from the various works, and there were probably 1,000 empty workmen's houses in the town. Many of the houses were owned by workmen subject to building society mortgages, and their savings were in jeopardy.[1]

A like tale of woe was told to a later Royal Commission in 1894. The north of the county had suffered worst, because in the south, where the soil was better, potatoes, roots and seeds could be grown and market gardening carried on. Rents had fallen on average land by 45 to 50%; on the best land 33%, on the worst 80%, though no farms had been abandoned.[2] The population was sparse, and there was little scope for selling milk; Danish butter was being sold in Lincoln. Wages had fallen, though lower prices reduced hardship, but there were a good many out of work.[3] By 1898 prices had risen. Chaplin claimed that there had been nothing the matter with agriculture except the low prices of the last 15 or 20 years. The competition of India and Argentina had been reduced by famine in the former and locusts in the latter.[4]

Meanwhile the engineers, already affected by the farm depression, were running into competition abroad in countries first beginning to make machinery themselves, and then raising tariff walls against foreigners. Germany first made her tariff really protectionist in 1879. Russia followed with general increases in 1881–2, France and Austria-Hungary in 1882. Presently the walls went still higher, and the United States became one of the most highly protected countries in the world. All Australia was protected in 1900.[5] When the Royal Commission on Depression of Trade and Industry was appointed in 1885 the agricultural engineers spoke of exports to France and Germany (to an extent diminishing yearly), Austria, Russia (diminishing with every increase of tariff), the Cape and India. There had been years of expansion from 1870 to 1877, and the depression began in 1879; its symptoms were falling demand, difficulty of getting payment, and increase of bad debts.[6]

[1] Press cutting, February 1886. Dunham Bridge tolls, let at £242 in 1885, made only £120 in 1888.   [2] See also Sir John Clapham, *Economic History of Modern Britain*, III (1938), 79.
[3] *Royal Commission on Agriculture*, 1894, IV, 104.   [4] *L.C.*, 8 January 1898.
[5] R. C. K. Ensor, *England 1870–1914* (1936), p. 276.
[6] *First Report*, p. 106. The Newark evidence can safely be taken to represent the views of the Lincoln firms.

The British Consul General for Hungary (which formed one customs territory with Austria) said Fosters of Lincoln had established large works in Budapest; Robeys were building portable engines, thrashing machines and corn mills there; and Clayton and Shuttleworth had a large establishment in Vienna. Some of their former agents had begun to manufacture in competition with them.[1] Two Lincoln trade unions gave evidence. The Loyal Free Industrious Society of Wheelwrights and Blacksmiths said there were upwards of 1,000 belonging to their trade; 5% were unemployed, the rest on short time. They dated the depression from 1875. The working week was 54 hours, but they averaged 43; they were paid by piecework, wages being 26s. for a full week. During the past 20 years piecework prices had gone down, but time rates had risen. The Friendly Society of Ironworkers spoke for Lincoln and the south of the county; they had 286 skilled men and 115 youths, and 60 were unemployed. They dated the depression from 1884. They were paid by the hour, from 5d. to 7d.[2]

Organised labour was making itself felt, though the friendly society aspect of trade unionism was still the most important, and relations with employers were still deferential. In 1871 the engineering employers promised to consider the nine hours movement, which had met with success elsewhere. They granted it, and were publicly thanked by the men; some other trades followed suit. Occasional strikes occurred for an advance of a shilling or two per week, or against unskilled labour being put on skilled work. The boys, who began at 4s. per week, rising by a shilling a year up to the age of 21, struck for a shilling a week and 2s. for the last year, in 1871; they paraded the streets singing 'hang old Robey on a sour apple tree', rolling a tarbarrel and throwing stones, forcing timid special constables to retreat to the Guildhall. The move seems to have failed. In 1873 fitters and turners struck against their work being done by labourers, and there were other sectional disputes.

The depression of trade was acutely felt in the industry in 1886. Robeys reduced wages by $7\frac{1}{2}$%, and men were discharged by Claytons. Rustons announced temporary reductions ranging from 1s. to 3s.; piecework prices had already been reduced. Ruston told a deputation bluntly that he would conduct his business on commercial principles, by which no doubt he meant that wage rates were dictated by the laws of supply and demand; and the men were incensed, and decided to strike rather than submit. Mass meetings inflamed feelings, though Ruston claimed with justice that he had kept the works on full time while other firms

---

[1] Second Report, App. part II, 106–7. In the Berlin district British machinery was being displaced by German (p. 160), and see Third Report, p. 489.

[2] Second Report, App. part II (1886), pp. 33, 34.

dismissed their men in large numbers. But he was vulnerable because he had become the city's liberal M.P., and his political enemies were using the wage reductions against him. He tried to explain. In 1875 the price of an 8-horse portable engine was £255; in 1886 it was £190. Claytons and Robeys had dismissed men, and Clarke's profit was down to £43. Fosters had earned no interest on capital, and Robeys were said not to have made 1 %. He offered to modify the reductions. But the strike began, and the men paraded with a brasss band. His earlier good treatment of his men was dismissed as electioneering.[1] In a fortnight the men began to drift back. As they entered they were attacked by pickets, and some were kicked and bruised. Police were drafted into Lincoln and dispersed the rioters. The strike collapsed, and some of its leaders were not allowed to go back.[2]

Men in the building trade were also becoming organised. In 1871 the stonemasons and bricklayers struck for a rise of a shilling a week and a reduction of 2½ hours; they wanted to stop work on Saturdays at 12.30 instead of at 4 o'clock, as the engineers did. They were successful, and in the following years secured further advances. They suffered greater hardships in wintertime than men in other industries, for they were often at the mercy of the weather. In 1878 they were forced to accept a reduction. Agricultural labourers were also attempting to organise, and they had some success. An attempt at a labourers' union did not do so well, and it was claimed that their fellows in the county were in advance of them.

Bitterness and distress continued for several years after the strike of 1886, and there were sporadic outbreaks, but by the end of the decade trade was better. Engineers were working overtime in 1891. After again and again increasing tariffs against imports, Germany reduced them. The Chamber of Commerce was formed in 1889 to watch over commercial interests, and in 1891 the Corn Exchange receipts were a record. In spite of the general trade depression and the slump in agriculture, Lincoln exports of machinery, especially to South America and Russia, were higher than ever; if the demand for agricultural machinery was poor, general engineering prospered. Trade held up until 1896, when affairs in South Africa, failure of harvests in South America and Russia, famine in India, and foreign and home competition reduced the volume of trade and the resulting profit.[3] By 1899 there

---

[1] From a remark that he hoped they would let him get bread and cheese out of his business he was known as 'Bread and cheese'. J. D. Jones, *Three Score Years and Ten* (1940), p. 43.

[2] Over 1,000 men had been out, and 800 were taken back.

[3] At the Ruston Annual General Meeting Colonel Hutton, the chairman, said that there was a 10-year cycle in their business, and it had been the same with Clayton and Shuttleworth. *S.M.*, 28 May, 4 June 1897.

was unmixed prosperity and the Ruston dividend, which had been $4\frac{1}{2}\%$, rose to 7%.

Meanwhile union activities were carried a stage further. In 1890 Tom Mann addressed the Lincoln branch of the Amalgamated Society of Engineers – one of the oldest branches, said to have been formed in 1848 – and called for a union of all workmen in the engineering trade. In 1892 the Lincoln Trades and Labour Council was formed, with a membership of over 1,100. It sought to organise the labourers, and it campaigned for an 8-hour day, and attacked the city council for its 'niggardly and ungenerous' treatment of gasworks labourers and scavengers.[1] Wage rates in Lincoln had naturally been related to farm wages in the country-side; an increase of a few shillings sufficed to bring a man into the town, even supposing he had work in the country at all; and so it was that industrial rates in Lincoln, Derby and East Anglia, the standard being from 27s. to 29s., were the lowest in the country.[2]

It would be tedious to recount the frequent attempts of the city to reduce the railway level crossing nuisance, which began in 1851; but the prospect of a loopline round the city was welcomed as likely to afford some relief. In 1878 the Great Eastern Railway Company proposed a line from Lincoln to its existing line at Spalding. The council welcomed the project: it would provide direct communication with the eastern counties, and so open the port of Harwich to makers of agricultural implements and engines, which hitherto had travelled by train to King's Cross, and thence to Harwich docks by horse power. It would also reduce dependence on the Great Northern, which was thought by one merchant not so obliging as the London and North Western, by whose route he sent his goods to London by Rugby. But the Great Eastern had to fight a hard battle with the Great Northern for its parliamentary bill, and in securing it had to agree to joint running on several lines near Lincoln. The Spalding line was opened in 1882; it included the high level bridges across the High Street and Canwick Road, south of the level crossings.[3]

[1] Both Lincoln and the Lindsey County Councils rejected the fair contract clause, demanded by a meeting presided over by Sir Hickman Bacon. Bacon, the wealthy premier baronet of England, whose home was at Thonock near Gainsborough, sought unsuccessfully to address the Diocesan Conference on Socialism in 1888, and he accompanied the Webbs to the Trades Union Congress in 1895. Beatrice Webb wrote of his 'doglike devotion to Sidney'; but he declined to subscribe to the Library of Political Science in 1896. *Our Partnership* (1948), pp. 48, 93.

[2] S. and B. Webb, *Industrial Democracy* (1897), I, 346n. After the First World War wages and other costs were becoming equal to those elsewhere, and an advantage in competition was lost. *Lincoln Review*, 1 September 1920.

[3] Passenger traffic was taken into the Great Northern station by a short branch line from Great Northern Terrace to Canwick low fields.

One main project remained in the proposal of a Lancashire Derby-shire and East Coast Railway from Warrington across country through Lincoln to Sutton on Sea. The initiative lay in the Chesterfield area, and the main purpose was to provide better outlets for Derbyshire coal. The bill came before parliament in 1891 and passed into law. With the help of the Great Eastern Railway the central section from Chesterfield to Pyewipe just west of Lincoln (where it joined the Great Northern and Great Eastern joint line) was undertaken. There were difficulties, both mechanical and financial, but at last the Lincoln–Chesterfield section was opened in 1900, the Great Northern station being used. It became known as the 'Dukeries route'. Although efforts were made to popularise the Dukeries, the picturesque group of ducal and other great estates round Edwinstowe, the line served chiefly for carrying coal. The eastern section of the line was never built, and the Manchester Sheffield and Lincolnshire line, since 1897 become the Great Central Railway, took over the company in 1907. The Great Central had in the previous year ceased to use the Midland station in Lincoln, transferring to the Great Northern. The new line had been regarded as important for Lincoln. Cheap coal would encourage the development of ironstone working, and the proposed harbour at Sutton, if it had been built, would have been a convenience to Lincoln firms, struggling against European tariffs.[1]

In spite of the railways the waterways still mattered. William Rain-forth, who was born in Gainsborough, where he owned two or three seagoing vessels, came to Lincoln in 1837, being described in 1841 as a sailmaker, and living on Waterside South. Ten years later he employed four men. Later he was in Canwick Road, a sail and rope maker and vessel owner, employing 19 men and 6 boys. In the face of the railway threat he bought a business carrying on a boat trade between Lincoln and Hull, including about ten keels. He also started a rope walk and a waterproof manufactory below the Stamp End locks. In 1884 his firm (by then William Rainforth and Sons) suffered a disaster when their *Waterwitch*, carrying lime for Doughty Son and Richardson, became a total wreck in the Humber.

Warrener the coal merchant was even more ambitious. He was the owner of the ship *Enchanter*, registered at Grimsby, c. 1876–86, carrying coal from Hull to Demarara, and bringing back Greenheart timber; and another time carrying wheat from New Orleans to Bordeaux. One of the Leslie Melvilles was registered as co-owner, indicating that Warrener was being financed by Smith Ellison's Bank. He was owner or charterer

[1] See George Dow, *Great Central*, 3 vols., 1959, 1962, 1965; J. Cupit and W. Taylor, *Lancashire Derbyshire and East Coast Railway* (1966).

of vessels bringing coal or rape cake or guano from Yorkshire, carrying sand to Leeds, wheat, stone and old iron to London, wood from Horncastle to Wakefield and Castleford, no doubt for pitprops.[1]

These two firms and others based elsewhere continued to use the Fossdyke to the end of the century and beyond. At the time of the Royal Commission on Canals and Waterways[2] Rainforths had 21 barges and Warreners 13 or 14, up to 110 tons, with no motor power, being drawn by horses. The journey from Hull to Lincoln took 24 hours, but by rail 30 hours, costing much more. There was a large traffic in grain, put on the Witham to Lincoln and thence despatched by rail.

Transport by rail had therefore not robbed water transport of all its advantages. It was not without reason that Brayford had on its banks corn mills and the Malleable Iron Works (Harrisons), the Witham Clayton and Shuttleworth, Ruston and Proctor, and Doughty Son and Richardson, the upper Witham Cannon's Glue Works and Ruston's Woodworks. The Fossdyke mattered the most, and anything that happened on the Trent might therefore affect Lincoln. It had passed under the control of the Great Northern Railway Company, first singly and then jointly with the Great Eastern.[3] A move by the railway company to take power to increase charges for the carriage of goods was opposed in 1892 by the city council, the Lindsey County Council and the Chambers of Commerce and Agriculture. It was arranged in 1893 that evidence should be given to the parliamentary committee by the mayor, W. W. Richardson, who was also a partner in Doughty Son and Richardson, large users of river and canal, Thomas Bell of Robeys, John Jekyll, chemical manure manufacturer, and Warrener and Rainforth. Several of them met the general manager of the company: he refused to modify the charge on timber and deals, raised by a penny a ton, and said that though he could not alter the classification of goods, which had been accepted by the Board of Trade, he would deal with particular grievances. He could help Doughty's over linseed, and he promised to withdraw a 5s. charge on lighters passing through Torksey lock; and other charges were to be modified or withdrawn. When they went before the parliamentary committee they had little to do, almost all the concessions they wanted having been granted. When the draft schedule of the Board of Trade was published they decided to support it against the opposition of the railways.[4]

[1] Warrener business papers in my possession.
[2] Below p. 212.   [3] Above pp. 113, 209.
[4] *S.M.*, 8 December 1893; *L.C.*, 31 March 1894. In 1897 the Chamber of Commerce petitioned against the North Eastern Railway's Hull Docks Bill, which would throw a great deal of traffic then using the Fossdyke into the railway company's hands.

The whole matter was reviewed by the Royal Commission on Canals and Waterways in 1906. Oliver Bury, general manager of the railway company, said the Witham made a loss if the rent payable to the Witham Commissioners[1] were included. Traffic had declined since 1898. Boston was not such a good port as Hull and Grimsby, whose traffic had increased out of all proportion. On the other hand Fossdyke traffic had risen. There had been a good deal of prosperity in Lincoln, several large works getting their timber in bulk through Hull and Grimsby, by the Trent and Fossdyke. The prosperity was in Lincoln rather than in the Humber. Lincoln had done very well in the last few years; its manufacturers sent their products to Hull, Grimsby, Liverpool and London. The dock basin at Lincoln – Brayford – could deal with any amount of traffic, and the railway had beautiful warehouses there. The farmers used the Witham very little indeed.[2]

When this evidence was considered by the Chamber of Commerce it was severely criticised. The maintenance of a waterway was about a third that of a railway, and the cost of transport a sixth. If Torksey lock could be improved and lengthened – and a few inches deeper would be better but not absolutely necessary – boats could be brought through holding 50% more cargo. Messrs Warrener, Richardson and Rainforth agreed to give evidence.[3] In doing so they made several points. In criticism of the company's estimate of costs it was recalled that in the original deal with the owners of the Witham and Fossdyke they had, free, 40 miles of embankment on which to lay their line. Most of the big works in Lincoln had a river frontage, and could take or give delivery at their own gates. J. D. Blanshard, a Bardney farmer, added that an old arrangement whereby the companies used to pay the carriage of any traffic put on boats to Lincoln station, and charge a through rate to the customer, had been discontinued in 1906. Now there was one rate for the boatowner, another for the railway.[4]

The threat of increased railway rates in 1913 again called attention to the Fossdyke. It was noted that boats leaving Lincoln often went empty. More motor boats would be an advantage: a boat had lately reached Hull from Lincoln in 7 hours, but 12 was considered a reasonable time. Freight would then come much more cheaply than by rail. The great difficulty was that there was not a constant water depth of five feet.[5]

---

[1] Above, p. 113.
[2] *Royal Commission on Canals and Waterways Report*, 1906, III, QQ. 22485, 24509–10, 24546.
[3] *L.L.*, 1 June 1907.
[4] QQ. 37206, 37220, 37222, 37271, 37542.
[5] *L.C.*, 2 August 1913.

The basic trouble was that the railways' own interests were against canals. They performed their statutory duties, where they had them, slowly and without zeal, but they did no more. They were required to maintain standards adequate in the 1840s, and that was all. An independent authority might have deepened the canal and enlarged Torksey lock, and the whole of the subsequent history of transport in the area might have been different.

The importance of the waterways for purposes of land drainage remained the same. The water above Lincoln of course affected the city the most. The upper Witham came under the jurisdiction of the Court of Sewers and not of the General Commissioners. In 1869 the court were engaged upon a scheme for improving the upper river which at once provoked cries of alarm from interests below them. The city council protested that they would bring flood water down to Lincoln faster, but Lincoln would not be able to get rid of it as long as there was an insufficient outfall at Boston; and they wanted to know the extent of the proposed works, and to have the evidence of an engineer as to their effects.[1] The trustees of Lincoln West Drainage warned them that they would be held responsible for resulting damage, and called attention to the inefficient state of the river banks in the parishes of St Botolph and Boultham.[2] Ruston said that the floods had been more serious in recent years, for while they used to continue not more than a week, last year 300 of his men were thrown out of work for three or four weeks. It represented a vast amount of suffering, with the immense added danger of fever.

The argument continued until it was agreed in 1873 to consult with the corporation of Lincoln and the authorities at Boston; a further resolution to proceed was rescinded, and it was settled not to proceed until a better outfall through Lincoln was provided.

The court then turned attention to wider questions of the Witham generally, and joined with Lincoln and Boston in representations to the General Commissioners. Making no progress, they discussed with Lincoln the improvement of the channel under the High Bridge, and a plan was approved but blocked by the Great Northern Railway engineer at Boston, who said that the enlargement of channels for passage of water from west to east of Lincoln raised legal difficulties of so grave and serious a character that they might involve the commissioners in increased risks and responsibilities, and that he could not assist.[3]

[1] *L.C.*, 3 December 1869.
[2] Court of Sewers papers, 2 December 1869.
[3] Court of Sewers papers, 3 August 1875.

The reply was typical of the unhelpful attitude of the railways towards water questions.

There were heavy floods again in 1872 and in January 1878, when it was feared that matters would be made worse by the breaking of the Trent bank between Fenton and Torksey. As the General Commissioners made no move, although 40,000 acres of land were under water,[1] there was a meeting of the principal proprietors of land at Lincoln Guildhall, with Lord Ripon in the chair. He urged that the whole river basin should be under one jurisdiction; Chaplin thought that the Witham navigation was no longer necessary as traffic could go by rail. They called in Sir John Hawkshaw to advise. He produced a plan for extensive works at a cost of half a million pounds, but when it was found that the only benefit of the scheme could be to lower the flood level by one foot in the lower river, without any improvement in the outfall to the sea, the landowners resolved to take no action.[2]

Floods therefore continued to oppress the city and the surrounding low lands. In 1880 water flooded the houses on Great Northern Terrace to a depth of three or four feet, and the level of the water only subsided because the river bank broke below Lincoln. Complaints recurred in 1883 and 1886, in spite of work carried out for the improvement of the outfall, enlargement of the Grand Sluice at Boston, and improvement of the channel up to Tattershall. In 1890 there was a further conference with all parties on the improvement of the outfall of the upper Witham and its tributary river Brant through Lincoln. Alderman Maltby commented that in his experience the commissioners were the most intractable people he ever came across. Complaints went on until after the turn of the century.

Agriculture was not all gloom. In 1892 a new ram fair was a great success, there being an unusual foreign demand for Lincoln rams, many of the best flocks going to foreign purchasers. In that year the Lincoln Longwool Breeders Association was formed to promote a breed which was already important, both for fleece and for milk. It published its own flock book, starting with 58 foundation members, and reaching a peak of 337 in 1899. Its export was chiefly to South America, especially the Argentine. In 1897, 5,561 rams and 1,382 ewes were sent aroad; the trade was interrupted during a closing of Argentine ports in 1900–2, and an outbreak of foot and mouth disease in 1910–12. Through the First

---

[1] In reply to an argument about protection of the produce of the land the Rev. C. C. Ellison replied that a few months' produce off a few acres of engineering works would bring in more than all the Brant district could grow in as many centuries.
[2] W. H. Wheeler, *Fens of South Lincolnshire*, n.d., pp. 174–7.

World War about 2,000 sheep per year were exported, but by the 1920s the market had virtually disappeared.[1]

The horse fair in Lincoln was reported as flourishing in 1900: the stables were full, and the streets resounded with clattering hooves.[2] But generalisation as to state of agriculture seemed to be impossible. Rider Haggard noted this: he wrote in 1902 that it was impossible to speak of the county as an agricultural whole. He thought that in the dry season of 1901 the lowlands were prosperous, whereas the higher country had suffered very much; doubtless in wet and sunless years like 1902 the tale would read otherwise. He feared that on the whole the balance was on the wrong side. Sheep were everywhere, on high land and low; and the ruinous fall in the price of wool, together with the closing of the South American ports, were shocks – and there were others – that it was difficult to bear. There were grave apprehensions for the future. The high price of store cattle and the low value of beef smote the grazing interest hip and thigh. Potato growers were happier, and there was plenty of labour, though much of it was Irish.

A movement having political rather than economic value was having some slight effect. As the result of a drive for small holdings, county councils were empowered to buy land for that purpose in 1892, and the Holland County Council took action on a small scale. The councils were given compulsory powers of purchase in 1907. Lord Carrington encouraged the movement, and Richard Winfrey and others pressed on at Spalding. The movement did not come to much. The south, however, was going over to seeds, fruit and market garden produce: Bishop Swayne saw the trainloads going to London and other great centres of population.[3]

Rider Haggard noted that young folk were leaving the land. This was a point which especially exercised the Lincolnshire Chamber of Agriculture. It was urged that education should be half-time and some, like Mr Laverack, thought education would be useful if farmers would adopt up-to-date machinery and employ energetic men fitted to cope with its use. Given these things, they thought, a higher wage could with profit be paid.[4]

A rather more cheerful picture was painted by Sir Daniel Hall in 1910–12. He noted that farms on Lincoln Heath were all let, and there

[1] L.A.O. *Annual Report*, XXII, p. 27; *Lincolnshire Magazine*, I, no. 7, II, no. 11; *S.M.*, 9 September 1892.
[2] *L.L.*, 21 April 1900.
[3] *Parsons Pleasure* (1934), p. 266.
[4] *Rural England* (1906), II, 239–44.

was considerable demand for any that might come into the market. With change of fashions in ladies' garments, Lincoln wool was at the top of the market.

But what has made the fame of the Lincolns has been their value for crossing with the Merinos in Australia, New Zealand and the Argentine, where the demand for a sheep that would yield a better carcase than the Merino – something that could be exported as mutton, and would yet retain part of the immense wool-producing capacity of the latter breed, has been chiefly met by the introduction of the Lincoln–Merino crossbreds.[1]

A ram might once have made 500 guineas: by 1906 1,500 guineas was paid for a single animal sent to the Argentine. In that year the whole of one famous flock, that of the Messrs Wright, was sold to go there.

The Lincoln Red Shorthorns became a registered breed of cattle in 1895, though some of them could be traced back for a hundred years. The Royal Agricultural Society first granted classes for them in 1901.[2] The race spread to other parts of the country, it being a dual-purpose animal, good for milk as well as meat. The Shorthorn Society's bull sale in 1907 was one of their most successful, nearly 7,000 head being exported.

The farmer, as Hall noted, was an individualist, and teaching him to cooperate was an uphill task; but facts were driving him to it. The Lincolnshire Farmers Union was formed at a meeting of nine men at the Albion Hotel Lincoln, on 2 September 1904, each paying £1.[3] No doubt the new enterprise was the subject of much talk when the Royal Agricultural Show visited Lincoln in 1907.

The Corn Exchange and Markets Company made its largest profit since 1847 in 1905; and the fairs still brought business to the city. The

---

[1] Sir Daniel Hall, *A Pilgrimage of British Farming 1910–1912* (1914), pp. 97, 98. And see Clapham, *Economic History of Modern Britain*, III (1938), 95. Tomlinson and Hayward, proprietors of Hayward's Sheep Dip, yearly sent pedigree stock to South America. *S.M.*, 13 September 1895. C. P. Hayward of that firm has left a vivid account of a voyage with sheep for Messrs Kirkham of Biscathorpe, and of the casualties his flock suffered on the way.

[2] G. E. Collins, *Farming and Fox Hunting*, n.d., p. 58.

[3] Edward W. Howard was in the chair, and a committee was formed consisting of Joseph Brocklebank, John Jekyll, James Cartwright, Bemrose, John Evens, W. B. Burtt, J. Mountain, F. Godson, F. Scorer, Colin Campbell. By 1907 it had 2,000 members, having spread beyond the county. The National Farmers Union was formed in 1908, and Colin Campbell, then Lincolnshire chairman, was elected national president, an office he held until 1917. I am indebted to Mr Newton Loynes for this information. The late Canon Leeke passed on to me a tale of the Rev. Thomas Hamilton of Skellingthorpe that at an annual puppy show at Harmston (Blankney?), during a heavy shower of rain Hamilton and some farmers sheltered under a tree, and then decided on the formation meeting. Bishop Edward Hicks found Campbell 'a rich, rude, hectoring farmer'. Diary, 26 June 1915.

horse fair kept its place as the largest in the country, though the uproarious days when High Street was impassable through a mass of plunging horseflesh had gone, and the fair was falling off. Motor cars were affecting the breeding of horses to ride, and it was mostly agricultural and cart horses that attended.

Like Rider Haggard, Bishop Edward Hicks, an acute observer, found a varied scene. He noted that when Ludford church on the wolds was built in 1864, the parishioners, then largely gentlemen farmers of the old sort, had helped generously. In 1914 'the farmers are a smaller sort, and mostly Methodists. The vicar told me that the old set had been killed off by 1879 and the bad years, and a meaner race took their place'. At Weston St Mary and Moulton, in the fertile fenland, he found rich farmers, a class of men who abounded in south Lincolnshire, having superseded the old gentry. 'They are very modern businessmen: often sons of clerks, labourers etc. Wealthy and sterling men, but "near" with their money, with quite limited outlooks: they accumulate farms, and manage them with foremen: the families and old fashioned farmhouses have disappeared. I doubt if the labourers have got any advantage out of it. But I liken the damage to the old *enclosure*.'[1]

In 1907 the British consul at Warsaw reported on the competition that British agricultural machinery was meeting in Russia; a Vienna firm was offering machinery very little, if at all, inferior to that of British manufacture, with easier terms of payment; the new Portuguese tariff had increased from 50% to 200% on steam and other engines imported, either with or without thrashing machines.[2]

Even so, trade was good. The Lincoln firms and Hornsbys of Grantham were selling about 4,500 thrashing sets a year, this trade having reached its peak in the period 1906–12.[3] In 1907 Clayton and Shuttleworth reported a steady increase of profit. Rustons had doubled their output in ten years, with corresponding increase of wages, and were increasing their capital. They were employing over 3,600 men and their output averaged 1,500–1,600 steam and oil engines, 950 boilers and 950–1,000 thrashing machines per year, besides steam navvies and pumps. Clayton's road rollers had spread over Europe, South Africa, China and Cuba. Robeys offered their drop valve engines, Duckerings their corn-grinding machines, Rainforths their waggons and trailers.

In the following year Robeys could report increased profit in spite of competition and the higher price of coal. Claytons, however, had been

---

[1] Diary, 28 September 1914, 21 November 1915.
[2] *L.L.*, 13 April 1907.
[3] Sir William Tritton in *Lincolnshire Magazine*, II (1934), 59.

caught by events abroad. In Roumania the harvest had failed, and there had been an insurrection, their depots escaping fire and plunder only by a display of armed force by the staff; and there had been drought in Austria and Hungary. Tariffs drove them to manufacture inside these countries; they moved their works in Vienna and trade improved. After drastic reorganisation of their management the company's prospects recovered, and in 1911 attained the largest profit on record. Happily, in view of approaching events, they sold their property in Austria, Hungary, Roumania and Bulgaria on satisfactory terms, and later reported that the new Austrian purchasers had bought more of their Lincoln goods than had been supplied to that market in any of the previous six years. The firm had strengthened its position in Russia where both the firm itself and two of the Shuttleworth family had invested largely in the company acting as their agents.[1] In Lincoln Alfred Shuttleworth had built a new foundry, pattern shop and pattern stores, and his brother Colonel Frank Shuttleworth a new smithy department. There was also a new iron turnery for the thrasher section and a complete electric power station for using wood waste from the sawmills.

Rustons twice increased their capital. They had put up new buildings in Lincoln and bought property in Odessa to supply stores to customers in South Russia.[2] By 1912 they occupied 52 acres of land and employed 5,200 men and 315 office staff. Robeys contended with unrest, bad trade and low prices, and after the coal strike could only pay $2\frac{1}{2}\%$. Fosters, after a bad spell, were redesigning their portable engine, doing well in road locomotives, especially for the showman trade, where nobody could come near them; but there were no dividends. Prospects generally were good.

But there was the other side of the picture. There was industrial unrest in 1907, when toolmakers, amalgamated engineers and gasworkers demanded 2s. per week on time rates and 5% on piece rates. The claim was refused and the situation was aggravated by numerous discharges from Stamp End. The building trade was depressed, and the typhoid epidemic and consequent troubles were responsible for many empty houses. These things however righted themselves, and the Boilermakers Society could claim that Lincoln was better off than other engineering towns; that only 7% of the men in their industry were not members of their union; and

---

[1]   These investments were lost in the Russian Revolution; this loss was one of the causes of the failure of the company.

[2]   Bornemann, the managing director, said in January 1910 that during the past few years there had been a general tendency for wages to rise and employment to increase, and he attributed this prosperity to free trade.

good conditions of employment were due to the confidence between employers and employed.

Unemployment came to the fore again in February 1910, when labour exchanges were devised under Winston Churchill's scheme. The Lincoln exchange was opened in February 1911, when Dean Fry said it would enable them to know, as they got lower down in the ranks of labour, who were the permanent unemployed, and those who need not be unemployed.[1]

Several wage disputes in 1911 were settled. Then in July the boiler-makers demanded an increase of 2s. a week, and handed in their notices, all the larger firms being affected. In support of the Lincoln firms, Marshalls of Gainsborough dismissed their boilermakers. Labourers and machinemen became involved in the strike, which merged in the national strike of railwaymen, with picketing and disorder. Trouble in Lincoln culminated in a riot lasting all night near the Great Northern Railway crossing. County police joined the city police, and an attempt was made to set fire to a signalbox. Troops marched down the High Street, and the crowd were warned that if they did not disperse the street would be cleared by the troops. Order was not restored for some hours.[2] After prolonged discussions, exacerbated by Marshalls' action, the employers offered terms which were accepted.[3]

The economic outlook was not cheerful. Costs for wages, railway carriage and raw materials had all increased at a time when foreign trade in the face of fierce foreign competition made it impossible to increase selling prices. Though the war that broke out in 1914 marked the end of an epoch, this grim prospect had to be faced when peace returned in 1918.

[1] *L.L.*, 11 February 1911.
[2] At the following assizes Mr Justice Ridley had before him 12 men of an average age between 20 and 30. He said they had behaved no better than untutored savages; as for the authorities, the mob had had its way from 11 until after 2 o'clock. The police charged several times, and the military came, though the judge did not know who sent for them. The chief constable arrived from his bed about 1 o'clock; no mayor, no magistrate, nobody to read the Riot Act. In evidence the chief constable put the crowd at about 4,000, throwing stones, bottles and brickbats. The prisoners were all found guilty but two, and given sentences of 3 or 6 months imprisonment. In summing up (following a communication he had received from a city magistrate) the judge admitted that some of his earlier observations were made in ignorance of the facts. (Papers kindly lent to me by Mr J. L. E. Phillips.)
[3] *L.C.*, 9 September 1911.

CHAPTER XII

RELUCTANT PROGRESS

The liberals had recovered power largely because they could blame the tories for adopting the Local Government Act of 1858,[1] though its adoption could not have been carried without some liberal acquiescence. When the matter had come to the vote, three liberals made varying contributions to the result: Doughty voted in favour, Ruston was absent, and Brogden abstained. He had helped to convert many of his colleagues to sanitary reform, but when the time came he was smart enough to leave the onus on his political opponents.

Popular feeling ran so high at the time of the municipal elections in 1867 that William Ashley, the retiring tory mayor, declined the compliment of a public dinner. The tories drifted away until Samuel Stephenson, elected in the upper ward in 1875, could be described as the representative of the dean and chapter and the only conservative on the council.

The new brooms were all for economy – reduction of salaries and open competition for lighting and repair of street lamps. Brogden, the new leader, declared that no notice whatever would be taken of tory complaints about the state of the river. There were many expressions of regret that some good men, tories, were withdrawing from municipal life, and that good men among the liberals – Doughty, Ruston and Henry Williams – were swamped by a caucus majority more concerned to hold power than to use it wisely.

Yet there were irresistible pressures towards greater expenditure. The city was growing fast, and there were new streets to be taken over and repaired by the inhabitants at large; and, moreover, furious protests about their disrepair and the neglect of scavenging made it clear that public opinion was calling for a raising of standards of public health. Footbridges over the river were needed to serve the foundries. Country practices must give way to urban ones; fairs must be removed from the street and pinfolds set up for stray animals on the edges of the built up areas. Successive additions to the strength of the police force had to be made. Even the town crier was becoming more expensive, for he could no longer get round the city in the traditional two hours. New by-laws were needed. And there was the impending threat of underground sewerage.

[1] Above, p. 45.

There was no escape from an increase in the municipal establishment. In 1874 the part-time treasurer's salary was increased from £50 to £70. The medical officer's salary was increased from £20 to £40 in 1877, and in 1878 an analyst was appointed under the Food and Drugs Act at a salary of £20. In 1874 the council passed and then rescinded a resolution to appoint a full-time surveyor; but in 1876 one was appointed at a salary of £300.

The only official buildings available for municipal purposes were the Guildhall, with an inner room which could be used for committee meetings, and the Sessions House, built in 1805–9 for the courts and the city gaol; there lived the chief constable, who also looked after the fire engine. Part-time officers provided their own quarters, and offices had to be taken over a bank for the surveyor. The central need for a town hall was increasingly felt as other boroughs were busy building their municipal palaces. In 1876 a special Town Hall Committee considered the financial position of the corporation and the funds available for the purpose; it appeared that after paying off some debt they had available from the sale of property about £13,000. They decided on application to the Treasury so to use this sum and to borrow a further £18,000. Enthusiasm was effectively extinguished by the Treasury intimation that money from the sale of corporation properties could only be used on condition that the whole was repaid over 30 years. As the council had already decided that no repayments that could not be met out of surplus income should be raised by rates, the scheme came to an end.

The matter came up again in 1889, when a central police and fire station was needed. There was much argument about sites. The chief constable said that the police station must not be far from the High Bridge, in the immediate vicinity of which by far the greater number of refractory prisoners were taken into custody. Then the idea that it could be coupled with municipal offices and baths was discussed and abandoned. Eventually the police and the fire engine remained at the Sessions House – the city prison there having been closed in 1878 – and the National Central Schools were chosen for municipal offices. The freehold was the property of the corporation and the school trustees agreed to surrender their lease on terms. This was in 1891. The building was to house the city surveyor, the waterworks engineer (the undertaking having by then been bought) and the rate collectors. In 1900 it also housed the newly appointed city accountant, who was provided with a clerk and a boy.

Specific issues had to be faced as they arose. The making of the Lincoln– Honington railway line through the south common, connecting

Lincoln with the Great Northern main line at Grantham, brought up the question of the division of the purchase moneys between the corporation as lords of the manor and the commoners; and both the railway line and the diversion of the turnpike road left small pieces of common cut off from the rest which would be better sold. Furthermore, there were, surrounded by the common, closes of land formerly the site of a leper hospital, the Malandry Closes, which had rights of common; and this property had come into the personal ownership of the town clerk.[1] The opportunity was taken of buying these rights. All these matters, including the diversion of the turnpike road, were dealt with together in the Lincoln Corporation (Canwick Common) Act 1868.[2]

Talk of the commons brought up the need to provide recreation grounds for the working classes, especially since the closing of Temple Gardens;[3] and there emerged the proposal to buy the Monks Leys common from the freemen and make an arboretum there. Ruston said the scheme would be a mixed blessing; it would mean more drinking, and he recalled that when there had been a gala at Temple Gardens his men had had a half day's holiday, and some stayed away drinking for two or three days. Nevertheless it was decided to proceed; and on their part the freemen, fearful of the loss of their rights, and recognising that the common was not much used by themselves, though it was, improperly, by non-freemen, welcomed the suggestion. They offered to sell for a perpetual payment of £200 a year. The council accepted the terms. They would also sell the Holmes, the other freemen's common, and small parts of the south and west commons. It was noted that the scheme had the nearly unanimous support of the freemen and the support of the vast majority of householders. The Lincoln City Commons Act 1870[4] carried these provisions into effect. The scheme was not painless. It cost much more than was expected, and half the council committee resigned; it was thought it would cost the corporate fund £9,000 plus the annual rent.

There followed much debate about the other commons. Land was needed for building more houses, and it was proposed to sell the cowpaddle, part of the south common severed by the turnpike road and further separated by the cemetery, and the fringes of the common. There was tremendous feeling on the subject. A petition signed by 1,200· householders protested against a parliamentary bill. Valuable recreation ground would be lost; it was said that as a result of the then recent Commons Act the commons were already overstocked; 800 cattle were

[1] M.L., p. 352.   [2] 31 Vic. c. xxii.
[3] Above, p. 13.   [4] 33 and 34 Vic. c. lxxxvii.

registered for depasture in 1876. The town clerk advised against the bill, and it was abandoned.[1]

With the growth of leisure as working hours were gradually reduced, new emphasis was being placed on the commons as places for organised games. A cricket ground was laid out on the south common; a bog on the west common was filled in; there was drainage, planting with trees, and stubbing up of gorse. It was urged that not one in 500 citizens had a cow, and that cattle should be confined to part of the commons. The freemen were roused again, and in 1894 formed a Freemen's Guild to protect their rights.

But the times were against them. Their common rights belonged to the time when the town still had its rural shell, and it was becoming more urban every year. In 1895 the Lincoln Golf Club were playing on the west common. By 1913 the corporation had provided 20 football pitches and 11 cricket pitches on the commons, and there were two golf courses. In emergency they had put an isolation hospital on the west common; they had received agricultural shows and accommodated the races; all activities that in some way impeded rights of pasture. The freemen, on the other hand, were declining in number as the city's population grew. The town clerk told a House of Commons Committee in 1915 that from and including 1845, 1,143 persons had been admitted to the freedom, and he did not think there were more than 500 freemen living. Only 310 were registered in the city for parliamentary election purposes. Few people exercised their rights of pasture; about 2% of freemen and 2% of householders did so personally. They were however entitled to let their rights to other qualified persons, with the result that dairymen and horse and cattle dealers were enabled to put on large numbers of stock, one man nearly 50. In 1915 the corporation sought to extinguish all rights of pasture, paying compensation to the freemen, and then allowing all householders to pasture one head on payment of a registration and branding fee, and more in the council's discretion on payment of £1 per animal. The freemen resisted, but without success. Their rights were extinguished and compensated; but their claim, partly sentimental, to be guardians of the commons, especially against a corporate body they distrusted, was dismissed. The commons were to be secured to the citizens as open spaces for ever, for their full enjoyment as places of public resort and recreation.[2]

---

[1] An exchange of some of the common with the Great Northern Railway and Messrs Robey was however approved.

[2] Minutes of Evidence on the Lincoln Corporation Bill, 1915; Lincoln Corporation Act, 1915, 5 and 6 Geo. V, c. lxxvii.

One of the greatest needs of the city from the point of view of public health as well as amenity, and one of the longest frustrated, was public baths. In the summer of 1852 there was a public petition for a public bathing place. Pressure led in 1858 to the formation of a committee to promote a scheme and to examine sites. Soon afterwards the Baths Committee of the council reported in favour of public baths: it thought that a 6d. rate would buy a site and build baths; they should be self-supporting, but if they were not, a small annual sum from the borough fund would supply the deficiency. The report was not confirmed by the council.[1] Then in 1874 a deputation from the Lincoln Swimming Club proposed an enclosure on the bank of the Fossdyke near the racecourse, and the plan was carried out.[2] The Public Baths and Washhouses Acts were adopted, but nothing followed.

The open-air bath was soon being denounced as an apology for a bath; it was too far away; it was unfit to use, and was in fact only used by the roughest of the working classes.[3] By 1889 2,900 people had signed a public memorial in support of the idea of a bath. The council decided by 9 votes to 6 in favour of a covered bath rather than an open-air one, though the realistic W. T. Page gave warning that if the citizens wanted baths they must be willing to pay for them, probably not less than £300 a year.

Ideas grew bigger, and the opposition did also. In 1893 a town poll was taken on a proposal for a swimming bath and 20 slipper baths on the site of Pacey's warehouse near Brayford head. The plan was carried. Then there was a petition against it. Another poll was taken in 1896, when there were 1,400 votes for the plan and 3,139 against, there being 8,545 people entitled to vote. The rates had just been increased by 4d. and that was enough.

At last in 1908 baths were provided at Boultham on the upper Witham, and it was noted that on one Bank Holiday they were used by 2,460 bathers. But the continuing need and the method of fulfilling it have been a subject of intermittent discussion through the years that have followed.

The incessant demand for land for building houses required the laying out of new areas, which meant new roads. At the same time increasing

---

[1] L.A.O. li 1/8/1, 14 May 1859. At a public meeting held on requisition a motion in favour of the adoption of the Baths and Washhouses Act of 1846 was carried. *L.C.*, 25 February 1859.

[2] L.A.O. li 1/8/6, 1/10/4. Agreement about the supply of water to the baths was reached with the Great Northern Railway Company, lessees of the Fossdyke, in 1875, and the Lincoln West Drainage Trustees in 1878.

[3] *L.C.*, 31 May 1884.

traffic was calling attention to the need for improvement of existing highways. One of the leaders in this field was Francis Jonathan Clarke, a chemist who built up a large business by the sale of patent medicines, notably Clarke's Blood Mixture, and devoted much of his energy and not a little of his money to the public good, becoming deservedly popular, and four times serving the office of mayor.[1] He was largely instrumental in removing the row of houses which stood down the middle of St Mary Street, seriously impeding access to the Great Northern Railway station. He also pressed forward the scheme which Richard Carline had proposed in 1854 for a Yarborough Road,[2] the first sod for which was cut in 1880. It was hailed as the best thing of its kind since Canwick Road was made.[3] There followed a widening and improvement of Brickkiln Lane and its extension to the west common, the whole becoming West Parade, and leading to a gradual occupation of the whole area between the city and the common by middle-class houses.

Clarke also played a part in improvements in the vicinity of the minster, where relations had been difficult. When the local board was set up in 1866, with the prospect of money for improvements, the dean and chapter had been willing to talk, and a minor concession was made for the improvement of a steep and dangerous Pottergate. The chapter then deputed two of their number – Massingberd and Mackenzie – to report on possible improvements of Minster Yard. They favoured a carriage way round to the west of Pottergate arch; an exchange of land for the improvement of Lindum Terrace; and they would have liked to close the road to the south of the minster to all but private carriages, so restoring to Minster Yard something of the lost air of a precinct. They would widen the road and get rid of the sheep pasturing in the churchyard of St Margaret.

There followed a delay for which the corporation were to blame. In 1868 the chapter refused to enfranchise land needed for the arboretum, and the committee, with Brogden in the chair, described this refusal as still further proof of the impolicy of leaving the management of large masses of national property in the hands of ecclesiastics who had nearly always shown their incompetence to deal properly with the estates of which they were but trustees. The council confirmed the resolution.[4] This egregious tactical blunder naturally caused resentment and the

---

[1] Dr O'Neill of Lincoln gave the *Lancet* an analysis of the Blood Mixture: it was free from metallic impregnation and had no injurious ingredient: one of its main ingredients was a pleasant stimulant. Clarke treated this as a personal vendetta, he having refused to pay professional bills wrongfully sent to him by O'Neill, who was said to have claimed, equally wrongly, that the mixture was made from a prescription of his. *L.C.*, 30 July 1875.
[2] Above, p. 51.   [3] Above, p. 62.
[4] 29 September, 2 October 1868, L.A.O. li 1/8/1/4.

chapter required a rescission of the resolution before they would receive a deputation.[1]

It seems that nothing happened immediately, but in 1881–2 the chapter again declared themselves willing to help. They gave up the idea of restricting the road south of the minster, and were willing to lower it both to the south and west. In 1883 Subdean Clements proposed that the corporation, the chapter, and the public (by subscription) should equally share the cost,[2] and a vast public improvement was effected, especially in Pottergate, where a road was made round the arch to the west (1884).

The Water Company's undertaking had been bought in 1871;[3] there were three more trading undertakings to come. In 1873 the Lincoln Gas Light and Coke Company was promoting a bill for further powers, and a committee of the council proposed to oppose it in order to keep down the price of gas. A town meeting gave a tepid consent; there were 80 people present, of whom a third voted in favour and the rest abstained. The company were willing to sell out on terms, which the council rejected, and the company obtained their bill.[4] Terms were however reached in 1880, and the council promoted a bill to effect the transfer; but the bill included provisions to increase the number of wards and take further powers for water and the markets and fairs. It was abandoned. The company then obtained another act;[5] but at last in 1882 terms were reached again and carried through in 1885.[6] By 1898 the price of gas was lowered by 2d. per thousand cubic feet.

When the Electric Lighting Act was passed in 1882 the council considered whether to apply to the Board of Trade for a licence to supply current in the city and adjoining parishes. It was not until outside companies began to apply that the council really bestirred themselves, obtained a licence (1897), appointed an electrical engineer, placed a contract for building a power station, and put the work in hand.

In 1880 the promoters of a proposed Lincoln Tramways Company, having waited until the sewerage works were complete, applied for the council's consent to a tramway from Lincoln to Bracebridge, and also to Carholme Road to the west, the arboretum to the east and perhaps

[1] L.A.O. Chapter Acts, 10 November 1868.
[2] S.M., 17 June 1883.
[3] Above, p. 169.
[4] 36 and 37 Vic. c. cxx. It extended the area of supply to Bracebridge, Boultham, Canwick and the south common; authorised the issue of new capital; and for protection of the public fixed a maximum dividend of 7% on ordinary capital and 6% on preference capital and a maximum price of gas.
[5] 43 and 44 Vic. c. lxxxvi.
[6] 48 and 49 Vic. c. xlvi.

Burton Road abovehill.[1] It was granted, and a tramway from St Benedict's church to Bracebridge, 1¾ miles, came into being. The trams were of course horse trams. Within a few years the company could pay a dividend of 3½%; by 1897, 6%. In 1902 the corporation decided to buy the undertaking, by which time the company had ten cars and 24 horses, providing a ten-minute service at a penny for the whole distance; it was carrying three-quarters of a million passengers per year. In 1905 the line was electrified on the Griffith–Bedell stud system, converted to overhead wires in 1919: the last car ran in 1929. By 1915 it was carrying 1¾ million passengers a year.[2]

There was no public library, although local authorities had had power to provide one since 1850. In default, free news and reading rooms were opened in Broadgate for the use of working men irrespective of politics, in the hope that they would spend their leisure hours in the newsroom in preference to the taproom. Within a few months from 500 to 600 readers were using the rooms daily; subscriptions were invited, and the corporation voted £10.

Perhaps it was this initiative that led Hinde Palmer, the liberal M.P. for the city, to propose that the city should provide a free library. The Mechanics Institute thought that they met the need: for 2d. a week anyone could use their library (with 6,000 books), museum and newsroom. The council declined to ask the mayor to call a public meeting: Brogden declared that he would not increase taxation for the purpose of obtaining cheap reading of newspapers and periodical light literature. A town's meeting might be called, and they could tax themselves if they would. Working men could pay for their mental as well as their animal food. That for the moment was that. The free newsroom continued to flourish, but with some unemployment their readers' demands were exceeding resources.

A letter in the press in 1884 said that, with the exception of Hull, Lincoln was the only place of any size without a library. In 1887 it was proposed to commemorate the Queen's Jubilee by providing a library, and the council offered to find a site and maintain a library if the

---

[1] Before then a few private waggonettes had plied for hire.

[2] In 1908 the public spirited W. R. Lilly proposed and planned a funicular railway, one-third underground, to accommodate the 109,000 people who passed between uphill and downhill every week. He estimated the cost at £10,000; it should belong to the corporation, and he would give the goodwill free. It would stimulate the erection, not only of workmen's but also of better class houses within the boundary of the city. The corporation turned the scheme down, pleading the cost of waterworks and schools. *L.C.*, 17 October 1908, 6 November 1909. Lilly, who had borrowed to buy property for the purpose, was believed to have been impoverished, and he left the city, with nothing more than a commendation of his patience and determination.

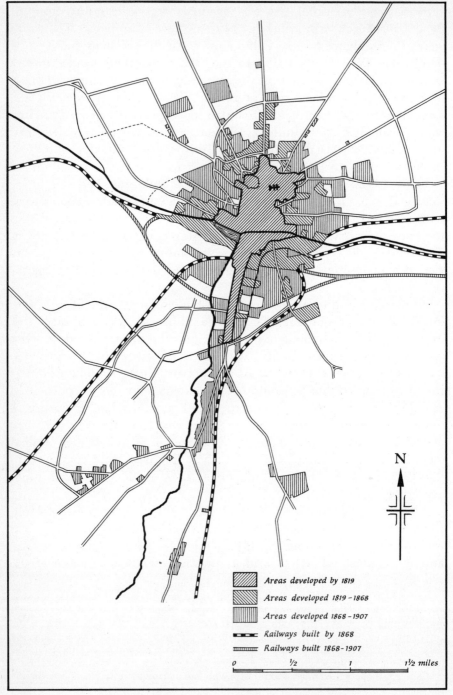

N

▨	*Areas developed by 1819*
▨	*Areas developed 1819-1868*
▥	*Areas developed 1868-1907*
▰▰▰	*Railways built by 1868*
▭▭▭	*Railways built 1868-1907*

0 　　　　 ½ 　　　　 1 　　　　 1½ miles

Map 4. Lincoln's nineteenth-century development

building were provided by subscription. There was another pause during which the Co-operative Society opened its free reading room and library. By 1891 there was sufficient public opinion to support the formation of a provisional committee, with A. C. Newsum[1] as chairman, to campaign for a library. Meetings were held in the works' messrooms; all were in favour save one, that thought that baths should come first. A public meeting proved unanimous, and a town poll was favourable: 2,819 for, and 2,330 against the idea.

The project required the rooms over the buttermarket then occupied by the Mechanics Institute, which was unwilling to move. They had to do so, and the scheme went forward. Colonel Seely gave £1,200 for books, the corporation £200 for technical books, and Crosfield M.P. £100. Mr Gladstone was the library's first visitor, and the formal opening was performed by Professor Jebb, M.P. for Cambridge. There the library remained until a gift of £10,000 by Andrew Carnegie in 1910 made possible a new building, designed by Sir Reginald Blomfield, in Free School Lane.

A like period of gestation preceded the establishment of a museum. There was a temporary one established for the visit of the Archaeological Institute in 1848, and the death of Sir John Franklin, a county worthy, in the Arctic in 1847 prompted the proposal of a Franklin Museum. Various premises, among them the old county hospital, now the Theological College, and the old gaol in the castle, now the Archives Office, were considered; but it was not until the sale of the Grey Friars by the grammar school governors to the corporation that the project came to fruition. A City and County Museum was opened there in 1907, though for many years it was regarded as a mere poor relation of the public library.

But these amenities lay far in the future when the city council were troubling about municipal finance in the 1870s. Up to that time the revenues of the borough fund had been fairly satisfactory, and ordinary revenue was creeping up, though there was little margin for extra-ordinary items. The position changed dramatically for the worse as a result of the election riots in 1874: the damage to property and the expense of keeping the soldiers were estimated at £800.[2] The town clerk reminded

---

[1] The eldest son of Henry Newsum the timber merchant. He graduated B.A. at Owens College, Manchester, and entered the business, of which he later became chairman. He served on the city council from 1900 to 1909 and was mayor in 1905. For many years he was a coopted member of the Education Committee and the Library Committee and chairman of the governors of the Grammar School and the Girls High School. He befriended many university students in days when grants were few and inadequate.
[2] Above, p. 192.

the council that they could not borrow, even from the bank, without Treasury consent, and if they did so, all the members authorising the loan would be liable in law. This brought the council to the desperate expedient, long threatened but always held off, of a borough rate. A precept for a rate of 2½d. in the pound was issued to the parish overseers of the poor. They had never heard of such a thing happening, and there was great indignation. They were given time to collect the rate, followed by a threat which the town clerk defensively described as a friendly caution. After payment there was a complaint that the amount collected was excessive, and the overseers wanted the surplus to be refunded to them; but the Rubicon was passed, and there was no return.

The district rate, levied by the council in its separate capacity as the urban sanitary authority, was bound to grow. The underground sewerage was expected to cost a shilling rate for 50 years. There was the new Yarborough Road, and there were the Minster Yard improvements; and applications to borrow were mounting. The inspector holding the enquiry on an application in 1884 remarked upon the improved condition of the city since he first knew it, and the comparatively small cost at which the improvements were being carried out.[1] The district rate was then 2s. 1d. per half year.

The state of the borough fund was reviewed by W. T. Page in 1886. Until lately (1881) they had had some surplus income, and had been able to hand part of it to schools and charitable institutions. But income was falling owing to the reduction of farm rents and tithes, and expenses were rising. A borough rate of 3d. was needed. Thereafter a rate was levied for two years, followed by a remission for a time; but it soon became an annual event. In 1900 the general district rate was ten times the size of the borough rate.

The real work of the council was carried on by a small proportion of the membership. The others often did not trouble to attend committee meetings, which had sometimes to be abandoned because nobody turned up, or there was not a quorum. In 1872 the habitual non-attendance of some members led the council to decide that they should apply to the Home Secretary to sanction by-laws imposing penalties for non-attendance. Some members were concerned only to keep the rates down, and their attitude to new projects was castigated by Page. He said he did not know why these matters were always treated humorously instead of being dealt with in an ordinary businesslike way. They had become the laughing stock of the town, and inside the corporation there seemed to be

---

[1] *S.M.*, 25 January 1884.

a sort of pride in laughing at any scheme that was suggested. Every member ought to feel that such a state of things was a disgrace. When in 1890 an increase in the number of wards and the size of the council was proposed Page told them bluntly that many members of the council were doing nothing, and more members would only mean more contests and more expense.

William Tomlinson Page was emerging as the dominant figure of the last quarter of the century. He was called 'the younger', as his father, the manager of the Lincoln and Lindsey Bank, bore the same name. He built up a large legal practice, and became a director of a number of local companies. In 1878 he was elected to the council as a liberal and quickly came to the fore, especially in the work of the sanitary authority.

His further municipal career was clearly planned in his own mind, and it must have been also in the minds of some of his colleagues. He resigned from the council in 1898, and was elected clerk to the urban sanitary authority and deputy town clerk in succession to Hebb. When at last Tweed died in 1910 he was the obvious successor, and he held the office to his death in 1912. In spite of his wide-spread private interests – he was chairman of the bank which held the corporation account – there is no hint that he ever abused his influence, and he served the city faithfully and well in his several capacities. He was a tall and dignified figure, with a reputation as an orator in the grand manner, though the irreverent noticed that his manner continued grand however trivial the theme.

Throughout almost the whole of the Page period the city was concerned with problems of water supply, both as to quality of the water and the adequacy of the supply. They were made more difficult by the growth of two small communities on the boundaries of the city. The large parish of Bracebridge had an area of 1,527 acres, partly in the valley of the upper Witham and partly on the heath. The Newark Road ran through the lower part of the parish; and the area that began to expand was the ribbon along the road, bounded on the west by the river and on the east by the Great Northern Railway line. The village nucleus, near the church, was about two miles from the centre of the city. The marked growth of population began in the 1870s. In 1871 it was 1,203; in 1881, 2,123.[1] By 1901 it had risen to 2,967. There was no sanitary provision at all, and the *Chronicle* wrote in 1880 of the flood of accumulated horror to be found eastward of the village, with overcharged vaults and middens near every house. What made it so serious to Lincoln was that the effluent drained into a meadow, flooded by rain which entered the river;

[1] The earlier statistical increase was evidently due in the main to the pauper lunatic asylum built by the county in Bracebridge.

the Lincoln water was taken at a point just opposite, and much sewage must have gone into the waterworks tank.[1]

Already in 1871 the Local Government Board, watching Lincoln, sent an inspector to enquire into the condition of the parish. The vicar, Charles Ellison, who was virtually also squire, attended as chairman of the rural sanitary authority, and not a single other ratepayer of the parish was there. As separate sewage works would be too costly, the inspector suggested an arrangement with Lincoln. Nothing came of this until ten years later the rural sanitary authority made a 50-year contract with Lincoln to receive and deal with the sewage.

The parish of Boultham lay a mile to the south-west of the city centre. The parish had a population of 114 in 1881. By 1891 it had grown to 527 and by 1901 to 671. The increase was in the north part of the parish (New Boultham), where several industrialists built factories.[2] Here too there were perils; there was no provision for drainage, and water percolated into the ground, and some of it must have found its way into the river. The city agreed to receive the New Boultham sewage in 1895.

In 1871 the city council's new waterworks committee were advised by an expert that the waters of the Prial Brook (Skellingthorpe reservoir) and Pike Drain (Boultham lake overflow) were wholesome and useful for general domestic purposes, though for drinking water he preferred the upper Witham. The committee knew that sewage came into the river above Lincoln, but they thought that this was only in such quantities that what was not carried off by evaporation was absorbed; and they were satisfied with their reservoir and catchwater.

Their satisfaction was not generally shared. The medical officer of health called attention to contamination of the sources in 1878; in 1883 (there having been an outbreak of smallpox in 1882) he said the water should be filtered, and if diarrhoea broke out, public warning should be given that drinking water should be boiled; in 1885 he warned the council of pollution of the river, especially at Grantham, and of an impending need for a greater supply of water.

Precentor Venables wrote to the board in London, pointing out that the death rate in Lincoln was in excess of the average.

[1] *L.C.*, 14 May 1880.

[2] Dawsons the belting manufacturers, Poppletons the sweet makers, Tomlinson and Hayward, makers of sheep dip. Foster the engineer built the Wellington Foundry. The area had been laid out by Commander Swan, who was an admirer of the duke; hence the street named Waterloo and others named after his generals, Beresford, Raglan, Clinton, Picton and Hardinge. Surviving gas lamp posts still bear Wellington's head at the base. The late Canon W. W. Leeke, rector of Boultham, gave me this information.

Water supply is in the hands of the Corporation, who are hoodwinked by their manager. The water professes to be taken from certain meres and large ponds to the south west of the city, but the greater part of it is really drawn from the Witham, at a point where it is liable to pollution by manure works, gas works etc. existing on its banks.

The letter was referred to the council, who received it with derision.[1] A crusade was led in the council by William Watkins the architect who called for enquiry into other sources of supply; but his resolution was defeated by 13 votes to 4, his supporters being Cannon, Bainbridge and Martin. Page carried a resolution that in the opinion of the council the quality of the water did not afford reasonable ground for complaint; that what steps were possible should be taken to limit the entry of contaminating matter and to improve the oxidation of the water. The Local Government Board warned them of grave responsibility if disease should spread. But plain business men and rational-minded lawyers were not to be rattled by alarmists.

Complaints continued, not only as to quality, but as to shortage of water. Diarrhoea was prevalent, but could not be proved to be due to the water; and pollution was not sufficient to secure condemnation by a chemist. The *Lancet* denounced the council, which appointed a committee. It duly reported that the water was sufficient in quantity, and in dry seasons better pumping into the Fossdyke at Torksey would obviate any shortage. It was a fair second-class water, and the risks were no greater than in many large towns which took water from rivers; and no alternative source of supply could be obtained at reasonable cost. The *Lancet* denounced the report.

The board continued to press the council, and not only about the water supply. Water closets should be substituted for earth vaults; a public slaughterhouse was needed; new by-laws were called for, especially about the keeping of pigs; and there should be better isolation provision for infectious diseases. The council said they had a report on the water, were converting privies in urgent cases, could not agree among themselves about the slaughterhouse, and were considering by-laws. They could not afford isolation provision.

The board returned to the charge in 1892. Members of the council visited the Pike Drain, the Prial Brook and the ballast pits of the Midland Railway, and congratulated the citizens that a large proportion of the water came from districts free of taint. Vegetation in the stream would take care of agricultural pollution, and the subsoil of the whole area

[1] *L.C.*, 10 January 1885.

formed a splendid filter bed; and when the water reached the water-works it was submitted to a further purifying process.

The great water question had become mixed in the minds of the councillors with the idea of extension of the city boundary to include Bracebridge and Boultham; and this in turn would affect an overdue redistribution of wards, which had become very unequal in population. Here, however, it seems desirable to deal with the subjects separately.

An attempt was made at a public meeting in 1891 to secure the adoption of the Infectious Diseases (Notification) Act of 1889. Familiar arguments were deployed in opposition – a low death rate, the expense, the inhumanity of taking a child from its mother. In vain the mayor pointed out that this was only a matter of notification, not removal: a resolution of disapproval was carried by a large majority, and a few months later the council took the same line. The Local Government Board said that nearly all the great cities had adopted the Act: adding that it was in force in 31 urban and rural district council areas out of 42 in Lincolnshire. It was in vain.

In 1894 there was another report on the water from the board, but its effect was blunted by the report of the city medical officer in 1895 that few towns had a better bill of health or a lower death rate than Lincoln. Perfunctory quests for new water supplies went on, and fever hospital buildings were undertaken in Long Leys Road. The council knew that the growing demand for water required larger provision for filtration, and that the building of houses and factories on the river bank increased the danger of pollution. In 1901 a borehole was sunk in the attempt to find a new supply, and in 1904 the area of filter beds was largely increased.

It was too late to avoid disaster. Inaction soon brought nemesis on the city. On 2 December 1904 a case of typhoid fever was reported, followed by a second on the 22nd; by 10 January 1905 there were 18 cases. A sample of water was taken from the tap of a domestic supply and analysed. The bacillus of typhoid was not detected nor was the total number of organisms excessive, but the presence of intestinal bacteria was regarded as evidence strongly suggestive of pollution with sewage. The report reached the town clerk on the 18th; on the 19th 13,000 handbills were ordered to be printed and circulated, asking consumers to boil water for drinking purposes. A full statement of the facts was prepared by Page as deputy town clerk, published by the council and entered upon the minutes.[1] Later the public was urged to boil milk also. Provision for scarlet fever patients was used for typhoid patients, and halls fitted up to receive the sick. An expert from the board declared that

[1] L.A.O. li 1/10/7 7 February 1905.

the water supply was absolutely safe after boiling for ten minutes. Water was brought from Newark, the gift of Alderman Thomas Smith of that town, and was carried free by the Midland railway, and householders were invited to fetch it in their own casks.

By 6 May the worst was over, by which time there had been over 1,000 cases and over 100 deaths. The catchment drain and the Pike drain were cut off, and additional water taken from the river with additional filtration. Boring began at Boultham, and reached a depth of 2,014 feet, a depth unprecedented in this country. It was concluded that at that depth the supply would only be half of the amount needed, and the engineer wished to go another 400 feet down.

By the end of the year the temporary supply of water was ended, and the public were told that thousands of people had been using the water delivered through the mains without ill effect. The Lincoln Medical Society inspected the alterations at the waterworks, where they were assured that the filter beds had been constructed to deal efficiently with the water supply. Three days later it was found that the filter beds were inadequate; and this at the very time when the special supply was discontinued. The doctors thought the warning of Dr Harrison in 1885 about the pollution of the river at Grantham still held good; and they urged that water be brought from Newark or Willoughby. The South Lincolnshire Water Company were willing to supply water from Bourne. This was found to be not good enough in quality, and the Newark supply not large enough in quantity.

Anxiety continued. The council relieved their Waterworks Committee from responsibility and took direct charge. They were told that as their boreholes went deeper, pure water from the Trent valley was coming through. It appears that the special supply from Newark was resumed, the amount being doubled at the cost of Sharpley Bainbridge; and it was recalled that the waterworks engineer Henry Teague (who died in 1898) had urged an increase in the filtering area.

By February 1907 the disease had almost gone, though business, badly affected, remained stagnant. The British Medical Association pronounced judgment on the outbreak:

taking into consideration the history of the nature and conditions of Lincoln water supply during the last 20 years, it might safely have been predicted that – sooner or later – an epidemic of typhoid fever would occur in the city with extensive and sudden violence...It is difficult to understand how the Corporation of Lincoln can have ignored for so many years the obvious and continuous risks to which the citizens have been exposed through using a water supply constantly liable to dangerous contamination. They have turned a deaf ear to the repeated warnings given to them by their medical adviser, by the experts who corroborated his views, and by the Medical Society of the city.[1]

In default of alternatives, attention turned to Elkesley, 22 miles from Lincoln, to the east of the Dukeries in Nottinghamshire. A scheme to bring water from there was estimated to cost £180,000; the corporation had already spent £160,000, and owed £94,000. A public meeting, duly chastened, voted in favour of Elkesley with only one dissentient.

When the bill to authorise the scheme was promoted in parliament the whole dismal history was rehearsed: the warning of the medical officer and the Local Government Board in 1885 – a cholera scare in 1893 – the events of 1904–5. In spite of opposition from Nottinghamshire interests the bill passed, and the first sod was cut at Elkesley in October 1908. The city water engineer (N. McK. Barron), appointed in 1905, said that the new water supply was the best that could be obtained; it might not be the softest water, but from the organic standpoint it was certainly the purest supply in the country. The tap was turned on in Lincoln in October 1911. To Page belongs the credit, once the need was proved to his satisfaction, of carrying the scheme through to the statute book; to Barron the successful execution of the programme.[2]

To return to the question of boundaries and wards. The County Government Act of 1888 set up county councils, the three administrative divisions of Lincolnshire, Lindsey, Kesteven and Holland, each being given a separate county council. A city that had enjoyed its own charter powers for centuries, and had had a popularly elected council for fifty years, would not lightly acquiesce in partial absorption in a countryside which was wholly dominated by the gentry and would be likely to continue to be so for a time at least. Lincoln's interest was taken up by Kerans M.P.; the Home Secretary invited representatives of cities and towns which were counties of themselves to a conference; and Lincoln in due course became a county borough. It was expected that there would follow legislation setting up urban and rural district councils, as in fact happened in 1894. This might well affect the question of relations with Bracebridge and Boultham. The city council decided to wait and see, and meanwhile petitioned for redivision of the city into six wards instead of three; an order to this end took effect in 1899, each ward to have three councillors instead of the former six.

The pros and cons of boundary extension were under discussion throughout these years. Bracebridge was dependent on Lincoln for

---

[1] Quoted in *L.C.*, 25 February 1907.

[2] Minutes of Evidence to the House of Commons Committee on the Lincoln Waterworks Bill, 1908; 8 Edward VIII, session 1908, Lincoln Corporation (Water etc.) Act 1908.

water, gas and sewerage; and it had a school board, which on incorporation it might get rid of and so save a 10d. rate. New Boultham had Lincoln gas and water, but it had no sewerage. William Watkins, ever alert, said both districts had some very indifferent houses, not conforming with city by-law standards, and there not being sufficient control by the county authority; at New Boultham, with no drainage system, water percolated into the ground and under the floors of some houses, and speculative builders there were a menace. A scheme for extension failed because Bracebridge only wanted to give Lincoln the part of the parish they did not themselves want.

In 1894 the Bracebridge parish council came into being with C. W. Pennell as chairman. He soon pointed out to them that they might save money if they had control of their own highways and sanitary business, and that if they could withdraw from the new Branston Rural District Council and become an urban district council on their own they might save a rate of 7d. in the pound. The parish was growing, and there was hope of a railway station. They decided to petition the county council for urban status; whereupon the city renewed its approach for amalgamation. The county council preferred to give the urban powers. The boundaries of the new area, however, seemed to Bracebridge too narrow; the city on the north, the railway on the east, Waddington on the south and the river on the west. It was, in fact, the ribbon along main road, and the boundaries were accepted under protest. Any advantage the city could offer by way of differential rate was outweighed by the advantages of the change to urban status.

As building began on the late F. J. Clarke's estate at Bracebridge the urban district council enquired whether the city would extend the area from which it received sewage, and later whether it would extend the area to the whole of the urban district. Terms were reached on the latter basis in 1912.

On the side of the city there was strong feeling that the newly built-up areas were benefiting from city enterprises without bearing a share of the burden of rates. Difficult questions were arising: a street was planned in New Boultham partly in Boultham parish and partly in Lincoln. In 1913 Colonel Ellison sold his Boultham estate for development, and the Branston Rural District Council resolved to apply to the board in London for a town planning scheme, and there was a conference with the city. There was an agreement that the density of building should not exceed 16 houses to the acre, and as to access roads and bridges. When war broke out in 1914 no decision upon boundary extension had been taken.

It was a surprise to many that the Boultham area would ever be fit to build on. In spite of drainage schemes of the various authorities, parts of Boultham and the lower city were still subject to the risks of flooding. In 1910 there was flooding of the upper Witham and the Sincil Dyke, and miles of planks were laid to get people along the streets. It was yet to be some years before the risk was materially reduced.

A new political symptom had appeared in 1883; in two wards the official liberal candidates were defeated by the votes of liberal working men. A separate electoral interest was beginning to emerge. Perhaps this had something to do with the change of heart proclaimed at the Queen's Jubilee in 1887; a desire to mitigate party warfare between tories and the older liberals. The mayoralty had been part of the spoils of electoral victory, but it was then agreed that the office should go by seniority among those members of the council who had not held it, regardless of politics. This rule is still observed. Thomas Martin, then chosen, was the first tory mayor since 1867, and he was followed by Watkins, another tory, and the champion of pure water.

Yet the liberals kept their grip, fortified by a Liberal Association, a Liberal Club, formed in 1892, and a newspaper, the *Lincoln Leader*, started in 1896. They could withstand the attacks of men like Thomas Bell of Robeys, who had the support of both parties and none. He was defeated in 1889 by Thomas Wallis, standing on a party ticket, and then a comparatively unknown man. Another good man, Sharpley Bainbridge, had been lost by liberal opposition. The liberals were embarrassed, and had to defend their caucus methods of cutting and drying everything beforehand, though the tories had to admit that they too consulted together. Dissensions within the liberal party led to the defeat of W. W. Richardson in 1892 at the end of his mayoral year. It was said that he had refused to bow the knee to the association and the club; he was a devoted Methodist, and may well have disagreed with them. Radical candidates were appearing. William Turner, a working man, won the upper ward on the 'fair contract clause' in 1893, and Stanley Udale, a merchant tailor and extreme radical, came in with Wallis.

In 1895 Udale, supported by Dr Collier and Turner, called for a better supply of houses for the poorer sections of the working classes. Lincoln, he said, like all old cities, was honeycombed with courts and alleys; and he enumerated 46 properties consisting of 280 dwellings which should be condemned. It was presently resolved to adopt part of the Housing of the Working Classes Act of 1890. A scheme for building 50 houses at New Boultham was adopted, and the board were asked to sanction a loan of £6,500. The case for the corporation was put by Hebb. Lincoln had some slum property which the city would not buy owing to the heavy compensation payable; but if they built new houses the slums would become tenantless. The site proposed was only a few yards outside the city boundary, and near large works; rents would be 4s. 3d. and 3s 6d. The surveyor said that out of 10,000 houses in the city, only 34 at rents from 4s 6d. to 6s. 6d. were empty, 10 of them dilapidated. The scheme would be self-supporting. The houses were not put forward as model houses.

For the opposition R. J. Ward said that the purpose of the Act was to buy and pull down houses and build on the sites, though there was power to buy other land. Mortimer the architect criticised low-bedroom houses like those proposed. Speculative builders were building good houses. There was no town of the size of Lincoln where so many people owned the houses they lived in.

The board refused to approve the plans. With necessary improvements the houses could not be let at the desired rents without a charge on the rates. The scheme was therefore abandoned. It was a choice between 'rabbit warrens' and houses at 5s. 3d. and 4s. 3d., which was too much. Wallis said later that they had proved that the Act was useless.

The radical wave for the moment was spent. Several socialist candidates stood without success, and both Udale and Turner went out in 1899. A new tory drive at municipal elections had some success, and the liberals only kept their majority because they held the aldermanic seats. They could not escape responsibility for the disastrous results of their long neglect of warnings about the quality of the water supply, and in 1905 hostile feeling brought into being a citizens' association to promote the candidature of suitable men without political commitment. Colonel Ruston was elected unopposed, and a few others came in. The liberal hold was assailed again from the left when a labour candidate, Ralph Thompson, a locomotive engineer, won a by-election in 1907 in a three-cornered contest. He lost his seat in 1909.

The liberal record was defended by Wallis. It was the citizens who had voted down the baths scheme at a town poll; and on the first proposal for a fever hospital the working men had held a meeting against it. It was the public who had kept out a school board and left the city with a heavy education rate and an inefficient school system. As to slums, he accused the champions of the poor of refusing to denounce their vices as well as their wrongs.

The trade unionist councillor, Bell, was attacked for supporting a liberal, Thomas Halkes, a master builder, and to escape from a difficulty he took a corporation post as pathways foreman and retired from the council. In 1913 R. A. Taylor, a labour candidate won the Park ward at a by-election. It was a solitary success, but it was a portent.

It could at least be said that the health of the city was comparatively good. In 1910 the medical officer reported a death rate of 13.2 per thousand, which was nearly one per thousand less than the average rate for the whole country, in spite of diphtheria at that time. Memories of the epidemic were strong enough to ensure that provision was made for a refuse destructor in 1911; but when by-laws were proposed to control the distance which pigsties must be from dwelling houses they were defeated by an overwhelming majority; hands off the poor man's pig. An abattoir had been opened in 1903, and an infectious diseases hospital in 1904.

Lincoln was still one of the lowest rated cities in England, but the rates were steadily rising, and this is what the ratepayers noticed. There was the new water supply; the burden of the new schools, brought on the city by the prolonged refusal of a school board; all manner of improvements, and the poor rate. Yet at least the manner of collecting the rate could be improved. The newly appointed city accountant was calling attention to the fact that there were in Lincoln 18 rating authorities: the city council levied the general district rate and the borough rate, precepting on the parishes, and 17 parishes independently collected poor rates on behalf of the guardians, with their own overseers and their own assessments. There were 24 spending authorities – the council in two capacities, the guardians, the parishes and four burial boards. He therefore recommended the consolidation of rate collection, the unification of civil parishes and the transfer of the powers of the burial boards to the council. There would then be five instead of 35 overseers, and one authority responsible for registration. When the old parishes ceased to be civil parishes the guardians would be distributed amongst the wards instead. Opposition by vested interests soon collapsed, and the order for the union of parishes was confirmed by the Local Government Board in 1906. The old parishes would no longer be used for civil purposes, even statistical ones.

CHAPTER XIII

CHURCH AND CHAPEL: II

In 1869 Disraeli transferred the orthodox and protestant Bishop Jackson to the see of London, and as a concession to the high church party, who had hoped that Samuel Wilberforce would go to London,[1] nominated Christopher Wordsworth, canon of Westminster and nephew of the poet, to the see of Lincoln. Although he was a high churchman he was decidedly anti-Romanist and opposed to ritualism. He had a powerful mind, and was never afraid to carry his principles to their logical conclusion without regard to expediency or indeed to realism: his biographers refer to his spiritual knight-errantry.[2] Cracroft wrote of 'dear grand hearted Bishop Wordsworth, who has every quality except discretion';[3] and A. C. Benson said of him that he lived three-quarters in the third century and the rest in heaven.[4]

In his refusal on principle to make concessions to current opinions he exasperated the dissenters and especially the Wesleyans. He declined to use his influence with the vicar of Owston to allow the title of 'Reverend' to be placed on the tombstone of a Wesleyan minister's daughter; a view upheld by the Court of Arches but overruled by the Privy Council.[5] In 1873 he issued a pastoral letter to the Wesleyan Methodists inviting them to return to the church of their fathers on the principles of John Wesley, and he told them that no well-instructed Christian of the first 1,500 years after Christ would have thought it safe to receive the Holy Communion at their hands. He arranged a conference between leading Anglicans and Methodists in London; and perhaps only the bishop was surprised that the clergy were dismayed and the Methodists indignant. While he wished to discuss ordination questions the Methodists dwelt on current grievances.[6] He opposed the Burials Act of 1880, which allowed

---

[1] See Standish Meecham, *Lord Bishop, Samuel Wilberforce* (1970), p. 289.

[2] Overton and Wordsworth, *Christopher Wordsworth, Bishop of Lincoln, 1807–1885* (1888), p. 241. A reviewer of the biography said that the bishop was 'too good, too kind, too easily influenced by plausible excuses. A bishop must be able to harden his heart.' *L.D.M.*, IV, 224.   [3] Cracroft, 27 March 1875.

[4] *The Leaves of the Trees* (1911), pp. 261–3; *The Trefoil* (1923), pp. 111–12. W. H. Brookfield wrote that some men – Bacon, Shakespeare, Milton – were born in advance of their age, and some a little behind it, like the Bishop of Lincoln. *Mrs Brookfield and her Circle* (1905), II, 532.   [5] *Law Reports*, 4 Ad. & Eccl., pp. 398–408.

[6] E. W. Watson, *Life of Bishop John Wordsworth* (1915), p. 97. He acknowledged that some of the blame for schism lay on the Church of England, and that the tendencies to Romanism in doctrine, practice and ritual which were then visible repelled the Wesley-

Christian dissenters to hold services in parish churchyards: there should be no surrender of God's acre.[1]

He entered with enthusiasm upon his life and work at Lincoln. He had a plan to sell the episcopal residence at Riseholme[2] and build a house in Lincoln on the site of the Old Palace,[3] but the project had to await the advent of his successor. He founded the Lincoln Theological College, the 'Scholae Cancellarii',[4] and bought for it the old county hospital building; and he presently brought Edward White Benson to Lincoln as chancellor of the cathedral. The latter conceived his function as that of a diocesan minister of education, and notably he fulfilled his charge in the city.[5] There came to help him John Henchman Crowfoot, lately a missionary to Delhi.[6] Wordsworth also revived the custom of episcopal visitation of the cathedral church (1870), called the first diocesan synod of the whole clergy of a diocese to meet since 1683 (1871) and a diocesan conference (1872).

His impetus carried forward a great outburst of church building in the city, then lately begun. In 1867 the parishioners of the fast growing parish of St Swithin asked the corporation to convey to them part of Sheep Square for a new church: the square had not been used for 20 years, and the parish need was urgent, for it had 1,400 houses and 7,000 inhabitants, and the church would only hold 260. The plan proceeded, and within a few months of his consecration Wordsworth laid the foundation stone of the new church, which was designed by James Fowler of Winterton, the spire being a copy of the superb spire at Louth, and was to be built at the cost of Nathaniel Clayton and Joseph Shuttleworth, many of whose employees lived in the parish. Eight years later, laying the foundation stone of a new church at St Paul's, Wordsworth could recall that he had seen seven churches either entirely rebuilt or begun to be built in the city:

At the north, on the side of this old Roman road, is the Training School new chapel; here is St Paul's; a little to the east is St Peter in Eastgate, which, I am

ans and widened the separation. Preface to the third edition of *The Bishop of Lincoln's Pastoral to the Wesleyans* (1873).

[1] He and some other bishops decided not to consecrate any new churchyards or parts of cemeteries, and drew up a form for clergy to consecrate separately each grave to be used for Anglican burial. P. T. Marsh, *Victorian Church in Decline* (1969), p. 261.

[2] See above, p. 173. [3] L.A.O. Massingberd 31/17.

[4] By this time several diocesan theological colleges had been founded. It seems that such a college had been mooted in Lincoln earlier. Richard Sibthorp, not liking the idea, had discussed it with Cracroft. Diary of the latter, 4 December 1849.

[5] A. C. Benson, *Life of Edward White Benson* (1900), I, 348, and see below, p. 277.

[6] The bishop gave Crowfoot his own stall in the cathedral, and Benson made him vice-chancellor. Lambeth Library, H5195, L5, Pamphlets.

glad to find, has an overflowing congregation, fruitful in good works;[1] to the south are the spacious new churches of St Martin[2] and St Swithin; further to the south is the new church of St Mark,[3] the spire of which has just been erected by the munificence of one lady, and further (south) is the church of St Andrew, now still rising from its foundations.[4] There is also the restored church of St Mary le Wigford with its new aisle. And to return to the neighbourhood where we are, we have also the prospect of a chapel of ease in the parish of St Nicholas and St John.[5]

St Mary Magdalene, rebuilt in the classical style in 1695, was regothicised and virtually rebuilt by Bodley in 1882. At St Peter at Gowts, which seated 300 though the parish had a population of 4,000, a new chancel and chancel aisle were built at the cost of the vicar, the Rev. J. W. Townroe. St Botolph, which was concerned with the area between the south end of Wigford and Bracebridge, rapidly building up, and already occupied by five dissenting chapels, was enlarged. The western suburb too was building up, and a move was made to provide a church for this outlying part of St Mary le Wigford; it began with a second-hand iron structure in 1885, its place being taken by the present St Faith in 1895.[6]

Wordsworth's episcopate and that of his successor were much troubled by the spread of ritualistic practices, with which the earlier Tractarians had had little sympathy.[7] The Public Worship Regulation Bill was introduced in Parliament in 1869 to restrain extravagant practices, and Wordsworth approved of the Bill, though he protested against the manner of its introduction.[8] In his Charge of 1873 he referred to 'that sentimental and morbid craving which is too rife among us, for the

[1] Designed by Sir A. W. Blomfield.
[2] By A. S. Beckett. The west door was ornamented by the heads of Bishops Jackson and Wordsworth. *L.C.*, 13 October 1871, said that of Wordsworth was admirable, that of Jackson not so good, though the sculptor was going to be employed further on it. Cracroft thought both good likenesses, though Jackson's did not bear looking into as the other did. Cracroft, 27 August 1875. The church was demolished in 1970.
[3] By William Watkins. The church was demolished in 1972.
[4] By James Fowler. Land for the church was given by Canon Swan of Sausthorpe, whose family had bought and developed much of the area; part of the fabric of old St Martin was bought by the bishop and used in the new church. It was built especially for Robey's workmen; it was demolished in 1970.
[5] Overton and Wordsworth, *Christopher Wordsworth*, 219, 341.
[6] By C. Hodgson Fowler.
[7] Dr Pusey declared that he had never had any sympathy with 'any innovations in the way of conducting the service, anything of ritualism, or especially any revival of disused vestments...I have looked with sorrow at the crude way in which some doctrines have been put forward without due pains to prevent misunderstanding, and ritual has been forced upon the people, unexplained and without their consent'. Davidson and Benham, *Life of Archibald Campbell Tait* (1891), i, 249 (26 April 1860).
[8] Tait, op. cit., ii, 223–5. Wordsworth's biographers would hardly give the impression that he supported the Bill. Overton and Wordsworth, *Christopher Wordsworth*, pp. 257–60.

reproduction of Romish Doctrine and Ritual, and even for the restoration of Romanism' and to 'the urgent need of vigorous measures of Ecclesiastical Discipline'.[1] And in 1875 he signed the Bishops' Pastoral, which referred to that interruption of sympathy and mutual confidence which ought to exist between clergy and laity:

Changes in the mode of performing Divine service, in themselves of small importance, introduced without authority, and often without due regard to the feelings of parishioners, have excited apprehension that greater changes are to follow...Refusal to obey legitimate authority is another evil.[2]

Subsequent and mostly one-sided discussion of the controversy – and especially veneration for Edward King – has so much overlaid the contemporary scene that these quotations are necessary to put the matter in its historical perspective.

The attitude of older high churchmen is neatly illustrated in the diary of Sir Charles Anderson. In 1852 he had presented the Rev. Richard Thomas Lowe to the living of Lea. In 1867 the rector lit the candles on the altar during Lent, a practice of which Anderson disapproved, commenting nevertheless 'that the sacrament does not lose its efficacy by the administration of a fool'. When his old friend Bishop Wilberforce visited him in the following year Anderson did not attend communion, in order to show that he did not countenance the new ritual by his presence, and the bishop refused to celebrate on account of the ritual and the candles. When the Privy Council gave judgment against lighted candles at the sacrament the rector delivered 'a silly tirade against the unrighteous judgment of an unrighteous judge'. Anderson let himself go in his diary upon the inculcation of simple obedience by men who disobeyed their bishops in the most determined way. 'They are to be petty popes and everyone is to yield to them.' He bitterly regretted his presentation of Lowe, to the rectory: but his sufferings came to an end when the Lowes sailed for Madeira and were lost at sea.[3]

In this atmosphere the smallest change in church came under suspicion. The abolition of pew rents and the substitution of collections; the introduction of *Hymns Ancient and Modern*; the use of the surplice by the choir;[4] trust was destroyed, and each change was enough. When the decision of the courts established that a cope was to be worn in cathedral

---

[1] Bradshaw and Wordsworth, *Lincoln Cathedral Statutes*, II, (1897), 683.   [2] Tait, II, 271.
[3] Lowe had held a chaplaincy in Madeira. Anderson noted (14 April 1874), 'It is said that *Liberia* came into collision and sank on this day.' See Standish Meecham, *Lord Bishop, Samuel Wilberforce*, p. 204.
[4] Surplices for the choir were introduced at St Michael in 1876, but the governors of the Bluecoat School decided by three (Wesleyan) votes to two (Anglican) not to allow the boys to wear them. *L.C.*, 16 June 1876.

churches by the principal minister on the great festivals (the *Purchas* case)
the *Mercury* commented:

We are asked to be thankful for the introduction of ecclesiastical finery thus
announced: but we prefer to express our regret that symbols should be revived
or introduced which, however pleasing to some members of the Church of
England, are very distasteful to others. Is the gaudy vestment to draw Roman
Catholics to the Church, or is it thought that Dissenters will be won by the
dazzle of crimson velvet, carbuncles and lapis-lazuli?[1]

The new vicar of St Peter at Gowts promised to steer a middle course
between opposing rocks of doctrine and ritual; but the vicar of St
Botolph told a vestry meeting that a clergyman had a right to carry out
services in his own way, so long as he kept within the law, though he
added that he thought no clergyman would carry out services to the
displeasure of parishioners. He aroused much greater feeling in 1879
when he refused to read the Anglican burial service in church over one of
his parishioners who had attended the parish church and the vicar's
Bible class, and sometimes the Independent and Unitarian chapels, but
who did not believe in the Trinity. The vicar refused to have the body in
church, though he was willing to read part of the service at the house and
the remainder at the graveside. Instead, the Independent minister
undertook the duty.

There was a dramatic change of scene in 1885. On the resignation and
death of Wordsworth,[2] Gladstone chose Edward King, professor of Pastoral
Theology at Oxford, described by Lord Acton as, next to canon Liddon,
the greatest high church influence at Christ Church, but quite without
his magic force as *allumeur des âmes*,[3] as the new bishop of Lincoln.
At about the same time he chose as dean on the death of Blakesley,
William John Butler of Wantage; he was only his fourth choice, not
having planned so strong a combination of high churchmen at Lincoln.[4]
As soon as King was appointed the extreme Protestants denounced

---

[1] *S.M.*, 5 April 1872.
[2] His death occurred at the time of the Lincoln races, which by direction of Henry
Chaplin were suspended during the time of the funeral service. It was afterwards said by
the police that more pockets were picked that day in the cathedral than on the racecourse. Ex inf. Canon W. W. Leeke. A. E. Collis used to tell of a visit by the bishop to an elementary school, where the schoolmaster introduced him to the boys as the nephew of the
poet. When he addressed them the bishop asked if any boy could give him an epitome
of the life of the poet. There ensued a frozen silence, broken by the unhappy master,
who said, 'I am afraid, my lord, they do not know the meaning of the word *epitome*.'
'Not know the meaning of *epitome*', said the bishop, 'why, it's synonymous with *synopsis*.'
[3] David Mathew, *Lord Acton and his Times* (1968), p. 279.
[4] Gladstone had wanted to appoint his son-in-law E. C. Wickham as dean, but was then
dissuaded. Owen Chadwick, *Edward King* (Lincoln Minster Pamphlets, 1968), pp. 23–4.

him for holding doctrines which, they said, disqualified him from holding the office of a bishop in the Church of England. Incidents quickly accumulated. He began to wear a mitre in his cathedral, the first diocesan bishop to do so since the Reformation. In the sacristy at the Palace he had a portable altar and a chasuble which had belonged to Dr Pusey. Most of the ritual practices condemned in the legal judgments of the 1870s, small things in themselves, were instituted.[1] All the distasteful events which followed were the natural and probable consequences of the spread of these ritualistic practices and the forcing of exasperating changes on unprepared congregations, so rousing, as Bishop Wand has said, the fanaticism, the rowdyism, the sheer ignorance which went along with that real and lively fear of Rome which was part of the national sentiment.[2] Indeed, the consequences were foreseen; when early in his episcopate King vetoed a prosecution against the rector of Clee for a ritual offence, Butler wrote, 'We in Lincoln are on a powder barrel, which a very little more will explode.'[3]

In 1886 it was complained that under the influence of the dean the members of the chapter, except the archdeacon Kaye, were adopting the eastward position during the communion service.[4] The Lincoln solicitor H. K. Hebb sought proceedings under the Clergy Discipline Act against the precentor, Venables, in that at communion service he did not stand at the north side of the table, but in the front or on the west side, with his back to the people, except when reading the Ten Commandments and the Offertory Sentences, when he turned towards them. As Venables' canonry was in the gift of the bishop the appeal went to the archbishop; the reason why complaint was not made against the dean was that the appeal would have gone to the bishop, which would have been useless. Archbishop Benson declined to issue the commission.

By then the bishops had decided to stop prosecutions for ritual offences, and the active Protestant body, the Church Association, faced with this veto, had to choose between abandoning the fight and prosecuting a bishop. They chose the latter course, and King was the obvious target. They instituted proceedings on eight counts in the archbishop's court arising out of incidents of St Peter at Gowts church. After the Privy Council had decided that the archbishop had jurisdiction, the case went on wearily until 1890. The archbishop ruled against King on two points

---

[1] The facts are summarised in E. R. Norman, *Anti-Catholicism in Victorian England* (1968), p. 112. On his monument in the cathedral Wordsworth was given a mitre, though he never wore one in his life.
[2] *Anglicanism in History and To-day* (1961), p. 102.   [3] L.A.O. King deposit, xvi, xvii.
[4] Kaye pointed out that he had not changed the position he had taken for 23 years; Canon Leeke also refused to adopt the new practice.

and in his favour on the rest, censuring both those who gave and those who took offence unadvisedly in such matters.[1] King at once announced that he would discontinue the actions of which the archbishop disapproved.

King was no fanatic; for example, he always respected the practices of the parishes he visited; but he was caught by his actions in the clash between two groups whose extremists were fanatics.[2] His suffering was not in vain. There followed a revulsion of feeling against ritual prosecutions. Uniformity of worship was not thus to be secured; and indeed it was not to be secured at all. It was breaking down, and those who did not like the form of service in one church went to another or fell away.[3] Denominational dissension was being diverted to educational issues, and public interest in ecclesiastical questions would wane to a point at which many people would think the whole controversy absurd. But it mattered then, and there were two sides; one has been forgotten, whilst veneration for King has kept the other side alive.

Benson himself seized every chance of showing his affection for the bishop. In 1887 he stayed with him at the Old Palace, which had been restored for him: 'an odd phenomenon if the next step is disestablishment'. He regretted the destruction of the old pantry and the conversion of the ancient bishop's solar into the clerestory of the chapel. 'But anything can be forgiven to the Bishop – so sweet and manly. Thank God for this Lincoln King.'[4]

He has been so widely acclaimed as a saint that it is not easy to write of him objectively. He was a man of great nobility and sweetness of character. His simplicity appealed to all save those who thought his

---

[1] *Read v The Bishop of Lincoln*. The plaintiffs had been de Lacy Read, churchwarden of Cleethorpes, William Brown, solicitor, Grimsby, and J. Marshall and Felix Wilson, working men, aggrieved parishioners of St Peter at Gowts. An appeal by the plaintiffs to the Privy Council was dismissed.

[2] A. J. Balfour wrote (6 February 1903) to Edward Talbot: 'I confess to entertaining the gloomiest apprehensions as to the future of the Church of England. I can hardly think of anything else. A so-called "Protestant" faction, ignorant, fanatical, reckless, but every day organising themselves politically with increased efficiency. A ritualistic party, as ignorant, as fanatical, and as reckless, the sincerity of whose attachment to historic Anglicanism I find it quite impossible to believe. A High Church party, determined to support men of whose practices they heartily disapprove.' Blanche Dugdale, *Arthur James Balfour* (1936), I, 284.

[3] R. C. K. Ensor, *England 1870–1914* (1936), p. 307.

[4] 'The Bishop went to the consecration of St Peter at Gowts at 8, in white cope. If he had a mitre he hid it.' At the cathedral Sunday evening service, '2000 people. They clearly enjoyed it. But the music was much too soft and the dean's sermon much too hard.' A. C. Benson, *Life of Edward White Benson* (1900), II, 151. The Master and Fellows of Trinity College, Cambridge, kindly allowed me to read the archbishop's diary. There appear to be no entries during the period of his Lincoln chancellorship.

sermons so simple that they were an insult to intelligence. Every hat was raised as he walked the streets of Lincoln. Canon Scott Holland wrote of him:

The porters loved him, the villagers loved him, the town loved him. Twice I went down to Lincoln Fair with him, all among the coconuts and the ginger-bread and the fat woman. It was a delicious experience to note the affection that followed him about. He draws out love as the sun draws out fragrance from the flowers.[1]

A local journalist wrote long after that:

he looked as if he had stepped out of a stained glass window when his bowed figure, his benevolent face, his twinkling blue eyes and shaggy brows were seen in a little village church. Here is a typical story of the grand old man, whom I heard in many village churches. At one country place a woman was fumbling in her bag when the offertory was taken, and the plate passed her. She went to the vestry after the service and said 'here's my penny, I meant to put it in the collection'. The Bishop, overhearing this, put on his cope and mitre, put the penny on a salver, went back to the Holy Table, and dedicated the coin with as much reverence and ceremony as that with which he had dedicated the whole offertory. A deputation once angrily went to interview King. He came out in a purple dressing gown and the well known smile, and after saying how pleased he was to see them, invited them to lunch. 'We went away', said the deputation, 'without having said any of the unpleasant things we meant to say.' In his presence it was impossible.[2]

This last incident seems to be evidence of something less exalted than sanctity!

His long drawn ordeal had been a great strain on him, and as he grew older something of power seemed to go out of him. Men came to think of him 'as a holy and delightful old man, but no longer as an intellectual'.[3] Perhaps he had stayed too long.

Veneration for the man did not prevent opposition to what he was thought to stand for. In 1900 a Church Association was formed in Lincoln to preserve the Protestant character of the Church of England. The Congregationalist J. D. Jones said that their fathers would have recoiled with bland incredulity from the suggestion that the Protestant Church would again be imperilled, and that it should again be imperilled by bastard Romanists doing their work within the pale of the Church of England as by law established. At the general election of that year not only did the liberal and Wesleyan candidate at Louth (R. W. Perks) denounce ritualism, but the tory and Anglican candidate at Horncastle, Lord Willoughby de Eresby, said that if the bishops could

---

[1] *A Bundle of Memories* (1915), p. 61.
[2] Letter from Harold Murray to me, dated 15 September 1951.
[3] Owen Chadwick, *Edward King*, p. 20.

not stop Romish practices he would support a measure to make them illegal.[1] During the liberal ascendancy after 1906 it became a matter of reproach that though for reasons of age King had become almost a stranger socially he could travel to the House of Lords to vote against Lloyd George's budget of 1909, the only bishop to do so.

When he died in 1910 a local liberal journalist wrote that Lincoln lay 'almost as under a pall'. A month later he hailed the new bishop as 'a messenger of a new spirit which demands that the captains of the church should be champions of a new democracy...Bishop Hicks is the man we have been looking for through many a long and weary year'.[2]

Edward Lee Hicks, canon of Manchester, was a distinguished classical scholar and a moderate high churchman accustomed to work with nonconformists in matters of social policy, and especially in the cause of temperance[3] which he held to be the foundation of all social and political progress. His advocacy of this cause, and his political views – he even favoured the disestablishment of the Church in Wales – ensured a lack of popularity in some church circles. He was a fighting bishop, and none certainly could cavil at his courage.[4] When a few months later the scholarly Dean Wickham died, and Hicks was joined as dean by Thomas Charles Fry, a vigorous member of the Christian Social Union, it was clear that temperance and social justice were to be the leading themes.[5]

Whilst in these years the Anglican Church was showing renewal it had to face the fact that nonconformists too had made great strides in numbers and social and political influence. Their advance exercised

---

[1] The Willoughby agent said in 1852 that dissenters were the staple product of the Fens. L.A.O. 3 Ancaster 7/23/62/63.

[2] *L.L.*, 12 March, 9 April 1910. The appointment had been offered to and declined by Dr E. S. Talbot, who later accepted the see of Winchester.

[3] He noted in his diary that his enthronement was attended by Lancashire and Yorkshire friends with whom he had worked for temperance reform, 'nearly all dissenters of the deepest dye, and radicals. It was no small embarrassment to me to have to take a leading share in the gorgeous piece of ecclesiastical ceremony *in their presence*. My Address had them largely in mind – no bad influence.' Diary, 30 June 1910.

[4] Hicks noted on his seventieth birthday that the needs of the diocese were more discipline, more zeal, more hope, and more definite ideals. The discipline he tried to supply with the aid of his archdeacons; he exercised control of ceremonies and vestments, and he complained in private of the Catholic 'spikiness' of some young curates. The zeal and hope he tried to infuse by word and example; and the definite ideals he found difficult to conceive or inculcate in the then state of confusion in the church. Diary, 18 December 1913 and *passim*. Later he reflected that his constant weekend visitation had (he hoped) strengthened many things; he was satisfied with his appointments, in particular those at the cathedral. 24 June 1914.

[5] J. H. Fowler, *Life and Letters of Edward Lee Hicks* (1922). Though he belonged to a different school from King, his respect for the Oxford Movement led him to value his teaching (p. 165).

Bishop King when he sent out his visitation articles in 1886, and he commented on the returns that 'the one overwhelming result is Dissent, Dissent, Dissent'.[1] Though nonconformists had no endowments they had advantages when it came to providing places of worship, for they were not hampered by ecclesiastical machinery and the parson's freehold, or by reluctance to use lay preachers. A mission chapel – perhaps only a tin tabernacle – could be put up cheaply and quickly, and the Methodists especially, with their circuit system and their local preachers, could easily man the pulpit. Their preachers moved every few years, and for purposes of local history are therefore almost anonymous, yet their frequent movement prevented staleness and kept interest alive. The influence of the chapels is perhaps best measured by the part taken by their laymen in public affairs. It was an era of huge bazaars and other money-raising efforts which were themselves a stimulus to enthusiasm; and social, political, religious and educational battles kept them on their toes.

The Lincoln Wesleyans found their buildings totally inadequate. A small chapel built in Alfred Street in St Peter at Gowts parish in 1864 gave way in 1875 to a new chapel in High Street, named in honour of Dr John Hannah,[2] to seat 1,000 people. At the opening 1,800 people attended, and in its turn it was at once small, and a new chapel was built further south, at St Catherine's, in 1878. The United Methodists pulled down their chapel and built a larger one on the same site. The Primitives built a large chapel in 1874, later sold it to the Great Northern Railway, and built in High Street. All three sections of Methodists built smaller chapels in outlying parts of the city. A visiting Wesleyan minister said in 1881 that he was greatly struck by the progress of Methodism in the last six or seven years.

The Congregationalists turned their chapel in Newland over to the British and Foreign School, and built a new chapel beside it in 1876 to house 1,100 people. They had already built a mission chapel in Far Newland, and were also to build in the south and east of Lincoln. In 1894 there was a membership of 500.[3] The Particular Baptists built a new chapel in Mint Street in 1871, and the General Baptists rebuilt in St Benedicts Square in 1886.

Nonconformists were assuming a new and improved status for them-

[1] L.A.O. Larken iii/10. Earlier Visitation Returns, frequently made by the churchwardens, give little information because little was asked for. Wordsworth's second visitation Queries in 1872 asked for much more, and his inquisition provoked protest in some quarters. See *The Ingoldsby Letters* (1879), II, 361–7. The returns are in L.A.O.
[2] As to whom see above, p. 181.
[3] See J. D. Jones, *Three Score Years and Ten* (1940); Arthur Porritt, *J. D. Jones of Bournemouth* (1942).

selves. The word 'chapel' with its implications of subordination to the parish church, once acceptable to Methodists, was giving way to the word 'church'. If their meeting houses were to be called churches, it seemed to follow that they should look like churches, and this meant Gothic. Wesley Chapel was classical; the new Hannah Memorial was classical, but St Catherine's, built almost at once, was Gothic, with a chancel, and to make it more Gothic a spire was added later. Current trends were illustrated in the Congregationalist buildings in Newland. The chapel built in 1840 was in a Regency Gothic style, and when it was altered to become a school it still had a Gothic arcade in front. The new church must of course be Gothic, and in order to stand up to the Anglicans it must have a stone front; and the architects, Bellamy and Hardy, a local firm, chose the Early English style. There was anxious debate whether to go so far as to include a spire, it being settled in favour by the offer of Joseph Ruston to pay the interest on the necessary loan for ten years. The rest of the building could be governed by business principles, and the work must be as cheap as was consistent with good construction. It must therefore be of brick. They did not share the doubts inspired by the Gothic revivalists whether it was proper to use iron in the building of churches, especially as gallery pillars.[1] Cast-iron pillars with capitals were no doubt commissioned under the superintendence of Ruston the ironfounder, and Henry Newsum the timber merchant would approve the use of pitch pine for pews and fittings rather than oak.

A slow approach to social equality was marked by occasional incidents. Ruston, whose achievements and wealth enabled him to take a lead, took the corporation in state to Newland when he was mayor in 1870, this being noted in the minute book as proof of the better feeling regarding dissenters. In that same year the city council resolved to withhold its annual subscription to the county hospital until the rule compelling its officers to be members of the Church of England was expunged. It could no longer be defended; the rule was abolished, and the subscription renewed. There were occasional gestures of good will, as when the Anglicans holding a mission in 1874, received from nonconformist ministers a cordial letter, to which they sent a cordial reply. The personal influence of Bishop King, in spite of his reputation as a ritualist, made for kindlier feeling, and the subdean could say in 1891 that there was a growing tenderness towards nonconformists.[2] Yet at parish level there was continuing hostility, kept alive by the education question, and

[1] C. L. Eastlake, *History of the Gothic Revival* (1872), p. 244; Sir John Clapham, *Economic History of Modern Britain*, II, 71; III, 196.
[2] *L.D.M.* vii, 25.

indeed aggravated by suspicion of Romish tendencies. A Free Church Council, formed in 1896, had for one of its objects resistance to the encroachments of sacerdotalism. When Anglican Sunday scholars had a service in the cathedral, and Leeke provided space for non-Church scholars, some of the clergy prevented their children from attending; and only one Anglican school joined a nonconformist party at the chapter house.

The social distinction between clergy and ministers was especially marked. When a survey of the county was published at the beginning of the twentieth century it contained biographical notices of a large number of clergy, but the only nonconformist minister included was the Rev. H. H. Carlisle, the Newland minister: he was a graduate, which was unusual; of Cambridge, still more unusual; and – perhaps more remarkable still – he lived in Minster Yard, where he had bought a chapter lease.[1] The book noticed one Roman Catholic priest, Father O'Donovan; no doubt the itinerant system of Methodism would tend to disqualify its ministers.

When King sent out his Visitation Articles in 1886 he had especially in mind the labouring classes, the strength of dissent and the numbers who attended no place of worship. The information provided then and in 1889, when it is given at all, is vague and impressionistic. At St Botolph about 300 adults and 300 children went to church, and 450 might represent the three chapels in the parish. St Peter at Gowts said, church, 1,200, dissent 1,500, nowhere 1,500. St Mark said, church 300, chapels 500, nowhere 200. St Martin forthrightly declared that people wandered to the cathedral and other churches, and that the cathedral evening service was crippling their evening service and their offertories. Uphill St Paul returned that perhaps 500 attended church, though not all at one time; 700–800 went to a chapel which served all the uphill district; and some in a family went to church and some to chapel. At St Mary Magdalene all were churchmen, and at St Peter in Eastgate nearly all. Several parishes noted that very few neglected worship entirely, though clearly the attendance of many of them was exceptional; and several said that their churches were well or fairly well filled.

In 1879 St Swithin had suggested that the bishop should prohibit the archdeacon (Kaye) from supporting and managing schools kept by dissenters. This was aimed at the Ragged School in Sparrow Lane.

[1] He used to tell of his first meeting in the Yard with the Archdeacon Bond, who expressed astonishment at finding him in such place, and whom he tried to reassure by telling him that he would pay his rent and try to behave like a gentleman. Later his relations were cordial, and especially in educational matters, with Wickham and Leeke.

I beg to call the Bishop's special attention to the fact that a dissenting *day* and *Sunday* school is carried on in this parish under the auspices of the Archdeacon of Lincoln and the Bishop's Secretary...It seems right that the Bishop's attention should be formally directed to the anomaly before the notice of Churchmen generally is directed to it.

In 1892 the same parish complained that people were attracted to the minster by the advertisement of special preachers. There they met dissenters who were similarly attracted, and who told them how much superior chapel preachers were to minster preachers: hence a generation of sermon critics and church and chapel rovers. In 1895 it was said that in Lincoln few people confined themselves to one place of worship: most people went sometimes to church, sometimes to chapel, sometimes to the cathedral (which must be doubted): those who neglected all public worship were very few. The emphasis on 'nominal' churchmen grew as the century drew to a close. Several parishes reported a lack of people able to take a lead in the parish, and complained that parishes over-stocked with such people did not come to their aid.

As the population grew the churches, even if well filled, represented a declining proportion of the citizens. Perhaps it was only after the turn of the century that there was an absolute decline in numbers. A clearer indication is given by the number of Sunday scholars. So far as it is possible to generalise the peak seems to have been reached in the 1890s; thereafter the number of confirmations fell and there was decline.

The nonconformist evidence is even less satisfactory. In the period following the secession of 1851,[1] Wesley Chapel reached its peak of membership about 1865, but the fall that followed is no doubt due to a redistribution of worshippers as other chapels were built. The Hannah Memorial chapel and several of those on the perimeter grew until about 1909, though by then the District Methodist Synod had reported a decline for several years. For the other Methodists the evidence is even less clear, but the broad conclusion seems not to be widely different.[2] The Congregationalists as a whole grew until about 1910, but they were distributed over four chapels, the growth being wholly in the outlying districts. Central churches were becoming downtown churches.

There are a few scattered pieces of evidence about the relative numerical strength of Anglicans and dissenters and non-churchgoers, though they were not official like that of 1851.[3] In 1873 a nonconformist committee took a census of church attendance on one Sunday. Anglican churches, morning and evening, had 4,963 attendances; nonconformists,

---

[1] Above, p. 183.
[2] See William Leary, *Methodism in the City of Lincoln* (1969).
[3] Above, p. 187.

8,722. This latter figure must have included many more twicers than the former, and there is no reliable way of translating figures of attendance into numbers of worshippers; and it has to be remembered that the faithful may have been specially whipped up for the purpose of the count. Yet there can be little doubt that the number of active nonconformists exceeded the number of active Anglicans. The largest figures of attendance are eloquent. At the cathedral in the evening were 495, and at St Peter at Arches 525. At Wesley Chapel were 1,232, at the Free Methodists 945. The Newland figure, only an estimate, was nearly 400 in the evening and between 500 and 600 in the morning. One 'competent judge' was quoted as believing that the aggregate number was not larger than that of 1851 in spite of the large increase of population.[1] In 1881 church Sunday schools mustered a parade of 1,700; and in 1886 2,300 elder children (probably from day schools) marched to the cathedral. In 1890 a Sunday School Union (nonconformist) anniversary of 20 schools had 4,771 scholars and 671 teachers.

In 1896 the Free Church Council undertook a house-to-house visitation to find out whether people went to a place of worship, if the children went to a Sunday school, whether a visit from a clergyman or a minister would be welcome, and if so which would be preferred. The bishop asked clergy and parishioners to cooperate. The result was: houses visited 9,147; attendance at places of worship 7,845; non-attendants 1,233; refused information 69.[2] The most striking fact was the absence of hostility and the desire of a vast majority to represent themselves as adherents of some place of worship, even if only for purposes of baptism, marriage or burial.

In 1903 a count was organised on one Sunday by the *Lincoln Leader*. It showed a total of Anglican attendances of 7,103, nonconformist 9,046. The newspaper commented that the figures hardly proved, with the most liberal allowance, that half the population came under religious influences during the day. Even so the result was nearly twice as good as that of a similar count in London.[3] An Anglican, after criticising the method of compilation of the return, commented that it showed that about one in five of the population attended Sunday morning services, and about one in three in the evening.[4] In relation to the growing population, in spite of messroom meetings and special missions, it seems that all the churches were losing ground. A Baptist minister said it showed that Baptist

---

[1] Appendix IV, ii.
[2] *L.C.*, 13 January 1897; *L.L.*, 18 January 1897.
[3] Appendix, IV, iii.
[4] *L.D.M.*, xix, 55.

churches were half empty. It was said by a Wesleyan minister in 1908 that half the population never attended any religious services, and that two-thirds were untouched by the churches.[1] It was a matter for frequent comment that on Sundays, during the time of evening service, the main streets were crowded with strollers wandering up and down, vapidly indifferent and killing time.[2] An unfinished review of parish churches written soon after the end of the First World War spoke of devoted work, a church full at its patronal festival, and uphill fighting. Bishop Swayne, who became bishop in 1919 on the death of Edward Hicks, said that all the churches were losing ground as the wellbeing of the people increased. They were like the *nouveaux riches* who took a great delight in their own advancement, and found that self-sufficing: they had no time for spiritual matters.[3] Society was becoming more secular in outlook, and the part played by organised religion in the community was on the decline.

[1] *L.C.* and *L.L.*, 18 July 1908.
[2] E.g. *L.L.*, 14 March 1903; *L.C.*, 18 March 1911.
[3] *Lincoln Review*, 8 October, 5 November, 3 December 1921.

CHAPTER XIV

THE MINSTER

In his reflections upon his Barchester novels Anthony Trollope records that he was struck by two opposite evils. The first was the possession by the church of funds and endowments which had been intended for charitable purposes, but which had been allowed to become income for idle church dignitaries. The other was the injustice with which the recipients of such income, who could not be considered the chief sinners, had been publicly assailed and denounced, though the fault was not due to worse than want of care and the natural tendency of any class to take care of itself.[1]

The paradox that a beneficiary of gross abuse could be in personal character a good man is illustrated by an account of the Lincoln cathedral body. George Gordon had been dean since 1809. He was believed to have from his several preferments an income of £20,000 a year,[2] and on his death his personal estate was sworn at £140,000. He opposed all change, and stood stoutly upon the rights of the church. Yet he was a kindly and hospitable old man. Anderson thought him the best of the chapter, and when he died in 1845 uttered the wish: 'may we get as good a successor of which there is little chance'.[3]

But the Barchester parallel and especially Hiram's Hospital come closer. Richard Pretyman, son of Bishop Tomline, was precentor of Lincoln (to which were added four livings) and was collated to the wardenship of the Mere Hospital in 1816 by his father, who created the vacancy for him. The rent of the hospital lands was £32, divided as to £8 to the warden and £4 to each of six poor persons. (The original number was 13.) The real income of the warden came not from rents but from fines on the renewal of leases: by 1837 his receipts from fines and the sale of timber exceeded £14,000. Pretyman found himself in Chancery, where the Master of the Rolls said his conduct was wrong and rather shocking; the chapter was not to appropriate rents beyond £24 per annum, and there were to be no fines; and the original number of poor

---

[1] *Autobiography* (World's Classics edition), pp. 86–7: James Pope Hennessy, *Anthony Trollope* (1971), p. 196.   [2] *G.L.*, pp. 270–1.

[3] Anderson Diary, 2 July 1845; his notes in *L.D.B.*, sub 1845; *G.L.*, p. 301. The sale of his goods on his death was successful, particularly the coins, which were mere rubbish, and sold beyond all bounds, the remains apparently of purchases made by the precentor Gordon his father from Sympson the antiquary. Letter from W. Brooke, Bromhead MSS, 9 December 1845.

persons was to be restored. Pretyman was, however, excused repayment of funds.[1]

It is a remarkable fact that men spoke well of Pretyman. E. B. Drury, an ardent reformer, wrote to Bromhead that 'I only regret that so amiable and fairminded a personage as Richard Pretyman should be the unlucky offender'.[2] The better informed Anderson noted in extenuation of his way of life, which included racing and gambling, that he was forced into the church by his father against his own inclinations.[3]

Drury went on, 'I hope Spital will be the next'. This was a hospital to the north of Lincoln to which the bishop had collated first his brother and then his nephew John. The commissioners could discover only two pensioners, though they learnt that the net income over 15 years exceeded £10,000. In 1844 the court pronounced against him a judgment he had not lived to hear.[4]

The bishop appointed his son George chancellor of Lincoln in 1814: he was also a prebendary of Winchester and rector of three livings. In 1846 the Ecclesiastical Commissioners sought to buy his interest in a lease of one of his prebendal estates. He declined. He was about to renew it 'for the benefit of my family, as my father always desired me to look at it in that light'.[5]

The life tenure of residentiaries made it impossible for reformers to effect any change in the chapter until vacancies were created by death. As the years went on the intense hostility of the reform period died down, and the survivors of an earlier age were regarded with tolerance. But when Richard died in 1866, the last of the Lincoln Pretymans, conventional eulogy provoked a protest against tributes to the most notorious pluralist in the English church. It was pointed out that he had £4,000 a year, while the minor canons had stipends of £150 a year, which showed at least that Lincoln had profoundly studied the parable of the Ten Talents.

The cathedral librarian received even worse treatment than the minor

---

[1] *Reports, Charity Commission*, 1839, pp. 394–9; *English Reports* xlix, 418–19; *S.M.*, 10 December 1841. *Parliamentary Papers*, 1852, xxxviii, 408. A scheme for the charity was settled in 1858.
[2] Bromhead mss, n.d. [3] Notes to *Lincoln Date Book*, sub 1817, in L.P.L.
[4] He died in 1842. *Charity Commission Report*, pp. 413–22; *A.A.S.R.*, xx (1890), 264–98. This scheme also was settled in 1858.
[5] L.A.O. Cor.B, 10/8. He was rector of Wheathamstead, where his reputation for kindness to the poor earned the eulogy 'that what was right in the sight of God on the road from Jerusalem to Jericho must be equally right at Wheathamstead-cum-Harpenden'. Quoted in *S.M.*, 17 March 1854. Cracroft described him as 'a fine medieval sample of well-fed prosperous priesthood', 2 May 1855. G. F. A. Best, 'The Road to Hiram's Hospital: A Byway of Early Victorian History' in *Victorian Studies*, v. He is commemorated by a window in the north choir aisle of the minster.

canons. He received a guinea a year, and, recording this, T. F. Dibdin reflected:

Here is one of the finest sacred edifices in Europe; but nothing seems stirring about it. It is a body without a soul. Melancholy seems to mark it 'for her own' ...there wants a vitality of devotion *somewhere* ...[1]

The state of the diocesan muniments was described by Charles Dickens:

decayed boxes filled with rotten wills...worm-eaten, spider-woven, dusty, ill-arranged...Mildew and rot are so omnipotent in this damp depository, that the shelves have in some places broken and crumbled away...

Thus, then...are documents, involving the personal or real property of seven English counties allowed to crumble to destruction; thus, is ruin brought on families by needless litigation; thus, do Registrars roll in carriages and Proctors grow rich; thus are the historical records of the great English nation doomed – by an officer whom the nation pays the income of a prince to be their conservator – to rottenness, mildew and dirt.

The registrar so pilloried was Robert Swan, nephew of Mrs Gordon:

He lives in great state: he keeps horses, carriages, dogs and a yacht; he is – could he be anything else – a staunch tory; he generally proposes the tory members for the county, and has been known to pay the entire electioneering expenses of a favourite tory candidate.

He lived in a house superior to the bishop's, and he put every obstacle in the way of all who wished to search in the records. In all this there is doubtless some of the usual Dickensian exaggeration, but even in much later days the condition of the diocesan archives was so bad that the description does not seem incredible.[2]

It was natural that to such an establishment the plans of the Ecclesiastical Commissioners (who included in their number Bishop Kaye) for cathedral reform were anathema. They wished to reduce the number of residentiaries to the dean and four others, to destroy their separate endowments, to confiscate their patronage for the benefit of the bishop, and to dissolve minor corporations like the priest vicars. The chapter opposed interference with the bounty of founders, and pleaded for preservation of the 52 prebendal stalls. They flattered themselves, and must have astonished everyone else, by claiming:

---

[1] *Northern Tour* (1838), I, 118–19. The music was poor, the canon in residence not liking music, the stalls were enveloped in dust, and the interior was of a jaundice tint, begrimed with dirt (p. 101).

[2] *Household Words*, 28 September 1850, reprinted in *Uncollected Writings of Charles Dickens* (1968), I, 170–2. Swan's pained defence is in L.A.O. Cor.B. 5/4/100/5. He was a learned ecclesiastical lawyer. He published *A Practical Treatise on the Jurisdiction of the Ecclesiastical Courts relating to Probate and Administration*, with an appendix upon the courts in the diocese of Lincoln (1830); and *Church Repairs and the remedies for enforcing them* (1841).

It would ill become us to speak of the individual utility of Residentiaries in their respective Cities: but, without reference to ourselves, we may be permitted to assert that their Charities, their exertions in the cause of Religious Education and Improvement, their superintendence of Local Establishments, their influence upon the character of Society, the respect and attachment often felt through them for the Church: are all uses which must ever exist in proportion to the consequence, in the eyes of the Public, which their situations have hitherto given to them.

They added that they feared there was moving abroad a mischievous disposition to magnify, at their expense, the pastoral office and ministerial duties of those who were invidiously called the working clergy.[1] Not surprisingly the protest failed, and the proposals for remodelling the constitution of cathedral chapters were carried into law, with some modifications, in 1840.[2]

Gordon was succeeded as dean in 1845 by John Giffard Ward, rector of St James, Piccadilly. Cracroft described him as a tall, plain, gentlemanly mannered man, very agreeable, and just what a dignitary of the church ought to be – at home. He wore breeches and black silk stockings, the only instance Cracroft knew to be left of this antiquated custom. It seemed doubtful whether he liked the change from Piccadilly.[3]

He soon conceived the idea of pulling down the Deanery on the north side of the minster, with some other old houses to the east of it, and opening the minster entirely to the north. He broached the matter to Lord Brownlow who proposed that the bishop should make over the palace as a deanery, as had already been done for the dean at Worcester. The dean replied that he had already put the idea to the bishop, 'who was most positive and decided in rejecting any arrangement that should at all interfere with the residence of the Bishop in the palace now or at any future time'.[4]

The dean therefore resolved to build on the old site, getting as far as possible to the east. Anderson regretted the demolition of the old house and Willson pleaded for the preservation of the entrance tower: it served

[1] L.P.L., Ross Scrap Books, Lincoln 1; L.C., 10 February 1837.
[2] 3 and 4 Vic. c. cxiii.
[3] Cracroft, 30 January 1846, 10 May 1850. The Rev. W. H. Brookfield, who became his curate at St James' in 1840, knew him better. He described him privately as 'a most friendly, honest fellow'; at dinner one night 'Jacky Ward pronounced that Miss Rowbottom's legs were the thickest legs under the table'; and when the Lincoln preferment came to him and he talked of the deanery, 'worldier talk was never heard from a stockjobber'. Mrs Brookfield and her Circle (1905), I, 46, 178. Truth, quoted by L.C., 3 September 1910, said Ward was expected to refuse. The deanery would then have been offered to F. D. Maurice, which would have pleased the King of Prussia. This must be a reference to the bishopric of Jerusalem.
[4] Anderson Letters, i, 30 October 1846.

well, he said, to give a scale to the noble tower of the minster that soared aloft far above its modest battlements.[1] Byrne was the architect, producing the gloomy pile that now houses the Cathedral School. Cracroft found the house comfortable and admirably arranged, though the dean wished the bedrooms were larger.[2]

When Ward died in 1860 Lord Palmerston chose Thomas Garnier, Dean of Ripon and son of the Dean of Winchester. Anderson comforted himself with the thought that it might have been Larken, for whom great attempts had been made.[3] With the double handicap of ill-health and twelve children Garnier was not able to take much part in affairs,[4] and he died in 1863.

When Dr Jeremie, regius professor of divinity at Cambridge – an office he held from 1850 to 1870 – was chosen, Gladstone wrote to commend him to Anderson, a task he evidently did not find easy. He was not, he said, aesthetic or archaeological *ex professo*.

But he is a very practical man, with more I think of energy than egotism in his activity: he has a desire to work with people, and is remarkably hardy and full of resource as well as very well armed with general experience. For finance he has an especial turn. He is rational but not a rationalist: anxious to make himself useful, not quarrelsome nor addicted to party. In Oxford he was not personally popular, but he carried weight from an honorable and grateful sense of real service to the University.[5]

With this qualified tribute before him Anderson formed his own judgment, adding to a letter from Jeremie inviting him to dinner the note 'One of those clever men who preach highly finished sermons, which people admire, but who do no good – a retiring shy bookworm, agreeable and kind, but as a dean utterly useless.'[6] Benson was to comment on his acuteness, wit and French quotations, and said he made him think of a French ecclesiastic before the Revolution: 'if deans and inferior canons live this life of elevated gossip always, it is very different from the earnest life of the Bishop's house'.[7]

[1] Ross Letter Books, 21 January 1849.   [2] Cracroft, 10 May 1850.
[3] He wished the deanery was an episcopal appointment. L.A.O. Massingberd 4/87.
[4] L.A.O. Massingberd 31/66. See also A. E. Garnier, *Chronicle of the Garniers of Hampshire* (1900). Cracroft described the wedding of a Garnier daughter in the cathedral. It failed as a spectacle, the whole place being turned into a bear garden or a badly ordered playhouse. There was a crowd in choir and nave, 3,000 or more, one fellow walking about whistling with his hat on. Cracroft, 16 September 1862.
[5] Letters, II, 26 December 1863.
[6] *Ibid*, I, 23 July 1868(?). Jeremie divided his time between Lincoln and Cambridge, and took little interest in the cathedral or its affairs. *L.C.*, 3 September 1910, quoting an article in *Truth*.
[7] A. C. Benson, *Life of E. W. Benson* (1900), I, 274. See also A. C. Benson, *The Trefoil* (1923), p. 116. Venables wrote in *D.N.B.* that he wrote much, was a good preacher, voice

On Jeremie's death in 1872 Gladstone appointed Joseph William Blakesley. He was described as a man of the world: he had been a friend of Tennyson at Trinity, and he was believed to be the 'clear headed friend' of one of the earlier poems. He was not in sympathy with the high church movement, being a whig of the old school and a broad churchman. When Bishop Wordsworth sought to bring the whole of the non-residentiary canons together as 'a greater chapter' and make of them a 'bishop's council', and to attach specific duties to each such canonry, making proposals to the Cathedrals Commission to this end, Blakesley opposed. He saw no practical benefit in them, and suggested that the idea 'is mainly due to the enthusiasm of medieval ritualists, whose imagination and eloquence have enabled them to exercise great influence over the spirit of ecclesiastical dilettantism now prevailing'. Since 1840, the link binding the prebendaries and the dean and chapter was almost evanescent, and existed mainly in virtue of the courtesy which may be expected to prevail among gentlemen, the equals of one another in education and social position, when brought together in any professional relation.[1]

One other member of the chapter calls for mention. Frank Charles Massingberd, of a notable Lincolnshire family, became rector of Ormsby-cum-Ketsby in 1825. As a young man he wrote for Archdeacon Churton *The English Reformation*, published in 1842; its keynote was given in a quotation from Bishop Ken's will on the title-page: 'I die in the communion of the Church of England as it stands distinguished from all Papal and Puritan innovations.' He was one of the earliest supporters of the revival (after 135 years) of Convocation, and thereafter he spent much time as one of its proctors. He was a much loved man, and admired by many including Cracroft, who wrote of him 'he is a most superior man, whether as a clergyman, as a gentleman, or a scholar – perhaps a little shy – would there were more like him'.[2] In 1853 Anderson wrote

weak but musical and sympathetic. He had a magnificent library, but with habitual indecision could not decide to whom to bequeath it, and it was dispersed at his death.
[1] The bishop's case for the non-residentiary canons rested on the *Novum Registrum* of 1440. The dean contended that it was not confirmed; and it was proved in 1880 to be only a draft. *L.C.S.*, III, 675n, 704. Memorials and Correspondence in *Report of H.M. Commissioners for enquiring into the Condition of Cathedral Churches in England and Wales upon the Cathedral Church of Lincoln, 1885*. The dean refused to sign the report. *S.M.*, 24 April 1885, said that, if less learned, he was shrewder and more acute than Wordsworth. Venables wrote of him in *D.N.B.* that, 'if not an ideal dean according to the modern type, for which his tone of mind and line of thought, essentially non-ecclesiastical, entirely unfitted him, he conscientiously fulfilled the duties of his office. In the city itself he helped to promote all well-considered measures for the welfare of the community.' He edited Herodotus, and was an active member of the committee for the revision of the New Testament.   [2] Cracroft, 21 November 1849.

that 'Massingberd ought to be archdeacon, but some of the bigwigs don't like him because of his being proctor; but he would do the thing much better than anyone, for he is the most tender creature possible, and would be as gentle as a child, whilst he knows how things are to be done'.[1] Anderson was delighted in 1862 when Bishop Jackson told him that Massingberd was to be chancellor. Some of his difficulties at the cathedral must be mentioned later.[2] He died in 1872.[3]

Though individual members of the chapter had social position and influence, it would be difficult to underrate the part played by the dean and chapter or the cathedral in the religious life of the community. The cathedral was normally kept locked, and representations to the dean about free admission were rejected as being impracticable, though the vergers were forbidden to charge for admission. The state of the interior is shown in the engravings of Charles Wild.[4] There were no seats in the nave, and no services were held there. In the choir there were two rows of pews in front of the stalls, and the seating capacity of the choir must therefore have been very small.

The vergers and stallkeepers had their instructions about persons to be placed in the stalls. The rule of church discipline was that everyone should be seated according to his rank, quality and station. They were therefore directed to admit to the stalls only those appearing to bear the character of a gentleman; and to remove all who habitually sat during the service, or persisted in laughing and talking, even to the extent of calling in the civil power of the constable to effect their removal. The instructions applied in lesser degrees to occupants of the pews and benches.

These instructions were denounced by Edward Horsman in the House of Commons.[5] Local agitation on the subject produced in the *Chronicle*

---

[1] Wilberforce MSS d.27, fol. 26v. Miss Wordsworth said that he looked like Keble, and recalled that 'a quaint little touch of conservatism long remained in the little brass candlestick (relic of the days before gas was introduced into Lincoln minster) which at his desire was left in front of his stall'. A. C. Benson, *Life of E. W. Benson*, I, 343. The Rev. James Hildyard, who did not approve of the revival of convocation and Massingberd's high church views, said he was 'ycleped by certain profane persons "the Lincoln Humming-bird"'. *The Ingoldsby Letters* (1879), I, 309n.   [2] See below, pp. 263–4.
[3] For a tribute by his son, see W. O. Massingberd, *History of Ormsby* (n.d.), pp. 346–53.
[4] Seely asked Sir Robert Peel to stipulate, on the appointment of a new dean that the cathedral should be open free of charge; he contented himself by expressing the hope that it might be open free as at Westminster and Durham. *S.M.*, 22, 29 August 1845. *An Illustration of the Architecture and Sculpture of the Cathedral Church of Lincoln*, 1819. John Britton published a second edition in 1837, using the same plates.
[5] *P.D.*, 3rd Series, 98, 1076–7, 16 May 1848. It was complained in 1882 by a vicar that when he and his wife attended a service in the choir they were not allowed to sit together in the stalls, or lower down; he ought to sit in the stalls and his wife two rows below. *L.C.*, 4 August 1882. Godfrey Lowe said that the passport to the stalls was a top hat.

the explanation that indecorum must be prevented; that people used to stand in the south-east transept, strolling in just in time to hear the anthem, and then clattering away with their heavy boots, laughing and talking.[1] But the congregation was growing. Even after forms with backs were provided, there were complaints that seating was insufficient; congestion was caused by the allocation of pews to the clergy, their families and a few friends. There remained a residue of eight pews for clergy servants and six for the public.[2]

By 1856, the loyal *Chronicle* said, complaints about the uselessness and inefficiency of the chapter were no longer justified. The dean, an able and earnest preacher, was resident most of the year, and his wife and daughters visited the sick in Newport and St Peter in Eastgate regardless of the danger of fever; and the subdean was a fine pulpit orator.[3]

Anderson had higher standards. After attending a volunteer service he wrote that 'that hard working individual Great Tom did duty for all, the only loyal member of the Dean and Chapter. It was quite disgraceful, no sermon, nor anything but a bit of shabby black cloth and an anthem. Mr Nelson, rector of St Peter's told me it was uphill work for the parochial clergy when the Minster clergy were so lifeless and idle.'[4] A few years later he told Wilberforce:

16 October 1865. The Bishop of Grahamstown preached in the dark at Lincoln Minster last week, for they never thought of lighting the choir any more than when the Archbishop of Canterbury preached there two years ago in November, and was obliged to have two lights brought up to the pulpit to see his book, and the Chancellor nearly came to a deadlock in the lessons. I had previously suggested *candlelight* prayers even at 2, for the Choir is very dark, but I suppose as they have always been in the dark there, except at the canonical hour of 4, they wished to remain so. It is hopeless to attempt to get anything done right *there*, for poor Massingberd is in a minority, and the rest have neither wish nor will to alter. At one S.P.G. meeting old Bonney and Kaye together managed to administer unconsecrated wine! It is a fact! all for want of a little timely preparation. What can we do, how can anyone ever have any pleasure in joining them in anything which might stir the deadly dullness of such a place. There is no pleasure in attempting it, and no likelihood of success.[5]

Something of Massingberd's struggle against the dead weight of inertia is shown in his journal. He was installed as chancellor on 12 December 1862. In the summer of 1863 he tried to hold a Sunday service in the

---

[1] *L.C.*, 8 January 1847.   [2] *L.C.*, 5 September 1851.
[3] *L.C.*, 10 October 1856.   [4] Anderson Diary, 23 December 1861.
[5] Wilberforce MSS, d.30, fol. 116v. At a thanksgiving service at the minster the clergy were not ready for the mayor and corporation, and the sword and the mace had to lie on the ground. The collection was taken in willow pattern soup and dinner plates, a 'ludicrous neglect of common forethought and sense'. Anderson Diary, 27 February 1872.

messroom of Clayton and Shuttleworth, and seemed likely to succeed but for the violent opposition of the vicars of St Swithin, first Dickson and then Fardell. As he wanted to have some work belowhill, he sought the use of St Benedict, then closed and united to St Peter at Arches, but did not succeed. Then he wanted to arrange Sunday Advent lectures in the nave of the cathedral, but 'all hangs in hand from having so many to consult'. Lent lectures in the nave in 1864 were opposed by the dean and the precentor, and Massingberd retired to the Morning Chapel, which was full. Multitudes in the nave, walking to the choir, caused much disturbance, and after explanations with the dean he held his second lecture in the nave, which he thought was probably the first sermon delivered there since the Restoration. To prayers and the sermon he would have liked to add a hymn, but did not venture to do so. The dean was present in spite of his objections: the seats were full, and many were standing.[1] Once begun, the annual lectures continued.

When Benson attended Wordsworth's enthronement as his chaplain in 1869 he recorded the same sense of the dead weight of the past.

The Dean and Chapter seem to have very little notion of how to manage and win the laity, and they are deservedly unpopular, though very amiable nice people. They somehow want working into an effective institution.

He added that the chapter stood on precedent as some people stood on etiquette.

It may be questioned whether the Dean would think it correct to put out the Bishop's robes if they caught fire, unless some Dean could be proved to have done it before. They would not allow a Canon's baby to be baptised in the Cathedral though there is a font there, on that ground.[2]

There was such strong criticism of the authorities both nationally and locally that the case for the defence was set out in the *Chronicle* by 'one who knows'. It is a useful summary of changes made in a comparatively short time:

The whole building has been warmed by stoves (1862). The choir has been lighted with gas (1866). The library, much augmented by gifts from the present

---

[1] L.A.O. Massingberd 8/2; *History of Ormsby*, p. 352. After Massingberd's death the chapter decided that it was desirable to continue his Saturday afternoon Lent lectures, the precentor offering to give them that year as the new chancellor, Benson, was then unable to reside. L.A.O. Chapter Acts, 24 February 1873. On 17 January 1874, the new chancellor was allowed to hold a service in the Morning Chapel according to the provisions of the Act of Uniformity Amendment Act for the behoof of his clerical students; it was not to exceed 15 minutes. Dr Godfrey Lowe remembered seeing students streaming across the Castle Hill in various stages of undress, completing their toilet as they ran. The cathedral workmen also attended the service.

[2] *Life of E. W. Benson* (1900), I, 263, 265.

dean (Jeremie), has been warmed by hot water, and the manuscripts enclosed in cases, all the clergy of the diocese being at liberty to take out books. Lectures on subjects connected with Divinity have been established in the Minster on a weekday in Lent. Sermons are preached by the canons in turn, in the nave, in the afternoon of all Sundays in the Year, before the afternoon service in the choir, except when the Bishop preaches in Lent. The nave has been thrown open to the public every day before the hour of morning prayer to after that of evening prayer. Weekly communion has been restored, being celebrated at an early hour, except on the first Sunday of the month and the greater festivals, and then at the usual time. The offertory is collected from the whole congregation by the lay clerks in their surplices. The sacred vessels with the bread and wine are placed beforehand on a slab behind the high altar by a lay clerk, and brought to the celebrant by a minor canon to be placed by him on the holy table, together with the alms, before the Church Militant prayer. What is left is reverently consumed, after the Communion, by the assistant clergy, and the sacred vessels removed by the same lay clerk, who is a constant communicant.

It was admitted that the voices of some of the choir were failing, and they needed to be pensioned; and the chapter were paying out of their private funds towards making up the deficiencies in the choir fund and the fabric fund. The excellent training and singing of the boys were being constantly commended.[1]

The fabric itself showed a few faint stirrings of life. There appeared the first impetus towards the insertion of painted glass which would reduce 'the white light streaming through the uncoloured panes flooding the interior with painful brilliancy'.[2] It came from Dean Ward and Anderson, who placed a window in the south aisle in 1847 in memory of his father. When the Archaeological Institute visited Lincoln in 1848 a lecture reflecting on the east window put in by Peckett in 1762 – once described as a gaudy Brussels carpet – prompted a move to replace it. An appeal for funds made slow progress, but at last in 1855 it was installed, with a design setting forth 'the Scheme of Human Redemption'.[3]

[1] *L.C.*, 26 February 1869. It had been complained also that the dean did not resign the living of Somersham attached to his regius chair at Cambridge; but he paid curates in each of the three parishes in the living. The guess may be hazarded that Massingberd wrote or inspired this defence. It was said that at an afternoon service in the nave the great majority of worshippers were evidently working men and women. *L.C.*, 20 July 1866. And see *L.D.M.*, v, 12, 28. The Rev. C. S. Bird wrote when he was chancellor that he suffered so much from the cold damp cathedral that he had proposed it be warmed with Gurney's stoves at as York; he hoped they would be ready before the winter (1862). *Sketches from the Life of the Rev. Charles Smith Bird* (1864), pp. 358–9. *L.C.*, 22 April 1870, complained that the choir was not large enough for the Easter service, forms were uncomfortable for sermons of nearly half an hour's duration. Seats might be put under the central tower where there was generally a draught.
[2] Williamson's *Guide through Lincoln, c.* 1875, believed to have been written by Venables.
[3] For the windows of the period see Canon P. B. G. Binnall, *The Nineteenth Century Stained Glass in Lincoln Minster* (Friends of Lincoln Cathedral, 1966). A scheme for the chapter

The dean and chapter had taken no part in the ecclesiological movement.[1] Repair work carried out at the cathedral by the Roman Catholic Willson was approved by ecclesiologists,[2] but a storm broke over the design by Westmacott for the tomb memorial of Bishop Kaye. It was complained that instead of the universal medieval custom of representing monumental effigies in an attitude of devotion, full length, gaze upwards, hands in prayer, they were being offered a person on a couch in an attitude of extreme exhaustion, exhibiting not the triumph of a Christian over death, but of death over the church. The battle was lost, although Ward opposed the design adopted; he told a meeting of subscribers where laymen (among them William Monson, Melville and Charles D'Eyncourt) were in the lead that the chapter would refuse to admit the monument to the cathedral if they thought such a course desirable in consequence of the nature and character of the work. But they did not venture to take that course.[3] Anderson later read a paper on monumental sculptures, saying that the idea that in a recumbent figure the head should be turned to show the features (as Kaye's did) savoured of the Green Room.[4]

Then the methods of repair adopted by the chapter's architect J. C. Buckler, appointed after the resignation of Willson, was attacked by the Royal Institute of British Architects and the Ecclesiological Society. At a meeting of the latter body Anderson said that he

might be permitted to allude to the Dean and Chapter of Lincoln under whose directions a very injurious process of scraping was going on; and, he believed, was to be extended to the Norman work...When he was told of this scraping he wrote to the Dean and Chapter; but their reply was, that they had had good advice, and believed the work was being well done. He went to see it; and

house windows was under discussion in 1873; Anderson disapproved of it. Diary, 25 April 1873. For the scheme, see *S.M.*, 10 September 1875. Professor Freeman made merry on the subject in a letter to Venables (22 May 1873): 'For subjects for the Chapter House windows, I should say that the two most prominent ought to be the Visitations of Bishop Robert in the thirteenth century and Bishop Christopher in the nineteenth; the difference of dress would make a pleasing diversity. Then you might have Remigius going to consecrate the minster and not doing it, and no end of subjects from the life of St Hugh – he might be carrying a hod, or the two kings might be carrying his bier, or he might, best of all, be trampling on Froude, with Dimock and me on either side as his henchmen. Or you may put it the other way, as a scene of martyrdom – Froude trampling on St Hugh and Dimock and I weeping.' W. R. W. Stephens, *Life and Letters of Edward A. Freeman* (1895), II, 68.

[1] Above, pp. 175–6.   [2] *Ecclesiologist*, IV (1845), 238.
[3] The monument was placed in the south-east transept, but was lately removed to the west end of the nave to make way for the Grosseteste memorial.
[4] *A.A.S.R.*, III (1854), xxxvii–xxxviii; *S.M.*, 8 April 1854. Charles Terrot published *Remarks on Sepulchral Monuments*, Horncastle (1854), in which he dissented from the views of the ecclesiologists.

though he would certainly say that the work was well done, he objected to it very strongly, being decidedly of the opinion that the appearance of the cathedral was injured by it...It appeared that the cathedral was in the hands of the Precentor.

George Gilbert Scott said he had visited the building, and found that the work was very much overdone, and that harm had ensued; the colour given to the cathedral was frightful, and destroyed its beauty in point of colour. The architects Street and Parker also joined in criticism.

The *Ecclesiologist* quoted with approval the comments of the local *Mercury*:

But against whose acts have these learned bodies spoken so loudly? Against those of the Cathedral Chapter, consisting of five persons. Of these, two from infirmity are utterly incapable of taking a part in the duties belonging to their position, and two others ingenuously confess that they have no knowledge whatever of architecture. It is left therefore to the remaining one to seize the reins of the capitular government, and to direct the repairs of the cathedral &c. What then does *he* do with the fabric fund?[1]

Pretyman was the precentor, and the man attacked, and Buckler confirms that it was he who managed the matter. He wrote in 1866:

I owe everything at Lincoln to him. He had an hereditary regard for me, and treated me like a member of his family. His father the Bishop and Mrs Tomline were among my father's most zealous friends. The son remembered this circumstance with pleasure.

This at least shows Pretyman's good nature. According to Buckler the local architects were jealous of him, which may well be true. Scott then joined in, and Buckler's wish was to settle the matter with him, but was persuaded against this course.[2]

When in 1870 the dean and chapter transferred their estates (except the houses in the Close) to the Ecclesiastical Commissioners, the cathedral was believed to be in such a satisfactory state of repair that the comparatively small sum of £20,000 was allotted for the repair and improvement of the fabric. When Buckler retired from the post of consulting architect J. L. Pearson was appointed; and the chapter were soon undeceived. Pearson estimated the probable cost of necessary repairs at not less than £70,470; and if the north side of the cloisters, 'which was

[1] XII (1861), 222–6.

[2] L.A.O. Misc. Don. 335/2–5, letters from Buckler to William Dyke, Fellow of Jesus College, Oxford; L.A.O. Anderson 6/2, p. 23b; Anderson Letters, II, Street to Anderson; Wilberforce MSS, 30 June 1861, denouncing the four old clergymen who would persist in scraping the façade. Massingberd wrote that he was abused in 'disgraceful and insulting language' on the subject of the west front. L.A.O. Massingberd 8/2, p. 272. For Buckler's counter-attack on Scott, see his *Description and Defence of the Restorations of the Exterior of Lincoln Cathedral*, 1866.

demolished in the middle of the 15th century, were to be replaced and a new library erected, which would be a necessary consequence of the restoration of the cloisters, an addition of £4,800 would be required'.[1]

There followed a public appeal, and a long series of reports from successive architects, Pearson, Sir Arthur Blomfield, Hodgson Fowler and Sir Charles Nicholson.

Adverse comment on Pearson's work was soon forthcoming. The Society for the Protection of Ancient Buildings inspected the work on the cloisters and the chapter house only after it had been half done. It denounced the amount of new stone carving in the cloisters, supposed to be an exact copy of what was there before; the new Purbeck marble shafts in place of the old, which still existed; the removal of the plaster from the rubble filling of the vaulting, and the rubble work pointed.

Lincoln Cathedral is still the most pleasant to visit of all our Cathedrals, for it has suffered far less than any of them at the hands of the 'restorers'; and had it not been for our member, Precentor Venables, we believe that this would not have been the case.[2]

Two years later they complained that the chapter house now appeared as a new building; much of the stone was new, and the rest had been smartened up to match. Three sides of the cloister had been rebuilt, not as they were, but as it was supposed they ought to have been.[3]

In 1891 H. K. Hebb for the city brought to the chapter a proposal by Alfred Shuttleworth, who lived at Eastgate House (now the site of the Eastgate Hotel), facing the cathedral. The proposal was to widen Priory Gate and Eastgate by buying land on the west and south sides of streets. The chapter welcomed the proposal, but said they could only consent if the properties affected were wholly removed, and an open space left for ever. The chapter would however reserve a small space on the west side of the area affected as a site for the cathedral library with a cloister beneath it. Shuttleworth met the chapter by proposing to clear the ground between the Deanery stables and Priory Gate, provide the chapter with investment income sufficient to compensate them for the loss of rents, the Deanery buildings being masked by the rebuilding of the library on the west side of the cleared plot, facing east. The chapter gratefully accepted the proposals and sent them to the Commissioners.[4]

It is astonishing today that Pearson's report could refer to the building of a north cloister in place of one demolished in the 15th century, without

---

[1] Answer of the Dean and Chapter to the Cathedral Commissioners in Appendix to their *Report*, 1885.

[2] *13th Report*, 1890, p. 33.   [3] *15th Report*, 1892, pp. 26–9.

[4] Chapter Acts, 17 October 1891, 18 January, 13 February 1892.

mentioning that the site was occupied by Wren's library; of course it was not Gothic, and A. C. Benson testifies that when he was a boy it was thought of as hideous.[1]

The proposals were published to the world at a meeting in the chapter house. They involved the removal of eight houses in all, and the removal of Wren's library, stone by stone, and rebuilding it on the western boundary of the cleared land, and providing a new north walk of the cloister. The dean quoted Pearson as saying that the present position of the library was extremely detrimental to the general character of the cathedral; it was not without dignity, and had certain admirable characteristics, but it was not satisfactory for the purpose it represented. The cloister existed 400 years before the library. A new library could be enlarged with a reading room.

The storm broke at once. A satirical article, using a thin disguise, in the *St James Gazette*, said that after the resolution about the removal of houses it quickly became known that this was not the main business of the meeting.

When clerics ask laymen to meet them for discussion, it generally appears that the former have designs on the purses of the latter: it is also a matter of common observation that increase of appetite for charities grows with what it feeds on. The Dean was undoubtedly asking for money; but for what? The suspense was not protracted. A shuffling of feet on the stone floor, a rustling of umbrellas, resettling in seats, marked the announcement that no less a measure was proposed than the removal of the Bishop's Stables, a noble Renaissance annexe of the Palace, and the erection in its place of a structure in thirteenth century Gothic (with all the latest improvements) in harmony with its surroundings.

It went on that the 'Archfriar' (clearly meaning Venables) who was wintering abroad, was not in the secret, and it became evident that there was discordance in the chapter house. He said that he would not stand by and see the destruction of Wren's masterpiece. Even an episcopal blessing was in vain.[2]

The *Builder* denounced the substitution of imitation Gothic for a Renaissance building. The proposal would no doubt have been generally popular 30 or 40 years ago, when probably Wren's building would have been pulled down without it being thought necessary to provide for rebuilding anywhere else. There was much clearer perception of the value of Renaissance buildings, and of the picturesque harmony of old architecture in mingled styles. The dean was rather behind the age. A writer to the same paper said that the barbarities of Wyatt at Salisbury were going to be repeated; the cloister had already suffered at Pearson's hands.

[1] *The Trefoil* (1923), p. 89. [2] *L.C.*, 30 April 1892, quoting *St James Gazette*, 22 April.

It was charged that a letter from the Society for the Protection of Ancient Buildings had been suppressed, and the Society of Antiquaries, on the motion of Sir Hickman Bacon, protested against this falsification of history and the demolition of the only example of a cathedral cloister of post-Reformation date in England. *Truth* said it seemed inconceivable that Bishop King, Dean Butler and above all Precentor Venables, could approve of such vandalism.

The proposal to tamper with the library was given up, but the clearance of the houses to the north-east of the cathedral went on to the great public advantage. The new green was soon to provide a site for G. F. Watts' statue of Alfred Tennyson. In 1909 Edward Charles Wickham, appointed dean in 1894, offered to build a library and reading room facing the green, and his offer was gratefully accepted. During his tenure of office much repair work was carried out.[1]

In 1909 Hodgson Fowler, then consulting architect, reported on the vaulting of the nave; and further work, advised by Sir Charles Nicholson, led to the great effort of money-raising led by Thomas Charles Fry, appointed dean in 1910; it was for heating, cleaning, rehanging the bells, restoring the library and repairing the house property.[2] The great drive for the fabric had to await the end of the First World War.

By then the cathedral had come to life as a place of worship. The efforts begun by Massingberd and Benson were carried further by William John Butler, founder of the Wantage Sisterhood, who became dean in 1885. He was a man of fine appearance, stern of face and rather alarming at first, but those who got to know him found him a man of tender disposition, though he would stand no nonsense.[3] Although he was a Tractarian his ritualistic views were not forced into prominence, and at his death he could be described as a decided but not an extreme high churchman.[4]

He cleaned up the cathedral, every part of it being used at some time for worship. Communion services were held more frequently. His greatest impact on the public was made by the Sunday evening services which he instituted in the nave. He could not endure that the cathedral should be closed at 5 o'clock on Sundays, when all the churches in the city were opened for public prayer. In doing so he upset some of the parish clergy, who feared the loss of their own congregations.[5] He also upset the musicians and liturgiologists by transferring evensong from

---

[1] Lonsdale Ragg, *Memoir of Dean Wickham* (1911), pp. 155–6, 193.
[2] *L.L.*, 28 September 1912.
[3] 'Lincoln Cathedral in the Eighties', memories of the late Dr Godfrey Lowe, of which he gave me a copy.   [4] *S.M.*, 19 January 1894.   [5] Above, pp. 252–3.

afternoon to evening on Sundays, and the litany from morning to afternoon with an anthem and a hymn; he was accused of creating 'fancy services'. But the result was what he wanted. When he or the bishop preached in the evening the nave was packed particularly with working men and women. He was not displeased when the cathedral on Sundays was compared with Clapham Junction on account of the rapid succession of services.[1]

Butler entered much into the life of the city, especially at the Free Library and the School of Science and Art. So also did his colleagues. To Subdean Clements was largely due the improvements in the vicinity of the cathedral. Leeke, who was a Second Wrangler at Cambridge and a classical scholar, found time to render unique service to education in Lincoln,[2] besides which he was vicar of the growing parish of St Nicholas from 1902 to 1919. Edmund Venables, precentor from 1867 to 1895, and a founder of the Cambridge Camden Society, devoted immense energy to study of the history and archaeology of city and cathedral, and did more perhaps than anyone else in the Victorian period to popularise local history in Lincoln.

Kaye, the stern evangelical, reacted against the high churchmanship of King and Butler; when King was enthroned the other archdeacon walked alone. The chapter acts of his later years are studded with his protests, and when one of the weather vanes on the central tower refused to move it was known as the archdeacon. For nine months in the year he resided at Riseholme Rectory, and for three months came into residence, bringing his baggage in on a horse dray crowned by a large hip-bath upside down, which looked like a cupola.[3] It is said that even when in

[1] L.D.M., II, 38; *Life and Letters of Dean Butler* (1897), the greater part of the Lincoln chapters being written by Canon Maddison; and MS Memoirs by E. F. R. Woolley, of which there is a copy in the cathedral library. There is an alabaster effigy in the cathedral.

[2] He was always in a hurry. He generally ran to and from the cathedral, and he was a cyclist in the days of the 'bone-shaker' and the 'ordinary', and he continued to cycle until he was nearly 80.

[3] After the death of Queen Victoria he was reading the Litany, and came to the suffrage for the reigning Sovereign 'Thy servant Victoria'. There was a long pause, after which he said, 'I have inadvertently made a serious error. I have prayed for her late Majesty, Queen Victoria.' Immediately one of the clergy said, 'It will do her Majesty no harm, Mr Archdeacon.' Woolley, MS Memoirs. Professor Hamilton Thompson used to tell of his going to preach in a small dark village church. Seeing the candles lit on the altar he blew them out. After the service he complained to the incumbent that he had not been able to see his notes; and when the incumbent told him he should not have blown out the candles, he said, 'Is that what they were for?' He walked with a jerky gait and nodded his head, giving rise to the riddle recorded by Anderson, 'Why is the archdeacon of Lincoln the most liberal man in England? Because he gives three or four bobs to everyone he meets.' L.A.O. Anderson 6/2, p. 369.

residence he preached at Riseholme on Sunday mornings, taking his family with him in a four-wheeled cab, lest they be contaminated by any Popish doctrine.[1]

Wickham, though he was a shy and retiring scholar, entered fully into the life of the city, and having been headmaster of Wellington rendered great service to the city schools.[2] His successor, Thomas Charles Fry, had also been a headmaster (of Berkhamsted), and he brought his school-masterly ways with him. He was quick to take offence. But he was kind-hearted and much given to writing little verses to his friends.[3] He was a man of small stature with a round bald head and a fine broad white beard, and he held himself erect, moving slowly and with dignity. His devotion to the fabric was thus described by Frank Woolley:

During his last ten years at Lincoln he gave himself completely to the great work of restoration when the cathedral was found to be in imminent danger of collapse. He worked with amazing energy and travelled three times to America, the third time when he was over 80 years of age, to appeal on behalf of the Restoration Fund, for which he gathered large sums of money.[4]

In some sense the cathedral is his monument.

[1] Janet Courtney, *Recollected in Tranquillity* (1926), p. 87.

[2] He never forgot that he was a son-in-law of Mr Gladstone. When he was headmaster of Wellington he one year forbade the boys to wear primroses on Primrose Day. The masters obeyed, but the boys disobeyed and were punished. It happened only once. *L.C.*, 20 August 1910.

[3] He and the equally irascible cathedral organist Dr Bennett did not speak to each other for several years; the latter on hearing Fry's voice one day said, 'The voice of the cocksparrow'. Yet Fry wrote to Bennett on one of his birthdays:

> If one is deaf or mute or blind,
>   The years go sadly by.
> The boisterous world soon leaves behind
>   Both big and little Fry.
> But if one has the magic hands
>   For organ reed and pipe,
> While others age the Master stands
>   The Muse's Archetype.
> And so the Muse the cure supplies,
> And helps the years themselves disguise.

(From the originals kindly given to me by Dr Bennett's daughter Mrs Olive Riggall.)

[4] Woolley, MS Memoir. Fry was no doubt the author of the chapter minute about the memorial to Bishop King. A first model submitted by the sculptor, Sir William Richmond, was disapproved. It could not, said the minute, appropriately consist of a figure in action; and the chapter could not accept four angels, diaphanously clad, as supporters. The suggested scene of the Virgin and Child was not based on any authorities or tradition, and the *toute ensemble* was not English. Chapter Acts, 24 February 1911. Bishop Hicks thought the attitude finally adopted was not restful. The bishop might just be saying a fine thing, or preparing to bring his hand down to slap his own knee, or (conceivably) to smack a child on his lap. Diary, 19 July 1915.

CHAPTER XV

THE SCHOOLS AFTER 1870

Prolonged political controversy led to the passing of the Education Act of 1870. For the first time it laid down the principle that a school should be placed within the reach of every English child, and the system adopted was the creation of new, elected school boards with power to levy an education rate. There was however a proviso that where voluntary effort had made provision in any district that was 'sufficient, efficient and suitable' there was to be no interference. If there was inadequacy the voluntary associations were allowed six months in which to supply the deficiency: in default there must be a school board and a school board rate. There would be no denominational religious teaching in board schools.

After seeking a return of school numbers the town clerk reported to the city council that it appeared that there was a deficiency of 1,000 school places in Lincoln. Two liberal nonconformist members of the council, Joseph Ruston and Charles Hughes, moved for a school board; but they were overruled by the majority of the liberal caucus, who found double advantage in warding off an unpopular new rate burden and at the same time enjoying the unusual support of the Anglican clergy. They carried a resolution that in view of the success which had already attended voluntary efforts, no requisition should be made 'at present' for a school board. It was never made, and a board was never imposed; and when the system was changed in 1902 Lincoln was one of only seven county boroughs which had never had a school board.[1]

It was left to the churches to fill the gap. A meeting was held in the Assembly Rooms, with the dean (Blakesley) in the chair, to consider the problem. The vicar of St Swithin (G. H. Pratt) thought a school board would be needed, and he did not fear it; he would be glad to be relieved of the work of the parish schools. Nathaniel Clayton doubted whether they could ultimately avoid a compulsory rate, but he welcomed the attempt.

The cost of a well-managed national school was said to be 20s. per pupil yearly. An appeal for funds was launched, and by November 1871 the Anglicans could say that of their need of £5,000, the sum of £4,000 was promised, some of it from nonconformists. They had decided to build

---

[1] The vicar of Bracebridge was unable to rouse his principal parishioners to stave off a school board, which was ordered in 1878. There was a board for New Boultham in 1894.

in five parishes: St Peter in Eastgate, St Swithin, St Mary le Wigford, St Peter at Gowts and St Botolph. The city council helped by leasing to them an infant school in Free School Lane to augment their numbers.

The Wesleyans decided to convert their chapel in St Peter at Gowts (Alfred Street) into a school and build a new chapel; and the Congregationalists similarly handed over their chapel in Newland to the British School and built a new chapel, thereby enlarging the school fourfold. The Roman Catholics built a school in Friars Lane.

But Lincoln was continuing to grow: and in 1873 the Education Department, keeping up the pressure, gave notice of a deficiency of 1,330 places. Furthermore, some of the schools needed to be made efficient as well as being enlarged. The Elementary Education Act of 1876 moved towards compulsory attendance, and said that where there was no school board the local authority could enforce attendance; by 1880 the power became a duty. So there appeared on the scene an attendance officer, known as the 'school board man'. In 1877 that officer visited 5,810 families, and found 3,803 children between the ages of 5 and 11, of whom 3,393 were at school. One hundred and eighty-seven notices for non-attendance were quickly sent out. Two years later 590 notices were served on parents of children picked up in the streets or reported absent from the schools; 507 were complied with, 66 parents were fined, and attendance orders were made for 19.[1]

It was a mounting struggle for voluntary schools. In 1877 it seemed probable that St Martin's would close. The number of scholars (409) had outgrown the space, and the school committee could not find the funds for additional buildings. The sum of £400 a year was needed for maintenance, yet the parish gave about £21 in collections and subscriptions. The laity were lukewarm and the vicar was weary; he said in 1889 that if religious instruction were allowed he would have a school board at once.[2]

On the other hand a new schoolroom was opened at St Peter in Eastgate. When in 1883 Bishop King opened St Andrews schools he dwelt on the dual need to keep down the rates and to give sound religious teaching; and he recalled that although Mr Forster (who had promoted the Act of 1870) had said the school rate would never exceed 3d. it was already double that sum in London, and in some Lincolnshire parishes was 10d. or a shilling. The bishop knew how to make his hearers' flesh creep and stave off a board.

[1] Some incumbents reported to the bishop that compulsory attendance had brought in an influx of the very ignorant; its result seemed to be in the main satisfactory.
[2] L.A.O. Visitation Returns.

By that time there were over 7,000 children on the school registers, and the School Attendance Committee of the city council told the Education Department that there was no deficiency of places. Yet there were grave problems. The raising of the standards for partial and total attendance from the fourth to the fourth and fifth standards in 1893 added to the still rising number of children, and some schools were facing crises. The National School in Silver Street had declined to 300 in 1891; the area had ceased to be suitable for a school, as by street improvements Silver Street had become a main thoroughfare. The managers, who held the property on lease from the city, agreed in that year to sell their lease to the landlords, who were looking for municipal offices.[1]

This measure called for a review of Anglican policy, and a meeting of managers and subscribers to church schools was held in the Guildhall with the bishop in the chair. The chancellor (Leeke) had already opened a continuation or seventh standard day school;[2] and it was decided to add to existing schools, bearing in mind that they were not well distributed. In the upper and lower districts they were full, but in the heart of the city there was room and to spare. Pratt of St Swithin tartly welcomed that interest of the dean and chapter in the parish schools which had been missing in his 25 years' experience. Joint action was not approved by all parishes, and St Botolph at once made its own public appeal for money to build a boys' school and add a classroom to the infant school.

On their part the nonconformists were not well provided. They had no school uphill, although they had 800 Sunday school children there. The Wesleyan schools were over full. Accommodation at the British school in Newland was poor, and in 1895 the school had to be closed, as the buildings could not be altered to comply with the official code.

The voluntary principle was hard pressed. Many nonconformists, with the support of the Free Church Council, were calling for a school board. Statistics were produced to show that 2,000 children were in some way neglected, that the schools were badly distributed, and that the quality of education was inadequate. A Lincoln Public Elementary Church Schools Association, formed to defend the voluntary system, admitted a deficiency of at least 1,000 places, and new building plans were put in hand, the subdean Clements pointing out that until 1870 there were large building grants from the state; now there were none.

---

[1] The rector complained that the school had been closed by the *ex-officio* managers. When the children were dismissed most of them were received in nonconformist schools. He thought a great wrong had been done to church education in the city. L.A.O. Visitation Returns.   [2] Below, p. 279.

At last, in 1898, the School Attendance Committee approved the raising of standards to the fifth and sixth, for without this change, elementary scholars had little hope of getting to the School of Science and Art.[1] The measure required the provision of 200 more school places, and the Free Church Council renewed its pressure for a school board. The by-laws, however, were not carried out; attendance was not well enforced, though there were two more attendance officers; and there was little support from the magistrates. Fear of a board and a rate inhibited action. The *Lincoln Leader* had pointed out in 1897 that there were 8,158 children on the school registers; yet 7,000 nonconformist Sunday school children went to the Arboretum on Whit Monday, and 12,000 children sat down to tea at the Queen's Diamond Jubilee celebrations. What were the facts? in 1900 Lincoln had an average attendance worse than that of any town of equal size in the country; many parents still thought that they could keep their children away for at least one day a week, and still be safe from the law.[2]

When a last effort was made to force a school board for the city, the mayor, Hugh Wyatt, although a Methodist, refused to call a meeting, and the matter dropped. Denominational zeal and ratepayers' parsimony were to cost the city dear.[3]

Meanwhile the Mechanics Institution[4] had made a last effort to establish a place in the new world of elementary education. They resolved to extend their night school, and the corporation agreed to provide extra buildings. The project failed. The night school was abandoned, the books and slates given to the Ragged School and the desks sold to the Grammar School. As a last blow the corporation gave the institution notice to quit the old assembly room over the buttermarket, which was wanted for the new free library. It continued for a time in other premises, but in 1899 its library of 12,000 books was sold to the Church House for a song and the institution was dissolved. It had outlived its usefulness.

What it had failed to do was done by Edward White Benson, who came to Lincoln as chancellor of the cathedral in 1873. He soon had a

[1] Below, p. 278.

[2] *L.L.*, 26 June 1897. When the chancellor, Leeke, was an incumbent of a parish in Cambridge, in order to prove that there were children who were not attending school, he hired a Punch and Judy show to tour the streets in school hours, and soon collected a crowd of children. Ex. inf. the late Canon W. W. Leeke.

[3] Miss Margaret A. Sterry kindly allowed me to read her thesis on 'Elementary Education in Lincoln 1870–1902', which she submitted as a degree thesis to the University of Nottingham in 1957.

[4] Above, p. 147.

Bible class for mechanics, and in 1875 he started night schools at the national schools. The initiative seems to have come partly from Susan Wordsworth and partly from the Reverend William Mantle who recalled later that he made the suggestion to Benson, addressed meetings in the foundry messrooms, and promised to teach any subject for which a class of six could be raised. Both he and his brother taught, and their father and another schoolmaster helped.[1] Graduates, theological students and others helped also, and classes were formed for reading, writing, arithmetic and other subjects. There was a fee of 1s. 6d. for a course from October to Christmas, half to be returnable for punctual attendance on 18 nights, the whole for such attendance on all nights. The cost was covered by guarantees.[2]

Canon Crowfoot has described the opening scene:

I remember walking down on the first night with the Chancellor and a few students, thinking it possible that we might find 60 pupils. To our astonishment when we came in sight of the Central School in Silver Street we found the street blocked with working men and lads. There were 400 waiting for admittance. As soon as the doors were open the Chancellor mounted the table and in stentorian tones shouted 'All over 40 years old go to such a room', 'All over 30 to another', and so in an incredibly short time the mass of men and boys was roughly sorted.

Test papers were set in writing and arithmetic, and classes were soon formed.[3] The building was found not to be large enough; there were 458 pupils that session. Another school opened uphill at North District. At St Swithin an evening school was started for women by the Misses Wordsworth, Mrs Venables, Miss Swan and Mrs Steeper; and another at St Nicholas by the Reverend F. B. Blenkin. In 1876 there were 1,186 scholars, 700 of them entitled to a reward for regular attendance and proficiency. Benson left Lincoln in 1877, and he told a farewell meeting how he and other teachers had shrunk from the first examination of the inspector, and how relieved they were when 93% of all they could present passed the required standard.[4]

Chancellor Leeke took over, and started a night school for girls and

[1] L.C., 2 November 1889.
[2] L.A.O. D. & C. A.4. 17.
[3] A. C. Benson, *Edward White Benson* (1900), I, 369. Two old ladies of the Cranfordian type subscribed out of regard for the chancellor, saying that for their parts they preferred an ignorant poor (p. 370). A. C. Benson recalled a time when many of the skilled workmen of the Bible class came to tea: they seemed to have a knowledge of all current affairs and topics, and the only thing that a little embarrassed them was being waited upon by the chancellor's children. *The Trefoil* (1923), p. 163.
[4] The workmen at Robeys presented him with a cast-iron dessert service, which, though not beautiful, generally appeared on his dining-room table.

women in St Martin's schoolroom, and, in 1885, a branch school in Robey's messroom. In 1893 the question arose whether the corporation should take over the night schools but it did not do so, and they continued to be managed by a voluntary committee, not all of whom were Anglicans: A. C. Newsum was secretary. No religious instruction was given.[1]

These schools had pointed to a need for something more, half school, half club, combining recreation with instruction. When the Bluecoat School[2] was closed in 1883, the buildings were taken temporarily for that purpose, a Church House and Institute being transferred to it from Westgate. The intention was to build on some central site if funds could be raised. By 1890 it had 500 members apart from night school students.[3]

Another movement was making progress at the same time. A School of Art established in 1863 by voluntary effort was an instant success. It began in the Corn Exchange, and in the following year was transferred to the National School. It owed much to the Reverend J. S. Gibney, one of the priest vicars. When he fell to his death through a skylight at the School of Art in 1875 he was heard aloud to say 'my God', which seemed to Arthur Benson an insupportable piece of realism.[4]

Science evening classes had been held at the Newland British School since 1877, and Leeke started a class for advanced mathematics, five of his pupils gaining Whitworth Exhibitions. There followed in 1880 a movement to promote technical education among mechanics, and the committee of the School of Art was asked to provide for it in a new building it was planning. Terms were reached and forces were joined.

By a great voluntary effort the new School of Science and Art was opened in 1886 on a site granted by the city council. Its activities were confined to night classes. A day school would interfere with existing schools, and, moreover, the trust deed excluded the holding of religious services. In the first science class there were 44 pupils, foremen, journeymen and apprentices; after a fall in numbers in the second year Canon Fowler, headmaster of the Grammar School, undertook supervision without payment, having persuaded the managers of most schools to

[1] There were other adult schools, one at the Thomas Cooper Baptist Church and one at Temperance Hall.
[2] Below, p. 284.
[3] There had already been a club of this kind at Robeys, where newspapers and a bagatelle board were available every evening. See *L.D.M.* v, 172.
[4] A. C. Benson, *The Trefoil*, p. 132, said he was a small dignified man with a high collar, like a Victorian statesman. The first exhibition arranged by the school was depicted in a woodcut in the *Illustrated London News* for 26 November 1864. It was so successful that the room had to be divided, and the floor supported with props.

send their pupils for science training. By the third session there were 534 students, a fair proportion of them from the artisan class, the subjects taught being mechanical and building construction, mathematics and applied mechanics, sound, light and heat, agriculture and mechanical drawing.

Leeke also started science classes at his school for boys who had passed Standard VII elsewhere, and were intended for the foundries, and placed Alfred Collis, a Ruston draughtsman to whom he had taught mathematics, in charge. This was in 1889; in 1891 he added a Standard VII of his own, and placed the school under the Department of Education; and in 1893 a Standard VI, the upper part of the school becoming an 'organised science school'. It had to be such to qualify for new technical grants; and it must not be an elementary school, to which only a school board could make grants. His boys were given instruction either in their own school or at the School of Science and Art on Monks Road, by teachers of the latter school.

The new technical grants came from money granted to local authorities in 1890 – known as whisky money, as it came from excise duties on whisky – which it was widely agreed to apply for technical instruction. There were several applicants in Lincoln: the School of Science and Art; the Continuation Day School (Leeke's); the City and Guilds of London Institute; the District Council in connection with the Worshipful Company of Plumbers; and the Lincoln School of Carpentry (begun in November 1890) which was housed at Church House but non-denominational. The Lindsey County Council favoured the School of Science and Art as one to which scholarships from other parts of the county might be most usefully awarded; many children from surrounding villages went there. The city decided to establish there a day scientific and technical school, and granted money for the building of workshops.[1] Provision was made for the teaching of ironwork, carpentry being left to the Church House.

On the advice of an inspector the various bodies worked together, sharing the grant, for an experimental period; but the whole position was thoroughly confused. The headmaster of the Continuation School at Church House – a religious and voluntary institution – had part of his salary paid by the Science School committee, and one of the Science School masters spent half his time at Church House giving science lectures. Of 110 science students in Lincoln paid for by the government,

---

[1] A proviso was added that if under the trust deed or otherwise the corporation should wish to take over the buildings no sum of money should be charged in respect of those so to be erected.

90 were in fact at Church House. The Department said that science grants should be earned at the Science School, and that Church House students should not use the Science School as a classroom. Leeke replied that they were cavilling at teaching practical chemistry in Monks Road to scholars who did the rest of their work uphill.

It was Leeke who was aimed at; the confusion was due chiefly to him, and indeed he was in hot water all round. To the parish schools his school was a pirate school, taking away their best older boys, affecting the influence of the parish clergy and injuring their appeals for funds when they were trying to fend off a school board. And what was he doing in the old Christs Hospital buildings, which by then had been dedicated to a school for girls? An anonymous 'Liberal Churchman' thought all this would be wasted on the prime mover of the mischief, whose rightheartedness and wrongheadedness he respectively appreciated and deplored.[1] On the other side it was complained that a church school had got into an undenominational school of science.

To all this Leeke replied in 1895. He did not deny that he had confused the whole picture. He said that the Continuation School had been pushed upon them during the last four or five years. They had taken no step in advance save where they had been forced to do so by the success of the previous step, by the Education Department or the Science and Art Department in London, or the necessities as they conceived them of the lads of the city. Now, he thought, they would feel that the school had reached a position to be thankful for. It was not started as a sort of fad that would run amuck against the other sources of education in the city, but they tried to fill the gap when it came.[2]

If he is the villain, he is also the hero of the story. In his passionate zeal for education he could not wait for the slow grinding of official wheels either in London or in Lincoln whilst lads were growing up and missing their chances. He cared little for denominational interests, though he could not wholly escape from them.[3] He was described as always in a hurry – and there can be little doubt that in spite of the confusion he created, things moved faster than they would have done without him. Collis, who was devoted to him, used to recall that he once said to Leeke that he did not proselytise among his pupils; to which Leeke replied, 'Ah, you've noticed that, have you?'

[1] L.C., 7 November 1891.
[2] L.C., 16 February 1895.
[3] Unlike other clergy, Leeke issued to parents of children in his parish (St Nicholas) forms for the withdrawal of children from church religious teaching. 25 were withdrawn. When parents were not thus told of their right the more usual figure was 1.

Confusion was resolved by the decision that in 1897 there should be a complete science school in Monks Road, and that the Continuation School should go on as a higher grade school[1] and prepare scholars for the science school. Collis, who as well as being head of the science school at Church House, had also taught technical drawing in the evening classes at the School of Science and Art, ceased to fulfil this dual role, and became headmaster of the science school. As some compensation it was agreed that the Science School Committee should carry out at their own expense classes of not less than 80 boys in elementary science, being scholars of the Continuation Day School, in the Christs Hospital buildings, with a view to some at least of the boys entering the Science School. To encourage all elementary boys to the same end, and to recoup managers, a grant of £1 was made for every scholar who passed from one of them into the Science School. It was intended to open the Science School as a day school with 50 scholars and the Wesleyan elementary school at once decided to form a preparatory class. The council took over the administration of the whisky money in 1898. In 1901 the Science and Art School was handed over to the corporation, and it was combined with the Science Day School to become the Municipal Technical Day School.

The Church House trustees bought the Christs Hospital buildings, the new school for girls having other plans, and opened a girls' department in 1898; another Continuation School was started at St Andrews by the Lincoln Council for Voluntary Schools.

Before the Act of 1870 the view was coming to be generally held that the Grammar School was doing well as a classical school[2] but failing as a commercial school. In this respect it was not above the average of a good parish school. This view was put by Joseph Ruston to the city council, leading to the conclusion that the school should be divided, with increased fees, in order to pay higher salaries. It was opposed on the ground that poorer children would thus be excluded: to which it was answered that they did not attend even when the fees were lower, and that if the council did not make the school more than an elementary school the Endowed Schools Commission would do it for them. Free places would provide for the poor.

[1] A child had to be at least 10 on admission and must pass an examination up to the fourth standard, and who could stay at school until he or she was 14–18. It appears that there were only 12 such schools in England and Wales.
[2] Several old boys went to Shrewsbury and gained distinction, among them H. W. Moss, who became headmaster, and T. E. Page, editor of the Loeb Classics.

The project of severance was agreed in 1875. The dean and chapter would keep all the buildings uphill for the upper school, and control the Mere Trust and the chapter endowment, and the corporation would retain all the buildings belowhill for the lower school. When the scheme was presented to Bishop Wordsworth for confirmation as Visitor under the deed of 1850[1] he refused his consent. He thought that the chapter ought to take the lead in all that concerned the religious, moral and intellectual welfare of the citizens; without them and the upper school the lower school would sink; and the upper school would probably become a seminary for the children of strangers. Furthermore, the master of the lower school was not required to be a believer in Christianity, and the approval of such a provision by the bishop, dean and chapter and the corporation of the city would dishearten those who were fighting to retain the religious character of the parochial schools.

Reasoning of this kind, so remote from reality, was not likely to weigh with the council, which, fortified by learned counsel's advice that the bishop could not prevent the separation of the schools, got on with the job. Steps were taken to admit to the modern school boys from any school, including the Ragged School, and to pass them by examination to the upper school, several places being free. As a visitor in 1876 Ruston was pleased with what he found. There were now 100 boys in the lower school instead of 40; they were well taught in Latin, English and French, and they were evidently receiving a sound commercial education. The master, the Rev. Markham Hill, had brought the school into good condition.

A charity commissioner ruled that if the schools were to separate they must do so completely, and a new scheme was approved in 1883. The upper or Grammar School moved to a new building just below the headmaster's house on Lindum Terrace, £10,000 being contributed by the Ecclesiastical Commissioners in acknowledgement of the chapter obligation to maintain a cathedral Grammar School, and the chapter's own contribution was increased from £90 to £300. The schools were to have two separate governing bodies, and there were to be 30 scholarships from the elementary schools to the Middle School (as the old lower school was to be called) and 12 from it to the Grammar School. The new building on Lindum Terrace was opened in 1885. Grammar School numbers at once grew to over 100, and a new wing was added in 1891. The ladder which had been built from elementary school to university was to be the theme of many speeches: here was progress.

[1] Above, p. 57.

The examiner of 1884 had no doubt that the Middle School would supply a need felt all over the county. The middle classes had been at the mercy of anyone who chose to call himself a schoolmaster, having no qualifications for the profession, and having failed in everything else had invested in a cane and set up a school. This was a bid to entice children from the private schools. Markham Hill harped on the same theme, and asked for scholarships to the School of Art and the School of Science. In 1890 he boasted that all the Grammar School scholarships to universities were being held by old Middle School boys; and in 1896 that his school had more Oxford local examination successes than all the other schools in the city put together. It was no doubt in getting these results that he earned the reputation, long remembered, of a martinet.

The division of the schools was presently adjudged not a success. Both schools were weak (though well taught), and they had to compete with a new secondary day school and the higher elementary school. In 1898 both bodies of governors sought reunion, and a scheme to this end was sealed in 1900. The whole school moved to the Grammar School site, and the Greyfriars passed back to the city council.

The other old school, Christ's Hospital, or the Bluecoat School, originally founded by Richard Smith for 12 boys,[1] had grown with its income from endowments, principally the manor of Potterhanworth, as the result of inclosure and drainage. By 1838 it had 56 boys, and measures were taken to provide for 100 more.[2] But the school was adjudged not to have adapted itself to changing times. The boys were being apprenticed at 14 instead of 16 so that they could complete their seven years at 21. The Charity Commissioners reported that having been taken from the poorest classes at 7, they were well clothed, fed, treated, lodged and educated; at 14 they were put to a mechanical trade, with hard work and harder fare, under a master perhaps ignorant of even the rudiments of that education in which the apprentice was skilled. It was not surprising, the commissioners held, that a boy should become dissatisfied and run away. This generally happened in the first year. Boys who took posts as clerks or book-keepers generally did well.[3] Certainly the boys were well treated in the school, and they showed their affection for the master William Wilkinson when he retired after nearly 30 years' service.[4] Dakeyne gave a glowing account of the school in 1844.[5] In 1854 an inspector found it below the standard of many national schools;

[1] *T. & S.L.*, pp. 135–6.   [2] *L.C.*, 20 April 1838.
[3] *Charity Commission Report*, 1837, pp. 357–8; *G.L.*, p. 285.
[4] When he died in 1841 a mural monument to him and his wife was erected in St Michael's parish church.   [5] L.A.O. Cor.B. 9/10.

and in 1868 the Schools Inquiry Commission noted that the boys were the sons of poor parents, labourers and small tradesmen, and although they were said to enjoy good health, did not grow up very big or vigorous. As there were only two masters for 120 boys, the staff was clearly insufficient.

Yet the school had gained the loyalty of its boys, and it had also attracted in a remarkable way the affection and good will of the citizens. In 1880, having already a drum and fife band, it added a brass band, and paraded the city occasionally. When the boys had their annual trip to the seaside they were accompanied by members of the council and about 2,000 citizens.[1]

In 1880 the Charity Commissioners were engaged upon their task of devising a new system of graduated schools in Lincoln, and they had to find money for a middle-class school for girls. The question whether Christs Hospital was founded primarily for the relief of poverty or for the promotion of education was settled for them, in law at least, by the Endowed Schools Act of 1869; it was an educational institution. The commissioners decided that the school was no longer needed; it must go, and the money be better used elsewhere.

When it was heard in Lincoln that they thought that, elementary education being fully provided for, the Bluecoat endowment must go to secondary school purposes there was an outburst of wrath. An institution providing clothes, board and lodging and education for 100 boys of the poorest class, probably orphans, to be converted into a middle-class institution, not even for boys, but for girls! There were already numerous private schools for them. Official protests, a petition signed by 6,000 people, and a deputation, left the enemy unmoved; if money could be found otherwise they would not interfere with the Hospital. It could not.

The final draft scheme provided for exhibitions open to boys of any elementary school in the Lincoln school district to be held at the Middle School or elsewhere. A girls' school was to be built, with some endowment, tuition fees being not less than £4 or more than £10 per year. The Hospital ceased to exist on 21 December 1883. All manner of doubts were expressed: could the elementary schools take up all the exhibitions with boys of sufficient ability to merit election to the Middle School? But they did. The Christs Hospital Girls High School opened in 1894.

Balfour's Education Act of 1902 provided another landmark in the history of Education in England. With increasing numbers of children to

[1] For a bright picture of the last days of the school see *Lincolnshire Magazine*, III, 19, 67.

be provided for nationally, it was impossible any longer to maintain enough schools by private subscriptions and church bazaars. Balfour accepted that if voluntary schools could not be abolished they ought not to be starved. The new Act made county and county borough councils the authorities for all secondary and technical education, and, in county boroughs, for elementary education also. Voluntary and board schools alike came under them. The managers of the former provided the buildings and retained the appointment of teachers, but current expenses were met out of the local rates. This was a great disappointment to nonconformists, who had seen that the voluntary system was breaking down, and looked forward to its end. Now it was being given a new lease of life. They had a real grievance in single-school areas, where the only school was a church school, and nonconformist children had to attend it, and nonconformist teachers had no hope of appointment to posts in it. Their leaders contested the Bill on the ground that it would put sectarian teaching on the rates; this was not a good ground, for voluntary schools had long been drawing grants from taxes. From the national point of view there was no other practicable way forward, and in retrospect, in spite of some injustice, it was seen to be a good scheme.

Local protagonists at once took up their positions. Dean Wickham said that short of a system of universal school boards, or universally denominational schools, neither of which was practical politics whichever party was in power, it was difficult to see what more could be wished for. With managers for denominational schools, one-man government for the parish school – the parson, of course – would be ended. For the Free Churches the Rev. H. H. Carlisle said the Bill was the bishops' Bill, and provided for one section at the expense of the rest. The Free Church Council asked the city council to determine not to administer the Act unless an appeal had first been made to the country at a general election. The city council, not going so far, unanimously resolved that the obligation to maintain and keep efficient all voluntary and public schools within the city, and to levy rates for the purpose as proposed by the Bill, would not be acceptable to the council unless it was accompanied by the right to nominate and appoint a majority of the management of such schools; and with this the Free Church Council were satisfied. In the end the council were given only one-third of the managers, the other two-thirds being left to the church representatives.

Passive resistance ensued. Those who felt most strongly refused to pay the rate, and were summoned before the magistrates. Nonconformist ministers led the movement. Some justices were courteous, making allowance for strength of feeling by allowing a speech; others refused to hear anything but legal objection. When seized goods were offered for sale in the police station yard there was a seething crowd, and a table was overturned, and the auctioneer prudently said he would give his fees to the Dispensary. As the years went on the feeling gradually grew that protest having been made there was no point in continuing it, and by 1910 only six stalwarts continued to resist. Excitement was kept alive by two attempts by the liberal government to carry education bills, but both failed to pass the House of Lords, and the Balfour settlement remained in operation.

The elementary schools in Lincoln were taken over on 26 March 1903, and an Education Committee appointed consisting of 16 members of the city council and eight coopted members. Dean Wickham could have become chairman, but he wisely elected to take the vice-chair,[1] leaving the chair to Benjamin Vickers, a Methodist and liberal council member. R. C. Minton, who had been secretary of the diocesan board of education, was appointed secretary of the committee and inspector. Every attempt was made at a conciliatory start.

When the inspectors of the Department of Education visited the elementary schools they concluded that on the whole the teaching was satisfactory, though they had many suggestions for improvement of the buildings. Shortage of accommodation would become worse as standards were raised. Proper provision was needed for scholarships for girls, and a better system for boys, with exhibitions to colleges and universities. Provision also was needed for defective children, and for more woodwork and cookery instruction.[2]

Two voluntary schools, the girls school in Free School Lane which had been handed over by the corporation to managers in 1874[3] and St Peter at Gowts Wesleyan School (Alfred Street), became council schools; St Marks was closed, and Sparrow Lane (the Ragged School premises) allowed only to continue until a new council school to serve the east end of the city could be built. The latter (Monks Road) was opened in 1905. The question whether .elementary education should be free came up quickly, and it was agreed that in principle it should, but that finance dictated delay; some schools continued to charge fees of 2d. or 3d. per week and the others were free.

Both the new authority and the church committees were engaged in

---

[1] He was also vice-chairman of the Grammar School, Christs Hospital Foundation and the Girls High School, chairman of the Training College and the Christs Hospital Terrace Management Committee. *L.L.*, 26 August 1910.

[2] *General Report on the Elementary Schools*, Lincoln, November 1905.

[3] Above, p. 274.

erecting or improving buildings, and trying to reduce overcrowding; yet they could hardly keep pace with the increase in the number of children. By 1912, 936 places had been lost by condemnation of buildings and 610 by alterations, and managers had provided 564 places and the authority 1,441. The net increase therefore only averaged about 50 places per year, and the number of children was growing at the rate of 120.[1]

The Education Committee were going as fast as they dared. There had been the most gloomy forecasts of the cost of the new authority and the level of the new education rate. It was soon clear that it would be more than the expected 4d; it would be 6½d.; it might even be 7d. By 1904 it was 9¾d. The defects inherited from the old order were not likely to be underrated by defenders of the new. Alderman Edward Harrison said that Lincoln was almost unique in the matter of its educational inheritance. The schools had too few teachers, and too many of them uncertificated, and even apprentices. There were few places of its size which, when the Act of 1902 was passed, had not a considerable amount of educational property: Lincoln had not, and everything was coming upon them at once.

The Department also reviewed the secondary schools, congratulating the authority on being called on only to make the most of what the city already possessed. The Board of Education could help with grants, and also by exercise of their jurisdiction over charitable trusts. The Girls High School, with very slight additional expense, should be able to earn grants, but it was cramped and needed to expand. At the Grammar School new buildings were urgently needed, and could not be provided without external aid. The board were pleased that the authority were disposed to take the view that it was their duty to consider both the schools as part of their local provision; if practical proposals were framed in that sense, and the board were assured that the schools would receive local support for maintenance, capital could be applied out of endowments towards the cost of building on much easier terms than were imposed where no such aid was forthcoming. The board would also consider strengthening authority representation on the governing bodies, and would encourage the county authorities to help. The friendly attitude of local engineering firms to the Municipal Technical School would probably make its development into an advanced school of engineering only a matter of time.[2]

Fees and grants and an appeal for funds for extension enabled the Girls

---

[1] *L.C.*, 17 February 1912.
[2] *L.L.*, 17 September 1904.

High School to open new buildings in 1911, by which time it had grown from the 51 pupils of 1894 to 253.

The Grammar School, with a much longer history, had more problems. The merger in it of the Middle School in 1900 had not been universally approved. Some thought it a backward step, and wondered if the scholarly Canon Fowler could conduct a commercial school with as much success as had attended his classical efforts. Lindum Terrace, where the school then lived, was remote enough for boys from downhill; but the new site on Wragby Road might as well be at Wragby so far as downhill boys were concerned: they would have to take their dinners with them. But the new building plans were approved by the local authority provided that the number of free places for elementary scholars was increased.[1]

It is clear that there was a marked prejudice against the school in the city, which F. H. Chambers, the headmaster, tried to dispel. Threequarters of the cost of the school was met by fees, a quarter of the boys being admitted free on scholarships, most of the endowment being so applied. The cost of the school was too high because the school was too small, and the governors had to meet the charge that the school curriculum was not sufficiently strenuous, and offered few advantages which were not offered by the Municipal Technical School or the higher elementary school. The headmaster pleaded that the authority should take the school entirely under their wing and make it their own.[2]

All turned on money. Leeke, who had had five sons at the school, said that the school could not lay its hand on money it needed the better to equip itself. If it wanted to do this in science it was too proud to go out and collect sixpences. Like the Girls High School it sought a grant of £300; if it could get it it would soon be under the Board of Education and get government grants. In spite of the common view that the schools were semi-private institutions it was realised, even by the unsympathetic, that if the schools were neglected they would die, and the children would go to schools maintained out of rates and taxes. The grants were made.

By 1910 the governors and the Education Committee were agreed that the school must be self-supporting. Scholarship places provided had not been filled, and the best boys at the elementary schools had not been won by them. In spite of a better all-round curriculum, the alternative practical courses at the Technical School had proved too strong to be ignored by parents. Voluntary municipal grants ceased, and the school

---

[1] The Lindum Terrace buildings were sold to a Roman Catholic order, who opened St Joseph's Convent as a private school for day girls and boarders.
[2] *L.L.*, 16 July 1904.

took its chance as a middle-class fee-paying school. A junior school for boys from 9 to 13 was established independently of the Board of Education. The bishop strongly supported the school, and Dean Wickham offered his services as a class teacher during the illness of the headmaster. Charles Brook, a governor, who went to the upper school in 1849, hailed the change of policy, which he thought gave prospect of a return to the earlier days of the school.

One reason why the Technical School was a serious competitor was that its fees were only £1 per year for boys from a Lincoln elementary school, and £3 for other boys, 45 scholarships being provided in 1904. It had begun with only five classrooms, but a large extension was made in 1908, with a target of 250 boys. It was later to break away from its technical origins, and become a good all-round grammar school.

CHAPTER XVI

ECONOMIC AND SOCIAL CHANGE: II

The population of the city continued to grow, on the whole at an increasing rate, until the 1870s; in that decade it increased by 39%, a rate which it never reached again. The period of economic depression is reflected in the growth rate of 11% in the decade 1881–91, though industrial recovery brought the rate of growth up to 17% in the two decades 1891–1911.[1]

The houses required to accommodate the new population were mostly built in long drab rows in three areas; in St Martin and further west, in the detached part of St Mary le Wigford, land of old enclosure, soon to become St Faith's parish; in St Swithin, towards Stamp End, near the ironworks; and in St Peter at Gowts, the Canwick Road area, east of Sincil Dyke, land once enclosed from the south common and let to freemen, and sold just before or after 1835, which was to become St Andrew's parish. At the turn of the century the Monks Liberty, east of St Swithin, was broken up for building and became All Saints parish.

Bad as some of the new houses were, they were not so bad as those built a generation earlier. Lincoln had the advantage, like other towns in the east Midlands, that it had been little affected by the first uncontrolled movement of population in the industrial age, and was therefore better off than towns in the south, west and north of the country. Furthermore, Lincoln was not afflicted by large areas of slums, and open country was never far away. Nearly all families had separate houses, and in 1911 the percentage of the population officially regarded as overcrowded – that is, more than two to a room – was 2.9, compared with 1.1 in Leicester and Northampton, 1.9 in Derby, 4.3 in Nottingham.[2] Throughout the period the ratio of inhabitants to houses did not change materially. In 1871 the average number of persons per house was 4.74; in 1901 it was 4.43.[3]

The building of houses was not all left to the speculative builder and the small men building for investment – the 'little landlords'; it was calculated in 1910 that half the tenement property in Lincoln had been

[1] Appendix 1. In 1889 the incumbent of St Swithin replied to the bishop's Visitation Articles that his parish consisted of 1,000 labouring class, 7,000 foremen, artisans, clerks, builders and shopkeepers, and a few professional men.

[2] Sir John Clapham, *Economic History of Modern Britain*, II (1932), 494; III (1938), 459–60.

[3] The figure for all England was 5.4.

raised by the help of building societies.[1] The terminating societies[2] usually ran for 12 years, and one passed £85,000 through its hands. The Lincoln Land and Building Society was formed in 1872, and in 1883 the Lincoln Cooperative Society began to provide its members with houses on the same hire-purchase principle.[3]

A Lincoln Industrial Dwellings Association had a few modest successes. In 1904 it built a central lodging house on the Waterside South; then Canon Crowfoot handed over to it a women's lodging house. In 1909 it bought seven cottages on the north side of Unity Square, repaired and let them. In the following year it paid a first dividend of 4%.

A first attempt by the corporation to build working-class houses to relieve a serious shortage had not been successful.[4] The need for such action was shown by the report of the inspector of nuisances in 1900, when he complained of overcrowding. When houses were demolished for improvements, the dispossessed could not afford to pay the rent of new houses. There was, however, the hope that cheap trams might bring cheaper building within range across the boundary: clearly Bracebridge was in mind.

In 1912 the sanitary inspector visited 2,676 houses with a view to forming an opinion of the necessity of houses for working men. Eleven were unoccupied; in 145 there were two families in one house; only 368 were let at less than 4s. a week. He thought more were required at 5s., but it was difficult to find a site where houses could be built at that rent near to work. In the following year Ruston and Proctor were urging action on behalf of their workpeople, and R. A. Taylor moved in the council for the provision of working-class houses; he suggested a site, and thought a house could be built for £180. The Boultham estate had lately been sold by Colonel Ellison to a Nottingham syndicate, on whom the city were trying to impose a rule against building more than 16 to the acre; and the mayor thought they would not stand a very good chance of success if they themselves proposed to build at 25 to the acre instead of 15. Under growing pressure of public opinion, a town planning committee was appointed in 1913, but the outbreak of war delayed further progress.

Interest in the housing question was resumed after the war. In 1923

---

[1] *L.L.*, 1 January 1910.

[2] Above, p. 130.

[3] Duncan McInnes, *History of Cooperation in Lincoln 1861–1911* (1911), p. 88. But the society had done some building of houses earlier. *S.M.*, 28 February 1873. It was said by the wits that McInnes had proclaimed that he looked forward to the time when every working man would own his own house and the house next door.

[4] Above, pp. 238–9.

over 15,000 houses were visited, and were found to include 1,356 where there were two or more families; there were 170 cases of overcrowding, and 826 families wanting houses. In the following year it was optimistically claimed that although an appreciable proportion of old houses fell short of modern requirements, there was nothing that could accurately be described as a slum. The average number of persons per house was 4.09, which was an improvement. There were 707 houses with no through outlets; and 20 houseboats and some vans were used as dwellings. There were probably 180 cases of overcrowding on the basis of more than three adults to a bedroom. The clearance schemes that slowly followed were chiefly concerned with small pockets of bad houses, mostly built in the early or middle years of the nineteenth century. Housing standards were steadily to rise.

Although the local data are too scanty to be marshalled statistically, there is no reason to doubt that the conclusions of economic historians as to conditions in the country generally apply to Lincoln. Taking the period as a whole, 'average real wages in 1914 may be estimated as from 70 to 100 per cent higher than in 1860, and, more certainly, as about 45 per cent higher than in 1880, the level in 1914, however, being only the same as in 1896'.[1] The pressure for reduction of working hours, which in some cases must have meant reduction of earnings, points in the same direction. A reduced working week in industry was slowly being achieved,[2] and with it an improvement in conditions in shops. Drapers began to close at 7 o'clock instead of 8 in 1846, and public opinion was invoked in aid of the movement. Collingham the draper set an example by giving, unasked, a Saturday half holiday to his assistants in 1876.[3] Presently many shops, which had remained open on Saturdays until 11 o'clock, decided to close at 10. An Early Closing Association agreed in 1885 to advocate closing at 4 o'clock on Wednesdays, and the principal tradesmen gradually agreed. By 1895 a public meeting, called on requisition by the mayor, approved of Wednesday closing at 2 o'clock, and public opinion, with the aid of a procession and a brass band which demonstrated before nonconforming shops, secured general adoption of the measure.

Public and private effort was still trying to cope with the grave social evils of crime, vagrancy and destitution. The number of vagrants in the Lincoln workhouse much increased in 1877, and the increase led to the

[1] W. Ashworth, *Economic History of England 1870–1939* (1960), p. 201, and see pp. 247–52.
[2] Above, pp. 154–5.
[3] He paid the subscriptions of his apprentices, many of them living in, to the Y.M.C.A., which was near his shop.

stricter enforcement of the poor law. More room was needed at the workhouse in 1879, and in the following year it overflowed into the militia barracks. Begging, said the county constabulary report for 1878, had become a formidable nuisance during the previous fifteen years, but had altered in character:

the action of the police has suppressed the class of sturdy professional beggars, families of whom infested all parts of the country, and found their calling lucrative: harassed by constant convictions, they have disappeared, and with them many of the lodging-houses they have frequented...the tramp of to-day is generally a weakly, diseased and miserable wanderer, lodging at the tramp-ward of the union (which his predecessor despised), and passing the greater part of his time in prison, an asylum he prefers to the workhouse; he is for the most part the product of vice and destitution, and will not easily be eradicated.[1]

In 1880 begging reached an unprecedented figure, and by the next year the cost of outdoor relief had so much increased that new rules were ordered. The increase was halted in 1886, but by that time the guardians were finding both city and country parishes backward in paying the calls made upon them for poor rates. The guardians did, however, reply to a Local Government Board enquiry about distress that they could deal with applications.

The country guardians complained that their parishes were paying £3,000 a year more to the union than the city parishes, although city paupers received £3,000 more in outrelief. The reply, however, was clear. Unemployed countrymen came into the towns; younger farm workers had come to work in Lincoln, and when their fathers fell out of work they came to join their sons, and applied for relief.

By the standards of the time the guardians were humane. The government inspector's tables showed in September 1890 that the rate for indoor and outdoor relief in the Lincoln Union was higher than that for any other union in the district except Boston; to which the chairman replied that to lower the rate would cause a vast amount of misery, and they would not economise at the cost of the flesh and blood of the poor.

In 1893 the Board in London sent out a circular about the provision of work for the unemployed. By then it could be said that as work in the foundries was plentiful there was no need for relief work in the city, though the problem of seasonal work, especially in the building trades, remained: in the previous winter 600 families had to be relieved during six weeks of frost. It was claimed that 1,000 were out of work during part of the winter of 1895, when the corporation provided a little relief work.

Under the Local Government Act of 1894 rural district councillors

---

[1] L.A.O., Lincolnshire Constabulary Report for 1878.

became guardians for their districts, and magistrates ceased to be guardians *ex-officio*. Women for the first time became eligible to serve. Charles Ellison, re-elected chairman after 25 years' service in the chair, said a cheap board meant the paring down of everything, the denial of little comforts, the guardianship of the pocket instead of the poor, sometimes the inadequate remuneration of relieving officers, to whom too many of the guardians looked for the information about relief cases that they ought to acquire for themselves.[1]

Another view is found in comments of the Local Government Board inspector in 1902. He pointed out that in the Lincoln Union outrelief costs were much higher than in other agricultural districts. The argument that it was better to give outrelief than drive old people into the workhouse could be demolished. Other unions went on the principle that it was better to take the sick into the workhouse and have them treated by trained nurses day and night than give 3s. 6d. outrelief, which was hardly sufficient to keep body and soul together. He though too much discretion was left to the guardians of each parish, and not enough enquiries were made; and he advocated several relief committees. Perhaps he was right: but the guardians had a stop in the mind. They would not, if they could help it, commit the poor to the hated Bastille. They would not forget that in 1900 Henry Chaplin, as president of the Local Government Board, issued a circular (the last of a series of ameliorating circulars) recommending that outrelief should be allowed to aged persons of good character. A workhouse hospital was part of the poor law, and bore its stigma: and if their outrelief costs were higher, their workhouse costs would be held down.

Voluntary efforts to mitigate the lot of the poor had long been made. Initiatives taken by the Minster Yard ladies led to a regular visiting of inmates. It had come to be thought unseemly that at the May hiring statutes women should stand in the streets waiting to be hired, and in 1872 the Guildhall was opened for their accommodation. In 1875 Mrs Bromhead undertook to help with the nursing at the workhouse, and earned the gratitude of the guardians, who were presently asking for trained nurses for the sick poor. Mrs Danby and others established a Girls Friendly Society Home for the preliminary training of girls going into domestic service, and for finding places for them. Girls were sent there from the workhouse on the same footing with respect to relief as boarding out cases. Ladies petitioned for the boarding out of children in 1870, and soon afterwards the practice was adopted. A Lincoln Work-

[1] *L.C.*, 5 January 1895.

house Boys Aid Society was formed by Miss Mitchinson for boys under 16 who were working, and the guardians agreed to subscribe 2s. weekly for each of their boys, to cease when the boy earned 7s. In 1893 the workhouse school was closed, and the children sent to schools in the city. After years of effort by Edwin Pratt and others all the children were got out of the workhouse and a receiving home opened for them in 1911. The clerk (W. B. Danby) recalled that 30 years earlier the children used to go walking, two and two, with dull and uninteresting countenances, almost shorn heads and a distinctive workhouse garb. All that had been changed without any appreciable burden on the rates.

Even in times of good trade there were men out of work, their numbers swollen in winter time when out-of-door work had to cease. Here charity came in, especially to help able-bodied unemployed to keep out of the workhouse. In the 1870s soup kitchens, uphill and downhill, had become a regular feature of the winter scene; on one day in January 1881 750 quarts of soup and loaves of bread were distributed downhill and 400 uphill.

When trade was bad the soup kitchens were not enough. A correspondent wrote to the *Chronicle*:

We have been out almost every night for the last eight weeks, and what have we found? Amongst other cases a man with a wife and five children, the man out of work for 8 weeks, and no food in the house; another with a family of three children; another with nine children, and, when we called, entirely without food, and we were compelled to go and buy bread for them on a Sunday. Another family of six children had had no work for nine weeks. Another family, where there were six children, had not a mouthful of food in the house of any description, and the little ones were famishing...The above are all respectable hard working men who have been paid off from the various foundries, and they do not like to make their trouble known: they would rather suffer starvation.

He distinguished professional beggars. He and a friend had been sent out by teachers of the Ragged Sunday School, and with the aid of funds they had supplied more than 60 deserving cases. The *Chronicle* confirmed the account from its own enquiries.[1] A further report added that poverty drove families to live together with consequent overcrowding. To the obvious question why the unemployed did not report to the poor law it was replied that:

amongst many of the poorest classes there is a feeling of pride – and a very admirable one too – which no matter how keen may be their sufferings, causes them to have a wholesome dread of anything that savours of parochial relief, and would rather endure unheard of privations than end their days in the

[1] 20 February 1885.

workhouse...parochial relief is disbursed by paid officials, who, I am afraid, in too many cases, wound the susceptibilities of those with whom they have to deal...'Oh,' says the officer to whom the application is made, 'we cannot grant you outdoor relief, but you are perfectly at liberty to come into "The House".' Nineteen times out of twenty for obvious reasons, this kind of offer is declined, and then the poor law (metaphorically speaking) chuckles over the result, and with remarkable shortsightedness thinks that because 'The House' is not accepted the applicant is not in want, overlooking the fact that a man, temporarily out of employment, loses all chance of obtaining work when once the workhouse gate is closed behind him. Moreover, such a course necessitates the breaking up of his home, and it is no wonder that he looks upon the entrance to the Workhouse as an 'abandon hope' sort of gateway.[1]

A Charity Organisation Society was formed at once, on the initiative of Dr Lowe. Help was offered on many hands, though some, like Charles Ellison, thought it would tend to pauperise the people. The policy adopted was to grant relief after visitation of the home, give it in kind and not in money, find work where possible, and repress begging. The city council and the guardians appointed members of the committee, though Ellison objected that ministers of religion had been excluded on the ground that they would probably give most of the money to people of their own persuasion.

Lowe reported that in three weeks 256 cases had been investigated and recorded, and 196 relieved, representing over 950 persons. In many cases all the furniture had been sold. The city council provided work for 150 men three days a week, improving the commons. By the end of the year 590 families had been relieved.

In the following winter the society provided halfpenny dinners for children, and by January 1886 were feeding 800 children with three meals a week, noting the improvement in their health and appearance, and finding work for 150 men. Winter frosts raised the number of children to 1,200 and the number of men to 200. The society found in March 1886 that 5,000 men were working on short time – 42 hours instead of 54 – earning 14s. a week. The short-time system had been going on for several years, and savings and furniture had gone. Operations were suspended in May, but resumed in December 1886: the archdeacon Kaye had started a parochial fund to work alongside the society. Though the number of distressed families was not so great, the poverty was deeper and the general conditions far worse. Things were better by March, and the society was giving warning that nine-tenths of the applicants at the doors of private houses were impostors.

[1] *L.C.*, 27 February 1885. He refers to the attitude of Betty Higden in *Our Mutual Friend* towards the thought of being buried by the parish.

There was distress again in November 1887, when it was said that some men had been out of work ever since the Ruston strike 18 months earlier. By that year the worst was probably over, and trade was recovering. Such exceptional relief measures were not called for again until after the turn of the century. But when he built the Drill Hall for the Volunteers in 1890, Joseph Ruston had it provided with a soup kitchen, fitted with coppers and every appliance for cooking food in large quantities, and he stipulated that in times of great distress in the city, when it became necessary to feed many poor people and children, the hall should be available without fee. Tables and seats for a large number were provided. In 1893 began a series of 'Robin Dinners', given yearly in the hall to perhaps 1,200 poor children at Christmas.

Meanwhile the problem of drunkenness had grown worse. In 1869 there were 183 public houses in Lincoln: 1 for every 25 families.[1] In 1871 the Lincoln Temperance Society made a new drive, and opened a hall in St Swithin's Square to which the city contributed. It sought to offer counter-attractions to the public house – floriculture, literary and scientific interests, outdoor recreation, railway excursions, charitable work, and encouragement of saving. The Licensing Act of 1872 to regulate the sale of alcohol to the public raised a fear that public houses might be allowed to remain open longer; and the churches and friendly societies joined in petitions to brewster sessions against any relaxation. The mayor replied that the magistrates had decided to keep open hours as they were, one reason being the good record of innkeepers and hotel keepers.[2]

In 1876 the county police reported that drunkenness had greatly increased during the last 20 years; higher wages and less work were the rule, and facilities for obtaining drink had not decreased. There was, however, in that year a decrease of drinking and an increase of vagrancy owing to the trade depression. The report for 1877 was more outspoken:

In the gross and increasing abuse of strong drink lies the source of the enlarged total of offences. It cannot be doubted that by indulgence in this vice, is stimulated the frequent assaults, and that the poverty resulting from drunken habits is the origin of much of the vagrancy and begging which have now assumed such formidable proportions, while to vagrants may be largely attributed the frequency of petty larcenies.[3]

Yet drunkenness continued to grow from year to year.[4]

[1] L.C., 2 April 1869.
[2] L.C., 12 September 1873.
[3] L.A.O. Lincolnshire Constabulary Report, 1877. And see L.C., 22 March 1878.
[4] L.C., 10 January 1879. The county police reported increases in 1895 and 1896.

The chancellor Benson testifies to the same effect. He wrote:

14 March 1876. We are now *plunging* into the Church of England Temperance Society, and are going to plough this extraordinarily fertile field by cross-ploughing – *rich* land, the 'fertile' is to be seen in the next 30 years. 'Temperance' must precede 'Faith', and any practical belief in 'Judgment to come'.

18 November 1876. I send you the new iron – my prospectus about Temperance. You'll think I meddle with 'ower many things' – but you couldn't help it if you lived in a place like this. Its awful to see so much wit and work take to drink and death.[1]

Among reformers there was usually a division between temperance men and total abstainers, and the division roused the more feeling because Anglicans, at least locally, tended to favour temperance and the total abstainers were mostly dissenters. Bishop Wordsworth did not support the total stopping of sale of liquor on Sundays: he thought it should be restricted.[2] On the other hand the city council signed a petition against Sunday sale in 1882. Bishop King's declaration in 1887 that beer was the gift of God roused vigorous protest.[3] Dean Butler said that if some of their excellent temperance people, instead of talking the nonsense they did, gave the people good drink, nine-tenths of the drunkenness would disappear.[4] They all lacked Benson's awareness of a grave social problem.

A new and larger temperance hall was built in 1902. Applications for new licences were resisted, and in 1909 a fall in drunkenness was reported in Lincoln for the second successive year. Powerful reinforcement came with Bishop Hicks, who held that temperance reform lay at the foundation of all social and political progress.[5] He said in 1911 that Lincoln was among the six worst counties for the number of convictions for drunkenness, and Lincoln itself was notable for its abundant facilities for drinking.[6]

One of the most striking features of the social scene was the growth of

---

[1] A. C. Benson, *Life of E. W. Benson* (1900), I, 396, 408.
[2] *L.C.*, 21 November 1873.
[3] *L.C.*, 8 January 1887.
[4] *L.C.*, 13 October 1888. A Lincoln Coffee Palace Company was formed by public spirited citizens in 1882, and was a useful auxiliary of the temperance movement. A branch opened by Robeys opposite their works in 1884 was closed by the trade depression.
[5] J. H. Fowler, *Edward Lee Hicks* (1922), p. 199. For his opposition to a 'Trust' Public House in All Saints parish, promoted by the clergy, see his Diary, 23 January 1911.
[6] *L.L.*, 18 February 1911. He added that the county was one of those pilloried by the Registrar General for a high proportion of illegitimate births with a lower proportion of illiteracy. The county death rate among infants and children was also bad.

the friendly societies.[1] By 1874 the eight lodges of the Manchester Unity of Oddfellows had 1,297 members in Lincoln; they had their own medical officer, and in 1879 they opened their Oddfellows Hall. The London Unity had three lodges with 119 members, and the Derby Midland Unity five lodges with 360 members.[2] As part of their propaganda the Manchester Unity instituted a brass band contest in 1882. The other friendly societies combined to provide a dispensary, and by 1886 their 13 orders with 27 lodges had 2,590 members and 115 family members.[3] The Ancient Order of Foresters could say in 1892 that over 500 adults had joined during the year. By 1900 the Manchester Unity had 6,209 members, and the annual friendly society service at the cathedral had become an established institution. The incentive to voluntary saving was however seriously eroded if friendly society benefit payable during sickness was deducted from poor relief. In 1892 the question was raised with the guardians, who resolved that in arriving at the amount of outrelief to be given, club money should not be considered when such money did not exceed 5s., and when it exceeded that amount it should be counted as half. No sick relief should be granted on a second application unless in the interim the applicant had become a member of a friendly society. This was something, but the societies were soon to seek further relaxation of poor law rules. An association to provide nursing for the poor was formed as part of the Queen's Second Jubilee celebrations in 1897: its funds were to be administered by Miss Henrietta Bromhead so long as she continued to be lady superintendent of the Bromhead Institute for Nurses.

Other public services were expanding their activities in ways that overlapped the work of the guardians. In 1904 the School Attendance Committee of the Lincoln Education Authority, ahead of statutory provision, began privately to seek out ill-fed children and provide them with breakfasts. By 1909, when the first public statements were made, 17,000 breakfasts had been provided. The city council had done a little for the relief of unemployment. All the local agencies of betterment were affected by the will of John Dawber, who died in 1904. He was the last surviving partner of the firm of Dawber and Company, brewers and maltsters, which had been founded by his father Robert Dawber in 1826. He had served on the Board of Guardians and the Welton Rural District Council, but lived almost unnoticed in the city. He had no family, and had contemplated retirement to Brighton, when late in life he inherited

[1] Above, p. 154.
[2] L.C., 19 June 1874.
[3] S.M., 5 February 1886.

the fortune of his brother, who had died intestate. By his will John Dawber left the bulk of his estate, which included the brewery and some 60 public houses, in trust for charitable purposes in Lincoln and Bracebridge, the corporation thus having a power of appointment of about £3,000 a year.

The corporation began to make grants from the estate: to the Education Committee for clothing and boots for poor children, to the county hospital, the Dispensary, for the provision of nurses in Lincoln and Bracebridge, and for the relief of distress. It also granted a number of annuities to needy people in the hope of relieving them of the necessity of seeking poor relief.[1]

The relief of poverty was becoming complicated. Old age pensions began to be paid on 1 January 1909. Questions inevitably arose of the effect of one form of aid on another, and the Dawber Committee of the council first agreed with the guardians that when an applicant for outrelief had no material means of support other than a Dawber annuity of £6, the guardians would not take account of the annuity in assessing outrelief. The Local Government Board ruled in 1909 however that the guardians *must* take account of all means of support, and cited cases where people were receiving relief, a municipal charity grant, a Dawber annuity and an old age pension. The Lincoln corporation replied that Dawber money was not for the relief of the poor rate, but for little extra comforts. In one case the guardians reduced relief on account of the annuity, and the corporation stopped the annuity. The corporation won: they had a discretion, but the guardians had a statutory duty.[2]

When severe unemployment recurred in the winter of 1907, the attitude of men without work towards the workhouse was in no way affected by these ameliorating activities. They still refused to go into 'the House', preferring starvation, mitigated by charity. A Charity Organisation Committee was formed; the mayor said that the corporation had 1,400 names on the list of applications for Dawber annuities. There were 380 on the city unemployed list, 148 being offered work. The charity allowance was 1s 6d. for each parent and 9d. for each child, with a bag of

---

[1] *L.L.*, 2 January 1909.
[2] The Report of the Royal Commission on the Poor Law in 1909 was followed by a communication from the National Committee for the Break up of the Poor Law, following the policy of the minority report; it offered literature for the guardians' consideration.

Mr Marshall: 'Is it Mrs Webb? Let her lie on the table.'

The Chairman: 'You are giving this woman full licence. She will knock your legs from under you before you have done.' (*L.L.*, 26 February 1910).

But she did not do so until 1929.

coal in addition. A trade union organiser said that 11 % of organised workers were unemployed, and he wondered how far short of a thousand men were out of work. John Richardson of Robeys said that in skilled workers throughout the country 1 in 20 was out of work, but in Lincoln 1 in 9. The numbers in the workhouse grew.

By the end of the winter (April 1908) the Charity Organisation Committee said that since January they had relieved 801 cases, the greatest number in any one week being 130, dropping to 34. They were satisfied that allegations by some members of the city council of widespread distress were absolutely unjustified, but there were some cases of dire distress. Half the men affected belonged to the building trade, which had been in low water during the winter, and another quarter were labourers dismissed from a local foundry.[1] Lincolnshire was reported as the only county in the North Midland Division that showed an increase both in outdoor relief and indoor pauperism.[2]

In 1908 the society, with Dawber aid, distributed 868 orders on tradesmen and 725 bags of coal, the greatest number of families relieved in one week being 136. It became the Dawber Relief Committee of the council.

Conditions in the winter of 1908–9 seem to have been better. But if trade was better the number of vagrants was on the increase; the figures in the Lincoln union for 1907 were 2,683, and for 1908, 3,521. It was said that the presence of the prison in Lincoln made the figures worse. There was some call for labour colonies, and Charles Roberts, the city M.P., said he had sympathy with the idea, but he thought the new labour exchanges would help, and that the government expected to legislate on the poor law. The corporation opened an employment register, but there was little they could do, and they were rather establishing a principle than adopting an effective policy.

Almost on the eve of the outbreak of war R. A. Taylor moved for a Distress Committee, and gave some figures of unemployment which he thought were approximately correct: absolutely unemployed, 223; working five days a week, 897; four days, 119; three days, 167; two days, 54; one day, 31; total on short time, 1,268, with 1,158 dependent children. The wholly unemployed had 219 children. The council were in favour of corporation action, but not a distress committee under the Local Government Board.[3]

Most of the working classes lived in the new housing areas, but not all.

[1] *L.L.*, 4 April 1908.
[2] *L.C.*, 19 September 1908.
[3] *L.C.*, 6 December 1913.

Some of them lived in the older parts of the city, which remained largely unchanged in appearance. The young A. C. Benson was familiar with the little streets and winding lanes that threaded the hill in all directions, with walls of ancient stone or rubble descending the hill at a precarious angle; the big brick Georgian houses, sometimes with high gateposts and iron gates in front, and walled tree-sheltered gardens at the back, dotted about among the old quiet streets behind the cathedral and near the castle, whose inhabitants, with the cathedral dignitaries, made up the innermost circle. Of the features in the lower city beyond St Peter at Gowts he could only recall 'a villa of flashy and new-fangled design, standing in a large parterre, set with ornamental shrubs and expensively crowded with plaster statues – heathen goddesses and Roman Emperors and Greek athletes – as much exposed to the weather as the statues in the Groves of Blarney, but more decorously adorned. This, I think, was the work of a citizen of Lincoln who had made a large fortune by the sale of a patent medicine.'[1] He was right. Bracebridge Hall was the new home of Francis Jonathan Clarke.[2]

Other business men had prospered. Tradesmen who had lived over the shop or the office were moving to villas a little way off. In 1869 houses were built on the fringe of the south common. On the hill, Lindum Terrace was followed by the development of the area between the Wragby and Greetwell Roads, laid out by a syndicate including Ruston and Charles Brook; there Ruston built his own great Monks Manor to house his collection of paintings and other treasures.[3] The *Chronicle* said in 1887 that:

during the recent years of great prosperity and public improvement no adequate effort has hitherto been made to provide a superior kind of residence suitable to the requirements of a genteel and refined class of persons at a moderate cost.[4]

The omission was gradually being redressed.

Apart from the areas of residence, perhaps the most marked distinction between the classes lay in the schools their children attended. Middle-class children did not go to the elementary schools, and few went to the Grammar School until it began to recover. Some private schools went on from one generation to another, and produced men who made their mark. Witton Dalton, after teaching in Thomas Bainbridge's school,[5]

[1] *The Trefoil* (1923), pp. 98–9, 113.
[2] Above, p. 225.
[3] It stood on a detached part of the Monks Liberty. It was built about 1870 and demolished in 1933.
[4] *L.C.*, 26 February 1887.
[5] Above, p. 182.

had a private school of his own before he was appointed to Christs Hospital. Among his boys were men who took a leading part in the city's life and beyond: Charles Akrill, John Jekyll, William Ashley, George and Sharpley Bainbridge, William Manby, Rev. Henry Moss, head-master of Shrewsbury, James Thropp, William Mortimer, Henry Watson, Frederick Watson and Edwin Teesdale.[1]

Mr Mantle had a school in Northgate to which his son the Rev. William Mantle succeeded; Henry Mantle had it later. George Hopkin Shipley kept the Lindum House School for 50 boys, putting over 1,000 boys through it. Henry Harris, the science master at Newland British School, opened a private school.

Until the Girls High School was opened in 1894, middle-class girls had only private schools to choose from. As the High School established itself, and the Grammar School recovered, followed by the Municipal Tech-nical School, the private schools gradually faded away.

In 1874 there was an attempt to bring Lincoln into a university extension movement deriving from Cambridge, which was especially successful in Nottingham. Joseph Ruston presided over a public meeting supported by clergy and ministers. But after this first flutter of interest little if anything happened, though Lincoln was still mentioned as a sub-centre of the Nottingham circuit in 1879.[2]

It was too soon; the soil was not ready. The Mechanics Institute was fading away, the night schools had only just begun, and there was not yet a public library. Lincoln could not sustain a continuing effort. Presently single lectures by notables at the public library or the Y.M.C.A. began to flourish, and adult schools and mutual improvement societies prospered. It was not until 1890 that university extension courses were offered again, this time by Oxford, and there followed a branch of the Workers Educational Association in 1911. Arts and crafts exhibitions had been popularised by the School of Art, and they became important annual events. Other cultural societies were beginning to appear; for example, the Lincoln Musical Society, which was formed in 1896.

Lincoln was slow to change. J. D. Jones, becoming Congregational minister in 1889, found life 'apt to get a little sleepy'.[3] Social life was governed by rigid convention; church or chapel going was still a mark of respectability; there were no Sunday trams or Sunday games, at least in public; shop blinds were expected to be discreetly drawn on Saturday nights; those who read Darwin or biblical criticism for the most part kept

[1] L.C., 15 July 1881.
[2] See J. L. Paton, *John Brown Paton* (1914), pp. 161, 163.
[3] Arthur Porritt, *J. D. Jones of Bournemouth* (1942), p. 33.

their thoughts to themselves. Mrs Benson, for a clergyman's wife, was thought very daring in her open advocacy of George Eliot's novels, in spite of all that was known about the novelist's private life. And then there was the sad tale of Edna Lyall, who wrote a letter of sympathy to the atheist Bradlaugh and signed it 'A Lady from Minster Yard'.

She might be sister-in-law to a Residentiary, but that did not save her. Was she not also the author of *Donovan* and *We Two*, novels with a purpose and that a 'dangerous' one, bordering upon free thought? Lincoln soon became too hot to hold her, and she had to bow her head and remove elsewhere till the storm was over.

Minster Yard was happiest at the sight of the high yellow coach of the Sibthorps, which went on well into the nineties. The ironworks crept uphill, and Clayton and Shuttleworth and Ruston at length made entrance even into the cathedral. Even a dean was a liberal and son-in-law of Mr Gladstone.[1]

In some respects Lincoln had become rather more separate from the county. The influence of the gentry, who had once themselves been 'the county', had declined. The reduction of their rent rolls, as the result of agricultural depression, had reduced their spending power; and for those who could afford it there were now other ways of occupying their time, such as foreign travel, which had become relatively easy. They no longer provided parliamentary candidates to the same extent, and the adoption of the three ancient administrative divisions of Lindsey, Kesteven and Holland as county council areas in 1888 took the southerners – already tending to separate[2] – to Sleaford or Grantham or Boston. While the country remained almost wholly agricultural, the city had become increasingly industrial; and it no longer found its markets in the countryside, but in the further parts of Europe and in the other continents, its fortunes influenced, not so much by home harvests, as by drought in India or a war in the Balkans.

The biographer of Dean Butler remarked that the city, though the capital of the county, was very unfavourably situated as a centre!

The service of trains is not convenient. Proud as Lincolnshire people might be of their Minster, they certainly did not regard Lincoln as a Yorkshireman does York. Grantham, Boston, Stamford and Louth had their separate interests and agencies.[3]

[1] Janet Courtney, *Recollected in Tranquillity* (1926), p. 89. See G. A. Payne, *Edna Lyall: an Appreciation* (1903); J. M. Escreet, *Life of Edna Lyall* (1904). Her real name was Ada Ellen Bayly; her sister was the wife of the Chancellor Crowfoot.
[2] Above, p. 79.
[3] *Life and Letters of Dean Butler* (1897), pp. 319, 362. Yet bishop Edward Hicks did most of his travelling in the diocese by railway.

The same point was made by the *Lincoln Leader* when it was proposed in 1900 to publish a county magazine. It asserted that there was no county unity:

Grantham takes no interest in Grimsby: Bourne none in Barton: Spalding and Gainsborough are oceans apart. Lincoln itself could scarcely be called the centre of county life, though it is ecclesiastically the chief town in the diocese. All the northern villages and towns look to Hull. Only this week a Scunthorpe correspondent complains, with much reason, that while systematic collection is made there for the Lincoln County Hospital, the needs of the Hull Infirmary are neglected, although the latter is the resort of the Scunthorpe sick and injured.[1]

The time had not yet come for people to get about the county and to know it. The railways would take the businessman to London or Manchester or Sheffield; the middle-class family to Scarborough or Brighton or Cromer; and the working classes, at the annual 'trips', to Skegness or Cleethorpes. 'Trip week', an early example of the staggered holiday, being the week before the August Bank Holiday week, began in the 1870s, and gave great numbers of people their first chance of getting more than a few miles away from home, and certainly the first chance of seeing the sea, or perhaps London.[2] But those who did not own or hire horses did not visit neighbouring towns or villages until the motor car and the country bus made it easy to do so; the motor car was still the rich man's toy, and there was no country bus. It was true that there was the bicycle, but only young and adventurous spirits, members for the most part of cycling clubs, travelled far. The first aeroplane arrived in 1912. It left Peterborough, came down at Scopwick, came down again at Rusking-ton, and after enquiring the way to Lincoln, finished the journey. It was late.[3]

[1] *L.L.*, 8 September 1900.
[2] By 1897 17,000 railway tickets were sold; many went only for the day, others for three, four or five days.
[3] *L.L.*, 13 July 1912. Another, more successful, followed. *L.L.*, 3 August 1912. The first cinema was opened in 1909, though Alfred Vidler took a film of 'The Lincolns' leaving for the Boer War in 1899. The Scout movement was gripping the attention of youth in 1910.

APPENDIX I

POPULATION

Parish	1801	1811	1821	1831	1841	1851	1861	1871	1881	1891	1901
St Benedict	547	550	628	654	693	690	653	631	628	519	432
St Botolph	354	455	585	614	727	917	1,027	1,209	3,347	4,456	5,473
St John	101	133	159	216	205	324	285	333	500	110	132
St Margaret	303	311	403	359	330	378	452	504	415	508*	463
St Mark	262	322	430	450	445	666	722	909	997	933	912
St Martin	1,187	1,487	1,768	1,942	2,283	3,020	3,232	3,978	4,331	4,546	4,561
St Mary Magdalene	659	708	701	646	613	630	625	593	610	564	538
St Mary le Wigford	503	599	590	702	912	1,187	1,746	2,504	3,555	4,452*	5,948
St Michael	468	509	716	843	1,135	1,363	1,296	1,391	1,253	1,171	1,170
St Nicholas	147	228	223	442	1,053	1,233	1,515	2,250	4,462	5,400	5,767
St Paul	316	387	423	447	492	746	789	919	820	1,574*	1,439
St Peter at Arches	413	420	498	534	548	625	562	588	528	456	350
St Peter in Eastgate	584	456	453	505	658	1,000	1,028	1,182	1,448	904*	887
St Peter at Gowts	413	481	549	661	875	1,430	2,055	3,197	6,560	8,133	9,900
St Swithin	940	1,553	1,869	2,202	2,634	2,961	4,665	6,294	7,328	7,373	9,134
County Lunatic Asylum	—	—	—	—	125	149	106	—	—	—	—
Castle Dykings	—	—	—	—	139	167	188	218	181	(added to St Paul)	
Castle Prison	—	—	—	—	29	47	16	—	—	—	—
South Common	—	—	—	—	—	—	—	43	242	333	445
Holmes Common	—	—	—	—	—	—	—		18	—	—
Bishop's Palace	—	—	—	—	—	—	7	9	6	11	11
Cold Bath House	—	—	—	—	—	—	5	5	5	5	5
Monks Liberty	—	—	—	—	—	—	21	9	79	43*	1,217

* Changes effected by Divided Parishes Act.

In 1906 Lincoln became a single civil parish, and in 1911 was enumerated by wards: Abbey, 10,530; Carholme, 9,288; Castle, 9,323; Minster, 9,781; Park, 9,813; Witham, 8,550.

Percentage increase of population

	Population	Increase	Percentage increase
1801	7,205	—	—
1811	8,589	1,384	19.20
1821	9,995	1,406	16.36
1831	11,217	1,222	12.22
1841	13,806	2,589	23.08
1851	17,536	3,730	27.01
1861	20,995	3,459	19.72
1871	26,723	5,728	27.28
1881	37,313	10,590	39.65
1891	41,491	4,178	11.19
1901	48,784	7,293	17.57
1911	57,294	8,510	17.44

APPENDIX II

HOUSING

Parish	1801 Inh.	1801 Bldg	1801 Uninh.	1811 Inh.	1811 Bldg	1811 Uninh.	1821 Inh.	1821 Bldg	1821 Uninh.	1831 Inh.	1831 Bldg	1831 Uninh.	1841 Inh.	1841 Bldg	1841 Uninh.	1851 Inh.	1851 Bldg	1851 Uninh.
St Benedict	113	—	2	127	3	5	139	—	1	135	—	6	131	—	7	133	—	7
St Botolph	87	—	14	105	—	—	126	—	2	134	—	10	155	—	3	187	—	8
St John	22	—	1	31	—	—	39	—	—	46	—	—	47	7	2	58	—	3
St Margaret	49	—	5	54	1	2	71	—	1	67	—	3	63	—	6	68	—	3
St Mark	55	—	3	71	3	—	90	2	3	86	—	9	92	—	—	137	—	13
St Martin	260	—	7	318	8	5	363	7	11	393	4	21	481	4	17	622	7	23
St Mary Magdalene	133	—	13	125	1	9	128	—	6	113	—	8	115	—	11	119	—	7
St Mary le Wigford	105	—	3	117	3	2	120	—	2	139	—	5	168	4	7	230	—	20
St Michael	99	—	9	103	—	—	130	—	5	175	1	10	230	—	13	244	—	14
St Nicholas	25	—	1	50	—	1	49	—	2	110	2	12	227	1	7	279	1	11
St Paul	77	—	5	94	—	1	102	—	3	111	1	10	117	—	9	176	1	7
St Peter at Arches	75	—	2	73	—	3	82	—	4	79	—	2	76	1	3	87	—	14
St Peter in Eastgate	77	—	—	81	3	—	82	—	2	90	5	4	102	1	5	173	—	8
St Peter at Gowts	89	—	4	110	—	3	119	—	5	150	1	5	182	—	7	285	1	12
St Swithin	230	—	7	315	3	—	382	—	13	465	1	34	563	1	23	617	15	34
Castle Dykings	—	—	—	—	—	—	—	—	—	—	—	—	32	—	2	32	1	2
South Common	—	—	—	—	—	—	—	—	—	—	—	—	—	—	—	—	—	—
Holmes Common	—	—	—	—	—	—	—	—	—	—	—	—	—	—	—	—	—	—
Bishop's Palace	—	—	—	—	—	—	—	—	—	—	—	—	—	—	—	—	—	—
Cold Bath House	—	—	—	—	—	—	—	—	—	—	—	—	—	—	—	—	—	—
Monks Liberty	—	—	—	—	—	—	—	—	—	—	—	—	—	—	—	—	—	—

Parish	1861 Inh.	1861 Bldg	1861 Uninh.	1871 Inh.	1871 Bldg	1871 Uninh.	1881 Inh.	1881 Bldg	1881 Uninh.	1891 Inh.	1891 Bldg	1891 Uninh.	1901 Inh.	1901 Bldg	1901 Uninh.
St Benedict	124	—	17	116	—	6	115	—	—	102	—	49	89	1	41
St Botolph	223	—	5	276	4	4	711	15	21	976	15	24	1,243	9	38
St John	60	—	1	60	—	—	74	—	5	1	—	—	3	—	—
St Margaret	76	3	4	81	—	4	77	1	6	92	—	4	92	—	4
St Mark	151	—	3	181	—	8	206	—	6	193	—	15	188	—	14
St Martin	677	—	20	839	—	13	924	4	33	985	2	79	1,035	—	73
St Mary Magdalene	124	1	5	126	—	3	123	4	3	109	—	12	114	—	13
St Mary le Wigford	364	10	25	542	5	20	733	6	29	936	6	39	1,310	40	80
St Michael	260	—	12	275	—	4	271	—	12	278	1	19	268	—	19
St Nicholas	350	—	1	513	—	11	867	5	46	1,072	—	69	1,247	4	50
St Paul	181	—	5	196	—	1	178	2	15	279	3	24	297	4	6
St Peter at Arches	93	—	4	93	—	4	80	—	26	71	—	30	52	—	58
St Peter in Eastgate	189	—	5	198	3	4	245	—	7	191	—	3	213	4	7
St Peter at Gowts	444	7	10	678	13	11	1,350	18	23	1,728	20	34	2,296	36	63
St Swithin	960	6	17	1,288	4	19	1,513	21	42	1,465	16	57	2,039	22	152
Castle Dykings	33	—	1	48	—	5	40	—	5	—	—	—	—	—	—
South Common	—	—	—	9	—	5	43	2	4	68	—	4	99	—	6
Holmes Common	—	—	—	—	—	—	5	—	—	—	—	—	—	—	—
Bishop's Palace	1	—	—	1	—	—	1	—	—	1	—	—	1	—	—
Cold Bath House	1	—	—	1	—	—	1	—	—	1	—	—	1	—	—
Monks Liberty	1	—	—	2	—	—	12	—	—	9	—	—	269	7	10

APPENDIX III

PARISH CHURCH ACCOMMODATION c. 1831

(L.A.O. Cor.B. 5/4/106/10)

Names of parishes and churches in Lincoln	Value of benefice £	Population of each parish	Sittings in each church	Proportion of sittings to population	Proportion of sittings to population (%)	Population of districts	Sittings in churches in the district	Population of the town in three divisions	Sittings in the churches in three divisions	Division
St John in Newport (City)	70	200	No church	—	—					
St Nicholas in Newport (City)	89	442	No church	—	—		265 (11%)		515 (15½%)	
St Paul (Bail)	68	447	100	2/9	23	2,578		3,341		Upper part of Lincoln
St Mary Magdalene (Bail Close)	120	646	100	2/13	15½				with Cathedral 815 (24%)	
Cathedral	—	—	300	—	—		with Cathedral 565 (22%)			
St Michael (City)	118	843	65	1/13	7½					
St Peter in Eastgate (City)	150 }	404 }	250	1/3	33					
St Margaret (Close)		359								
St Martin (City)	138	1,942	400	1/5	20	—	—	4,678	1,250 (27%)	Middle of the town
St Swithin (City)	108	2,202	300	1/7	13½	—	—			
St Peter at Arches (City)	79	534	550	Surplus	Surplus	—	—			
St Benedict (City)	90	654	200	4/13	31	—	—			
St Mary le Wigford (City)	115	702	250	5/14	36	—	—	3,081	1,050 (34%)	Lower part of the town
St Mark (City)	80	450	200	4/9	45	—	—			
St Peter at Gowts (City)	94	661	250	5/13	38	—	—			
St Botolph (City)	116	614	150	1/4	24½	—	—			
Total value of 14 benefices	1,435				With Cathedral 28					
Average value of each benefice	102.10									
Total		11,100	3,115		Without Cathedral 25					
Average				2/7	25					

CHURCH ATTENDANCE

(i) 30 March 1851 (H.O. 129/428/2)

	No. of sittings		Morning		Afternoon		Evening	
	Free	Other	General	Sunday scholars	General	Sunday scholars	General	Sunday scholars
St Botolph	—	140	—	—	44	49	—	—
St Peter at Gowts	35	165	96	50	—	—	71	(Singers) 12
St Mark	115		—	—	49		—	—
St Mary le Wigford	100	185	104	45	70	—	—	—
St Benedict	90		60	—	—	—	46	—
St Peter at Arches	About 200	700	285	300	53	300	440	—
St Swithin	—	About 338	71	—	31	—	—	—
St Martin	122	204	140	—	—	—	130	—
St Michael	45		44	63	—	—	39	—
St Paul	10	80	—	—	40	—	—	—
St Peter in Eastgate	135	165	188	78	—	—	146	—
St Mary Magdalene	—	—	130	—	84	(rainy)	—	—
St Nicholas	800	One pew	180	—	—	—	200	—
Cathedral	—	—	205	—	283	Charity scholars 116	—	—
Wesley Chapel (Wesleyan Methodist)	820	1,276	508	164	66	—	674	—
Newport Wesleyan	190	205	135	190	—	—	120	—
Primitive Methodist (St Mary)	122	198	85	56	80	60	300	—
Primitive Methodist (St Nicholas)	100	90	—	40	106	—	143	—
Corn Exchange (Wesleyan Reform)	320	222	340	—	—	—	560	—
General Baptist (St Benedict)	120	—	13	40	—	40	16	—
Particular Baptist (St Martin)	84	316	200	114	—	—	150	—
Zion Chapel (St Swithin)	60	200	—	—	—	—	—	—
Independent (St Peter at Gowts)	172	328	100	165	—	184	180	—
Newland Independent (St Martin)	200	850	315	—	—	—	306	—
Presbyterian or Unitarian (St Peter at Gowts)	—	130	30	—	—	—	20	—
Catholic Chapel (St Swithin)	100	100	250	54	70	—	—	—

Estimated number attending divine service on Sunday, 30 March 1851

[Additional information given in the returns. Particulars of endowment omitted. Where two figures of attendance are given, the first relates to the general congregation, the second to Sunday scholars.]

St Botolph. Average attendance 60, 50 in morning, 50, 50 in afternoon. Divine service is once every Sunday, alternately morning and afternoon. Many parishioners attend other Churches in the city of Lincoln.

St Peter at Gowts. Average attendance 100, 50 in morning, 50, 50 in afternoon, 140, 12 singers in evening. Divine service is twice every Sunday, always in the evening, and alternately morning and afternoon. Many parishioners attend other Churches in the city of Lincoln, as owing to a want of Church accommodation, they cannot have pews or sittings allotted to them.

St Mark. Part of the parish situated at considerable distance from the Church, with another parish intervening. One service on the Sunday alternately morning and afternoon. The congregations in the morning are always much larger than the afternoon.

St Benedict. Average attendance 50, 0 in morning, 50, 0 in evening. My parish is small, consisting principally of Dissenters. The church is filled with 90 people.

St Peter at Arches. The National School attend the morning and afternoon service, and are put down as Sunday scholars. The evening service is a lecture, and the lecturer is paid by a committee and not in any way under the control of the Rector. The National School is in the parish.

St Swithin. No free sittings, though there may be one or two unclaimed pews. No means of saying the average number of attendants, having never counted the congregation before 30 March.

St Martin. There is no Sunday School. The children of the poor attend the National School, which is open to all parishes, and the scholars attend another church. We could not accommodate them without excluding the adult poor. I do not consider the numbers 140 and 130 as by any means representing the usual attendance at St Martin's Church. The attendance yesterday was much diminished by the prevailing influenza, and as regards the evening service still further by a violent storm of thunder and lightning which occurred just before the time of service. Not having been accustomed to compute the numbers, I have no data from which to state the average attendance in figures. I can only state generally that the morning attendance is good, and that there are usually but few seats vacant in the evening. The churchwardens also have many applications for pews and sittings which they are unable to satisfy.

St Michael. Church accommodation lamentably deficient in proportion to population. A prospect of the church being rebuilt. Population nearly all poor.

St Paul. Average attendance 60, 0 in morning, and 60, 0 in afternoon.

St Peter in Eastgate (with St Margaret). Average attendance 200, 80 in morning, 240, none, in evening. A part of this parish is detached at an average distance of half a mile and about 70 yards from the Church, and although of late years much built upon and having also the Union Workhouse standing upon it, for which latter however there is a provision for religious services, the distance from the Church and the uncertainty of obtaining accommodation within it are such as to deter the inhabitants of this part of the parish from attending its services, although regularly performed on the mornings and evenings of every Sabbath day.

A thunderstorm with hail and rain which came on before and continued for some time after the commencement of Divine service this evening prevented the attendance of nearly the whole of the usual female attendants.

St Mary Magdalene. Average attendance very uncertain. They go from Church to Church, from Chapel to Church, and from Church to Chapel.

St Nicholas (with St John). Average attendance very uncertain, as is always the case in towns where there are many churches.

Wesley Chapel. Average attendance morning 700–800, about 180 scholars; afternoon, general 80 to 100, evening, general 1000 to 1200.

Primitive Methodist, St Mary. Standing space for 50. Average attendance morning 100, 80; afternoon, 50, 87; evening, general, 400.

Primitive Methodist (St Nicholas). Standing space for 50. Average general congregation, morning nil; afternoon 106, evening 143.

Wesleyan Reform. Standing room 200.

General Baptist (St Benedict). Average attendance, morning 15, 40; afternoon, scholars 40; evening, general 20.

Particular Baptist (St Martin). Average attendance, morning, 200, 120; afternoon, school only; evening, general 250 to 300. The evening congregation on the 30th was much below the average in consequence of a violent thunderstorm which came on just at the commencement of the services.

Zion Chapel (St Swithin). Average attendance, morning, 40, 40; afternoon, scholars 40; evening, general, 50. We have no afternoon service in the chapel. A small day school meets in the vestry, but it has been commenced very recently.

Independent Chapel, St Peter at Gowts. Average attendance, morning 110, 180; afternoon, scholars, 200; evening, general, 200.

Newland Independent Chapel, St Martin. Average attendance, morning, 350, 130; afternoon, none; evening, general 380.

Presbyterian or Unitarian Chapel, St Peter at Gowts. Average attendance, morning, general 30; evening, general, 40.

Catholic Chapel, St Swithin. During the harvest time many Irish labourers attend in the yard and outside the chapel door.

(ii) *26 January 1873* (Lincoln, Rutland and Stamford Mercury,
31 January 1873)

Last Sunday the number of persons attending the various places of worship in the city morning and evening were enumerated, with the view of ascertaining the comparison between attendance and accommodation at each place. The following were the number who attended.

Churches:	Morning	Evening
St Martin	212	196
St Peter at Arches	255	525
St Swithin	81	275
St Peter at Gowts	118	172
St Botolph	89	—
St Mary le Wigford	150	254
St Michael	215	236
St Mary Magdalene	124	181
Cathedral	205	495
St Mark	85	121
St Peter in Eastgate	149	197
St Anne	20	24
St Nicholas	190	181
St Paul (only one service)	—	93
Chapels:		
Catholic	199	173
Wesley St Peter at Gowts	258	276
Wesley Marketgate (*sic*)	970	1232
Wesley Newport	228	139
Primitive Portland Place	272	281
Primitive Rasen Lane	124	156
Unitarian	28	63
Temperance Hall	—	43
Independent High St	155	109
Free Methodist Silver St	656	945
Free Methodist Saxon St	270	230
Baptist Mint Lane	169	293
Baptist St Benedict	101	111
Disciples	33	31

The exact number for the Independent Chapel Newland has not come to hand, but the morning was between 500 and 600, and the evening nearly 400. Newland Mission Chapel was about 100. St Botolph was not taken in the evening. It is the opinion of a competent judge that the aggregate number is not larger than that of 1852, notwithstanding the large increase in the population of the city since that time.

(iii) Lincoln Leader and County Advertiser, 14 March 1903

We give below a census of attendance at religious worship in the city, taken by our enumerators on Sunday last. The day was brilliantly fine, and though this may have, to some extent, interfered with certain evening congregations, the general influence of a fine day on church attendance is decidedly good.

In making our calculation we have disregarded early morning services, and have taken no account of children of school age. It would be impossible to adequately account for these without enumerating the Sunday Schools, some of which adjourn in procession to the churches, whilst others do not. It is fairly safe, we think, to assume that those parents who themselves attend religious worship will see that the spiritual welfare of their children is not neglected.

We shall therefore confine ourselves to the adult worshippers, and compare the returns with the estimated adult population, secure in the assurance that the children are being looked after at least as well as and probably better than their parents.

The adult population of Lincoln is probably, in round figures, some 30,000 people – rather less if anything. This is how the figures work out:

Denomination	Morning M	Morning F	Afternoon M	Afternoon F	Evening M	Evening F	Total M	Total F	Total for the day
CHURCH OF ENGLAND									
Cathedral	174	197	212	307	328	388	714	892	1,606
St Peter in Eastgate	79	125	—	—	52	110	131	235	366
St Peter at Arches	48	56	—	—	167	202	215	258	473
St Mary le Wigford	27	29	—	—	39	67	66	96	162
St Martin's	46	95	—	—	63	164	109	259	368
St Mark's	69	60	—	—	104	168	173	228	401
St Peter at Gowts	95	106	—	—	114	157	209	263	472
St Faith's	78	92	—	—	89	174	167	266	433
St Matthias	111	145	—	—	88	107	199	252	451
St Nicholas	46	89	—	—	72	86	118	175	293
St Michael's on the Mount	18	10	—	—	28	17	46	27	73
St Mary Magdalene	27	34	—	—	38	40	65	74	139
St Andrew's	65	105	—	—	134	256	199	361	560
St Botolph's	49	63	—	—	73	137	122	200	322
St Paul's	14	28	—	—	27	63	41	91	132
St Swithin's	80	140	—	—	182	237	262	377	639
All Saints Mission	14	24	—	—	22	51	36	75	111
Long Leys Mission	—	—	—	—	21	13	21	13	34
Vernon Street Mission	—	—	—	—	30	38	30	38	68
WESLEYAN									
Clasketgate	209	223	—	—	290	327	499	550	1,049
High Street Wesley	175	139	—	—	316	380	491	519	1,010
St Catherine's	52	76	—	—	73	134	125	210	335
Bailgate	79	51	—	—	92	107	171	158	329
Stamp End Mission	—	—	8	9	48	59	56	68	124
Burton Road Mission	—	—	20	14	30	37	50	51	101
Well Lane Mission	—	—	—		20	19	20	19	39

11-2

Denomination	Morning		Afternoon		Evening		Total		Total for the day
	M	F	M	F	M	F	M	F	
CONGREGATIONAL									
Newland	115	128	—	—	174	292	289	420	709
Far Newland	—	—	—	—	67	104	67	104	171
Monks Road	27	44	—	—	58	85	85	129	214
South Bar	30	29	—	—	65	125	95	154	249
FREE METHODIST									
Silver Street	88	75	—	—	151	191	163	342	505
Portland Street	24	15	—	—	42	53	66	68	134
Saxon Street	43	32	—	—	81	119	124	151	275
PRIMITIVE METHODIST									
Portland Place	74	69	—	—	134	131	208	200	408
Rasen Lane	94	72	—	—	85	115	179	187	366
Carholme Road	18	13	—	—	29	53	47	66	113
Croft Street	33	11	—	—	48	46	81	57	138
Portland Place Mission, Coultham Street	—	—	—	—	46	58	46	58	104
Newark Road	41	31	—	—	55	85	96	116	212
CATHOLIC									
St Hugh's	78	81	—	—	107	205	185	286	471
BAPTIST									
Thomas Cooper Memorial	33	31	—	—	44	65	77	96	173
Mint Street	54	62	—	—	107	171	161	233	394
Monks Road	32	24	—	—	30	50	62	74	136
OTHER AGENCIES									
Salvation Army									
No. 1 Corps	74	92	140	145	136	154	350	391	741
No. 2 Corps	10	14	14	26	32	38	56	78	134
Christian Meeting Room (Oddfellows' Hall)	11	12	—	—	13	17	24	29	53
Christadelphians (Oddfellows' Hall)	12	6	—	—	18	11	30	17	47
Foster Street Mission	4	5	—	—	2	6	6	11	17
Ashton's Court Mission	—	—	24	26	—	—	24	26	50
House of Israel	—	—	—	—	2	2	2	2	4
St Anne's Mission	4	19	4	26	—	—	8	45	53
Friends	10	21	—	—	23	22	33	43	76
Plymouth Brethren	—	—	—	—	44	47	44	47	91
Christian Brethren	12	12	—	—	14	23	26	35	61
Ragged School	28	31	—	—	—	—	28	31	59

Below is an arrangement of the Churches according to numerical superiority. It will be noticed that the afternoon congregations are included in the totals for the Cathedral and the Salvation Army.

	Morning	Afternoon	Evening	Total
1. Cathedral	371	519	716	1,606
2. Clasketgate	487	—	562	1,049
3. High Street Wesley	314	—	696	1,010
4. Salvation Army	190	325	360	875
5. Newland	243	—	466	709
6. St Swithin's	220	—	419	639
7. St Andrew's	170	—	390	560
8. Silver Street	163	—	342	505
9. St Peter at Arches	104	—	369	473
10. St Peter at Gowts	201	—	271	472
11. St Hugh's	159	—	312	471
12. St Matthias	256	—	195	451
13. St Faith's	170	—	263	433
14. Portland Place	143	—	265	408
15. St Mark	129	—	272	401
16. Mint Street	116	—	278	394
17. St Martin's	141	—	227	368
18. St Peter in Eastgate	204	—	162	366
19. Rasen Lane	166	—	200	366
20. St Catherine's	128	—	207	335
21. Bailgate	130	—	199	329
22. St Botolph's	112	—	210	322
23. St Nicholas	135	—	158	293
24. Saxon Street	75	—	200	275
25. South Bar	59	—	190	249
26. Monks Road (Congregational)	71	—	143	214
27. Newark Road (Primitive Methodist)	72	—	140	212
28. Thomas Cooper	64	—	109	173
29. Far Newland	—	—	171	171
30. St Mary le Wigford	56	—	106	162
31. St Mary Magdalene	61	—	78	139
31. Croft Street	44	—	94	138
32. Monks Road (Baptist)	56	—	80	136
33. Portland Street	39	—	95	134
34. St Paul's	42	—	90	132
35. Stamp End Mission	—	17	107	124
36. Carholme Road	31	—	82	113
37. All Saints Mission	38	—	73	111
38. Coultham Street	—	—	104	104
39. Burton Road Mission	34	—	67	101
40. Plymouth Brethren	—	—	91	91
41. Friends	31	—	45	76
42. St Michael's	28	—	45	73
43. Vernon Street	—	—	68	68
44. Christian Brethren	24	—	37	61
45. Ragged School	59	—	—	59
46. St Anne's Mission	23	30	—	53
47. Christian Meeting Room	23	—	30	53
48. Ashton's Court Mission	—	50	—	50
49. Christadelphians	18	—	29	47
50. Well Lane	—	—	39	39
51. Long Leys Mission	—	—	34	34
52. Foster Street	9	—	8	17
53. House of Israel	—	—	4	4

DENOMINATIONAL TOTALS

	Morning		Afternoon		Evening		Totals		
	M	F	M	F	M	F	M	F	
Church of England	1,040	1,398	212	307	1,671	2,475	2,923	4,180	7,103
Wesleyan	515	489	28	23	849	1,084	1,392	1,496	2,888
Congregational	172	201	—	—	364	606	536	807	1,343
Primitive Methodist	260	196	—	—	397	488	657	684	1,341
Free Methodist	155	122	—	—	274	363	429	485	914
Baptist	119	117	—	—	181	286	300	403	703
Catholic	78	81	—	—	107	205	185	286	471
Salvation Army	84	106	154	171	168	192	406	469	875
Other agencies	81	106	28	52	116	128	225	286	511

This means that the episcopal Church of England compares as follows with the Free Churches of the city:

	Morning		Afternoon		Evening		Totals		
	M	F	M	F	M	F	M	F	
Free Churches	1,464	1,418	110	246	2,456	3,352	4,130	4,916	9,046
Church of England	1,040	1,398	212	307	1,671	2,475	2,923	4,180	7,103

We thus obtain a total attendance for the day of 16,149 which will give an average aggregate church attendance of one in $1\frac{7}{8}$ of the population over 15 of the city. A total number of 5,320 were present at morning service, making an average of nearly one in five of the adult population, 875 attended afternoon, and 9,954 evening service, the latter yielding the excellent average of one in three of the adult population. This is one of the best census results we have seen, and it is so far creditable to the old city, which has from time immemorial been a stronghold of religious endeavour. But it reveals the fact that during the time most convenient for divine worship, some 20,000 adult citizens were finding occupation in other directions, and it is but too true – the circumstance has been noted by every one of our enumerators – that a large proportion of them were promenading the streets. The figures scarcely prove, with the most liberal allowances, that half the population of Lincoln came under religious influences during the day. At the same time the result is nearly twice as good as the best London census which has so far been revealed by the *Daily News*.

APPENDIX V

THE ELECTION: A LEGEND

by Thomas Ingoldsby junior

[The original of this work is in the possession of Mr Edward Mason of Lincoln, by whose permission it is printed.

The 'legend' comes from a source unfriendly to Sibthorp. Mr Mason's great-grandfather was town clerk of Lincoln (see above, p. 39). It seems likely therefore either that Mason was himself the author, or was closely associated with him.

The *Ingoldsby Legends* were first published collectively in 1840, and this 'legend' was clearly composed at the time of the election of June 1841.]

Whiskerandos awoke one morning in June,
At Canwick Hall, twas nearly noon;
With nerves all shaken, and out of tune,
For he and old Ben had sat out the moon,
Though she had not withdrawn herself soon:
And he stared around in maudlin surprise,
And rubb'd his swollen and blood shot eyes,
Then caught at his watch, but there he found
No sign of the time by motion or sound
As well he might not, for it had not been wound
And he said as he pok'd out his hand to ring,
And vainly endeavoured to find the string,
    The Devil take this late carouse
    This aching head and lengthen'd snoose
    My true old Pinks will patience lose
    And some perhaps, worn out, refuse
      Longer to wait
      At the great Bar-gate
    For me their worthy candidate
And thus oh horror and sore dismay
Some beams will be lost to the grand array,
Arrang'd for my glorious Entrée.
Whiskerandos then threw off his cap
When he heard at the door a gentle rap
And his Tiger entered, a little chap,
Who stood in his shoes about four feet four
Or a little less, or it might be more!
Be that as it may, 'twas his proud fate
To be the sole prop of the liveried state
Then known in the Hall of the Candidate.
And he said, Please Sir! a man below
Has just come up to let you know

That the folks at the bar, which he left just now
Are beginning to make a terrible row.
Because you're so late before you show –
  And they all exclaim
  Its a monstrous shame
  That the world should see
  The true and free
  With hands so pure
  And hearts so sure
Thus treated like slaves in Bonds secure
The Committee he says are all in a funk
And the drums and trumpets getting quite drunk
The Saracen's tap is gushing forth streams
More copious than ever possess'd the dreams
Of thirty old Pinks; and the Rendevous teems
With Notaries guzzling ad libitum
  The Committee are puzzling
  On Measures for muzzling
For they knew that they dare not prohibit'em
The worthies had forc'd the Committee room door
Where limping Geordie on sand'd floor
Was eying his papers and *virtuous* books
With anxious air, and terrified looks
Protesting he could not provide such hosts
(Tho' he would if he could) with places and posts,
And he really believ'd that Humphrey's bags
Would hardly sustain such terrible drags –
In short the messenger waiting below
Says, that if you dont rouse, and quickly go,
There'll very soon be the Devil to do.
Whiskerandos then sat up in bed
And smooth's his moustache and scratch'd his head
  Looking about
  As if in doubt
As to the safest course to tread
  Whilst in his face
  A strange grimmace;
  (Not not in his face,
  For that whole space,
  So bristl'd with hair,
  That you could not there
Safely essay expression to trace)
  But his rolling eyes
  Denot'd surprise
  With symptoms beside
  Of scorn and pride
Which he did not just then affect to hide;
Then turn'd to the little Tiger and said

'So now that your message is fully sped
Say, are all things done and ready quite
As I commanded over night'.
And the Tiger replied 'An' please you Sir
The City below has been long astir.
Since the first grey streaks of day appear'd
The glossy pink flag has been proudly rear'd
And coquettishly flapping the Saracen's beard
   As if it would say
   Its just in this way
We'll lick the rads like fun and play.
   The address is out
   And handing about
And nobody seems to have a doubt
That its all very fine, and very good
If it were only understood:
But highly as people wish to commend it
Nobody seems to comprehend it.
The Saracen's hacks have arriv'd for the chaise,
And Powell has cut the laurel and bays.
And Tuke has sent up the gilded flags
And the Rector has pass'd with the money bags.
And the men have arriv'd with ropes at the bar,
Ready to yoke their backs to your car
And draw you gloriously forward instead
Of the more respectable quadruped.
And the nice little boys of the National School
All drill'd and train'd by clerical rule
Bearing with pride, new pink cotton banners
Are there to take lessons in morals and manners
   And join the route
   And drink and shout
And their reverence show for Church and State
Through you their idol candidate',
Whiskerandos exclaimed 'enough, I see
You've done my bidding quite punctually,
It's all very well, and as to the rest,
I must now be up and quickly drest,
So put me out my clothes – the best
Grey check & trousers and satin vest
A dickey and collar, and brown surtout
My brooches and seals, and or-molu,
Chains and guards, and the ladies' ring
And all the rest of that sort of thing'
Put the Macassar oil with the cork secure
And Espirit de Lavandre aux millefleur
On the table which stands beside the Ewer
The Tiger quickly did as desired,

And making his bow, he then retir'd.
Whiskerandos, that illustrous Tory
Thus left in silence 'alone in his glory'
After two or three yawns and as many sighs,
Did thus to himself soliloquize.
  But just by the way
  I wish to say
That as some of the exclamations might
Jar the tympanum of ears polite
  I think it discreet
  Not to repeat
Pungent expressions, slipt out in heat
Sounding like some stile heard in the street
But quite out of vogue and obsolete
With persons of fashion, the new elite
Modify'd then, as I've premis'd
The great man thus soliloquis'd
'To my worthy independent and free
Are exhibiting signs of mutiny
Ungrateful Varlets! am I thus repaid
For the efforts I've made and zeal displayed
Twice I've been sent to represent
My native city in Parliament
When in my place I've stood erect
Midst wild uproar and cold neglect
  And contemptuous sneers
  And ironical cheers
And pour'd anathemas in the ears,
Of the great Lord John and his proud Compeers;
Who in peals of laughter conceal their fears:
And do they forget above all beside
That stroke of my senatorial pride
(When the Court with radical Whigs allied)
I took the van, and did not wince
To mulct the allowance to the Prince
Tho' hate of pensions I seldom evince
And have not impeached one before or since.
And in this manner the cateffs requite
The horrors I've suffer'd thro' many a night
When I've condescended to do the polite
  Amongst the unwashed and greasy
  At the curs'd free and easy
  Midst toasting and shouting
  And amateur spouting.
  And guzzling and soaking
  And fuming and smoking
  And practical joking;
  Which the clamour and din,

Both without and within,
Of bells wildly ringing
And villanous singing;
Midst the rattle of mugs
And bottles and jugs
And rummers and spoons
And pipes and spitoons
With the hot glare of gas
And the stench too, alas!
And the crashing of glass
Prevail's till clamour and hubbub have grown,
Far too great for a head so weak as my own –
And do the recreants crew forget the doles
They yearly receive of my Christmas coals,
A boon which I deem, without disparity
To others gifts, a starting charity
Tho' some I believe are inclined to think
It a little too highly ting'd with pink,
But as charity ever begins at home
I cannot perceive why my own should roam,
And which of the Renegades now reflects
On the toils I've endured in "paying respects";
And wading this alley and lane to see
The worthy independent and free
Each at his home individually
How all uncover'd I've stood at the door
And blandly smil'd on the sullen bore
And wheedl'd and coax'd, whilst he bluffly swore
"He'd be blest if he serv'd the pinks any more
For he had not been paid like the rest before"
A thing which I could not too much deplore
And hint'd at benefits yet in store.
How I've press'd his grimy and horny fist,
And, with rising gorge, his wife have kiss't
And humor'd and flatter'd and gammon'd the flats
And ogl'd their daughters and slobber'd their brats
And if these were vain, and fail'd to do
Have left my kind friends to apply the screw.
But ne'importe, the villains may bounce and fret
They're safe enough in my gild'd net
The City is mine and Newcastle has shewn
A man may do what he likes with his own
As long as I list I'll hold my seat
And when I'm disposed to make a retreat
Or am doom'd to bow to the common lot
And am call'd to the shades, to be soon forgot
Why then they shall have young Waldo Tot.
A youth I ween who may aptly aspire

To tread in the steps of his honor'd sire
To bear his honors and don his laurels
And radiate all his talents and morals.'
But lo' our gallant hero's now array'd
In high costume to grace the Cavalcade
And if he linger still awhile, perchance
To give the mirror yet one parting glance
And feel his heart dilate with joy to see
His glittering chains and gay bijourterie
But most that glory of his upper lip
The fierce moustaches curl'd at the tip;
Forbear awhile, for that short gaze, alas!
In the bright, truthful, tell-tale, toilet glass
Brings sterner things before his anxious eye,
Which amidst all his triumphs force a sigh
For the wan face, and fallen cheek are there
And the blanch'd locks of thin and flowing hair
Telling of follies past, and years gone bye
In the wild and fever'd dreams of vanity,
And furrows too – not the brave warriors scar
Earnt in his Country's cause, in glorious wars
(Tho had it been so order'd by his Stars
They might have been, for he was a Son of Mars
And valor too, befitting his profession
Being ever largely temper'd with discretion
But this I must admit is mere digression)
The lines were such as times is wont to trace
With his stern graver on the brows and face
Of all who largely occupy his space
And most on those who have not wisely used him
But cast away his treasures and abus'd him.

INDEX